BURT FRANKLIN: RESEARCH & SOURCE WORKS SERIES 747
Essays in Literature and Criticism 134

BALLADS & BROADSIDES

chiefly

Of the Elizabethan Period

BALLADS & BROADSIDES

chiefly

Of the Elizabethan Period

And Printed in Black-Letter

Most of which were formerly in the Heber Collection

and are now in the Library at

Britwell Court Buckinghamshire

Edited with Notes and an Introduction by

Herbert L. Collmann

BURT FRANKLIN
NEW YORK

Published by LENOX HILL Pub. & Dist. Co. (Burt Franklin)
235 East 44th St., New York, N.Y. 10017
Originally Published: 1912
Reprinted: 1971
Printed in the U.S.A.

S.B.N.: 8337-30843
Library of Congress Card Catalog No.: 77-80261
Burt Franklin: Research and Source Works Series 747
Essays in Literature and Criticism 134

Reprinted from the original edition in the Ohio State University
Libraries.

DEDICATED AND PRESENTED

TO

THE PRESIDENT AND MEMBERS

OF

The Roxburghe Club

BY THEIR OBEDIENT SERVANT

SYDNEY RICHARDSON CHRISTIE-MILLER

BRITWELL COURT
May 1912

The Roxburghe Club

MCMXII

THE EARL OF ROSEBERY, K.G., K.T.
PRESIDENT

INTRODUCTORY NOTE

THE word 'Ballad' is in the mind of the ordinary reader usually associated with a popular form of anonymous verse, legendary or local, and often set to some well-known air. Ballads such as these, various editors, from Bishop Percy down to Francis Child, have gleaned since the middle of the eighteenth century. The broadside poems, however, which form the contents of this volume, though they pose as ballads and assume something of their outward garb, have little or nothing in common with them.

They are, with but few exceptions, of an ephemeral character, and may be regarded as a literary creation of the sixteenth century, fostered by the increasing popularity of the printing press, and with the news-letters sowing the seeds of modern journalism.

Several papal bulls and indulgences printed by Caxton and his successors are described by Mr. E. Gordon Duff in the ninth volume of the 'Transactions of the Bibliographical Society', 1908, yet the earliest English poetical broadside on record is one issued in 1540 on the execution of Thomas Cromwell, Earl of Essex, which was reprinted in the 'Reliques of Ancient English Poetry'.

As the sixteenth century advanced the poetical broadside became more and more popular, so that by the year 1560 there are said to have been as many as seven hundred and ninety-six copies of ballads stored at Stationers' Hall. Ballad writing offered an easy livelihood to a number of obscure and not too reputable rhymsters, few of whose names have survived. Their prolificacy, and the audacity with which they levelled their verses against those in authority, explain the reason why the ballad-writers were the objects of decrees made with a view to their suppression. The government and the bishops were not alone in opposition to this lower order of poets. Considerable profit attended the production of ballads, and this soon excited the envy and disgust of the better writers of the day, as Henry Chettle and others clearly testify.

The Stationers' Company was incorporated in 1557, and though its charter was ostensibly granted to confer a benefit on those engaged in printing and publishing, and was successful in this object, yet there can be little doubt that the sovereign and her advisers saw in it a readier means of controlling the press, as well as a machine for the detection and apprehension of any person who might be engaged in the production or distribution of seditious literature. The incorporation of the Company, aided largely by the restoration of the Protestant religion, brought about a rapid change in the tone of the ballads, until at length their language closely reflected the opinions of nine-tenths of the population of London at the time of their issue.

The Registers for the first forty years of the Stationers' Company abound with licences for ballads, fourpence being the usual fee charged for each item. Many of these entries have been identified with ballads preserved at Britwell and elsewhere, yet by far the greater number are not to be found in any of our older libraries, and must therefore be regarded as irrevocably lost, and to this fate they were by reason of their form and popularity particularly exposed.

The principal ballad collections in England, the Roxburghe and Bagford at the British Museum, the Douce, Rawlinson, and Wood in the Bodleian Library, the Pepysian at Magdalene College, Cambridge, the Halliwell-Phillipps in the Chetham Library at Manchester, and that formed by the Earl of Crawford at Haigh Hall, Wigan, contain many hundreds of broadsides printed in the seventeenth century, yet of those of the preceding one the number is extremely small. A large and very important series of broadsides of the Tudor period, however, is preserved in the library of the Society of Antiquaries, and this was rivalled only by that formerly the property of George Daniel of Canonbury Square, Islington.

The Antiquaries' broadsides are too well known through Robert Lemon's admirable Catalogue (1866) to need description here, and it is sufficient to say that they consist of no less than one hundred and seven articles which were published prior to the accession of James the First. These, together with a large number of ballads of a later period, and the

Society's unequalled collection of Proclamations, were the gift of Thomas Hollis of Lincoln's Inn, who had purchased them in 1756 at the sale of Charles Davis, a bookseller in Holborn.

The history of George Daniel's collection has been recorded by William Chappell in his introduction to the 'Roxburghe Ballads' (1871); by Mr. Henry Huth in some prefatory remarks to 'Ancient Ballads and Broadsides' (Philobiblon Society, 1867); and by Mr. W. Y. Fletcher in his 'English Book Collectors' (1902). From these sources we learn that the 'Suffolk' collection, as it has been named, originally rested at Helmingham Hall, the seat of the Tollemache family. Thence, early in the last century, it is supposed that they were rejected and sold by a housekeeper whose discrimination, or lack of it, in matters antiquarian was no more reprehensible than that of many of her superiors at that time. Tradition continues that they were purchased by William Stevenson Fitch, the postmaster of Ipswich, who shortly afterwards sold them for fifty pounds to George Daniel, who in 1832 parted with half of the parcel to Thomas Thorpe, the bookseller, in exchange for some Shakespeariana.

Thorpe had little difficulty in finding a purchaser for these in Richard Heber, a wealthy bibliophile, whose accumulations are said to have taxed the capacity of eight houses at home and abroad. From the following letter, the original of which is at Britwell, it will be understood how eagerly Heber accepted the suggestion that he should become the possessor of the ballads, and hinted that Thorpe's client would at any time find him prepared to accept the remainder of the Helmingham ballads or indeed any further parcel of equal interest and rarity which he might feel disposed to sell.

> Hodnet Hall near Shrewsbury.
> Saturday 15th. April. 1832.

Thank you for your offer, which observe I answer by return of post. Though I feel ashamed of my own folly and extravagance, I cannot resist the bait thrown in my way, and have accordingly written to my bankers to pay you on demand £200.

Of course I keep the list, and will thank you to let no other be made, and to say nothing of the transaction to anybody whatever. In fact, to lock up the portfolio till my return.

Mr. D. has certainly fallen into the inheritance of the Stationers' Company, or some ancient enchanted stall of ballads from which these sleeping beauties issue in their clean smocks after a lapse of 250 years and upwards. We have Fit the First, and Fit the Second,—when may we expect Fit the Third. He issues paper like the country banker—I wish I could find Bank of England notes as fast as he does old ballads. For alas, he has spoiled the old proverb of buying for an old song. 'R. H.'

Mr. Thorpe, Bookseller
    Bedford Street, Covent Garden, London.

Richard Heber died on October 4, 1833, and in the following years his vast collections were sold. The ballads formed ten lots in the fourth part of the 'Bibliotheca Heberiana', which contains so many rarities in English poetical literature. Most of them were purchased by Mr. William Henry Miller, of Craigentinny, Midlothian, and Britwell, Buckinghamshire, for a sum little more than half that which Heber had paid to Thorpe. Something of a mystery surrounds lot 386, which consisted of three ballads, translations from Horace, Martial, and Francisca Chavesia. It is impossible to believe that these could have failed to arouse the interest of a classical scholar like Mr. Miller, yet the ballads did not come to Britwell, nor has any attempt to trace them proved successful.

In 1856, George Daniel printed a catalogue of those ballads which he had reserved under the title of 'An Elizabethan Garland', and at the sale of his library, which took place after his death in 1864, the ballads were secured by Mr. Henry Huth, who in 1867 had them reprinted as 'Ancient Ballads and Broadsides', with an introduction and notes, for presentation to the Philobiblon Society.

Under the generous conditions of the late Mr. Alfred Huth's will, the Trustees of the British Museum have been enabled to make a liberal selection from that famous collection. Exercising particular wisdom in their choice, the Trustees, among other works of great literary and bibliographical importance, have selected the seventy-nine black-letter ballads and broadsides. Here within the National Library these venerable sheets, literary and historical relics of Elizabeth's England, will always be objects of the highest interest. An official catalogue of the Huth Bequest, wherein the broadsides will be found fully described and annotated, is about to be published.

The Britwell broadsides are eighty-seven in number, of which eighty-three were formerly Heber's, the remainder having been acquired from other sources. Except in a few instances, where copies of the original or of later editions exist in other collections, the ballads are unique. A selection from them was reprinted by John Payne Collier in the first volume of the 'Publications' of the Percy Society, 1840-42, and the same writer made frequent references to others in his 'Extracts from the Registers of the Stationers' Company', 1848-49. In 1872, Mr. William Henry Christie-Miller compiled an 'Alphabetical List of the Black Letter Ballads & Broadsides known as the Heber Collection', of which twenty copies were privately printed.

From a literary point of view this collection may be thought to suffer when compared with that in the British Museum, which includes several of the popular type, yet its range over the social and political features of the earlier years of the reign of Queen Elizabeth is comprehensive, and many of the verses throw an interesting light on some of the leading events of the period. The epitaphs and mournful ditties written for the illustrious dead, with the admonitions and confessions of others less enviable in their ends, form a third of the entire collection. The rest of the ballads deal chiefly with moral and religious subjects, and with historical episodes, among which the Catholic Rising in the North figures conspicuously; others with monstrous births and fishes; while a few are of the narrative order.

Of the authors whose names appear on the ballads there is little to note. Thomas Churchyard alone survives, Will Elderton is a typical ballad-writer, and Lodowick Lloyd is better known to posterity as the writer of a quantity of miscellaneous prose.

The thanks of the Editor are due to Mr. Horace Hart, of the University Press, Oxford, whence this volume issues; also to Mr. W. Aldis Wright, who has kindly supplied information respecting books in the libraries of Trinity College and of St. John's College, Cambridge. A particular expression of indebtedness is due to Mr. Robert Edmund Graves, late an Assistant Keeper in the British Museum, whose acquaintance with the Britwell Library extends over many years, for valuable assistance and advice during the progress of the work. Lastly, it is interesting to record that the late Dr. F. J. Furnivall, but a short time before his death, readily acceded to a suggestion that he should visit Britwell, where he examined the ballads and strongly supported the proposal for their reproduction.

BALLADS
AND BROADSIDES

I

¶ An Epitaphe vpon the death of
Mayſter *Iohn Viron* Preacher.

THou ſoule whych on Chriſtes breſt, doeſt reſt as Iohn loued,
And corps whych art lyke hys alſo, wyth earth en*Viron*ed :
Full ioyfull mayſt thou be, but we (alas) may wayle,
Thy preſence to forgo ſo ſoone, thy voyce ſo ſoone to fayle.
But oh thy payne and toyle, in God thee prayſe we ſhall,
That thou enſample now mayſt be, vnto thy fellowes all.
Whych ceaſedſt not at morne, at noone, nor yet at nyght,
To preache Gods woorde, to beate downe vyce, and to put ſynne to flyght.
Thyne natiue countrye thou, regardedſt not a whyt,
When God dyd call thee foorth to preache, but out thou wentſt wyth it.
Whych when in thyne owne toung, thou mightſt not preache in Fraunce,
Yet foorth thou wentſt, and by God led, to vs waſt brought by chaunce.
Where thou wyth paynefull watche, dydſt learne our Englyſh tounge,
And wyth as paynefull diligence, dydſt preache Gods truth among.
No Tyraunt, nor fierce lawes, coulde make thee vs forſake :
But in the mydſt of ragyng ſtormes, wyth Gods Sayntes part dydſt take.
And ſynce thou haſt well ſhewde, whoſe ſeruaunt thou haſt bene.
In preaching and in writing both, whych to Gods prayſe is ſene.
But now who ſhall lament? or who may ioy now flee?
Euen euery ſtate from top to toe, both hygh and low degree.
The poore may wayle hys myſſe, whych wyth both tounge and hand,
Dyd well refreſhe theyr weary ſtate, whych often they in ſtand.
The ryche may mone wyth them, hys barkyng voyce to want,
That kept from them that karking beaſt, whych rycheſſe dayly haunt.
And though hys lyke yet lyue, and many ſuche there be :
Yet ſhall we myſſe hym in our lyfe, and nombers more then he.
But oh London, London, thou oughteſt chiefe to wayle,
The people ſuche, and vyces great, may at hys want ſore quayle.
For twyſe ſo many as there be, and myllions lyke to hym,
Were not ſufficient to draw backe, thy people from theyr ſynne.
But ſhall I ſhewe the thankes, whych in thee he hath got?
Oh London, London, Sodome was, not ſo yll vnto Lot.
His paynes deſerued prayſe, but ſome in thee hym gaue :
Obprobrious woordes, and ſclaunders vyle, euen to hys bodyes graue.
But what for that they thus, haue vſed hym ſo yll :
Hys vertues were thereby more knowen, in ſpight of their yll wyll?
And eke theyr lying blaſtes, are ſo layde in their face :
That they may ſhame and weepe thereat, if they haue any grace.
But now thou flocke and folde, whych he in lyfe dyd guyde :
What cauſe haſt thou to wayle hys want, and count thee wo betyde?
Whych hadſt a Shepheard good, that dyd hys duty ryght :
In ſauing Rammes from daunger neare, and helpyng Lambes to myght.
From paſture vnto paſture, he dyd thee bryng to feede,
And neuer ceaſed to make thee from fayth to fayth proceede.

There reftes no more for you, hys paynes now to requite :
But fo to walke as he you taught, and fpeake of hym the ryght.
And thou O England now, to ende and mone wyth theefe :
Lament thou mayft alfo wyth vs, a woorkeman thus to leefe.
Thy harueft is fo great, and Laborers fo fewe,
Yea of thofe fewe fome Loyterers, full yll themfelues do fhewe.
And let vs here by take, a warning to vs all,
That feing harueft is fo great, and woorkemens nomber fmall :
Our fruit muft needes be loft, ourfelues to famifhe brought,
Our Land layde lyke a wyldernes, and brought at length to nought.
But thou O Lorde and God, of this our harueft great,
Spare thou our woorkemen, and more fend, that labour wil with fweate,
That as we mone for Iohn, en*Viron*ed by death,
Thou wylt vs glad wyth many a Paule, enfpirde with heauenly breath.

Quod Iohn Awdelie.

Finis.

❡ Imprinted at London, by Iohn
Awdely, dwellyng in lytle Britayne ftreete by great
Saint Bartelmewes.

John Awdeley otherwise John Sampson, whose name appears as the author of this and the two following ballads, was a younger son of Sampson Awdeley, verger of Westminster Abbey. The son was made free of the Stationers' Company towards the close of 1556, and from its Registers we learn that he obtained licences to publish a number of ballads, some of which he wrote himself, and a few books of importance. From the same source it transpires that on several occasions he incurred fines for pirating, and in July 1561 he paid twelve pence in consideration 'for that he ded reuyle Rycharde Lante with vnseemly wordes'.

Owing to a break which occurs in the Stationers' Registers between July 1571 and July 1576 we possess no further knowledge of Awdeley's press, except such as is supplied by products of it which have been preserved. He died in 1575, and his will was proved September 16th in that year (Plomer, *Abstracts from the Wills of English Printers*, Bibliographical Society, 1903). The printing-press in Little Britain Street, by Great St. Bartholomew's without Aldersgate, he left to his son Sampson Awdeley and his son-in-law John Simpson, to remain, however, under his widow's control until one of them should prove himself competent to manage it. The Stationers' records are silent as to the subsequent fortunes of the family.

Awdeley's chief claim to literary fame rests on his 'Fraternitye of Vacabondes', 1565 (Early English Text Society, 1869, and New Shakspere Society, 1880), to which Thomas Harman is said to have owed something for the 'Caueat or Warening for common cursetors vulgarely called Vagabones'. Awdeley was the author of two other ballads, now in the British Museum, which were reprinted by Mr. Henry Huth in his 'Ancient Ballads and Broadsides' (Philobiblon Society, 1867)—'The wonders of England,' 1559, and 'A godly ditty or Prayer to be song vnto God for the preseruation of his Church, our Queene, and Realme', undated, but about 1570. Awdeley may have been the writer as well as the printer of an epitaph on Francis

Benison (p. 18).

Jean Véron, protestant reformer, was born at or near Sens in France, and settled in England about the year 1536. He was ordained by Bishop Ridley in 1551, and in the following year received the living of St. Alphage, Cripplegate. On August 16, 1553, Gilbert Bourne preached a sermon at Paul's Cross in defence of Bonner and against Ridley. The congregation became infuriated and Bourne narrowly escaped injury from a dagger which was hurled at the pulpit. Véron and the reformers Bradford and Rogers were present, and they, though opposed to Bourne, made efforts to quell the tumult and were successful in getting the preacher away into safety. The service, however, did not avail, for Bradford and Véron were arrested by order of the Privy Council and sent to the Tower. Véron was deprived of St. Alphage and remained a prisoner until the accession of Elizabeth, when he received valuable preferment. He was instituted to the rectory of St. Martin, Ludgate, and made Vicar of St. Sepulchre and Prebendary of Mora, all of which he held until his death in 1563. He was buried in St. Paul's Cathedral.

Numerous entries in Henry Machyn's 'Diary' (Camden Society, 1848) attest that Véron occupied a prominent position among the London clergy and that he preached at the obsequies of several distinguished persons. From Machyn we also learn that on November 2, 1561, 'a yonge (man) stood with a (sheet) abowtt hym for spykyng of serten wordes agaynst Véron the preacher'; and on the 23rd Machyn himself sat in the place of penance for repeating further slander against the reformer. Véron published several works and translations, chiefly of a controversial nature.

In the Stationers' Registers, 1562–63 (Arber's *Transcript*, vol. i, p. 214), this ballad is entered thus: 'Receuyd of Iohn Awdelaye for his lycenfe for pryntinge of the Ephitaphe of mafter Veron.' It is printed in single column and is contained on three sides by an ornamental border of eight pieces.

Ecclesi. XX.

¶ Remember Death, and | thou shalt neuer sinne.

YE Adams broode and earthly wightes, which breath now on the earth,
    Come daunce thys trace, and marke the song of me most mighty Death.
Ful wel my might is knowen & sene, in al the world about,
    When I do strike, of force they yeld, both noble, wise & stout.
Of liuing things which breath and bray, I raigne as puisant Prince,
    No sooner take they lyfe, but I, pursue it to conuince.
In Mothers wombe the Babe I slay, in birth sometime I strike,
    No place nor state may me exempt, to me all is a like.
The Prince with Begger to graue I take, the yong eke wyth the old,
    [The] wise graue men with fooles and dolts, I lodge them in one fold.
Y[ea] courtly Dames, & town wyues fine, though neuer so trim they be,
    W[i]th Malkins, Sluts, & sloyes they trudge, in graue I make thē gree.
The seming braue fine Courtiers, which square it out in gate,
    With Hob and Lob I close in clay and bring them to one state.
The tchuffe with tchinckes and ruddocks red, wherin is all hys trust,
    In moment I wyth mysers poore, do hyde hym vp in dust.
The Iudge seuere, and Counceller sage, with me they all must trudge,
    I force not for their hye estate, nor feare their hate or grudge.
I wayting am on euery one, as shadow wyth body am I,
    And when the myghty God doth byd, I slay them by and by.
Sometyme in game, sometyme in myrth, somtyme in sleepe I kyll,
    In eating, drinking, and in sport, I many tymes them spyll.
No place so sure, no food so good, no exercise at all,
    Me Death can barre, but at Gods becke to earth I make them fall.
And yet behold how ech one thynckes, to scape me and my dart,
    Though neuer so nere I come them to, and grype them to the hart.
My Minstrell Sicknes pipes ech houre, by aches, stitches and cramps,
    It soūdes my daunce styll in their eares that they must to my damps.
The lusty Brute with snuffing lookes, by manhood doth hope to lyue,
    The Coward out, yᵗ feares to fight, though wounds him daily greue.
The Coward agayne thinkes long to lyue by sleeping in a whole skin,
    With shunning wars and forayn broyles, which countries oft be in.
The rytch by gold, the wyse by wyt, do thinke to shift me of,
    To Beggers that starue, & careles fooles, but yet themselues thei scof.
For one wyth other I take them all, feare they, or feare they not,
    The desperat foole and fearefull one go all into my pot.
The youthfull Lads by stout courage, thinke to driue me away
    To crooked age, yet many times by ryot I oft them slay.
And old old age, hopes styll to lyue, by keepyng a merry hart,
    With youthful sports and wanton toyes, though it be to their smart.
Yea my nere Syb and Beldam Trot, that croompled is for age,
    By youthly tyre & wanton trickes, thinkes deathes power to aswage.

It makes me laffe oft times to fee, their gate, their lookes, their walke,
    How halting tryps, and fine wryde ieftes they counterfet in talke.
They would me blere, and make folkes think, they wer to yong for me,
    And yet forfooth if ftript they were, faire Notamies might ye fee.
What fhall I fay to thefe old folkes, when nature cannot them teach?
    By ftübling fpech & paines ech wher, which death at hand doth preach.
Nay vfuall is it wyth all ftates, though fences all be gone,
    And I at hand to ftrike the ftroke, yet thincke they not thereon.
Thus all would fhift and driue me of, though I them follow & trace,
    And dayly fend vnto the graue all ftates before their face.
But fooles they are that dread me fo, which cannot be auoyded,
    Syth God the maker of all thinges to lyfe hath fo me ioyned.
Yet nede they not to fhun me fo, if all were wayde aryght,
    For I the worldly griefes do end, which vexe them day and nyght.
Yea and befides the guyde am I, to heauen and ioyfull blys,
    Of thofe that vertuoufly do lyue, and feare to do amys.
And to thefe folke welcomde am I, though neuer fo fharpe I pere,
    Becaufe with Chrift they fhal then raigne, and fee his glory clere.
But as for thofe that wicked be, and fo ftill leade their life,
    Good caufe they haue to dread me fore, for I begin their griefe.
With death I bring an endles wo, which neuer fhall haue end,
    Wherefore if me you would not dread, your yll lyues then amend.
For precious is the death of thofe, which dye in Chrift their Lord,
    Who hath faued them from fynne and hel, and ended their difcord.

                             Quoth Ioh. Awd.
    FINIS.

Imprinted at Lon|don by Iohn Awdeley, dwelling in litle Britaine ftreete | wythout
Alderfgate. 1569. | The .xxx. of Aprill.

This ballad is printed in two columns. The initial letter of the first line is a large ornamental capital similar in design to that reproduced in R. Lemon's 'Catalogue of a collection of printed Broadsides in the possession of the Society of Antiquaries of London', 1866, p. 15.

3

¶ The cruel aſſault of Gods Fort.

BY Edward the ſixt, of England kyng,
A Fort was made gods truth to ſhield
In whoſe lyfe time, by good rulyng,
Both friend and foe to it dyd yelde.
    But when for ſynne of hys owne flocke,
The Lord in wrath tooke him away :
Leauing the Fort to his next ſtocke,
The enmies then ſought out theyr pray.
    Then blew vp trūpets of Papiſts ſoūde
Souldiers to call, and wages gaue :
Come who ſo would, was armed rounde,
None they refuſde, but dreſt them braue.
    The field was pytcht of Papiſts part,
With corned caps, tippets and gownes.
Theyr ordnaunce lay redy in cart,
To beat the fort of gods truth downe.
    The generall Gardner [1], braue and ſtout
And Captaine Boner [2], marcht foorth amain,
Bourne [3] with ſtanderd, cryed out,
Al arme, al arme, our ſhauelinges traine.
    The Auncient which that Bourne bare,
Were fierce wolues teeth, wt blood beſprent
Fire and Fagot, whych did declare,
Their rauenous hartes to Chriſtians ment.
    Then doctour Martin [4], as clarke of army
With Doctour Story [5], the maſter Gonner :
Theſe two in office, were as truſty,
As Gardner, Bourne, or byſhop Bonner.
    A cry was made, throughout the hoſt :
With fire and hempe, all to deſtroy :
Where euer they were, in al the coſt,
That dyd the Popes power ſeke to noye.
    The Fort thus ſieged on euery ſyde,
With crye ſo fierce, to kyll them all :
A ſorte for feare durſt not abyde,
But from Gods Fort to them dyd fall.

---

[1] Stephen Gardiner, Bishop of Winchester from 1531 to April 1552 and from August 1553 to 1555.
[2] Edmund Bonner, Bishop of London from 1539 to 1549, when he was deprived. Bonner was restored to his see by Queen Mary in 1553, but again deprived in 1559, when he was committed to the Marshalsea where he died ten years later.
[3] Gilbert Bourne, Bishop of Bath and Wells from 1554 to 1559.
[4] Thomas Martyn, a zealous Catholic writer.
[5] John Story, chancellor to Bishop Bonner.

Then might ye heare the Canons rore,
Which Bourne and Watſon [6] falſely ſhot:
Yelde, yeld theſe cryde, from heretickes lore
Or batter we ſhal, both wall and fort.

No, no (quoth they within the Fort)
We yelde vs not Gods truth to ſtayne:
Though you deſtroy vs in this ſort,
God ſhal our Fort, wyth force maintayne.

Wyth that they all the Fort wythin,
Wyth ſighes and ſobs to God out cryde:
Thou Lord of hoſtes, may not our ſynne,
But ayde thy flocke ſo wo betyde.

For though with ſinne, we cauſde this day
That our good king yu ſhouldſt thus take:
Yet Lord with bitternes of ſoule we pray,
Strength vs againſt this firye lake.

This done they blowde a chereful blaſt,
Vnto the ſouldiers in the Fort:
Arme ye, arme ye, in all the haſt,
Our enmies now to Fort reſort.

The Auncient which was ſpred on wall,
Had a white Lambe, with red ſpots thicke:
And in gold letters were theſe wordes all,
Why do ye Sauls, againſt me kicke?

Forth came Rogers [7], Hooper [8] & Saunders [9]
Vpon the walles the Fort to fende:
We yelde not (ſaid they) to ſuch deſtroyers,
But fight we will vnto the ende.

To theſe Steuen Gardner, gaue onſet,
And layde on lode, as wolfe on pray:
He tooke them priſoners, with his falſe net,
And ſent them to the fire ſtraightway.

Then Story the maiſter of the ſhot,
On Papiſts rampire braue and proude:
For ſpilling bloud he cared not,
Aſſault, aſſault he cryde aloude.

Theſe were no ſooner of the wall,
But vp lept Rydley and Latimer [10]:
To reſcue Gods fort, ſo nere to fall,
And did with force, the foes encounter.

And biſhop Cranmer [11], tough with gyle,
The enmies ſtole him from the Fort:
Yet boldly fought with them a whyle,
And folowed his mates, in lyke ſort.

[6] Thomas Watson, Bishop of Lincoln from 1557 to 1559.
[7] John Rogers, burned at Smithfield Feb. 4, 1555, the first of the Marian martyrs.
[8] John Hooper, Bishop of Gloucester and Worcester, burned at Gloucester Feb. 9, 1555.
[9] Laurence Saunders, burned at Coventry Feb. 8, 1555, was a younger brother of Sir Edward Saunders, judge. An epitaph by Lodowick Lloyd upon the death of the latter is in this collection.
[10] Nicholas Ridley, Bishop of London, and Hugh Latimer, Bishop of Worcester, burned in company at Oxford Oct. 16, 1555.
[11] Thomas Cranmer, Archbishop of Canterbury from 1533, burned at Oxford March 21, 1556, after submission and revocation.

Then doctour Wefton [12], at thefe out fhot,
The pellets of Rome, and them did mayme:
So that away they paffed not,
But were deftroyed with fire and flame.

But Bradford [13] then on wall vp lept,
And Philpot [14] eke by hym did ftand:
Cardmaker [15] and Taylour [16] alfo vp crept,
And thefe by truth dyd noy theyr band.

Bifhop Boner, on thefe laide hand,
And to Smithfield fent them in haft:
But to the death, thefe did withftand,
And would not yeld to enmies blaft.

Then blewe the Papifts to affault,
And fet a watch about the Fort:
Of knightes and yemen to finde fome fault,
To make them yelde after this fort.

And fworen men in euery coft,
They did compell to watche and fpye:
If any did refift their hoft,
They muft prefent them for to dye.

The Fort with enmies laid round about,
And al the captaines fo cruelly flaine:
The foldiours therof with courage ftout,
Kept yet the walles with might and maine.

Now fcale the walles (quoth Boner then)
Behold the captaines we haue flaine:
Ranfacke the Fort, deftroy all men,
Both wemen & children let none remaine.

Then fcaling lathers were vp rearde,
And Iohn Auales [17] on them with targe:
His knees had croffes becaufe he fearde,
The fteps wold breake and hang him large.

Vp came Beard [18], by Vales his man,
Armed al round as dronkardes vfe:
His head was clofde, with goodale can,
And in his hand a Tauerners crufe.

But they in Fort, did with them play,
And caft them bribes, which made thē yelde,
They ftriuing who fhould haue the pray,
Fought one with other in their owne fielde.

Yet battred was this Fort full fore,
With vehement fhot on Papifts part:
The walles they bet ftyl more and more,
But yet the fortmen would not ftart.

[12] Hugh Weston, Dean of Westminster, transferred to Windsor, and subsequently deprived.

[13] John Bradford, martyred July 1, 1555.

[14] John Philpot, Archdeacon of Winchester, burned at Smithfield Dec. 18, 1555.

[15] John Cardmaker (alias Taylor), burned at Smithfield May 30, 1555, after recanting.

[16] John Taylor, Bishop of Lincoln, deprived 1554.

[17] John Avales is mentioned towards the close of 'A Complaynt agaynft the wicked enemies of Chrift', p. 49. The name also occurs in connexion with 'A Commemoration or Dirige of Baftarde Edmonde Boner . . . Compiled by Lemeke Auale', 1569, a copy of which is in the British Museum (Corser, Collectanea Anglo-Poetica, 1860–80, vol. i, pp. 76–81). The nature of the 'commemoration' does not lead one to imagine that John and Lemeke, if related, shared the same religious views.

[18] Richard Beeard, divine and author.

Then puffhed the Papifts wt their pikes,
The Hargabuffes fhot out amayne :
And dyms the ayre and many ftrikes,
Of them that did the Fort fuftayne.

The Holberts and the Bowmen eke,
Came preafing toward the Fort with fpede :
Thefe were the rakehels that did feke,
To haue mens goodes playde Cains dede.

There might ye fee the Fort about,
Great ftreames of bloode & bodies flayne.
The handes of al the hoft throughout,
With blood of Saints they did them ftaine.

In this affault the infants out cryde,
And eke their mothers as wydowes left,
To fee theyr friendes before them dyde,
And al their goodes from them bereft.

Though thus the Fort, was almoft gone,
By cruel affault of enmyes bolde :
Yet fome within the Fort alone,
To God did crye, Lord keepe thy holde.

The God did fend his flaue Death down [19]
Into the Papifts hoft among :
Which flew the chiefeft in all the towne,
And greateft captaines in the throng.

By thys great ftroke of mightie Ioue,
The vehement force of Papifts fell :
And fent this Fort (which is hys Loue)
A godly captaine [20] to keepe it well.

Which when in Fort fhe did appere,
And flag of truce fpred in her hand :
Aloud fhe cried, ceafe nowe your yre,
And yelde to me right heyre of England.

Then fcattred were the Papifts hoft,
Their flags of fire to ground did fall.
Their flaming brandes which oft they toft,
Were clene out quentch at our Quenes call.

Crye was then made to God on hye,
Of al the fouldiours in the Fort :
Oh praife the Lorde for victorye,
In helping vs after this fort.

Now yelde (they cried) our brethren dere,
Which haue againft Gods truth fo ftoode :
Behold our Quene doth profer here,
To graunt ye peace to chaūge your moode.

Which if her clemencie you refufe,
And pleade not for your liues graunt :
The law of armes fhe muft nedes vfe,
On fuch as are to her repugnaunt.

[19] This is doubtlessly a reference to one of the plague visitations by which England was invaded in the sixteenth century. The most severe of these was that which occurred during the summer of 1563, when in London alone the weekly mortality rose to two thousand.

[20] Though the accession of Elizabeth (Nov. 17, 1558) lent immediate relief to the Protestants, yet the Queen gave those of Mary's bishops who survived an opportunity of taking the oath of supremacy. This invitation with one exception was refused, whereupon the recusants were deprived.

Yelde, yelde therefore ye chiefe captaines
Example geue to all your hoſt:
Or els wyll God reuenge with paines,
The bloud of thoſe whom ye haue roſt.
    An all ye Chriſtians of this England,
Your trumpets found to Gods hie praiſe,
On Gods head let a Bay garland,
For your triumphe of all theſe fraies.
    Yeld now your liues after ſuch ſort,
As God may not this Fort ſo plage.
Strength now your ſelues in this gods fort
That ye yelde no more to enmies rage.
    So God wil ſpare vs our Quene long,
So God will make our land encreaſe:
So God wyl builde our fort ſo ſtrong,
That no enmies dare to it preaſe.

To this ſay al right Chriſten men,
God ſaue our Quene.   Amen.   Amen.

ꝗ.   I. A.

Τελως

❡ Imprinted at London by Iohn Awdeley, dwelling by great S. Bartelmewes
beyonde Alderſgate.

John Payne Collier, who included this with 'Old Ballads' (Percy Society, 1840), suggested that it was a moralization of 'The Cruell aſſaute of Cupydes forte', a ballad entered 1565–66, and expressed a hope that the latter, which is not extant, might have been less dull than 'the cruel aſſault of Gods Fort' (*Extracts from the Registers of the Stationers' Company*, Shakespeare Society, 1848–49, vol. i, p. 126). As a fact it is an interesting allegorical poem in which are depicted the leaders of the reformation struggle. It may have been licensed 1571–76, or not at all.

The ballad is printed coarsely in three columns and without border.

4

¶ A free admonition without any fees,
To warne the Papiſtes to beware of three trees.

I F that you be not paſt all grace,
O Papyſtes heare mee ſpeake,
Let reaſon rule, and truth take place,
   Ceaſe you from that you ſeeke.
Can you God or his woord deface?
   Can you the truth wythſtand?
Can you our noble Queene diſplace,
   And yet lyue in England?

Take heede beware the Deuyll is a knaue
   He wyl you ſure begile:
In cruelty he would you haue
   To ſerue hym here awhile.
Wyth lying and hipocriſy,
   His kyngdome to mayntayne:
Contemning truth and equity,
   This is hys ſubtile trayne.

Let curſed Cain example be,
   That ſlew Abel his brother:
Whom neither God with Maieſty,
   Could moue to leaue his murder.
Nor yet the godly lyfe of hym,
   That gaue hym none offence,
Tyll he had heaped vp hys ſynne,
   In practeſyng his pretence.

Let Core and Dathan come frō hell
   Where now they do remayne,
That they their minds at lēgth mai tel
   Wherfore they ther remain.
Namely, for that they did rebel,
   And would not be perſwaded,
But would be Lordes in Iſrael,
   Tyll hel had them deuoured.

What could make Abſalon meeke & tame
   And to deſiſt from rage?
His father Dauids worthy fame,
   Or yet his counſel ſage?
No, no, theſe things wil not preuail
   With hym that feares not God,
The force of doctrine ther doth fail,
   Tyl God ſtrike with his rod.

And as the Deuil in thefe did rage,
   To worke his wycked wyll,
That nothyng coulde theyr furye fwage
   Tyl they did it fulfyl.
So that the law of God and Man,
   They fought to ouerthrow,
Euen fo of late I truly can
   The lyke vnto you fhow.

When Kyng Edward of worthy fame
   Had Antichrift put downe,
And to the glory of Gods name,
   Had placed truth in her roome:
The denfhire [1] dolts like Rebels ranck,
   In rufty armour ranged,
But hangd wer fom, their cariōs ftāck,
   The world was quickly changed.

And then dyd Ket [2] the tanner ftout
   In Norffolke play his part,
Affemblyng fuch his Rebels rout,
   That Innocents might fmart.
But hanged he was, this was his end,
   And fo ende all the fort,
That Rebels are, and wyll not mend,
   A rope be their comfort.

Such bleffings as the Nortons [3] had,
   And fuch as Felton [4] found,
God fend them all that are fo bad
   Wyth heeles to bleffe the ground.
If that you lyke not for to haue,
   This bleffyng in a rope,
Leaue of you Rebels for to raue
   And curffe your Dad the Pope.

Which makes you oft fuch Crowes to pul
   Then leaues you in the mire,
In fending you to fuch a Bull,
   This is but fymple hire.
Behold the end of thys attempt
   That laft here was begun,
Loe God your doyng doth preuent,
   The Rebels race to run.

[1] A rebellion, flamed by the introduction of the English liturgy, which broke out in the villages of Devonshire and the western counties during the summer of 1549.

[2] Robert Kett, 'the tanner,' hanged as a rebel at Norwich, Dec. 7, 1549. Kett had led a popular movement which offered a resistance against the injustices of the existing land laws.

[3] See William Gibson's ' A difcription of Nortons falcehod of Yorke fhyre, and of his fatall farewel' (p. 149).

[4] See 'The end and Confeffion of Iohn Felton' (p. 144) and Stephen Peele's ' A letter to Rome, to declare to yᵉ Pope, Iohn Felton his freend is hangd in a rope' (p. 203).

Synce God by grace doth guyde hys flock
  That none can them anoy,
If you be grafted in this ftocke,
  He wyl you not deftroy.
Feare God, flee fyn, the truth embrace,
  And feeke your Prince to pleafe,
Obey the lawes and call for grace,
  So fhall you lyue at peace.

God faue our Queene Elizabeth.

ꝗ. G. B.

FINIS

℩ Imprinted at Londō by Iohn Aw|dely, for Henry Kirkham, dwelling at the mid|dle North doore of Paules, at the figne of the | blacke Boy.   The .xij. of December.
1571.

These initials have been ascribed to William Bald-win, contributor to and editor of 'The Mirrour for Magiftrates', 1559.   A satirical piece, 'Beware the Cat,' supposed to have been first printed in 1561, of which a unique though imperfect copy of the edition of 1584 formerly in the Corser and Huth Collec-tions and now in the British Museum, is signed in the same manner. Evidence of Baldwin's authorship of this is furnished by a contemporary broadside (Society of Antiquaries) entitled ' A fhort Anfwere to the Boke called Beware the Cat'. This is described in Lemon's Catalogue as a scurrilous poem of fifty-six lines denying that the book called ' Beware the Cat' was written by one Stremer, but that it was the production of Wil-liam Baldwin.   The ' Dictionary of National Bio-graphy' suggests that Baldwin may have written ' A newe Booke called the Shippe of fafegarde, wrytten by G. B.' (1569).   It is possible, however, that the author of this book and the ballad reprinted above may have been William Birch, the writer of three ballads in Heber's collection.   The ' free admonition' was reprinted by Collier in ' Old Ballads' (Percy Society, 1840).

The ballad is printed in two columns within orna-mental borders.   The initial letter of the opening stanza is the same as that used by Awdeley in print-ing ' An Epitaph of Maifter Fraunces Benifon', a facsimile of which is included in this volume.

5

Of the horyble and woful deſtruccion of Ieruſalem.

And of the ſygnes and tokens that were ſeene before it was deſtroied : which
diſtruction was after Chriſtes aſſenſion .xlii. yeares.   To the tune of the Queenes Almayne.

AS Emperour Vaſpaſian
  Some tyme in Rome there was,
Through whom much dolors then began
  Of mortall wars alas,
With in two yeares that he did rayne
He put the Iewes to myckill payne
With fyer and ſword both take and ſlayne,
  His power brought ſo to paſſe,
His Sone Tytus hauing no dread
His army ouer Iudae ſpread
The people to the Citie flead
  Hoping to haue redreſſe.

¶ Before Titus Vaſpaſians ſonne
  Vnto this warres dyd goo
Was after Criftes aſſencion,
  Longe .xl. yeares and two
Then did the Romayns with ſuche pride
Be ſet theyr land both far and wyde,
And hemd them in, on euery ſide
  To theyr great payne and wo,
They brought the Iewes in ſuch a caſe
The propheſye, to bryng to paſſe,
Spoke by our Lord when he here was
  The ſcripture doth ſaye ſo.

That prudent Iewe Ioſephus ſayes
  Who did no wryte in vayne,
That he was preſent in thoſe dayes
  And ſawe this mortall payne,
When that Tytus both bold and ſtout
Be ſet Ieruſalem a bout,
That none mought in, nor Iſſue out
  No waye but to be ſlayne.
For Tytus his chyef capteyn was
The ſeige when he had brought to paſſe
Great was the cry woe and alas,
  The ſtory doth ſaye playne.

¶He ſtopt their pypes and Conduyts all,
   That no water mought paſſe :
With famyne they were in great thrall,
   Moſte wofull was their caſe,
They were conſtraynyd in ſuch need
With Horſſe, and Aſſe, them ſelues to feed
Both Dogg, and Catte, this do I reed
   Moſt ougle meate it was,
The honger ther it was ſo great,
Ones vomit was anothers meate
Ther was no waye for to intreate
   But preſent death alas.

Sixe mounthes the ſiege it did holde on
   About that Citie gat,
Whearin was manie a mothers ſonne
   Did ſtarue for lacke of meate,
The famous Ladies of that towne
That weare before of hie renowne,
For fault of foode fell in a ſowne
   Ther was nothinge to geate :
The ſtorye this doth ſpecifie,
The mothers moſte vnnaturally,
They ſlewe their Children rufully,
   And Roſtyd them to eate.

This Titus then of hye renowne
   Moſt valyently and bold,
The walles ſo ſtronge he did caſt downe
   Reſyſtaunce waxyd colde,
The people in the ſtreetes laye dead,
They had no Succour drynk nor bread
Muche was the blood that then was ſhead,
   Alas lament wee ſhould :
The Romains entred with ſuche might,
With Polaxe, ſpeares, & ſwerdes ſo bright
They ſlew all that came in their ſight
   No mercie they did hold.

The Gates that couered were with golde
   They threw them to the ground,
That famous Citie to behold
   For ſinne it was confound,
Aleuen honderid thowſande ſlaine
Through honger, ſwerde & peſtelent paine
In this the ſtorie doth not faine,
   Of manie a blooddy wound,
The ſtinke of carkas in the ſtreete,
The feble ſoules that could not fleete
For faint with honger ſkarce could creepe,
   Full heauie was their ſounde.

Then Titus gaue this fentence bliue
  Which Romayns lykyd well,
As many as you fynd a lyue,
  After this Rate them fell,
As Crift was fold for thyrtye pence,
By Iudas and his falfe pretence,
So Titus made their recompence
  The ftorie thys doth tell,
XXX. Iewes for a penie bought,
As manie more were folde for nought
Ther owne confufion thus was wrought
  Becaufe they did rebell.

And manie prifoners mo I weene
  To Egipt they weare fend,
Fowerfcore thoufand, and feuenteene
  In prifon all their ende,
And Titus in his companie
Tooke manie fuche as were worthie,
And lead them bounde all captiuelie,
  To Rome with him to wend:
Ther was no helpe for to reuoke,
As Ihofephus faith in his booke
His Chronicles who lifte to looke,
  On truth they do depend.

Thirtie years God gaue them fpace
  That they mought yet repent,
Their liues amend and call for grace
  For them Chrift did lament,
This louinge Lord oft did them call
By fundrie fignes as heare you fhall
Before his wrath on them did fall
  Or anger fullie bent,
Twelue dayes eclipfed was the moone,
That they mought bee conuerted foone,
But they wift not what to bee doone,
  But finne ftill did augment.

Before the feige or anie warr,
  The fpace of all one yeare
Ouer that towne was feene a ftarre,
  Moft blafinge bright and cleare
So like a fworde in fhape it was,
Wher at great feare and wonder was,
Yet left they not their wickednes,
  when thefe fignes did appeare:
More ouer in the ayre fo light,
In plate of maile and armore bright,
Were feene men redie for to fight,
  To fhewe theyr time was neare.

A feftifall daye, in Apriell,
　To halowe they were dight,
And fodainlie amongeft them fell
　A merueylous ftraunge light,
So bright and cleare with fuche aleame,
Paffing the fonne as it did feeme,
But what it ment no man could deeme.
　But were all in fore flyght
And whyle the priftes did this in dure
To offer a Calfe they did their cure,
Whiche Calfe a thinge againft nature,
　Brought forth a Lambe in fight.

Suche manie tokens contrarie
　Whiche doth Prognoftikate,
And to the Iewes did fignifie
　Their wofull fall and fate,
Before that Titus warr began
Fower yeares of fpace, this proue I can,
How that the fonne of one rude man,
　Ananias lowe of ftate,
He ran the ftreates in fuche a rage
Beinge a child of tender age,
To call and crie he did not fwage
　Repente eare it be late.

But for his paines he was well beat
　This had he for his hire,
For truthe they did him euill in treate
　Againft him did confpire,
But yet he cried and would not blen,
While he was able yet to ren,
Sayenge wo be to Ierufalem,
　For kindling of Gods yre :
Wo be to thee and to thy land
Thou art be fet in wofull band,
Thy dayes of forowe is at hand
　Of famine fwerd and fyer.

This [sic] was that famous Citie then
　Diftroyed with fier and fword,
That mightie towne Ierufalem,
　The Citie of the Lorde :
Becaufe their God they would not knowe
Chrift being .xxx. yeares belowe
His word to them plainlie did fhewe
　This fcripture doth recorde,
That they mought be his chofen firfte
To liue and raigne a mongft the iuft,
And to no other for to trufte
　But to belyue his word.

Nowe feinge that this Ierufalem,
  As fcripture doth tell true
Was plaguyd for the finnes of men,
  Which Romaines ouer threw,
What fhall that Lorde to vs expreffe
That fo doth liue in fuche exceffe,
Of whordome, Pride, and couitoufnes
  More now then did the Iewe,
·Therfore is our example this,
A mend the thinge that is a myffe
That we maye haue eternall bliffe,
  By Chrifte our Lorde Iefue.

Finis.   Qd. Iohn Barker.

¶Imprinted at London, in Fleeteftreate | Beneath the Conduit, at the figne of |
S. Iohn Euangelift, by Tho|mas Colwell.

In the Stationers' Register, 1568–69 (Arber's *Transcript*, i. 380), this ballad is entered as 'Receuyd of Thomas Colwell for his lycenfe for pryntinge of a ballett in[ti]tuled *ye horable and Wofull Dyftruftion of Ierusalem*'. Three of Barker's other ballads—'A Balade declarying how neybourhed loue, and trew dealying is gone . . .', undated; 'The true defcrip-tion of a monfterous Chylde, Borne in the Ile of wight . . . M.D.LXIIII. the month of October . . . in the parys of Frefhwater . . .'; and 'The Plagues of Northumberland . . .'; undated, reprinted by Mr. Henry Huth in 'Ancient Ballads and Broadsides' (Philobiblon Society, 1867)—are now in the British Museum.

6

An Epitaph of Maifter Fraunces Benifon.

[See facsimile.]

Francis Benison is mentioned by Stow as having a monument in the parish church of St. Peter-upon-Cornhill, but no such name occurs in the Register of Burials there, as printed by the Harleian Society. The ballad was licensed to John Awdeley in 1570–71 (Arber's *Transcript*, i. 442), and it is not unlikely that it may have been written by him. The ballad from which this facsimile is made measures twelve inches by nine and a half inches.

¶An Epitaph, / of Maiſter Fraunces Beniſon, / Citizene and Marchant of London, and of the Haberdaſhers Company.

¶I Death this Coffyn beare,

Therfore ye lyuing prepare.

For you that lyuing are:

The dead are paſt my feare,

If lacke of health be ſuch a let,
as doth diminiſh ſtore:
And loſſe of goods doth care procure,
with ſobs and ſighings ſore.
Much more is leſſe of frendly friend,
whom GOD hath cald by death,
But vnto vs the leſſe redoundes,
which liue by vitall breath.
Man may to health reſtored be,
if Gods good wyll be ſo:
And wealth again mai grow in time
euyll hap to ouerthrow.
But friendly friend whom God by
death, hath cald to liue in ioy:
Cannot agayne to vs returne,
but reſt with out anoy.

Faith being fixed firme in hart, and hope of Heauens bliſſe:
Sure then in happy ſtate they reſt, this ſequel cannot miſſe.
¶Oh Fraunces Beniſon (I ſay) Gods Beniſon no doubt:
Thou waſt the bleſſing ſure of GOD, to wyfe, and all the rout
Of thy good friendes and kinred to, GOD bleſſed them in thee:
And bleſſed twiſe waſt thou of GOD, ſuch happy dayes to ſee
Of Marchauntes all he was the floure, for wyſdome and good ſkill:
And right experte in euery trade, delightyng therein ſtill.
This three and twenty yeares, or moze, in traffike he did toyle:
His wyll and ſkyll was alwaies ſuch, he thought it no tormoyle.
With foecaſt he and diligence did comprehend no doubt,
The vnderſtanding of all trades, nere Chriſtendome throughout.
And hauyng oportunitie, no tyme he would omit:
His full pretence to bryng to paſſe, and purpoſe for to hit.
When wynde and tyde dyd ſpaede require, all one was night or nowne:
His watchings he did nothing way, tyl his attemptes were done.
He oft would ſay that Diligence, good Fortunes Mother was:
Which brought his enterpriſes all, more luckely to pas.

Full quicke and ready with hys pen, and cunning to likewiſe:
Of right good ſkyll for to endight, to ſerue eche enterpryſe.
As well for frend, as for him ſelfe, when nede the ſame did craue:
Whether it were in Marchaunts trade, or other matters graue
Beſides his natiue Engliſh tong, the French and Dutch he ſpake:
With pen and ſpeeche in pleaſant ſtile, he arguments could make.
And for his tyme his trade hath bene, as ample I am ſure
As any Marchant of thys Land, whyleſt here he dyd endure.
The Quenes reuenues of her crowne, he thereby did enlarge:
With great preſerment of all youth committed to his charge.
Beneficiall eke he was, to eche ſorte and degree:
He traded ſo by Sea and land, it could none other bee.
¶Theſe paſt, he with good name and fame, to eche mans contentacion:
That with him dealt in any trade, to his great commendacion.
And though beſides his propper ſtocke, he vſed credite large:
Yet eche contract in traffike done, right well he did diſcharge.
And hys corragious attemptes, by forecaſt ſo did frame:
That diuers men did muſe therat, and ſome malignde the ſame.
Which to him knowne, full wyſely he, could temper Nature ſo:
That he vnquiet would not be, but let all malice go.
And leaue to GOD the whole reuenge, ſtyll ſeeking quietnes:
So his affaires they framed well, and better had ſucces.
To taſte the ſower wyth the ſwaete, hym ſelfe ſo did prepare:
When any loſſe he did ſuſtaine, that patience conquerd care.
Citizen lyke in euery poynt, himſelfe he did behaue:
With comely geſture and attire, right decent, ſad, and graue.
With chearefull ſalutacions, right curteous to all men:
And how to vſe audacitie, he knew place, tyme and when.
To noble and to worſhipfull, ſure knowne he was as well,
As vnto the inferiour ſorte, this iuſt reporte can tell.
And alſo knowne in Princes Court, by his ſollicitacion:
As well for cauſes of his own, as others of hys nation.
He left behinde hym worldly goodes, all men to ſatiſfie:
And for to comfort wyfe and frendes alſo aboundantly.
And where he was a Gouernour, for thimpotentes defence:
He charitably vnto them, gaue his beneuolence.
Hys Wyll long time lay by him made, which he from yeare to yeare:
Dyd ouerſee and order ſo, as Death were euer neare.
Sicknes ſo ſharpely did him take, all hope it did expell:
No way there was Death to eſcape, which he perceiued well.
Straight therupon he did commit, to perſons of great ſkyll:
The ordering of hys temporall goods, accordyng to hys Wyll.
And gaue himſelfe cleane from the world, and onely dyd depend:
On Chriſtes death to be his lyfe, and ſo he made an end.
Whoſe ſoule no doubt remaynes in ioy, with Abraham and the reſt:
Of good and faythfull Patriarkes, who ſure of God are bleſt.
His good example to enſue, graunt Lord we thee deſire:
And that we may them imitate, we humbly thee require,
Thus I conclude, yelding to GOD, all honour, laud and prayſe:
With thanks for this our brother deare, I wiſh to walke his waies.

FINIS.

Imprynted at London
by Iohn Awdely, dwellyng in little
Britayne ſtreete, wythout
Alderſgate.
1570,

7

The complaint of a finner, vexed with paine,
Defyring the ioye, that euer fhall remayne.

After W. E. moralized.

THe God of loue, that fits aboue,
Doth know vs, Doth know vs,
How finfull that we bee:
Sent his word, the two edged fword
To fhew vs, To fhew vs,
Our fin and iniquitie.
That euery vice may vanquifhed be,
Oh Lord arife for thy mercye
Doe this our God and bynd vs,
For euer and euer thine owne:
The truth wyl alway fynd vs,
By the feedes that we haue fowne.
The truth wyl tel if we wold lye,
The touchftone doth y⁰ tree wel trye.

¶And as we haue a foule to faue,
Vprightly, Vprightly,
Though troubled ftil with fin:
We fhuld not take, that did vs make,
So lightly, So lightly,
This worldly wealth to win.
But if we wyl the Lord prouoke
We may loke for his heauy ftroke,
As his word hath appointed
The Scripture doth plainely tell:
Yet fhal not his holy anointed
Once taft the paynes of Hell.
Now haue I told the ieoperdy,
But Chrift is our iuft remedy.

¶With woful harts though god forbeares
To plague vs, To plague vs,
We ought for to lament:
Thy word alway, both night & day
Perfwade vs, Perfwade vs,
Inwardly for to repent.

And euery one to call for grace
Since the touchſtone in euery place,
Doth floriſh freſh and ſhyne
That the whole world may ſee :
And all that wyl be thyne,
Muſt come with teares to thee.
We wyl not boaſt our merites Lord,
Since thy deare ſon made the accord.

¶ We reade of olde, what Prophetes tolde
Full truly, Full truly,
And wrote it long a go :
A Mayden myld, ſhulde beare a child
Full duely, Full duely,
And it prouen euen ſo.
But yet God wot, the Iewes of kynd
Beleued it not, but were ſtyl blynd,
And are vnto this day
Refuſyng the Triumphant truth :
That the Prophet Eſaye did ſay
And wrote it to age and youth.
But therto they wold not accord,
But cruelly crucified the Lord.

But let vs now, both bend and bow,
And ſpede vs, And ſpede vs,
To follow the true trace :
For he hath ſent, his Teſtament,
To feede vs, To feede vs,
And call vs vnto grace.
Vnworthy now although we bee
Yet ye ſee how his deare mercye,
To vs he doth ſtill geue
And liberall gyftes vs ſend :
That we might ſure beleue
And our lewde liues amend.
Therfore let vs our harts enclyne,
That pearles be not caſt vnto ſwyne.

¶ The fleſh (I ſay) both night & day,
Doth hold vs, Doth hold vs,
From followyng the true trace :
But thy deare ſon, doth bid vs come,
And bold vs, And bold vs,
To call to thee for grace.
Thus ſayeth our ſauiour Ieſu
Come vnto me, and I wyl eaſe you.
If ye wyl cal and knocke
That are ouer laden with ſin :
Then wyl I open the locke
And be ready to let you in.

For I am he that bought you deare,
Therfore behold, and draw ye neare.

FINIS.   W. Birch.

⁊ Imprinted at London by Alexander
Lacy, for Richard Applow, dwellyng in
Pater noſter row, hard by | the Caſtle Tauerne.

William Birch, the author of this and other ballads in Heber's collection, is an individual of whom nothing is known. The Society of Antiquaries possesses a ballad by Birch entitled ' A Songe betwene the Quenes Maieſtie and Englande ', without date (reprinted in the *Transactions* of the Bibliographical Society, vol. iv, p. 74). Permission to print this was granted to William Copland in 1558–59 (Arber's *Transcript*, i. 96), although the Antiquaries' copy was issued by William Pickering (Lemon, *Catalogue*, p. 17). There is a volume in the Britwell Library entitled ' A newe Booke called the Shippe of Safeguarde, wrytten by G. B. Anno 1569 ', which may have been written by Birch. Ritson (*Bibliographia Poetica*, p. 196) states that ' the complaint of a ſinner ' is a moralization of Elderton's ' God of Love '. The opening lines of the original ballad, now lost, are quoted in ' Much Ado about Nothing ', Act V, scene ii, ll. 25–28, where Benedick sings :

' The God of love,
That sits above
And knows me, and knows me,
How pitiful I deserve.'

Richard Applay or Apple was an original member of the Stationers' Company. He is mentioned in its records as having taken apprentices and paid fines, yet the licence for this ballad, 1562–63 (Arber's *Transcript*, i. 205), is the only evidence of his having published.

The Britwell ballad did not belong to Heber, but was purchased at the Bandinel sale in 1861 (Catalogue, No. 1115). It is printed in two columns.

8

A new balade of the worthy feruice of late
doen by Maifter Strangwige in Fraunce, and of his death.

ENgland hath loft a Soldiour of late
Who Strangwige was to name:
Although he was of meane eftate
His deedes deferued fame.

¶ For as the Plowman plowes yᵉ groūd
And toyleth to til for corne:
So Strãgwige fought a deadly wound
For Brittaine where he was borne.

¶ In deede of birth he was borne bace
Although of worfhipful kyn:
In youth he fought to runne the race
Where he might prowes wyn.

¶ In his yong yeares he walked wyde
And wandred oft a ftray:
For why, blynd Cupid did him guyde
To walke that wyldfome way.

¶ Thus here & there I wot not where
He founded where to ryde:
But happy hauen he found no where
Nor harbour for to abyde.

¶ But when he had the courfe out run
Where Pyrates prict the Carde:
Twyfe at the leaft, he thought vndone
And looked for his rewarde.

¶ For by legall lawes he was condemd
Yet Mercy bare the mace:
And in refpect he wold amend
He found a Princes grace.

¶ And in that ftate he vowed to GOD
And to his righteous Queene:
He wold no more deferue fuch rod
Nor at Iuftice barre be feene.

¶He thus contented for a whyle
And laughed Fortune to fcorne:
Tyl weeds did worke by fubtil guyle
To ouergrow the corne.

¶And then occafion ferued iuft
That Martiall men muft trudge:
He vaunced himfelfe with valiaunt luft
To go he did not grudge.

¶And to the fea he fought a charge
Where he might take his chaunce:
And there with fpred his fayles at large
To feke a porte in Fraunce.

¶And paffed by a warlyke towne
Where municion lay a land:
He fpoyld and cut their chaynes a down
And paffed by ftrong hand.

¶Where as he caught a deadly wound
Yet his courage neuer quayled:
But as he had ben fafe and found
On his way forth he fayled.

¶And paffed through euen to that porte
Where he vowed to aryue:
And ftyl he did his men coumfort
And courage did them geue.

¶Then ATROPOS did him affayle
That al Adams kynd doth call:
Againft whofe force may none preuayle
But fubiect to him all.

¶This life (ꝙ he) which was me lent
From iudgement feat in perrill:
I came with heart for that entent
To fpend in my Queenes quarell.

¶Therfore this debt here wil I pay
This life which is not mine:
O Lord receyue my fpirit to ioy
That by Chriftes death is thine.

☞ All Subiects now, loke and forefee
That to trade the warres pretend :
Offendours eke (if any there bee)
Make ye no worfe an end.

W. Birch.

❡ FINIS.

❡ Imprinted at London by Alexander | Lacy for William Owen, and are | to be fold at the little fhop at | the north dore of | Poules.

The Foreign and Domestic Series of the Calendar of State Papers contain several references to Strangways the pirate. On February 4, 1553, the Council ordered Sir William Pickering to request the French king to apprehend and deliver three pirates, 'Strangwisshe' and two others, fugitives, so that they might be brought to England. In May following it was reported that these had evaded capture 'by reason of official impediments and delays' and that the chance of taking them was remote.

Henry Strangways and his companions were not captured until August, 1559, when the ringleader was committed to the Tower (Machyn, *Diary*, Camden Society, 1848, p. 206). Towards the end of September sentence of death was passed on the offenders, but on the twenty-third day of that month Sir Nicholas Throckmorton addressed the Queen asking her to stay execution until he 'may speak with her'. On the thirtieth, Philip II. wrote to Elizabeth demanding restitution on behalf of one of his subjects who had been plundered by 'Enrieux Tranguaz'. This testimony of Strangways' activity against the merchants of Spain may have caused the Queen to exercise her prerogative on his behalf, for in June 1561 he was recommended by Throckmorton for employment in a proposed scheme for opening up trade with Morocco. In the autumn of 1562 Strangways joined the expedition to France, and on the eighth of October it was reported to Cecil that 'Captain Leighton and his band have embarked towards Rouen, with whom Strangwiche is gone'. This attempt to pierce the lines of the catholic troops with which Guise had invested the town fared badly. Numbers were killed or wounded, while others fell prisoners into the hands of the French. Strangways was wounded at Caudebècque and died at Rouen (Calendar of State Papers, Foreign, Oct. 30, 1562).

William Owen, bookseller of London, is known to posterity alone by the licence which he obtained for this ballad (Arber's *Transcript*, i. 203). It is suggested, however, that he may be connected with William Owen, who dwelt at the sign of the Cock in Paternoster Row, whence was issued the Earl of Surrey's 'Fourth boke of Virgill', without date. The only extant copy of this volume is in the Britwell Library. The ballad was reprinted in Collier's 'Old Ballads', 1840. The text of the original is in two columns.

9

A warnyng to Englan[d], let London begin :
To repent their iniquitie, & flie from their fin.

¶ Ifaie. 1.

¶ The Oxe knoweth his owner, and the Affe his mafters crib, but Ifraell hath not knowen : my people hath not vnderftand. Ah, finfull nation, a people laden with iniquitie : a feede of the wicked, corrupt chyldren : they haue forfaken the Lorde, they haue prouoked the holy one of Ifraell to anger : they are turned backewarde.

OH Endland [*sic*] be vigilant, and repent thee with fpede,
And marke well the myrours of thy vifitation :
Prepare thee to prayer, for it was neuer more neede,
And langwifh for thy lewde life, with great lamētation.

¶ When God drowned the worlde in the dayes of Noye,
For that fin onely (I faye) which we dayly do frequent :
He fent Noye to preach to them, or he dyd them deftroye,
And gaue them fixe fcore yeares, a fpace for to repent.

¶ Zodome and Gomorra alfo, were funke in fyre ful hot,
Burnyng all in Brimftone, vntyll they were deftroyed :
And yet they were forewarned long, by the prophete Lot,
With Repentance vnto them, continually he cryed.

❧But that happye citie Niniuie, among all the reft,
They heard Ionas his preachyng whē he came thither :
Repentyng ftraight wayes, and of God they were bleft,
A goodly myrour to LONDON, yf they wolde confider.

¶ O London, London, Ierufalem I may thee call,
For whye? thy conuerfation agreeth thereto now :
They wolde take no warnyng before the plague did fall,
And at this prefēt day O LONDON, nomore doeft thou.

¶ What tokens haue bene of late, of Gods feareful yre?
The lyke before was neuer feene, in no time (I trowe)
Thy cheef and beautifull Temple was defaced with fyre,
A goodly admonition fure (yf thou couldeft it knowe).

¶ Neither coulde the Peftilence prouoke vs to repent,
Nor cruell warres warne vs that the end is at hand :
No, we mocke at Gods threatnīgs lyke beafts impudent,
No doubt, Gods iuftice muft needes plague the lande.

¶ For we wyll not repent, nor our wicked lyues amend,
But continue ftyll in wickednes, procuring Gods curfe :
What earneft preachers doth the Lorde vs dayly fend?
It is but pearles before fwyne, for we ar wurfe & wurfe.

⳹If a man rebuke drunkennes, ſwearyng or blaſphemie,
He ſhall in this wyſe be mocked of one iauell or another:
[Thi]s good godly man, [is farr]e toe holy for our companie,
[You] ar a preciſian I t[rowe o]r ſome vnſpotted brother.

⳹Alas, is this your repentance after ſo long preachyng?
I pray you read the .xii. chap. of S. Mathewes goſpell:
Chriſt faith, of euery idle worde we ſhal geue a reconyng,
Then ſwearers and blaſphemers, ſhal be puniſhed in hell.

⳹Deare chriſtians, conſider our ſtate this preſent yeare,
Both w͗ war and other plagues, we are round encloſed:
Let vs turne to the Lorde our God w͗ tremblyng & feare,
With harty thankes geuyng for his great mercies offred.

⳹Remember the .x. Lepers, in the .xvii. of Luke certaine,
When the Lorde had clēſed them of their ſore infirmitie:
One poore Samaritane come to Ieſus Chriſt agayne,
To geue him hartie thankes for his great benignitie.

⳹So let vs geue thanks to God in hart both al & ſome,
And repent our former liues, without any longer delay:
In feare left a greuous plague among vs haſtely come,
Without ſpeedye repentance, looke for it we may.

Bryng forth the frutes of the goſpel, I meane a godly life,
Leaue your filthy hipocriſie which ſtinketh in Gods ſight:
Leaue your abominable pryde, amend both man & wyfe,
Leaue your horrible blaſphemie wherein you ſo delight.

Pray England pray, and London leaue thy wicked trade,
Eſpeciallye Couetouſnes, Glotonie, and al fylthy luſt:
And remember our merciful God who hath vs all made,
A body that is mortall, and ſhall turne to duſt.

⳹For our noble queene Elizabeth, let vs al hartely [praye,]
And for her honorable counſell, that God geue th[em grace:]
To maintayne his glorious Goſpell both night [and daye,]
To the advancement of Vertue, all wickednes to ra[ſe.]

⳹ FINIS.   ℘William Birch.

⳹ Imprinted at London, in little Britaine: by Alexander Lacie.

It is easy to account for the despondent tone which runs throughout this ballad. On June 4, 1561, the spire and roof of St. Paul's Cathedral, struck by lightning, fired, and were completely destroyed. This accident was regarded by many as a sign of divine displeasure at England's hostility to papal authority. On July 29, 1563, the English expedition to France ended disastrously with the surrender of Havre. The survivors of the siege were permitted to return home, but brought with them the plague, which soon raged throughout London and the provinces.

The Register of the Stationers' Company for 1564–65 (Arber's *Transcript*, i. 266) mentions a licence which was granted to Alexander Lacy for printing 'a ballett intituled a Warnynge to Englande and lett London begynne'.

Between the title of this ballad and the text is a woodcut representing Death and his victim. The text is printed in two columns and is somewhat damaged, but the defects in the text have here been restored conjecturally.

I O

A worthy Mirrour, wherein you may Marke,
An excellent difcourfe of a breeding Larke.

To the tune of new Rogero.

By reading whereof, perceiue well you may,
What truft is in friends, or in kinfefolke to ftay.

A Larke fometimes did breed,
   within a field of Corne:
And had increafe when as the graine
   was ready to be fhorne.
She wary of the time,
   and carefull for her neft:
Debated wifely with her felfe,
   what thing to doo were beft:
For to abide the rage,
   of cruell Reapers hand:
She knew it was to perilous,
   with fafetie for to ftand.
And to diflodge her broode,
   vnable yet to flie:
(Not knowing whether to remooue)
   great harmes might hap thereby.
Therefore fhe ment to ftay,
   till force conftraind to fleet,
And in the while for to prouide,
   fome other place as meete:
The better to prouide,
   the purpofe of her minde:
She would forthwith go feeke abroad,
   and leaue her young behinde:
But firft fhe bad them all,
   attend their mothers will:
Which carefull was for to efchew,
   each likelihood of ill.
This Corne is ripe (quoth fhe)
   wherein we neftled are:
The which (if heede preuents not harms)
   might caufe our mortall care.
Therefore to fence with fkill,
   the fequell of mifhaps:
I will prouide fome other place,
   for feare of after clappes.

Whilſt I for this and foode,
  am flowen hence away,
With heedfull eares attentiue be,
  what commers by do ſay.
Thus ſaid, ſhe vaunſt herſelfe,
  vpon her longeſt toe :
And mounted vp into the ſkies,
  ſtill ſinging as ſhe flowe.
Anon ſhe home returnde,
  full fraught with choice of meat :
But loe, (a ſuddaine change) her Byrdes
  for feare could nothing eat.
Therewith agaſt ſhe cried,
  what howe what meaneth this?
I charge you on my bleſſing, tell
  what thing hath chanſt amiſſe?
Are theſe my welcomes home,
  or thanks for food I haue?
Ye wonted were with chyrping cheere,
  to gape before I gaue.
But now ſuch quames oppreſſe
  your former quiet kinde :
That (quite tranſſformde) dumbe mute things
  and ſenceleſſe ſoule I finde.
The prime and eldeſt Byrde,
  (thus checkt) began to ſay :
Alas deare Dame ſuch newes we heard,
  ſince you were flowen away :
That were it not the truſt,
  that we repoſe in you :
Our liues were loſt remedileſſe,
  we know it well yneuw :
The owner of the plot,
  came hither with his Sonne :
And ſaid to him, this Wheat muſt down,
  it is more then time it were done.
Go get thee to my Friends,
  and bid them come to morne :
And tell them that I craue their helpes,
  to reape a peece of Corne.
The Larke that was the Dam,
  ſtood in a dumpe a while :
And after ſaid, his friends (quoth he)
  and then began to ſmile.
Tuſh, friends are hard to finde,
  true friendſhip ſeeld appeares :
A man may miſſe to haue a friend,
  that liues olde Neſtors yeares.
True Damon and his friend,
  long ere our time were dead :
It was in Greece, a great way hence,
  where ſuch true loue was bred.

Our Country is too colde,
  to foſter vp a friend :
Till proofe be made, each one will ſay,
  ſtill yours vnto the end.
But trie in time of need,
  and all your friends are flowen.
Such fruitleſſe feed, ſuch fickle ſtay,
  in faithleſſe friends be ſowen :
Therefore be of good cheere,
  reuiue your dulled ſprights :
Expell the care, that cauſeleſſe thus,
  bereaues you of delights.
Let not ſurmized feare,
  depriue your eies of ſleepe :
My ſelfe will be amongſt you ſtill,
  that ſafely ſhall you keepe.
And ſweare eene be the Tuft,
  that growes vpon my crowne :
If all his helpe be in his friends,
  this Corne ſhall not go downe.
The young aſſured by her,
  that ſuch an oth did ſweare :
Did paſſe the time in wonted ſleepe,
  and baniſht former feare :
And when the drouſie night,
  was fled from gladſome day :
She bad them wake and looke about,
  for ſhe muſt go her way.
And ſaid I warant you,
  theſe friends will not come heere :
Yet notwithſtanding liſten wel,
  and tell me what you heare.
Anone the Farmer came,
  enraged well nigh mad :
And ſware, whoſo depends on friends,
  his caſe is worſe then bad :
I will go fetch my kinne,
  to helpe me with this geare,
In things of greater waight then this,
  their kindred ſhall appeare :
The Larkes, theyr Dam returnd,
  informed her of all :
And how that he himſelfe was gone,
  his kindred for to call.
But when ſhe heard of kin,
  ſhe laughing cried amaine :
A pin for kin, a figge for friends,
  yet kinne the worſt of twaine.
This man himſelfe is poore,
  though wealthie kin he haue :
And kindred now a daies doth quaile,
  when neede compels to craue.

No, no, he ſhall returne,
   with ill contented minde:
His paines ſhall yeeld his loſſe of time,
   no ſuccour he ſhall finde.
They all are ſo addict,
   vnto theyr priuate gaine:
That if ye lacke power to requite,
   your ſuits are all in vaine.
My ſelfe am ouer chargde,
   with harueſt ye may ſee:
And nearer is my ſkin then ſhirt,
   this ſhall theyr anſwere be.
Therefore as earſt of friends,
   ſo ſay I now of kinne:
We ſhall receiue no hurt by them,
   nor he no profite winne:
Yet liſten once againe,
   what now his refuge is.
For kindred ſhal be like to friends,
   be well aſſured of this:
I muſt go furniſh vp,
   a neſt I haue begun.
And will returne and bring you meat,
   aſſoone as it is done.
Then vp ſhe clam the Clowds,
   with ſuch a luſtie Lay:
That it reioyſt her yonglings hearts,
   as in theyr neſt they lay:
And much they did commend,
   theyr Mothers loftie gate.
And thought it long till time had brought
   themſelues to ſuch eſtate:
Thus whilſt theyr twinckling eies,
   were rouing too and fro:
The ſaw whereas the Farmer came,
   who was their mortall foe.
Who after due complaints,
   thus ſayed in the end.
I will from henceforth truſt my ſelfe,
   and not to kin nor friend:
Who giues me glozing wordes,
   and faile me at my need:
May in my Pater noſter be,
   but neuer in my Creede.
My ſelfe will haue it downe,
   ſince needs it muſt be ſo:
For proofe hath taught me too much wit,
   to truſt to any mo.
The birds that liſtening lay,
   attentiue to the ſame:
Informde their mother of the whole,
   as ſoone as ere ſhee came:

Ye mary then (quoth fhe)
    the cafe now altered is.
We will no longer here abide,
    I alway feared this :
But out fhe got them all,
    and trudged away apace :
And through the corne fhe brought thē fafe
    into another place.
God fend her lucke to fhun,
    both Hauke and Fowles gin,
And me the happe to haue the neede,
    of friens, not yet of kinne.

Imprinted at London, by Richard Ihones, dwelling neere vnto Holborne Bridge. 1589.

A seventeenth-century edition of this ballad exists in the Roxburghe collection (*Roxburghe Ballads*, vol. iii, pp. 86–93), while in the library of the Society of Antiquaries is an early issue, undated, printed by Richard Jones, but differing from that at Britwell by the fact that it is signed 'Arthur Bour', whereas the later edition is anonymous. Bourchier further wrote a poem entitled 'Golden Precepts', contributed to 'The Paradise of Dayntie Devises', 1585, and which was reprinted in 'Select Poetry' (Parker Society, 1845), p. 297; as well as a prefatory poem to Geoffrey Whitney's 'Choice of Emblemes', 1586.

The story of the lark is taken from Aesop. A prose version is given in Painter's 'Palace of Pleasure', 1566 (vol. i, p. 43), while another in metre appears in H. C.'s 'Forrest of Fancy', 1579. Neither of the earlier copies of the broadside was licensed. The Britwell ballad was included in Collier's 'Old Ballads' (Percy Society, 1840).

Richard Jones, printer and bookseller, carried on business successively at no less than seven addresses in London; that at the Rose and Crown over against the Falcon, near unto Holborn Bridge without Newgate, being the last, and there he resided between 1581 and 1602. Jones printed and published a quantity of popular literature, including many ballads, some of which are in this collection (Bibliographical Society Publications, *Dictionary of Printers*, 1557–1640). The Britwell ballad is printed in three columns within a narrow ornamental border. The Antiquaries' edition has two vignettes which do not appear in this issue.

II

An Epytaphe
vpon the Death of the Right Reuerent Father in God
I. Iuell, Doctor of Diuinitie and Biſſhop of Sariſburie.
Who deceaſed the .22. of September. 1571.

IF Publique Weale, or Countreies clame, might languiſh and bewayle,
The late deceaſe of ſuche Deuines : as chiefely did preuaile
And cleane extirp ſuche ſhadowed workes : as Antichriſtians Ire
   Or Arius flocke, moſte Tityrus lyke, began for to conſpire,
To ouerwhelme the Verytie : then may we Chriſtians ſaye,
   We doo ſuſtayne a double loſſe, of Iuell at this daye :
Whoſe name doth not import ſo much the value, or the price :
   As is his miſſe accompted off, by Fathers ſage and wiſe.
No Pearle, or precious ſubſtance may, ſo much bewailed bee,
   As Countrey ſoyle hath cauſe to mone, deare Iuell now for thee.
Who hath detected prudently, and publiſht very playne :
   Suche Errours, as vnworthy are, in Chriſtians to remaine.
As Warrierlyke, thou Iuell haſt, laide Battry to thy Foes,
   As Hardyng, wᵗ like Popiſh Sectes, that Papiſts Captain choſe
For to defende their Hereſies : By thee his fond Deluſion,
   Apparantly as proued is, was brought vnto confuſion.
Thy zealous mind, thy ſacred ſpright : by Weſt, by North, by South,
   Hath driuen of raging Papiſts Sect, a Snaffle in the mouth.
Wheron ſo longe time they haue fed, that Chriſtes Ghoſpell cleare
   Vnto the Laye and common ſort, moſte brightly doth appeare.
So that deſeruedly of right, by golden Trumpe of Fame :
   Thou doeſt deſerue the Title of a Iuell vnto name :
For why ? by thee moſt worthily, thy Vertues ſtood inſtead :
   By thee likewiſe the Flocke of Chriſt, moſt preciouſlie were fed.
By thee, the Path of Heauēly health : by thee, true faith was ſhowen
   By thee, the fruites of Charitie, in deedes & wordes were knowen.
By thee, the inwarde man was clad, and nouriſht verie well :
   In any ſoyle, ſcarſe is there founde, ſuche Iuelles for to dwell.
Thy deedes agreed with ſtedfaſt wordes, faſt fownded on the Rocke,
   To Chriſtian ſtate, a Father deare, and Patron to the Flocke.
Whiche beares the Title of the Church, or Sheepefould of the Lord,
   Approued by teſtimoniall Actes, as Scriptures do record.
If thus much then, thaccompt, was made, what Creature can denay
   But England ſhe, too ſoone hath loſt, a Iuell at this daye,
Whom neither benefite of wealth, could cauſe to wander froe
   The Compaſſe of the heauenly Card, his Dutie to beſtowe
Amonge his Bretherne deare in Chriſt : then as we haue begon,
   Let vs ſuppoſe that we haue loſt, this Iuell all too ſoone.

Defiryng God, that as he is, no doubt with him on hie,
    We may become true Iuelles all, vntill the time we die.
So fhall the heauenly Verytie, moft brightly flooriſh ſtill,
    And ſpred her Branches fayre abroade, all ouer Sion Hill :
Wherby the Popiſh trayne may fall, that erſt hath ben ſo hie,
    And cleane diminiſht frō the Earth, as withered Plants that die.
Graunt this (O God) for euermore, and pearſe thy Paſtors hartes,
    That valiantly (as Iuell did) they playe true Paſtors partes.
And leaue behinde ſuche worthy workes, to gloryfie Goddes name
    As he hath don : and ſo confound the Popiſh Sect with ſhame.
That by ſuche meane no Papiſt may, the perfect Scripture wreſt,
    As Hardyng hath don heretofore, whom Iuell hath ſuppreſt.
¶ And thus farewell, (deare Iuell now) ſith Gods good pleaſure is
    To haue thee hence from vs among, to his Eternall bliſſe.
With teares I ende this ſimple Verſe, proceedyng of good wyll,
    Let learned fort take Pen in hand, and frame their filed Quill
To ſpread this Iuelles Fame abroad, though Corps be clad in Clay,
    His worthy Workes & Vertues rare, Dame Fame ſhal ſure diſplay.

FINIS.   N. BOVR.

Imprinted at London in the

vpper ende of Fleetelane, by Richarde Iohnes : | And are to be ſould at his Shop, ioynyng to the Southweſt Doore | of ſainct Paules Churche. 1571. October .2.

John Jewel, perhaps the most intellectual of the English reformers, was born in 1522. His protestant views abruptly ended a distinguished career at Oxford, and to avoid persecution he fled from England and remained abroad until the accession of Elizabeth. On Jan. 21, 1560, he was consecrated Bishop of Salisbury, and then entered upon a long course as literary champion of the reformed church, his chief contribution being 'Apologia pro Ecclesia Anglicana', 1562, a work which kept the author long busy with its critics, the foremost of whom was Thomas Harding, a former treasurer of Salisbury, who is mentioned in this ballad.

The author of the epitaph on Bishop Jewel and of that on Sir William Garrard, which follows, was probably Nicholas Bourman. His name is preserved in three licences which appear in the Stationers' Registers—'yᵉ fawltes facoultes', 1570–71, 'A ffrendelie well wiſhinge to ſuch as endure &c.', Mar. 10, 1581, and 'An Epitaphe vppon the Death of the Ladye Marie Ramſey', Feb. 24, 1602 (Arber's *Transcript*, i. 437, ii. 390, iii. 201). The last entry may be identified with a quarto which is preserved at Britwell and which answers to this description. The licence for printing Bourman's epitaph on Jewel may have been amongst the lost entries of the Stationers' Registers, 1571–76. Elderton also penned an epitaph on Jewel which is included in this volume. The ballad is printed in two columns within ornamental borders, and has at the upper right-hand corner of the sheet a small cut representing Christ and his disciples.

12

An Epytaphe
vpon the Death of the Right worſhipfull, Sir William
Garrat Knight : and chiefe Alderman of the Queenes Maieſties Citie of London.
Who deccaſed the .27. of September. 1571.   Anno aetatis ſue 64.

EVen as the Pylate traines the reſt, that trauaile would attayne :
And by the compaſſe of his Carde, deſcribes his Iorney playne :
Euen ſo the trauayle of this worlde apparant ſeemes to bee,
   From Childhood firſt to middle ſtate : Then finallie wee ſee :
From crooked Age vnto the Houſe, that mortall Creatures win :
   Our Mother deare the Earth, of whom our Subſtance did begyn.
Whiche full Effect conſidered well, as Flowers in the Field :
   we may conceiue this outwarde man, in tract of time ſhall yeld,
And hange the head : for as the ſhade that glydeth on the wall,
   compared with the Lillie faire, ſo ſodaine is our fall.
As here before our eyes we may proſpectiue plainly trie,
   A Mirrour and a lookyng Glaſſe, for euerie Wight to ſpie,
In Countrey ſoyle, (O Lector deare) of Conſulſhippes degree :
   A Lanterne bright to Iuſtice Seate, heare playnly thou maiſt ſee
Bereaued of breath : a Knight no leſſe, then Worſhips Title clame :
   for Rector of the Publique weale, that Garat had to name.
From middle Age by ſage aduiſe, purſuyng Vertues lore :
   Whiche is the cauſe that doth augment, his Worſhip euermore.
In Godlines, or ſacred lyfe, his ſteppes the Lorde hath bleſt :
   whoſe endleſſe Fame reuiueth ſtill, though Corps be now ſuppreſt
By Natures courſe.   In time, vnto the poore a perfect ſtaye :
   maintayning Iuſtice equallie, from euerie daye to daye.
A Patron of his Countrey deare intombde he hath, to name :
   For as the Senate graunts him right, the Cōmons ſay the ſame.
Though then that Fate hath him aſſignd, his Pageant thus to play
   Still puttyng vs in Memorie, that we ſhall walke that waye.
There is not one, that can reproue, one Title of his right,
   But as he was, (euen ſo he died :) to lyue a faithfull Knight.
And gaue the Onſet to the fleſh, and conquered hath the ſame :
   As Champian bould, by Shield of Faith, to glorie of his name.
Diſdayning Earthly trade, or meane : embracing Heauenly light :
   Committyng to the handes of God, his inwarde man or Spright.
If that as then ſuche noble Actes, enlarge his loyall prayſe :
   And by accompt of iuſt deſertes, his treble Honour rayſe.
What rufull loſſe hath all the ſtate, of Senatours degree ?
   with whome for Counſaile graue, he was accepted wont to bee.
Or els what teares may Publique weale, effuſe in wofull plight ?
   Since fatall Doome hath pluckt frō them, ſo ſage & wiſe a Knight.
What double loſſe hath Ladie his ? (that vertuous Matron graue,)
   Whom God had linckt to him as Spouſe, for terme of lyfe to haue.

What loſſe hath Children deare, of him? what loſſe hath ſeruants al?
  what loſſe hath eche that ſtood in neede, for Counſell his to call?
What loſſe hath rich? what loſſe hath poore? what loſſe hath eche eſtate
  what remedie? nought helpes herein, but wayle our wofull Fate.
Yet nought at all preuailes our teares, therfore to God I pray,
  (Sith he is gone :) the reſt may walke, his redy Path and waye :
And ſpecially, his Brethren ſage : that ſit on Iuſtice Seate,
  Their Worſhips hartes, the Lorde direct, vnto his glorie greate.
Mayntainyng iuſtly euerie cauſe, and plantyng Vertues right,
  So that therby the Cōmon Weale, may flooriſh cleare and bright.
In happie ſtate, moſt proſperouſlie, great ioye for to be ſeene :
  To ſpred her Branches in reſpect, as doth the Olyue greene.
Graunt this O God eternally, that when this race is ronne :
  Their Worſhips may obtain the Fame that Garrat hath begon.

FINIS.   DIXI.   N. BOVR.

¶ This Race preſents a Pilgremage,
  Or Tragicall Diſcourſe on Stage :
    Whiche once begon, drawes to an ende,
    Let Death therfore be thought on frends :
    And feare no whit the Campe to yelde,
    So longe as Fayth may be thy Shield.

Imprinted at London in the

vpper ende of Fleetelane, by Richarde Iohnes : | And are to be ſould at his Shop, ioynyng to the
Southweſt Doore | of ſainct Paules Churche.   1571.   October .2.

This epitaph, and another by John Phillip, also in Heber's collection, refer to Sir William Garrard, described by Stow as 'haberdaſher, a graue, ſober, wiſe and diſcreet citizen, equall with the beſt and inferior to none of our time, deceaſed 1571, in the parriſh of St. Chriſtopher, but was buried in this Church of St. Magnus as in the pariſh where he was borne. A faire monument is there raiſed on him. This monument is lately reedified and new fenced by ſir Iohn Garrard, his ſonne and L. Maior 1602'. Garrard was Lord Mayor 1555–56, when he was knighted. Machyn in his 'Diary' gives a description of his pageant. From Feb. 12, 1567, until his death Garrard was senior alderman or 'Father of the City'. He was a prominent haberdasher, and presented the members of that company with 'a great standing cup'. Sir John Garrard, his son, filled the office of Lord Mayor, 1601–2, as also did another of his descendants, Sir Samuel Garrard, 1709–10. His grandson, Sir John Garrard, was created a baronet, Feb. 26, 1622. Sir William Garrard of Dorney, Bucks, was a son of the first Lord Mayor and brother to Sir John Garrard, knight (Harleian Society, *Visitation of Bucks*, p. 61). In point of arrangement, borders, and woodcut this ballad is identical with Bourman's epitaph on Jewel, which bears the same date of imprint.

13

¶ Againſt filthy writing, and ſuch like delighting.

WHat meane the rimes that run thus large in euery ſhop to ſell?
With wanton ſound, and filthie ſenſe, me thinke it grees not well
We are not Ethnickes, we forſoth, at leaſt profeſſe not ſo
Why range we then to Ethnickes trade? come bak, where wil ye goe?
Tel me is Chriſt, or Cupide Lord? doth God or Venus reigne?
And whoſe are wee? whom ought wee ſerue? I aſke it, anſwere plaine
If wanton Venus, then go forth, if Cupide, keep your trade
If God, or Chriſt, come bak the beſt, or ſure you will be made
Doth God? is he the Lord in deed? and ſhould we him obey?
Then his commaundement ought to guide, all that wee doo or ſay
But ſhew me his commaundement then, thou filthy writer thou
Let feet, I ceaſe, if not, geue place, or ſhameles ſhew thee now.

WE are not foes to muſicke wee, a mis your man doth take vs
ſo frendes to thinges corrupt and vile, you all ſhall neuer make vs
If you denie them ſuch to bee, I ſtand to proue it I,
If you confeſſe (defend them not) why then doo you reply?
But ſuch they bee I will mainteine, which yet you bothe defend
And iudge them fooles, that them miſlike, would God you might amend
But, ſubſtance onely I regarde, let Accidencis go
Both you and wee, bee that wee bee, I therfore leaue it ſo
And yet I wiſhe your tearmes in deed, vpon ſome reaſon ſtayd
If mine be not, reproue them right, Ile blot that I haue ſayd
And that I wrote, or now doo wrighte, againſt you as may ſeeme
What cauſe I had, and haue, I yelde, to modeſt men to deeme
I wiſhe you well I doo proteſt, (as God will, I will ſo)
I cannot helpe, as frend ye wot, nor will not hurt as fo
But for the vile corrupting rimes, which you confeſſe to wrighte
My ſoule and hart abhorres their ſence, as far from my delight
And thoſe that vſe them for their glee, as you doo vaunte ye will
I tell you plainly what I think, I iudge thee to bee ill

This boafting late in part hath caufd, mee now to fay my minde
Though chalenges of yours alfo, in euery place I finde.

Thomas Brice.

❦ Imprinted at London by Iohn
Alde for Edmond Halley and are to be folde in Lumbard ftrete at the
figne of the Egle.

Thomas Brice, proteftant divine and poet, is beft known as the author of 'A compendious Regefter in Metre, conteinyng the names, and pacient fuffrynges of the membres of Iefus Chrift, afflicted tormented and cruelly burned, here in Englande, fince the death of our late famous kyng . . . Edwarde the fixte: to the entraunce and beginnyng of the raign of our foueraigne . . . Elizabeth . . . Anno 1559', a work which may have lent affiftance to John Foxe the martyrologift. Brice also wrote 'The Couurte of Venus moralized', 1566–67, and 'Songes and Sonnettes', 1567–68, both of which were entered in the Registers of the Stationers' Company (Arber's *Transcript*, i. 343 and 359). In 1570–71 was licensed to John Allde 'an Epytaph of Mafter Bryce preacher' (Arber, i. 442). Apparently the 'compendious Regefter' alone survives. Leave to print the ballad was granted to Halley in 1561–62 (Arber, i. 181): it is the earliest licence that appears in his name. Herein Brice with dignity rebukes the licentiousness of some ballad-writer and his supporter, whose names are not revealed. The ballad was included in J. P. Collier's 'Old Ballads' (Percy Society, 1840).

14

An Epitaphe declaryng the lyfe and end
of *D. Edmund Boner* &c.

LO now the lingering hope is paſt,
  that late the Papiſtes had :
Their braggyng breſts which boild in hate,
  their hartes with care haue clad.

They looked long for wiſhed tyme,
  of Antichriſtes returne :
When they in wonted wiſe might ſpoyle,
  and heapes of Martyrs burne.

But ſee the prouidence of God,
  their malice to aſſwage :
He hath bereft theſe Papiſtes proud,
  the piller of their rage.

Their whip, their ſword, their fire brand,
  of wrath their chefeſt ſtay :
The ſpoyler of the Chriſtian flocke,
  of whom he made a praye.

For bloudy burnyng Boner now,
  hath made exchaunge of lyfe :
That whilelome was the murtherer,
  of infant, man, and wife.

Yet ſometyme he a fauorer,
  and did profeſſe the troth :
Defiyng Pope and Popiſhnes,
  fiue tymes with ſolemne oth :

And letted not for to accuſe,
  and note of haynous crime :
Such as were ſlacke to do the lyke,
  duryng Lord Cromwels tyme.

A learned Epiſtle eke he wrat,
  in prayſe and in defence :
Of Byſhop Gardiners worke the booke,
  of true obedience.*

Wherin he doth accuſe the Pope
  his Churche and Romiſh rable :
Of haynous crimes right horrible,
  and deedes deteſtable.

* Bishop Bonner wrote a preface to Stephen Gardiner's 'De vera Obedientia', 1536.

As tyranny, vſurpyng ſtate,
   reprochefull vnto God :
Of England eke a very ſpoyle,
   to Chriſt his flocke a rod.

He names the Pope a greedy wolfe,
   he ioyes in his decay :
Hopyng the truth long troden downe,
   at length ſhould beare the ſway.

He prayſeth much the noble Prince,
   and calles K. Henry vertuous :
That in ſuppreſſyng Popiſh power,
   he is ſo ſtudious.

Wherby moſt playnly may appeare,
   how Boner had a taſt :
Of Chriſt and his Goſpell pure,
   tho he them ſcorned at laſt.

In Denmarke eke Ambaſſadour,
   he publiſhed with ſpeede :
The booke and Epiſtle named before,
   as worthy workes in deede.

Then ſent Ambaſſador to Fraunce,
   from Henry puiſaunt Kyng :
He furthered with free conſent,
   the Engliſh Bibles Printyng.

And cauſed diuers of the ſame,
   it ſemed of godly zeale :
For to be plaſt within Paules Church,
   Chriſtes truth for to reueale.

He cauſde fiue hundred Teſtamentes,
   be Printed, this I know :
And thoſe as precious iewels did,
   vpon his frendes beſtow.

But as a wauering weather cocke,
   Lord Cromwell beyng dead :
Forſaking Chriſt and all his lawes,
   to papiſtry he fled.

And of a Paule became a Saule,
   a Herode thirſting blood :
As on young Mekins well was ſene,
   his cruell killing moode.*

* In 1540 Richard Mekins, a youth of fifteen years, was burned for heresy at Smithfield.

For when one queſt had cleard the boy,
  and iudgd him giltles quite :
He cauſd another Queſt be cald,
  and him condemnd by might.

Thus draue he forth kyng Henries dayes,
  but when his noble ſonne :
In fathers place to regall throne,
  by due deſent was come.

Then cald to count for his offence,
  as iuſtice thought it fit :
In humble wiſe before the Lordes,
  himſelfe he did ſubmit.

But afterward moſt ſtubburnly,
  with great contempt and ſcorne :
He did deny his former facte,
  as one, ere then forſworne.

For which offence in priſon caſt,
  where he with wealth was fedde :
Without regard of God or prince,
  a peruerſt lyfe he ledde.

But when in brothers ſacred ſeate,
  God would Queene Mary place :
This wilfull man from priſon cald,
  by her eſpeciall grace.

Abuſing much the lenitie,
  and mercy of the Queene :
Such bloody broyles began to brue,
  as earſt was neuer ſeene.

And lyke a roaring Lion he,
  of Plutoes poyſoned band :
Made hauocke of the ſaintes of God,
  his Chriſt he did withſtand.

He trode his goſpell vnder foote,
  as much as in him lay :
With tormoyle great, and torments huge,
  the Church he did affray.

And pitie none would he alow,
  no mercy might him moue :
His broyling breſt enflamed ſo,
  with popiſh fathers loue.

With coales and candle light alſo,
   of ſome the handes he brent :
Of ſome the haire, from of their face,
   with cruell clawes he rent.

Some men he beate vpon the face,
   but ſome, moſt like a beaſt :
He ſcourgd with whips & rods (O wretch)
   that dede, all men deteſt.

And breathing forth his tiranny,
   conſumde with fire and flame :
The olde, the yong, the riche, the poore,
   the halt, the blinde, and lame.

What ſhould I ſay, my hart it rues,
   the peoples teares recorde :
The wayled woes for ſaintes ſo ſlayne
   which is to be abhorde.

But all this might not moue his mynde,
   for witte gaue place to will :
Both grace and reaſon fled him fro,
   his hart was hardened ſtill.

But when God of his prouidence,
   our famous Queene did ſende :
To ſtay the rage of tiranny,
   and waſtfull wreakes to ende.

The mercy of Elizabeth,
   tho it doth farre exceede :
Could not reclaime his cureles hart,
   which errors ſtill did feede.

But that he vſde vnreuerently,
   with ſcoffes in mocking wiſe :
Her graces high Commiſſioners,
   both worthy, graue, and wiſe.

So when the people prayd for him,
   reprochefull wordes he gaue :
Moſt vile, not chriſtianlike, as one
   that had a ſoule to ſaue.

The ſecond tyme to priſon brought,
   where he his lyfe did leaue :
Where learned men perſuaded him,
   vnto the truth to cleaue,

And flie the fancies of the fonde,
   wherwith he was abuſde :
Vnwilling ſtill to heare them ſpeake,
   good Councell he refuſde.

So that vntill his dying houre,
  he fhewed no perfect figne :
Of a repentaunt hart or mynde,
  that would from finne decline.

But as he liude a lothed lyfe,
  vnconftant, vile, and vayne :
Forfaking faith and natures kynde,
  which God hath in difdayne.

His glory aye the peoples griefe,
  the poore mans payne his pride :
(A wofull flocke where fuch a wolfe,
  appointed was for guide).

Euen fo his ende was dolefull to,
  wherin did well appeare :
On him the iudgement iuft of God,
  right wonderfull to heare.

For dead his face as blacke as coale,
  and monftruous withall :
His grifly looke fo terrible,
  as might a man appall.

Was to the good a very glaffe,
  wherin they all may learne :
To fhunne, the way that Boner went,
  and better path deferne.

Yet tho in lyfe he would not graunt,
  Chriftes mercy for to craue :
He wild his wretched Corps with pompe,
  brought fhould be to the graue.

Vnto the Church whereas fometyme,
  a Prelate plaft was he :
Euen there his folemne obfequies,
  and funerals to be.

But fith it was fo farre vnmeete,
  a place for him more fitt :
Within the Churchyard of S. George,
  he hath a homely pitt.*

And fith he loued not the light,
  but did the fame defpife :
At midnight was he buryed there,
  from vewe of peoples eyes.

Wherfore ye Papiftes all beware,
  forfake the Romifh whore :
And feare the Iudgementes of the Lord,
  which will you els deuoure.

* Bishop Bonner died in the Marshalsea, Sept. 5, 1569, and was buried in St. George's churchyard, Southwark.

Recant ye all your herefies,
    and leaue your peruerfe way :
Wherin you walkt fo ftubburnely,
    fo long and many a day.

Loue God, obey your foueraine,
    and pray for her eftate :
Renounce ye all your Maummetry,
    leaft ye repent to late.

T. Bro. the younger.

℣ Finis.

℣ *Imprinted at London, by Iohn | Daye, dwellyng ouer Alderfgate.*
℣ Cum gratia & Priuilegio Regiae Maieftatis.

The fignature above is that of Thomas Broke, or Brooke, the younger, fon of Thomas Broke, alderman of Calais and a prominent fectary, who is mentioned in the 'Dictionary of National Biography', where is given a lift of his works. The younger Broke was the author of a book preferved in the library of St. John's College, Cambridge, entitled ' An Epitaphe declaring the life and end of D. Edm. Bonner. &c. An other Epitaphe made by a Papift, in the prayfe of D. Edmund Boner, and fet vp in Paules Croffe : with an anfwere therto. Alfo a reply to a flauderous lying Libell caft abroad in the defence of D. Edmund Boner' [Col] 'Finis. T. Brooke the younger'. This contains twenty-four leaves. There is an imperfect copy in the library of Trinity College, Cambridge. The ballad was published without licence. It is printed in three columns.

15

The Refuge of a Sinner,
Wherein are briefely declared the chiefeſt Poinctes
of true Saluation.

SOyled in ſinnes (O Lorde,) a wretched ſinfull Ghoſte,
To thee I call, to thee I ſue, that ſheweſt of mercie moſte,
Who can me helpe but thou, in whom all healpe doth reſt?
   My ſinne is more than man can mends, and that thou knoweſt beſt.
On whom then ſhall I call, to whom ſhall I make mone?
   Sith man is mightleſſe ſinne to cure, I ſeeke to thee alone.
In thee I knowe all might and power doth remayne,
   And at thy handes I am well ſure, mercie I ſhall obtaine.
Thy promiſſe can not fayle, wherein I me repoſe:
   To thee alone, (els to no man) my hart wyll ſinne diſcloſe.
The Sinner thou doeſt ſaue: no Sauiour els I finde
   Thou onely ſatiſſied haſt for the ſinnes of all mankynde.
The Sacrifice whereof, thou offeredſt once for aye:
   Whereby his wrath for Adams gylt, thy father put awaye.
And by thy death alone, Mankinde reſtored is,
   There was no meanes mercye for man to get of hym but this.
Nowe thou haſt mercye bought, if man by thee will craue:
   And who that ſeeketh by other meanes, ſmall mercie might he haue.
Wherefore (O Lorde) on thee, for mercie do I call:
   Let not my ſinnes conſume me cleane, and I dampned to fall.
The merites of my workes, were they neuer ſo iuſt:
   I here forſake, and them reſigne, to ſuche as in them truſt.
There is no mummynge Maſſe, can make amendes for me:
   Nor of the Sainctes, departed hence, I truſt in none but thee.
No pardon can me purge, but thy pardon alone,
   Nor yet no pillynge Pilgremage, made vnto Stocke or Stone.
No Pſalter nor yer Pſalmes, ſaide to thy Creatures:
   No ryng of Belles, no Organe Pypes, nor Song that my ſoule cures.
Thy bloud hath bought my ſoule, and booteth all my bale.
   And not mans workes nor chaunted charmes, deuiſde in Māmons dale.
Thou ſitteſt where thou ſeeſt, our workes all and ſome:
   The ſecrete thoughts of euery hart, before thy iudgement come.
Shall I then pleade my workes? thou knoweſt them bett than I,
   Forget them Lorde, I claime them not, for mercie do I crie.
Haue mercie on me Lorde, forgeue my treſpaſſe wrought,
   And frō henceforth graunt me thy grace, to guide me, dede & thought.
That all my workes maye ſounde, due glorye vnto thee:
   That Heauen and earth, and all therein, may yeld thee praiſe for mee.
For where as ought is done, by man after thy wyll:
   That worke is thyne, and thyne the praiſe: man can do nought but yll.

For of my felfe I knowe, in me is nought but finne,
  In Sinne I walckte, in Sinne I fuckte: in Sinne I did begin.
And haue I not thy grace, to Sinne againe I fhall:
  Without thy grace fo weake I am, no choyce for me but fall.
Shall I than ceace to call, thy grace that I maye haue?
  Thy faithfull promiffe is to giue, to them in faith that craue.
Of mercy than and grace, my faith doth me affure:
  And by thy death to haue at ende, the Ioyes that fhall endure.

Ro. Burdet Efquyer.

℩ Finis.

℩ *Bonum quo communius eo melius.*

℩ Imprinted at London by Richarde Iohnes: and are to be folde | at his Shoppe in Paules Churchyearde, at the | Southweft Doore of Paules Churche. | Anno. *1565.* Aprilis. 14.

This is entered in the Stationers' Register for 1564–65 as a ballad entitled 'Spoyled in fynnes o Lorde a wretched fynnful gooste' (Arber's *Transcript*, i. 271), and appears to have been the earliest example of Jones's printing for which a licence was obtained. Further than that the name Robert Burdet is contained in the initial letters of some lines of verse which appear after the prologue in Robert Vaughan's 'Dyalogue defenfyue for women, agaynft malycyous detractours', 1542, nothing is known of this author, nor are any other ballads by him recorded. The opening lines of the ballad were reprinted in 'Select Poetry, chiefly devotional, of the reign of Queen Elizabeth' (Parker Society, 1845). The ballad is decorated with a deep border containing biblical subjects, typographical ornaments, and heraldic shields.

16

❧A Complaynt agaynſt the wicked enemies
of Chriſt in that they haue ſo tyrannuſly handled the poore Chryſtians.

Alas what grefe is this
  vnto all chryſten men:
That tirants ſtil do raine
  to worke miſcheif agen.
    They proſper in the land,
  whoſe practyſe late hath bene,
Both to deſtroy our realme
  and Eliſabeth our Quene.
    How dyd they Tower her
  and kept her there in thrall,
When they could not charge her
  with any cryme at all.
    But they beyng thyrſty
  woulde fayne haue ſuckt her bloud,
For when thei put her there
  they ment her grace no good.
    Whiche was the prelates fetche
  for why thei ſtode in awe,
That if her grace did raygne
  ſhe would reiect ther Lawe.
    Wherfore this curſed ſorte
  dyd geue many a ſaye,
To take her in a tryppe
  to make her cleane away.
    Such ympes of Sathans kynde
  do ſtand and floryſh ſtyll,
Whiche do ſuppreſſe all truth
  and do maynteine al yll.
    For they haue ſpoild this realme
  and made it very Poore
They brought in Foren power
  to Turne vs out of doore.
    Suche fruteles trees do growe
  they ſpred abrode and ſtande,
Whoſe curſed Branches lyue
  and do Corrupt the lande.
    For when the Olyue trees
  and eke the pleaſaunt Vynes
Did bringe vs forth good frutes
  and delectable wine .

They fharpened theyr Toles
to cut them by the grounde,
That they might fpringe no more
nor neuer more be founde.

For fume they brinte with fyer
and fome agayne they pinde,
And fum they tare and rackt
and fum remayne behinde.

Againe this curfed forte
dyd fcrape out of the moulde
The carkes of the dead
and many mo they woulde.

Yf tyme had ferude theyr turne
according to ther truft,
Kynge Harry and his funne
had both ben Burnt to dufte.

Doth it not nowe appeare
what loue and eke what feale
They had vnto our Kinges
that Rulde our commonweale.

Howe did they raile on them
in pulpettes euery where,
With vyle opprobrious termes
and that without all feare.

Alas that fuche fhould lyue
that feke all to deftroy,
Suche members woulde be ryd
that do nothinge but noye.

For where they hunt to fpoile
ther natures cannot feafe,
Tyll they haue murdred thofe
that be the funnes of peace.

Alas I rue it muche
that fuche Pypicked pates
Shoulde be about a Quene
or come within her gates.

Ther counfels be corrupt
for they fmel al of bloude,
Ther practys be all yll
how can they then be good.

Who can or will commende
this charitie of preiftes,
That be fuche murtherers
and haue fuche blodye fyftes.

Howe coldly doo they praye
for Elifabeth our quene,
Ther doinges haue ben heard
ther practys haue bene fene.

O curfed fede of Cayne
and members of the Deuill
All deftitute of grace,
replenifhed with euyll.

Who loue the name of you,
but fuche as ye do brybe,
O ye blinde balamites
o vyle and curfed Trybe.

The infantes in the wombe
haue caufe to Curfe your fede,
And eke the fatherles
for your accurfed dede.

Howe many liue this day
whofe Parentes ye haue kilde,
And turned ther Children out
into the ftretes and filde.

Ther to lye and pyne
and fayd that it was Synne
Eyther to geue them foode
or els to take them in.

What pitie were it nowe
to toffe and to turne them,
To hewe them in peces
to Broyle and to burne them.

To fle them from the Croune
to the foules of theyr fete.
To trye if fuche tormentes
be Pleafaunt and fwete.

And fpecially Bonner
the fier woulde fayne taft him,
But burne him it coulde not
his grece wolde fo Baft him.

Wolde god it might trye him
for if that day were cume,
Many handes would be redy
to geue Fyer to his Bum.

That fmithfelde might fmel him
and here the tyrauntes voice,
That fatherles Children
and infantes might Reioyce.

Whofe fathers and mothers
this tyraunt hath furthered,
To be cruelly burnt
and moft fhamefully murthred.

O trayterus tyrant
o falfe periured Beft,
Thy broylinge and burning
is knowen and manifeft.

And all thy tyrannes
which thou haft frequented
And alfo haft practyft,
and lewdly inuented.

How haft thou tried them
with torche and with taper
Burning their handes and feete
to make them wauer.

'Yea how didſt thou ſtock them
o murtherus thefe,
Ther necke there handes and feete
onlye for their beleif.

    Both within thy Cole houfe
and in the lollers tower,
The poore and ſimple men
had many a ſharpe ſhower.

    Through thy good counſelers
Clunnye and Iohn auales,†
Theſe are the two rake helles
that brought the all the tales.

    How were the poore lodgyd,
how were their bellys fedde.
With hunger and Coulde
and ſtones to reſt ther hed.

    Alas what beaſtes are they
that lurke vnder that wede,
Are they not Raueninge wolues
iudge them by ther deed.

    What iniurie were it nowe
to rid thoſe blody beſtes,
That ſeketh frendſhip now
with monye and with feſtes.

    Now thei haue ſpoild our realme
they fere and ſtand in dout,
If briberie helpe them not
then will ther knauery out

    But god for his mercy
ſeaſe the blody ſtreme,
And graunt that his glory
may floriſhe in our Realme.

Finis.

---

† Richard Cluney or Cloney was Bonner's ſumner, and keeper of the bishop's coal-house, into which many of Bonner's prisoners were thrust. Foxe often mentions him in the ' Acts and Monuments ', and at the end of Book VIII gives a Latin letter addressed to him by Bonner 'for the abolishing of Images', dated Oct. 14, 1541. Cluney appears, however, to have been an illiterate man who could scarce read English. He and John Avales are named together in ' The Trouble and Deliueraunce of Iohn Lithall ' (Foxe, Book XII). They were evidently Bonner's bloodhounds. Avales is also mentioned in ' The cruel aſſault of Gods Fort ', p. 7.

This ballad was licensed with a number of others to William Pickering on Sept. 4, 1564 (Arber's Tran- script, i. 262). It is coarsely printed in three columns without ornament or border.

17

THere bee many that fpeake much of Iefus Chrift, and beare a faire fhew of his holines and vertue : but | none are able to conceiue (much leffe to declare) the fweete comforts of his heauenly grace, fauing | fuch as hold faith in a good confcience, without hypocrifie, pride, and couetoufnes, and be reformed in | their liues with charitie, peace, and vnitie.

THE HEARTIE CONFESSION OF A CHRISTIAN,
Deuifed for his owne comfort, written for his remembrance, and now publifhed
for the vfe of M.H. and others his faithfull and priuate friends onely.

1 Cor. 3. 18, 19. Let no man deceiue himfelfe, if any man feeme to be wife amongft you in this world, let him be (*as*) a foole : that he may be(*come*) wife. | For the wifedome of this world is foolifhnes before God, &c.

The argument of the fong.

I. COR. I.

30. But you are of him in Chrift Iefus, who was *made* vnto | vs *wifedome* from God, yea, and *righteoufnes,* & *holines,* | and *redemption.*
31. That, as it is written ; he that *boafteth,* or reioyceth, let | him *boaft, and* reioyce in the Lord.

A fpirituall fong of thankes-giuing,
with praier vnto God, containing the full
effect of true religion in a
Chriftian.

The forefpeech with the drift and fub-
ftance of the Song.

THe fomme of all the comforts, which I finde
In holy writ to eafe my troubled minde:

* The vniting of two natures in the perfon of Chrift, who is our Emmanuell, that is, God with vs, very man as wee are finne excepted.

Is this, that God *my nature did vnite
Vnto his Godhead full of *grace,* and *might?*

In Chrift who ftandeth betweene God and me
For euer more my Sauiour to be.

Ruling me, as my *Prophet, Prieſt, and King,
On me beſtowing euery needefull thing.

Not onely for my preſent conſolation,
But alſo for my eternall ſaluation.

I will therefore ſing of his wondrous praiſe
For his exceeding loue to me alwaies.

The Song.

Doctrine by way of example.

1. WHere I by nature *through my parents fal,
Am ſo diſtemper'd in my members all,
And bent to ill (which beareth in me full ſway)
As from all goodnes drawes me quite away
And thus in *ſin originall* am drown'd :
Chriſt is my *perfect innocencie* found :
Him, as that *brazen ſnake*, if I adore,
In me ſhalbe no ſicknes nor no ſore.

Application of the Doctrine
praier wiſe.

O Chriſt forgiue my naturall infection,
Which to thy law will not be in ſubiection,
And ſo prouoketh me to dayly ſtrife,
Whileſt I am noufled in this *noyſome life*,
And grant me thy *pure nature* to expreſſe,
Henceforth in my behauiour, more or leſſe,
Til fleſh and blood by death thou ſhalt ſubdue,
My ſtate in heau'n for euer to renue.

Doctrine.

2. *Where through my *folly, & mine own ignorance,
I know not how Gods glorie to aduance,
Nor to diſpoſe my ſelfe in any ſort
For others helpe, nor for mine owne comfort :
And thus am *blinde*, and no truth I can ſee ;
Chriſt is moſt *perfect wiſedome* vnto mee :
Him, as that *faithfull guide*, if I attend,
I ſhall not neede any way to offend.

Application.

O Chriſt forgiue my iudgement darke & weake,
Which cauſeth me thy bleſſed Lawes to breake,
And ſo prouoketh me to daily ſtrife,
Whilſt I do wander in this *wau'ring life*,
And grant me thy *deepe knowledge* to expreſſe
Henceforth in my behauiour more or leſſe,
Till fleſh and blood by death thou ſhalt ſubdue,
My ſtate in heau'n for euer to renue.

*The annexing of three offices in the perſõ of Ch[r]iſt, namely of Prophet, Prieſt, & King, who is our full and perfect Saniour.

*Againſt our birth ſinne, commonly called originall ſinne.

*The proper remedie is, the vniting of two natures in Chriſt by his incarnation vpon earth.

*That is diuine ſubſtance, maieſtie, or godlines : as, Mat. 5. 48. Ioh.13.15.and17.20.21. 22. 1.Cor.11.1. Ephe.5.1. Coloſ.1.10. 1.Theſ.2.12. Heb.1.3. 1.Pet.1.15. 2.Pet. 1.4.&c.

*Againſt all our other ſinnes, commonly called actual ſinnes, the proper remedie is the annexing of three offices in Chriſt by his heauenly diſpenſation. And firſt of his Prophecie.
*Againſt our ignorãce, which is the mother of all ſinne and miſchiefe.
*The proper remedie is his wiſdome, which is the roote of all grace, and welfare.

Doctrine.

Further of his Priefthoode.
Againſt our vnholines, and breach of the firſt table.

3. *Where I *vngodly am, and fuperſtitious,
Vnreuerent, profane, and irreligious,
Leading my life after a worldly faſhion
Againſt the rule of my heauenly vocation,
And thus am fet in an *ilfauor'd cafe*;
Chriſt is my *perfect holines, and grace :
Him, as that *holy of holies*, if I frequent,
My blottes, and blemiſhes ſhall foone be fpent.

The proper remedie, is his holines.

Application.

O Chriſt forgiue my foule and vgly vice,
Which dooth my foule, and body both difguiſe,
And fo prouoketh me to dayly ſtrife,
Whileſt I am foiled in this *filthie life*.
And graunt me thy *faire beautie* to expreſſe,
Henceforth in my behauiour more or leſſe,
Till fleſh and blood by death thou ſhalt fubdue,
My ſtate in heauen for euer to renue.

Doctrine.

Moreouer of his Prieſthoode.
Againſt our vnrighteouſnes, and breach of the fecond table.

4. *Where I am *toyl'd with care of earthly pelfe,
And doe not loue my neighbour, as my felfe :
But hurt his ſtate, life, bed, goods, and good name
In thought, word, deede, and luſting for the fame,
And fo am filled full of *all iniquitie :*
Chriſt is my *perfect righteouſnes, and equitie :
Him, as that *vpright iudge*, if I obay,
I cannot hurt my neighbour any way.

The proper remedie, is [h]is righteouſnes.

Application.

O Chriſt, forgiue my violence and treacherie,
Which makes me offer others mickle iniurie,
And fo prouoketh me to dayly ſtrife,
Whilſt I am carking in this *carefull life*.
And grant me thy *high iuſtice* to expreſſe
Henceforth in my behauiour more or leſſe,
Till fleſh and bloud, by death thou ſhalt fubdue.
My ſtate in heauen for euer to renue.

Doctrine.

Laſtly of his kingdome.
Againſt our bondage & [mi-]ſerie, which is the iuſt puni[ſh-]ment of all our ſinnes.

5. *Where I am *bond-flaue to al kinde of mifery,
Solde vnder fin, and fubiect to all infamy,
Falling downe headlong to vtter deſtruction,
By naturall, and actuall corruption,
And thus am feeble, *fraile, and tranſitorie*;
Chriſt my *redemption is, and perfect glorie :
Him, as that *Lord of hoaſts*, if I doe ſerue,
From force of foes he will me fure preferue.

The proper remedie, is his [re-]demption and glorie, whi[ch is] the due rewarde of his ex[cee-]ding mercie towards vs.

Application.

O Chrift forgiue my wretched imperfection,
Which pulleth me from thine happie protection,
And fo prouoketh me to daily ftrife,
Whilft I doe warrefare in this *wearie life*,
And grant me thy **free ranfome* to expreffe
Henceforth in my behauiour more or leffe,
Till flefh and blood, by death thou fhalt fubdue,
My ftate in heauen for euer to renue.

Amen.

* Namely by relieuing of the needy, after thy Royall example, according to the power of thy grace in me. Io.13.14.15. Rom. 12. 16. Ephe. 5. 21. Phi. 2.5.6.7.&c. 1.Pet. 1.17. 18.19. Ephe.4.7.8. Iam 2. 8. &c.

FINIS.

AT LONDON | *Printed by* Thomas Orwin, *for* Chrifto|pher Hunt.   1593.

A licence for printing this ballad does not appear in the Stationers' Registers.

18

The Cronycle of all the Kynges : that haue
Reygned in Englande : Sythe the Conqueſt of Wyllyam Conqueroure.   And
Sheweth the Dayes of theyr Crownacion.   And howe many Yeres
They dyd Reygne.   With the Dayes of theyr Death.
And where they were buryed.

❡ *Wyllyam Conqueroure.*

THis myghtye Wyllyam,
Duke of Normandye
As Bokes olde, maketh mencion
By Iuſttytſe, and by his Cheualrye
Made Kynge by Conqueſt of Brutes Albion
Put out Harolde, and toke Poſſeſſyon
And bare his Crowne .xx. yere .vi. mōthes, and .xxii. dayes
And buryed at Cane as the Cronycle ſayes,
❡ Crowned the .xxv. daye of Decembre,
The yere of our Lorde God a .M. lxvi.
And dyed the .xi daye of Septembre,
The yere of our lorde a .M. lxxxvii.

❡ *Wyllyam Rufus.*

NExte hym in ordre, by Succeſſyon
Was wyllyam Rufus his ſonne crowned Kynge
Whiche to Godwarde had no deuocion
Deſtroyed Churches, of newe and olde buyldynge
To make a Foreſt pleaſaunt for huntynge
Bare the Crowne .xii. yere .xi. mōthes, & .xvi. dayes in dede
Buryed at weſtmynſter, the Cronycle ye may rede.
❡ Crowned the xxvii. daye of Septembre,
The yere of our lorde a M. lxxxvii.
And dyed the fyrſt day of Auguſt
The yere of our lorde a M. and a C.

¶ Henrye the Fyrſte.

THan his brother nexte, called the fyrſte Henrye
Was at London Crowned as I fynde
Whoſe brother, Robert Duke of Normandye
Made hym warre, the Cronycle maketh mynde
Reconſyled, all rancoure ſet behynde
XXXv. yere iiii. monthes, and .xi. daies, by recorde of wrytynge
He reygned and lyeth buryed at Redynge,
　¶ Crowned the .v. daye of Auguſt,
　　The yere of our lorde a M. a C.
　And dyed the ſeconde daye of Decembre,
　　The yere of our lorde a M. a C. xxxv.

¶ Stephen his Coſen.

STephen his Coſen, when Henry was deade
Towarde Englande gan to croſſe his ſayle
The Archebyſſhop ſet vpon his heade
A ryche Crowne, beynge of his Counſayle
And xviii. yere xi. monthes, and xiiii. dayes with trauayle
Bare his Crowne, and had neuer reſt
And lyeth at Feuerſam buryed in a cheſt,
　¶ Crowned the .xxvi day of Decembre
　　The yere of our lorde a M. a C. xxxvi.
　And dyed the xxv. daye of Octobre
　　The yere of our lorde a M. a C. liiii.

* * * * * * * * * * * * *[* *

¶ Edwarde the Thyrde.

THe thyrde Edwarde, borne at Wyndſore
Whiche in Knyghthode had, ſo great a pryce
Enherytoure of Fraunce, withouten more
Bare in his Armes quarterlye, thre Flowerdelyce
And he gat Calys by his prudent deuyce
He reygned in Englande l. yere v. monthes, and vii. dayes
And lyeth at weſtmynſter, as the Cronycle ſayes.
　¶ Crowned the ſeconde daye of Februarye,
　　The yere of our lorde a M. iii. C. xxv.
　And dyed the xxi. daye of Iune,
　　The yere of our lorde a M. iii. C. lxxvii.

❡ *Rycharde the Seconde.*

SOnne of Edwarde, Rycharde the feconde
In whofe tyme was peace great plentye
wedded Quene Anne of Cenme, as it is founde
Elyzabeth of Fraunce, after who lyft to fe
And .xxii. yere .iiii. monthes, and ii. dayes he reygned parde
And at Langley buryed fyrft, fo ftode the cas
And after to weftmynfter his body caryed was,
❡Crowned the xvi. day of Iulye
The yere of our lorde a M. iii. C. lxxvii.
And dyed the xxix. day of Septembre
The yere of our lorde a M. iii. C. lxxxxix.

❡ *Henrye the Fourth.*

HEnry the fourth, next crowned in certayne
A famous knyght, and of great femelynes
From his exyle whan he came home agayne
Trauayled after, with warre and great fycknes
Xiii. yere .v. monthes, and .xviii. dayes in fothenes
He reygned and lyeth in Cauntorbury in that holy place
God of his mercy do his foule grace,
❡Crowned the xiii. daye of Octobre
The yere of our lorde a M. iii. C. lxxxxix.
And dyed the .xx. daye of Marche
The yere of our lorde a M. iiii. C. xii.

❡ *Henrye the Fyfte.*

THe fyfte Henry of Knyghthod lode ftarre
Wyfe and ryght manly, playnely to termyne
Ryght fortunate, proued, in peace and warre
Greatly experte, in marcyall dyffyplyne
Able to ftande amonge the worthyes nyne
Reygned ix. yere v. monthes, & xxiiii. daies who lyft regarde
Lyeth at weftmynfter, not farre fro S. Edwarde.
❡Crowned the ix. daye of Auguft,
The yere of our lorde a M. iiii. C. xiii.
And dyed the xxxi. daye of Auguft
The yere of our lorde a M. iiii. C. xxii.

❡ *Henrye the Syxte.*

HEnrye the ſyxte, that in his tendre age
Crowned was kynge of realmes twayne
Endewed with grace, and heauenly wyſdom ſage
Drade and doubted, he was for certayne
And ouer that, as it is wrytten playne
He reygned .xxxviii. yere vi. monthes, and xviii. dayes
And lyeth at wyndſore as the Cronycle ſayes,
❡ Crowned the .xvi. day of Nouembre
The yere of our lorde a M. iiii. C. xxiii.
And dyed the .iiii. day of Marche
The yere of our lorde a M. iiii. C. lx.

❡ *Edwarde the Fourth.*

AFter whom, of noble memorye
Was Edwarde the .iiii. of that name
A noble prynce, a gouernoure moſt worthye
Full excellent were his actes withouten blame
And enrolled within the houſe of fame
He reygned xxii. yere. one month .viii. dayes and no more
And his body lyeth buryed at wyndſore
❡ Crowned the .xxviii. daye of Iune,
The yere of our lorde a M. iiii. C. lxi.
And dyed the .ix. day of Apryll,
The yere of our lorde a M. iiii. C. lxxxiii.

* * * * * * * * * * *

This may be a poetical synopsis of John Rastell's 'Paſtyme of People', a chronology of English history from the earliest times to the reign of Richard III. Its historical accuracy is somewhat faulty: Stephen was crowned in 1135, and Edward III in 1327, while Richard II abdicated on Sept. 29, 1399, but did not die until Feb. 14, 1400.

The broadside is imperfect and may have been complete in two sheets. It is printed in two columns which are separated by a border containing woodcuts of Prudence, Faith, Charity, &c. Above the first stanza is a woodcut portrait of William the Conqueror, holding the sceptre and bible.

THOMAS CHURCHYARD.

The thirteen ballads which come next introduce the name of a writer who is the most conspicuous of those who appear in this collection. Thomas Churchyard, though his productions in prose and verse are numerous rather than of such a character as to place him in the front rank of English literature, is an exceedingly interesting personality. Churchyard's long and active life began under the patronage of the Earl of Surrey and ended as late as the reign of James I. Many of his works are autobiographical and recount his military adventures in Scotland, Ireland, France, and the Netherlands. His career was at all times attended by poverty and neglect, and his disappointments are clearly reflected in his writings. The Reverend Thomas Corser summarized this author thus: 'there is a simplicity and straightforwardness, a truth, a good sense in some of his writings, which are quite refreshing, and although deficient in invention render them deserving of notice.' 'The Worthines of Wales', printed in 1587, is an important contribution to Welsh topography.

In the Britwell Library there are five ballads bearing Churchyard's signature, and a sixth written by one Ralph Smart on Churchyard's behalf. From the Registers of the Stationers' Company it appears that licences for all these were obtained between July 1565 and July 1566.

Besides the Churchyard ballads which are at Britwell, there is an earlier series in the possession of the Society of Antiquaries. It consists of fourteen broadsides, parts of a poetical 'flyting', in which Thomas Churchyard, Thomas Camell (an individual of whom little is known), and certain interlopers were engaged. Within a few years of their first publication in 1552 these were collected in a volume entitled 'The Contention bettwyxte Churchyeard and Camell, vpon Dauid Dycers Dreame sett out in suche order, that it is bothe wyttye and profytable for all degryes . . . Anno. M.D.LX.', of which the only copy known is preserved at Britwell. Since this date the ballads, with a single exception, have not been reprinted, and it has occurred to the Editor of Heber's collection that it might endow this volume with additional interest if a selection from this earlier series were included. With this object in view it has been found possible to furnish a facsimile and reprints of the most important; namely the four written by Churchyard himself, commencing with 'Dauy Dycars Dreame', a short ballad and one so little provocative in matter as scarcely to justify the appearance of others so numerous and lengthy, and the remaining three which are the replies of his spirited antagonist, Thomas Camell. To carry this into effect it was necessary to obtain the permission of the Society of Antiquaries for photographing these ballads. The application was favourably entertained and granted by the Council of the Society, to whom best thanks are due. There has also been added 'Sorrowfull Verfes made on the death of . . . Queene Elizabeth, my Gracious Miftreffe', a single sheet which is in the library of the British Museum.

Beyond those already mentioned no other broadsides by Churchyard are known. The 'Dictionary of National Biography' mentions 'The fantafies of a troubled mannes head'. This ballad is the first of four poems printed on a broadside formerly in the Huth collection and now at the British Museum, and is signed I. C., so that it is difficult to understand the reason for its ascription. The verses may have been written by I. Canand the accredited author of two stanzas entitled 'O euyll tovnges' which appear on the same sheet (H. Huth, *Ancient Ballads and Broadsides*, 1867, pp. 217-20). The 'Dictionary' further attributes to Churchyard 'An Epitaph vpon the deth of Kyng Edward' (Society of Antiquaries), yet a comparison with Churchyard's epitaph on the death of that sovereign as given in his 'Generall rehearfall of warres', 1579, shows that the two are not identical.

19

Dauy Dycars Dreame.

[See facsimile.]

This ballad was also reprinted at the close of ' A pleafaunte Laborinth called Churchyardes Chance', 1580, and is described there as having been 'Written in the beginnyng of King Edwardes raigne'.

The dimensions of the original ballad are the same as those of the facsimile.

Dauy Dycars Dreame,

When faith in frendes beare fruit, and folysh fancyes fade,
& crafty catchers cum to nought, & hate gret loue hath made
When fraud flieth far from towne, & lewterers leaue the sielde,
And rude shall runne a rightfull race, and all men be well wude:
When gropers after gayne, shall carpe for comen welth,
And wyly workers shall dildayne, to frygge and lyue by stelth :
When wisdome walkts a loft, and folly syts full low,
And vertue vanquish pampred vice, and grace begins to grow.
When Justice ioynes to truth, and law lookes not to meede,
& bribes help not to build fair bowres, nor gifts gret giotōs fede
When hongre hides his head, and plenty please the poore,
And niggerdes to the nedy men, shall neuer shut their doore:
When double darke deceit, is out of credit worne,
And fauning speche is falshed found, & craft is laught to skorne
When pride which picks the purs, gapes not for garments gay
No iauels weare no veluet weeds, nor wandring wits bere sway
When riches wrongs no right, nor power poore put backe,
Nor couetous creepes not into Courte, nor lerned, liuings lack
When slipper sleights are seene, and far fatchers be founde,
And priuate profit & selfe loue, shall both be put in pounde :
When dette no sergeant dreeds, and cowrtiers credit keepe,
& might mels not with merchandise, nor lords shal sel no sheepe:
When lucre lasts not long, and hurd great heaps doth hate,
And euery wight is well content, to walke in his estate,
When truth doth tread the stretes, and lyers lurke in den,
And Rex doth raigne & rule the rost, & weeds out wicked men :
Then baesfull barnes be blythe, that here in England wonne,
Your strife shal stynt I vndertake, your dreedfull daies ar done:

Finis. Quod. T. Churcharde.

Imprinted at London in Aldersgate strete
by Rycharde Lant.

20

¶ To Dauid Dicars when.

¶ To him that doth dreame, Dauid Dicars when,
And euen fo from hym, to fuch other men.

FRom when vnto when, to come to this when.
Whē fooles of your folly, wyl worke lyke wyfe men
And know theyr owne fautes, & leaue faulting other
And fyrſt mende them felues, & thē warne theyr brother,
Enuiyng none, for that theyr forte is not
Such as they would be, lyke others I wot.
Goddes of degree, to rule and beare fwaye,
Whofe maners mete not, to ſtand in fuch ſtay,
And yet wold haue mouthes, to rore lyke the Lyon
Beyng but Affes, brute of condicion.   Efopus de
Forgettynge that order doth thus aſke and craue,   afino rugēte
That eche ſhould hym felfe in order behaue.
As beaſtes of lowe forte, to be meke of theyr mynde,
To thofe that be hygher, and greater of kynde.
The Bore not to bragge, to ſtryue wyth the Lyon.
The Hart not to ſtand, wyth the Bull in contencion,
The Oxe that doth draw, to thyncke hym felfe able,
To runne for a wager, wyth the Horfe of the ſtable.
It grees not, it cordes not, nor orderly fyttes
That men ſhould fynd fault, wyth Gods and theyr wyttes,
Iupiters feate ſtandes fomewhat to hye
For vs to iudge it, that come it not nye.
And iudgementes of geffe, in any fuch forte,
May ferue to the Gods, for a laughter and fporte.
To fe how Iudas, would fayne become *Iuda*,
To iuſte at the life, of *Iuli apoſtata*.
Let Beaſtes that be meete, for carte and caryage,
Leane to theyr laboure, as manne to hys maryage.
And fynce we be members of one common wealthe,
Let vs ioyne aptly, as fyttes for our health.
The eye as the eye, let hym ſtare and looke,
And let the leg learne, to bowe and to crooke.
Let the hand anfwere, to helpe and to dooe,
As the wyl of the hert, ſhall wyll hym vnto.
And let not the foote, make murmur and cry,
To aſke why our head is placed fo hye.
Our inſtrument iarres, it makes no ryght melody,
If we thus tune not to order our armony.
Then mayſter when, when bothe you and I,
And euery man els wyl learne to applye,

To our ryght metyarde, and kepe oure iuſt compaſſe,
And looke not ſo deepe in an other mannes glaſſe.
And leaue dreaming dreames of dead Dauid Dicar,
And ſend ſuch whens home, to our perſon or vycar.
And therwyth remember, thys verſe of Cato,
Whoſe wyſdō doth warne vs, with theſe wordes I trowe
Que ſoles culpare, ea tu ipſe :
ne feceris, when wee marke this nipſe,
And leaue drawyng dialles, on other mens dooyng
And learne for to looke to our owne woorkes and brewynge, ·
Then I ſay then, when you agayn when :
wyll ſay well your ſelfe, and ſuche other men,
And all folke wyll doo well.   Lo thus I ende then,
All thynges ſhall be well, whiche god graunt. Amen.

Domine ſaluum fac Regem
& da pacem in diebus noſtris.

Quod T. Camel.

Imprinted at London by Hary Sutton, dwellyng in Poules
Churchyarde, at the ſygne of the blacke boye.

Henry Sutton printed at the sign of the Black Boy in St. Paul's Churchyard or Paternoster Row, where about 1552 he issued several of the ballads in this controversy. He was an original member of the Stationers' Company and printed up to 1563 (E. Gordon Duff, *A Century of the English Book Trade,* 1905). On each side of the ballad is an ornamental border containing winged boys and foliage.

21

A Replicacion to Camels Obiection.

IF right or reaſon, might moue you to ſpeake,
I wold not you blame, your malice to wreake:
Or if your iudgement, were vpright and cleane,
  You wolde not ſo rudely conſtrue what I meane.
How ſhould your folly, ſo plainly be knowne,
  If that your wiſdome, abrode were not blowne.
You byd me amende, whoſe life you know not,
  As though that in you, there were not a ſpot.
A tale of a tubbe, you bragge and you brall,
  wherin you do rubbe your ſelfe on the gall.
You touch not one poynt, wherof that I wrate.
  You leape ore the hedge, and ſeeith not the gate,
I muſe what you meane to diſcant and preache,
  Vpon a plaine ſong, ſo farre paſt your reache.
why Camell I ſay, wyl you needes be fyne,
  what wyll ye be knowne for a durty deuine.
It ſeemes you are learned, paſt reaſon or wyt,
  Or els you coulde not, the marke ſo well hyt.
You haue ſo good laten, you can want no pewter,
  Though ye are no foole, yet you are a newter.
You writ like a clerke, ore ſeene well in Cato,
  Forgettīg your name, which Therēs cals Gnato.
I can do no leſſe, but ſhew what you are,
  Synce you ar a Daniell, darke dreames to declare
Your knowledge is great, your iudgement is good,
  The moſt of your ſtudy, hath ben of Robyn hood
And Beuys of Hampton, and ſyr Launcelet de lake,
  Hath tought you full oft, your verſes to make:
By ſweete ſaint Benet, I ſwere by no foole,
  You are not to learne, you plyde well your ſcole.
Your wyts are not breched, who liſt you to preeue,
  You flocke and you flout, and ſmils in your ſleeue,
I prayſe you no more, leſt you thinke I flatter,
  I muſt now retourne, to the pith of my matter,
How can you well proue, that I do enuye,
  At any eſtate, be they low or hye,
Or that I ſpye fauts, in Iuppiters ſeate,
  why are you ſo mad, on me thus to bleate,
It grees not, it cords not, it fyts not you ſay,
  That mē ſhuld find faut, with gods that bere ſway
If plaine Dauy Dicar, with wiſe men be ſkande,
  He ſpeaketh vprightly, I dare take in hande.
I write not ſo raſhly, but I rule my pen,
  In faith you miſtake, Dauy Dicars, when,

You take chauke for chefe, and day for darke night,
  Of like you are fpurblinde, or ye loke not a right:
Your purpofe I know, you were in fuch care,
  Againft this good tyme, your purs was ful bare.
You thought to optaine, fome garment or gift,
  Then dyd you inuent, to make a foule fhift,
To flatter the Gods, & get a new cote,
  That made you to fyng, fo mery a note.
You faine me like Iudas, you thinke me not fo,
  For if I were he, then you wold me know,
I beare not the bagge, that mai you rewarde,
  But yet my good wyll, I pray you regarde,
You fay that order, would haue eche degree,
  To walke in his calling: then how may this be,
That you out of frame, do blother and barke,
  So like a curre dogge, at euery good warke,
Is this the order, that Camels doo vfe?
  Bicaufe you are a beaft, I muft you exfcufe:
A Camell, a Capon, a Curre fure by kynde,
  I may you well call, fynce fo I you fynde:
Bicaufe you haue ratled and railed to mytche,
  Now giue me good leue, to claw you wher ye ytch
And if that you thinke, I rubbe you to fore,
  Then giue me no caufe, to fcratch you no more.
Holde this for certayn, and for a fure thing,
  The ofter you ftyrre me, the more I wyll ftyng.
Syns that you wyll needes awaken my wyttes,
  I wyll feeke for you, both fnaffuls and bittes.
To holde in your head, and make you to rayne,
  And byte on the bridle, for angre and payne.
Then will I deuife for you fuch a burthen,
  As long as you liue, you fhall beare a lurden:
A Camell by kinde, wyll beare more at once,
  Then .iii. great horfes, pickt out for the nonce.
More meeter for you, to be in fome ftable,
  To beare heauy burthens, I thinke you more able
Then being as you are, walking abrode,
  Your limmes ar well made, to carye a great lode:
All beaftes that be made for carte and cariage.
  Shuld leane to their labour, as mā to his mariage
with horfes and Affes, you are well acquainted,
  Their maners in ordre, right wel you haue painted
I dout of your fhape, fome monfter you are,
  Bicaufe fuch a name, to me you declare.
Your wordes and your workes, ar tokens right fure
  You ar fome brute beaft, in mans forme & picture.
Right happy he were, that had you in charge,
  He fhuld gaine moch money, to fhew you at large
what caufe, or what toye, dyd trouble your mynde,
  To make you feeke fauts, wher non you can finde:
Your inftrument iarres, your myrth is not fweete,
  You play on falfe ftriings, which thing is vnmeete

Your eare is not good, you know no fweete founde,
    You can not efpie, where faut may be founde.
So farre out of tune, I neuer hearde none,
    Nor fo much paft fhame, nor yet fo farre gone,
As you in this cafe, God fende you to amende,
    which feekes to learne me, to bow and to bende:
Direct well your fteppes, by order and lyne,
    And fclaunder me not, nor no workes of myne.
In all my writinges, right honeftly I ment.
    If thei be taken, to my true entent:
Thei fhall breede no ftrife, nor no error fowe.
    when truth fhalbe tryde, and vertue fhall flow.
Thus yet once to, when, againe I returne,
    Bicaufe that you feeme, againft it to fpurne,
Vntill this long, when, do well come to paffe,
    This world fhalbe nought, & you fhalbe an Affe:
Since you doo inuey, alle vice to maintaine,
    You fhew that you haue, a folifh light braine:
God fend you more wit, now kepe your head warme
    Or els the next winter, mai doo you fome harme.
Thus here I do ende, and reft for this time,
    Excepte you procure me, to make a new rime.

           Finis.   Quod.   Thomas Churchard.

      Imprinted by Rychard Lant.

Richard Lant, the printer of five ballads in the Churchyard-Camell controversy, was made free of the Stationers on September 6, 1537. He is mentioned as a member at the incorporation of the company in 1557. His earliest book printed with a date, 'Heuy Newes of an horryble erthquake, which was in the Citie of Scarbaria,' was issued in 1542. At the beginning of his career he printed in St. Sepulchre's Parish, in the Old Bailey. He subsequently moved to Aldersgate Street, then to Paternoster Row, and lastly to the Parish of St. Bartholomew's Hospital in Smithfield. He last obtained a licence in 1562–63 (Arber's *Transcript*, i. 211). This ballad is printed in two columns.

22

¶Camelles Reioindre, to Churchyarde.

To Churchyard or Mānaring, or for lack of a name :
To Dicar the dreamer, if you knowe the fame.

MAye a man be fo bolde (an order to kepe :)
To bid you good morow, now after your flepe?
If I may be fo faucy, and make no miftaking :
God fpeede mafter Dreamer, yf you be wakynge.
But Dreamer or Dicar, or as you faye Dauy :
Whych fhal I now cal you, as our Lorde faue ye?

He hathe .v.
Dreamer.
Dicar.
Dauid.
Mannaring.
Churchyard.

Three names are to many, for one man alone :
And two mo makes fyue, for faylyng of one.
If you had twoo other, that men myght you feeke :
Then had you a name, for eche daye in the weeke.
But no man dothe doubte, that fo fundrye names :
Shuld haue other loomyng, thē out of good frames.
And therfor I thyncke, they come euery chone :
Out of fome olde houfe, tho the poftes be gone.
Or els kept in memory, for that they were founde :
In fome old ftocke, in fome noble mans grounde.
And fo do remayne, for mynde of your aunceftry :
As Syb to Sybbel, fibbes very properly.
So Iermaines lyps ioynde, & fo M. Churchyard :

Afke him
where he na-
med hym felf
Lorde Man
marynge, and
howe he vfed
it.

And Mannaryng met, both in an Orcharde.
And Dauid the Dicar, came in wyth hys fpade :
And dolue vp the Dreamer, tyl the line was made.
And thus percōfequēce, fins your writing doth gre it :
Youre name for my parte : Dauid Dreamer be it.
And good M. dreamer, your reafō long fought for
Hath combred your capar, I fe very fore.
Snap of the cafe, and yong and whot bloude :
Haue al to be fumed you, and moued your moode
That daunger it were, in you of a feeuer :
If heate and coller, fhoulde cuple together.
But thankes be to God, a vomet hath rydde :
A culpin of collops, farre inwardly hydde.
And now ẏ your reafon, hath fair brought it fourth

Parturiunt
montes.
Nafcetur ridi
culus mus.

It is a fayre reafon, and a reafon well wourth.
And fyrft you reply, to myne obieccion :
Wyth wordes of pleafure, as a man of correccion.
Wherby you would feeme, a learned man of arte :

Churchards
aunfware
doth but rail.

And yet Mafter Mome, you are out of your parte.
For as your aunfwere, doth but talke and tomble :
So you anfwer not me, but rayle out and romble.
And yet had you markt, my then to your when :
I no more falted you, then I dyd other men.

I meane mad raungers, that fo raunge at large :
To medle with matters, not ioynd to their charge.
And fuch men I bad, as then I bad you :
To fend fuch whens home, theyr vycar vnto.
And leaue dreaming dreames, to bufi mēs braines :
Wyth nedeles matters, and as thankeles paynes.
And thys lytle neded, to haue netled your noddye :
If you were (as you wold be) fom prety wife body.
But you wyl choplogicke, and be Bee to buffe :   Churcharde
will bee the
buffinge be.
But good Mafter Bufferd, be good yet to vs.
And tel me in truth, and lye no whyt then :
Haue not I touched, no parte of your when ?
If you ftyl dreame not, as you do yet :
I trowe I haue touched, your when euery whyt.
I nede not to byd you, turne my text againe :
But take your owne text, to aunfwer your brayne.
I touch not one poynte, that you wrote you faye :   His replica
cion.
And yet you cal me, a Daniell ftrayghtway.
Lo how thefe two now, agree in them felues :
They both fhame their mafter, thefe .ii. eluifh elues.
If you gyue me a name wythout an effect :
your mafterfhyps brayne, is madly infect.
And foule ouerfhot, to bryng two for wytneffe :
Whych are in thē felues, cleane contraries I geffe
But if my fyrft aunfwer, doo feeme fuch a miftery :
That you fee not your whē, ther anfwered alredye.
Then to awake you, and rayfe you from flepe,
Good Mafter Dreamer, marke thys & take kepe.
your when hath in it, a meanyng of who fay,   Hys when.
Whych ryghtly to meane, is thus ment I fay :
That whē thofe things be, which thefe dais be not
Then knit you your thē vp, in fuch fort as you wot
But whome you accufe, in whenning fo large.
I meane not to open, nor put to your charge.
But way with your felf, and fober your braines :
And defend not a when, mighte put you to paines,
I coulde perchaunce, make your when larger.
And ferue it before you, as brode as a charger,
And point you your when, by lyne and by Leuel.
Againfte Iupiters feate, and Iupiters Counfell.
But I lift not fo narow, to loke to your whanning
Nor make to your whanning, fo open a fkanning
You bid me not flaunder you, I flaunder you not.
If your felfe hurte you your owne is the fpot.
You afcribe to me, the manners of Gnato.
Full clarkelye applyed good mafter Thrafo.
A tytle as meete, they faye that doo knowe me.
As your title of dreame, to the matter of Dauye.
But vices in ftage plaies, whē theyr matter is gon
They laughe oute the refte, to the lookers on.
And fo wantynge matter, you brynge in my coate.
In faythe mafter dreamer, I borowed it not.

Tho I haue hearde, that good fellowes and ſo.
Graculus or natus eſt Plu mis Pauonis
Not you (goddes forbod) in borrowed geare go,
But when euery ſoule, hathe puld home his fether
The ſoule and the body, may then dwel together
And make a right ſommer man, to let in the heate
For clothes in whot wether, do but make mē ſweat
Whiche you ſir perchaunce, er ſommer come out:
Wyl vſe for a medicine, in trauailinge aboute,
And colloure the matter, wyth a title of ſeaſon:
As doutles your maſterſhip, hath very good reaſō
By which al y^t know you, wil thinke you wel hable
To thruſt a poore Camel, to lurke in ſome ſtable.
And doubtles if dreaming, may eny thinge ſpede,
I knowe Dauid dreamer, wyl do it in dede.
But tho I haue hearde, a Lion oft rore,
I neuer hearde aſſe, ſo rore oute before,
With bitings & bridellings, and raining of necks
Churchard is a fyne aſſe.
O fine maſter aſſe, howe ſharpe be your checkes.
You threaten to bitte me, to trim me and trick me:
Wehe maſter aſſe, what, wyl you nedes kick me.
Camelles and aſſes, be bothe mete for burden.
Then gip fellowe aſſe, then ioſt fellowe lurden.
No nerer my buttocke, ioſt iade are you winſyng?
It is mery to ſee, maſter aſſe fal to minſing.
De Aſino au reo.
Did you neuer here tell of the aſſe trapt in golde?
Lo maſter aſenoll, lo do as you ſhulde.
The french almes, perchaunce hath altred him.
you ſaye I knowe you not, and yet as I trowe:
you caſte your olde coat, a greate whyle a go.
But if I miſtake you, for that a newe ſpringe,
Hath wrought as a workmā, to geue you a new ſkī
And that I may not, now know you by eare mark
The aſſe wolde haue a Bell to be knowen by
Then for a more knowledge, to know you in dark
Tye a Bel at your tayle, to make ſome tinginge,
And ther goes the aſſe (I ſhal ſay) by the ringing.
But whether I knowe you, or els do not knowe:
Thus muche I knowe, and am certaine I trowe:
An aſſe bindes no camels, tho he bray nere ſo loud
Churchards Poetes. Robin hoode Sir Launcelot & Beuis. Qualia vis metere: talia graua ſere,
Robin hoode ſo ſhewed me, out of a cloude.
And when aſſes forget, to know what they are,
Sir Launcelot then biddes, to nip them more nar,
And Beuis of Hampton, whoſe cleargy I knowe:
Biddes me ſerue you, with the ſame ſede you ſow.
And not to contende, for the aſſes ſhadowe.
Whoſe ſhadowe I leaue you, and bodye alſo.
And thus, M dreamer, your folli hath brought me
To followe you further, then firſt I bethought me
Beinge muche ſorye, my pen ſo to ſpende,
To anſwere your follyes, and thus lo I ende.

Domine ſaluum fac Regem
& da pacem in diebus noſtris.
Thomas Camell,

¶ Imprinted at London by Hary Sutton, dwellyng in Poules churchyard.

The ballad is printed in two columns, and is without border or ornament.

23

The Surreioindre vnto Camels reioindre.

WHat lyfe may lyue, long vndefamde, what workes may be fo pure,
What vertuous thing, may florifh fo, that fautles may endure :
What things be paft, or yet to come, that freely may reioyce,
  Or who can fay he is fo iuft, he feares not fclaunderous voyce.
This Sclaunderous peales, doth ryng fo loud, he foundes in euery eare,
  Whofe craft can fayn, fuch plefaunt tunes, as truth wer prefent theare.
But it is falfhed, fraught with fraude, and fyngs a note to hye,
  Though that he bring, fome plefaunt poynts, for to maintayn a lye.
The fimple wyts, ar foone begylde, through fclaunders fweete deceayt,
  But thofe that knowes, fuch fifhing hokes, fhal fone perceyue the bayt.
Vnto whofe eares, and iudgements eke, I doo cōmende my workes,
  To faue me from, the Serpents ftynge, which vnder flowers lorkes.
With healpe of truthe, I hope to flee, the venome of this Beaft.
  Or els I truft, in his owne turne, to caft him at the leaft.
Although he whet, his teeth at me, and ftyngs me with his tonge,
  Yet with the iuft, I am content, to learne to fuffre wrong.
Synce Princes peares, & Kyngs themfelues, their Actes & godly lawes,
  Are fclaundred oft, through euyl tonges, and blamed without cawes.
Looke what is doone, and truly ment, to put things in good ftay,
  Are wrefted, & peruerted oft, by euyll tonges I fay.
The Preachers voyce, which thretneth wrath, the fynfull to redufe,
  Doth purchafe hate, for tellyng truth : lo, this is mans abufe.
The chylde doth blame, the byrchen rod, whofe ftrypes may not be fparde,
  Bicaufe his wyts, vnto his welth, hath very fmall regarde.
The wycked fort, whofe vice is knowne, by thofe which writes their lyues,
  Can not abyde, to heare their fauts, but ftyll againft theym ftryues.
The horfe, can not abyde the whyp, bicaufe it mends his pace,
  Thus eche thing hates, his punifhment, we fee before our face,
Therfore I blame, this man the leffe, which fclaundreth me fo mouch,
  And cafteth venome, lyke the Tode, bicaufe his fauts I touch :
What caufe in me, what hate in him, what mattier hath he fought,
  Within this Dauy Dicars Dreame, which for the beft was wrought.
Vnto the good, it is not yll, nor hurtfull vnto none.
  Nor vnto thofe, that loues the lyght, it is no ftumblyng ftone.
But thofe that ftands, to watch a tyme, the innocent to fpyll,
  May wreft the truth, cleane out of frame, & turne good thyngs to yll.
Out of the fweete, and fayreft floure, the fpydre poyfon takes,
  And yet the Bee, doth feede theron, and therwith hony makes.
The Caterpiller, fpyls the fruit, which God made for mans foode,
  The fly likewyfe, wher he doth blow, doth ftyl more harme thā good.
Thus may you fee, as men doo take, the things wheron they looke,
  Thei may it turne, to good or bad, as they applye the booke.

But euery man, to his owne worke, an honeſt meanyng hath,
  Orels thoſe haſty, ſclaunders tonges, might do good men moch ſcath.
He feeles moch eaſe, that ſuffre can, all thyngs as they doo hap,
  Who makes a pyt, for other men, may fall in his owne trap.
who flynges a ſtone, at euery dogge, which barketh in the ſtrete,
  Shall neuer haue, a iuſt reuenge, nor haue a pacient ſprete.
Therfore I ſuffre, al your wordes, which is myne enemy knowne,
  I could you ſerue, with taunting tearmes, & feede you with your owne
But I mynde not, to chocke your tale, before the worſt be tolde,
  Then may I haue, free choyce and leaue, to ſhew you wher you ſcolde.
Good ſyr if I, ſhulde you ſalute, as you ſaluted me,
  Then ſhuld I call you, Dauy too, and ſo perchaunce you be.
Ye multiply, fyue names of one, a progeny you make,
  As your deſent, dyd come from thence, wherof you lately ſpake.
Though ſuch as you, haue nycknamed me, in geſt and halfe in ſcorne,
  Churchyard I am, in Shrewiſbury towne, thei ſay wher I was borne.
You put your name, to others workes, the weaklings to begilde.
  Me thinke you are, ſomwhat to younge, to father ſuch a childe.
The truth therof, is eech to know, a blynde man may diſcus,
  Ye are in nombre, mo then one, ye ſaye, bee good to vs.
You ſay, I did not anſwere you : I could no mattier fynde,
  Nor yet can ſee, excepte I ſhulde, at folly waſt my wynde.
The greateſt ſhame, and moſt reproch, that any man may haue,
  Is for to write, or ſcolde with fooles, whoſe nature is to raue,
Synce railing ryms, ore coms your wits, talke on & babble ſtyll,
  I not entende, about ſuch chats, my pen nor ſpeche to ſpyll.
I neither fume, nor chaunge my moode, at ought that you haue ſayde,
  The world may iudge, your railyng tong, full like a beaſt hath brayd.
And where you ſay, you can poynt out, by lyne and leuell both,
  Of all the, whens, of Dycars dreame, you ſay you knowe the troth.
It is a wilfull ignoraunce, to hyde, I knowe full well,
  A faute, agaynſt Iuppiters ſeate, or agaynſt his counſell.
You ſhew your ſelfe, not Iuppiters frende, if you can truly proue,
  A faute in me, and doth it hyde, for feare or yet for loue.
As for my worke, and thankles paynes, in this and ſuch like caſe,
  I ſhall be redy to defende, when you ſhall hide your face.
Thinke you I feare, what you can do, my grounde is iuſt and true,
  On euery worde, which I dyd ſpeake, I force not what ye brue.
Fyll all your chargers, as ye liſt, and diſhes euery chone,
  when they be full, and runneth ore, I will caſt you a bone.
whiche ſhall be harde, for you to pyke, though that your wits be fyne,
  I can ſone put, you out of ſquare, from your leuell and lyne :
I wyll not anſwere worde for word, to your reiondre yet,
  Becauſe I fynde no matter there, nor yet no poynt of wyt,
But brabling blaſts, and frantike fyts, and chyding in the ayre,
  why doo you fret thus with your ſelf, fye man do not diſpayre :
Though that your wyts, be troubled ſore, if you in Bedlem weare,
  I thinke you ſhuld be right wel kept, if you be frended theare :
yf you were ſcourged once a day, and fed with ſome warme meate,
  You wolde come to your ſelf againe, after this rage of heate.
This may be ſaid without offence, if that your wyts you had,
  you wolde not lye nor raile on me, nor fare as you wer mad,

But as it is a true prouerbe: the threatned man lyues long,
  your words can neither hang nor draw, I feare not your yll tong.
The world is fuch it doth contempne, all thofe that vertue haue,
  An euell tong hath no refpect, whofe name he doth depraue.
what is the caufe of mortall foed, whiche dothe in frendes aryfe,
  But comenly thefe fclaunder tonges, which ftyll delyts in lyes:
who maketh war, who foweth ftrife, who bringeth Realmes to ruine:
  But plenty, pride, and euell tonges, whofe voyce is nere in tune,
The roote and braunche and cheefeft grounde, of mifcheefs all and fome,
  Is euyll tongues, whofe fugred words, hath wyfe men ouercome,
The proofe wherof you put in vfe, your words ye frame and fet,
  To creepe into fome noble hertes, a credit for to get.
The eatyng worme within the nut, the fweeteft curnell feeke,
  fo doo you drawe where gayne is got, and there you loke full meeke.
But vnder thofe fayre angels lokes, is hyd a deuelifh mynde,
  I durft lay odds who truft you long, full falfe he fhall you finde.
Now to returne vnto the caufe, which made you firft to write,
  you fhew your felfe to be a foole, to anfwer me in fpite,
The firft and laft that I haue feene, of all your nipping geare,
  Is not well worth when fruite is cheape, the paring of a peare.
your fodayn ftormes and thundre claps, your boafts and braggs fo loude,
  Hath doone no harme thogh Robyn Hood, fpake with you in a cloud.
Go learne againe of litell Ihon, to fhute in Robyn Hoods bowe,
  Or Dicars dreame fhalbe vnhit, and all his, whens, I trowe.
Thus heare I leaue, I lyft not write, to anfwer wher you rayle:
  He is vnwife that ftriues with fooles, wher words can not preuayle.

Finis.

Domine, faluum fac Regem:
& da pacem in diebus noftris.
         Thomas Churcharde.

Imprinted at London in Alderfgate ftrete
by Rycharde Lant.

The ballad is printed in two columns, without ornament or border,

24

Camelles Conclusion.

Camelles Conclusion, and laft farewell then,
To Churcharde and thofe, that defende his when.

A Man that hath mo thynges then two, to put hym vnto paines,
Hath euen fo many cares the mo to worke hym wery braynes.
So I, that late haue laboured harde, and plucked at my plowe,
Am come to towne, where nowe I fynde mo matters then ynowe.
Mo then I looked for by muche, mo matters to then needes,
Mo makynges and mo medlynges far, then I haue herbes or wedes.
And all agaynft me one alone, a fory fymple man,
That toyles and trauailes for my foode, to earne it as I can.
And gladly would in quiet be, to fwinke and liue in refte,
But dreamers wyl not fuffer me, they nettle fo my neft.
A furreioinder, dreamer bringes, the fecond a decree,
A mariner brings in his bote, and he the thirde wil be.
And fo they ioyne and iompe in leafe, god graunt them well to runne
For I fhall fhewe them if I can, a courfe er I haue done.
The dreamer firft full wel I know, I fhooke hym by the fleue,
Whereat the other .ii. I trowe, are angrye and do greue.
But that no force be as he may, here gothe the beaft abroade,
Dreamer awake, maryner rowe, decree man looke abroade.
The beafte will turne I laie a grote, and giue you all a tryp,
Why nowe fyrs nowe, nowe foote it well, this beaft begyns to fkyp.
And fyrft to maifter dreamer turnes, and his furreioyndre to,
Wherin all thyngs be well he faith, that he dooth dreame and doo.
He dreames he faies and truely meanes, to put thynges in good ftay
Shorte fyr dreamer, a bandy ho, that ball muft nedes away.
If that your dreame haue fuche entent, then hath it an effecte,
And that effect your Wefterne Wyll,* would not haue men fufpect:
But take it as a dreame faies he, and fantefy of the head,
A fyner freke by Roode then you, I haue his workes well read.
Altho he chop in chorles termes, and carpes in vncouth fpeeche,
Yet knowe I with a fynger wet, where wyfe men myght hym feeche.
That if he whyp his whirry fo, he may chance licke a clowne,
To whyp it vnder water quite, and craire and cariage drowne.
But fens he is become my iudge, and iudgeth me amyffe,
In notyng me quite oute of rule, as his wide wyfedome is,
He fhall well knowe, and fo fhall you, and the decreer too,
That for my rule, when I was yonge, this was I taught to doo.
My father put me firfte to fchoole, where I a maifter hadde :
Of whom I had preceptes and ftrypes as fitted for a ladde.

* A ballad bearing this title was contributed to the controversy by some unknown hand. For a description of it see Lemon's ' Catalogue of a collection of Printed Broadsides in the possession of the Society of Antiquaries of London ', 1866.

He taught me there to feare my god, and loue hym with my might,
To ferue the kyng, and pray for hym, and all his counfell ryght.
Then next to honour thofe my frendes, that kept me fo at fchoole,
And this whyle I a fcholar was, was euery day my rule.
And fyns that tyme, my vycar hath full lyke a chriften man,
Taught me to treade in goddes hygh waie, and kepe it as I can.
To be obedient to the kyng, and to the lawe alfo,
And doo my duetie to the powers, and lette their matters go.
Que noftra funt curare lo, he titled at my doore,
And bad me printe it on my poftes, and fpread it on my floore.
And leele loue and labour eke, he bad me learne to knowe,
And kepe my plowe for profite fake, and thanke god to I trowe.
And tolde me howe there hanges a bell, within our paryfhe churche,
whyche he dothe twange eche mornyng rathe, before we go to wurche,
That tales to me, and others mo, our neighbours there about,
This terme whiche I fhall tell you nowe, as I can bryng it out.
Que fupra nos, nihil ad nos, this bell tynges vs to kenne:
And this he fayd the bell warnde me, as it dyd other men.
And when I fawe this Dicars when, I was fo bolde to tell:
That Dicar in his draffyfhe dreame, had not herd this bell well.
And then for thy, forfooth and god, my horne and fcrape I tooke:
And fcratched in a fewe fret lynes, for dreamers on to looke:
And fo fir thus I ment no more, but mynded hym to know
His duetie (as I ment myne owne) and farther not to goe,
Tyll in his toyes he tickled me, as lofty ladde on lowde,
And fhope me fhares to fharpe me with, to carpe out of a clowde.
And if you rolle thus out of tune for raynyng hym this way,
To kepe hym felfe in order fuche, as he fhoulde doo I faie:
And take the iudgement to your hande, and terme me oute of rule,
Then trowe me well, you turne me wide from Camell to a mule.
Whiche camell can not crouche withall, nor cary with hym home,
But fhape and fhake it to your felues, like lumpes of your owne lome,
But welaway, I wander wide, for Churchyarde ment it well,
And fo he faies, and fo fay you, and fo your writynges tell,
So fometymes houfes fyred are, by meanyng well in lyghtes,
And then the meanyng is but marde, & they mad meanyng wightes.
But fens you will needes haue me feke the meanyng of this whan,
Meane it to thofe whom it dothe touche, and fcufe it as you can.
And then let wyfe men deme and iudge atwene Dicar and me,
Whiche of vs two is out of rule, I meane or I or hee.
And fyrft let me nowe axe you all, what fignifies this whan?
That caries with hym at his tayle, fo great a iarryng than.
Holde is it in hand a prefent tyme, or future tyme to come?
Or is it *admirantis* woorde, as fchoole men call it fome.
It muft needes meane a matter madde, as farre as I can fee,
But on go to, your wittes are fyne, meane you it out for me.
Dreamer dothe dreame, and whens vs out, a wondre of thefe whens,
Wherof fome whens are wonders well, and meete for whens mens
But fome from gammuth gront and grone aboue ela a note:
And thofe wilde whens ar whend to large, I dare you gage my cote,
what when is this, that he whens out, when iuftice ioynes to truthe?
whofe feate is that? howe ioynes iuftyce? dreamer faie on in footh.

And nodde your noddles nowe in one, and make a trinitie.
Full workmanly to worke this when, if that it will fo be.
And fyrft waie well what iuftice is, to whom it dooth pertayne,
who fwaies the fwoorde, who dooth decree, looke to the matter playn.
Frō whens he comes, what brāche he beares, & who & which him vfe,
And anfwere iuftyce to the wronge, wherwith you hym accufe.
And meane your meanyng as you meane, & dreame not in your flepe,
And fhewe what ioly ordre nowe, in this your when you kepe.
But fhorte to make of all your whens, to take the principall,
This is among the reft the worft, and ftandes the laft of all.
when Rex dothe reigne and rule the rofte, lo thus you raunge at lafte,
A meruailous when that fuche a when, fhould out in print be pafte.
Doth not Rex raign fir dreamer now? what whennyng term is this?
If Rex reigne not? who reigneth then? a faucy when this is.
And whend at length and large in deede, beyonde a fubiectes wit,
That god defend that I fhould dreame, or that, or like of it.
And yet I trowe I haue a byll for cattall that I folde:
That faies howe Rex hath raigned vi. yeare almoft I dare be bolde.
And eyther is your when full falfe, or my byll is not true,
And whiche is trueft of them bothe, let me nowe afke of you.
As for my felfe I make no doubtes, but that your when is wrong,
And that Rex raignes as he hath doon, and fhall I truft raigne long.
Which as in fchoole I was fyrft taught, to praie that he may doo.
So euery fubiect let hym feeke to haue that prayer too.
Thus coulde I touche fome other whens, wherin you when at large,
A great deale pafte your compaffe to, and as muche paft your charge.
But thofe I leaue by lyght of this, for to be fcande and fene,
To thofe that better iudgementes haue, then you or I, I wene.
And now wyl take your thē in hand wherwyth you knit your when
In publyfhing it thus to me, and to all other menne.
Than balefull barnes be blithe you fay, that here in England wonne:
Our ftryfe fhal ftynt you vndertake, our dredful dayes are donne.
An affuraunce here you make, that baleful barnes we be,
And that in ftrife we are alfo, and dreadfull daies doo fe.
But God defend it fhould be true, whych your ful frantycke hedde:
Hath publyfht to fo open eyes, for to be feene and redde.
For once for me I make no doughtes, nor no good fubiect elles:
But we a noble foueraygne haue, as al our ftatutes tels.
And as al orders els befydes do wyll vs for to know:
Who gouernes vs and is our head, and rules vs al alfo.
And vnder hym haue other powers to fee that lawe be donne:
To gree and tune vs in accorde, if wee be out of tune.
Vnder whofe rule and order eke, al we that fubiectes be:
Do lyue and ioyne as fytteth vs, in one for to agree.
And in the town where I do dwell, I know no ftryfe or dread:
But euery man there lyues in tune as fubiectes to theyr head.
And meddels not but with theyr plowes, & fomtime with their bow:
And prate wyth Peter and wyth Paule, theyr dutyes for to know.
And learne fo for to kepe them ftyll in order as they can:
Except fuch wranglers wrangle them, with fuch large whan & than
And fo I trufte they do els where, whiche for my part I pray,
That longe we may fo ioyne in one, what fo your when dothe fay.

But yet fuche dreadfull whans & thens, which doth the matter marre
were better quight, pulled out of fyght, then fhewed as they are.
And fo fhewe wefterne will from me, and wat and Herman too.
And wyll them wynde their takle well, not as they wont to doo.
For if they leane to learne fuch whens, it will be longe I feare,
Ere they will channell well their craire, that fhulde them fafely beare.

Domine faluum fac regem,
& da pacem in diebus noftris.   T. Camel.

The harteburne I owe you is, yf you come to Lynne,
I praie you to take my poore howfe for your ynne.

Imprinted at London by Hary Sutton, dwellyng in Poules
Churchyarde, at the fygne of the blacke boye.

This ballad is printed on both sides of two sheets.

25

¶A playn and fynall confutacion :
Of cammells corlyke oblatracion.

YE vpright men whiche loues the light, whofe heartes be voyd of gyle :
condemne no caufe till trueth be tryed, gyue eare and lyft a whyle.
And marke my tale from poynt to poynt, let no worde fkip vnfkande :
And heare them with indiffrent eares, and way them as they ftande.
Fyrft laye afyde affeccion blynd, for trueth my caufe muft pleade,
let nether foe nor fayned frend, this matter Iudge nor reade.
And then I truft to clere my felfe, and Cammell cleane confound :
that blowes the trompet of defame, which geues vnfertayn found.
The tune wherof femes yet full ftraunge, fo boyftous is the blaft :
but quiet calmes fettes forth ftill windes, when ftormes be gon and paft.
Whiche quyet time I wifh to haue, that I may be well harde :
and then I hope this vypars byrde, fhall haue his iuft rewarde.
That forgeth fautes and feeketh holes, to crepe and fteale therin :
and flattereth for no other caufe, but fame or gayne to winne.
What thinkes this man he hathe more witte, and learning in his head :
than hathe fyue thoufand other men, that Dycarres dreame hath read.
Or thinkes he that I am fo rafhe, to run fo far from fquare :
or that I make fuche obfcure thinges, that I dare not declare.
Than is he blynde and very fond, and fcarce him felfe doeth know :
let him loke on his booke agayne, his rule is nothinge fo.
To you I fpeak frend Camell now, which wrefteth ryght to wrong :
you faye you haue ben kept at fchole, in foothe I thinke not longe.
Your mafter did but ftroke your head, he did forbeare the rodde :
I dout he did not teache you well, howe you fhould feare your God.
For if he had you would haue ftayed, to wryte agaynft this dreame :
to fpye a mote within my eye, fynce in yours is a beame.
Yf you might fitte and iudge my caufe, I fhould foone feele your worft :
but God forbyd there were long hornes, on beaftes that would be corft.
I call you beaft becaufe you fayde, here goeth the beaft abrode :
the beaft will turne you gage a grote, yf he be prickte with goade.
Now turne fyr beaft and come aloft, fling not for fear of whip :
in dede it is a monftrufe thing, to fee a camell fkippe.
You fay you fhoke me by the fleue, than rubde I your gall backe :
yf I know howe to do you good, my healpe you fhould not lacke.
We Iompe in leaffe, ye gab fyr beaft, I am but one alone :
but I can proue (O beaw Camew,) that you are moe then one.
My furreioynder doeth declare, this dreame was for the beft :
and yet you crye, a bandye ho at tenues thus ye iefte.
What can you laye vnto my charge, of malyce or of hate :
fince I do wyfhe that euery wyght, fhulde walke in his eftate.
This verfe you hyppe, and yet it ftandes, next that when rex doeth rayng :
bothe thefe be good and godlye to, here fhall I fhowe you playne.

But as I fayde, out of fayre flours, the fpyder poyfon takes:
and yet the bee doeth feede thereon, and therewyth hony makes.
I do compare this fpyder nowe, to you whiche fo appeeres:
for that you run a patheles way, to leade me in the breerres.
Wheare fynde you this that dreames can haue, any effect at all,
be not they fancies of the hed, and fo wyfe men them call,
Why do you wryte againft a dreme, whiche hath a fmall effect,
why turn you yt to meanyng leawde, to brynge it in fufpect,
You ment no more but me to lerne, fo you wolde you excufe:
Syr yf you mynde to kepe a frynde, do not your frynde fo vfe.
You bragge you of your mafter muche when you to fkoole dyd goe:
You fayde ye learnd your duetye well, good fyr it feemes not foe.
To ferue the kyng and praie for hym, I learnde as well as you:
to loue hym leall for concyens fake, this leffon well I knew.
His councell eeke for to obaye, my duety learnes me too:
and with ther matters not to mell, nor therin haue to do.
This leffon hetherto I kept, and fhall here after kepe:
tyll I to earth retorne agayn, where flefhe and fell muft fleepe.
What is the caufe you anfwerde not, to that whiche I wrott laft:
You do conclude muche lyke a thefe, whiche is condemnde and caft.
For at the barre he prateth long, and can no reafon fhew:
to clere hym felfe and faue his lyfe whan trueth doeth hym orethrow.
So you althoughe with matter now, I do you ftyll affault:
yet with great fhame you are content, to yelde vnto your fault.
I wrate more thynges than one or two, yet reade them ons agayn:
I do perceyue a lyttell thyng, wyll foone orecom your brayne.
You haue fought councell fourteen daies, it feemes that you dyd dreame:
or els ye thought to run awaie, into fom other realme.
But now I heare a fodayn fownde, the beaft begyns to braye:
it is muche like a camels voyce, that dwels in lyn they faye.
Be as be may you fay your felfe, ye byd me foet it well,
why will the beaft now lead the daunce, with beafts I will not mell.
But wheare you faie, I when out whens, aboue eala a note,
you gront and groen from gammuth farre, I dare you gage my cote.
Sins you will put me to my trompe, with a falfe carde of ten,
marke howe iuftice fhall ioyn to trueth, I will make large this when.
Note.   Though iuftice doeth belonge to *Rex*, whofe fworde puts that in vre,
yet euery iuftice vnder him, is not fo iuft and pure.
Becaufe there be knightes of the poft, whiche wil them felues forfwere,
and fained troeth will forge a tale, fometymes in iuftice eare.
And worke fuche wiles, iuftice to blynde, and make him credit lies
fuche crafty miftes thefe men can caft, before true iuftice eies.
Thoughe iuftice of him felfe is pure, and clean deuoide of crime,
yet falfe witnes may alter him, and chaunge his minde fomtime.
The faut therof is not in hym, he woulde fayn ioyn to truthe:
But flatteryng faith, may him corrupt, alas the more is ruthe.
Whan truth is forman of the queft, and right fhall vardyt gyue,
Than iuftice fhall ioyn ftill to truthe, and fo together liue.
Thus is this when made manifeft, truely as I it ment,
and yet it was full plain before, to euery true entent.
Here haue I waide what iuftice is, to whom it dothe pertain,
who fwayes the fworde, who dothe decree, here haue I fet out plain.

Now ſtaye a while, and marke this when, which you call principal,
and is the beaſt among the reſt, and ſtandeth laſt of all.
Note. When *Rex* doth reign (*And*) rule the roſt, a coniunction copulatiue,
your maſter taught you not to knowe, coulde he ſuche thinges diſcriue?
Now *Rex* doth rayne whom god preſerue, in long life on vs here,
and ſende him rule the roſt him ſelfe, as prince withouten pere.
That he may fynde thoſe ſecrete ſlighes, whiche now in corners lye:
And ſuche as do abuſe his lawes and liue ſo wickedlie.
It ſemes they lyue as they delight, and leane not to his lore:
Bycauſe he doth commende them lawes and they paſſe not therfore.
Howe doth the maſter of the ſchole, his ſchollers rule and tame:
whan he dothe geue preſeptes and rules, and none doth kepe the ſame.
How doeth the kyng his people rule, let this be better wayde:
whan he doeth geue them lawes and actes, and none of them obeyde.
For thoughe that Rex do rayne and rule, as I beleue in dede:
yet dothe not he for mercy grete, the wicked all oute wede.
And like as God is mercifull, ſo doeth our kyng in dede:
enſwe and folowe in his ſteppes, (whom God defende and ſpede.)
His Iuſtice is to poniſhe ſinne, with death and payne extreme:
which is moſt godly exerciſde, and ſo doeth ſhewe and ſeme.
Yet yf all thoſe that do offende, ſhoulde haue ſuche punyſhmente:
what man is liuing nowe a dayes, that ſhoulde eſcape vnſhente?
But folowyng the exaumple of, the Lorde and kynge of kynges:
dothe often ſuffer vs vnkynde, in vyle and greuous thynges.
Becauſe he woulde (as it doethe ſeme, ſo mercifull and deare:)
bee rather loued then obeyed, for only dreade and feare.
And thys hys mercye godly mente, doothe make vs worſe in dede:
as ſcollers when they lacke the rodde, do lyue withouten drede.
But when he ſhall begynne agayne, to punyſhe wyckednes:
whiche is hys iuſtyce (or more playne,) to vs but ryghtouſnes.
Then folke for feare (but not for loue,) ſhall better ende theyr lyfe:
as horſes whipte ye then for feare, ſhall ſtynte and ceaſe oure ſtryfe.
Wherfore yf euery kynge this daie whyche oughte in dede to raygne:
do raygne and rule the roſt and weede, the wicked oute full playne.
Then haue they welthe withouten ſtryfe, whyche God geue vs ryght ſone:
that all oure wyckednes were paſte, and dredfull dayes were done.
If Dycar ſayde, when *Rex* doth raygne, and all men doe obey:
how could you Camell, thus conclude? he raygneth not to daye.
Note. Or if he ſayd, when Chriſt is God, and you a faythfull man:
would ye conclude? ergo, (to him,) he is not God now than.
Wherfore yf Rex do raygne and rule, as I beleue he doeth:
and I beſeche almyghtye God, he maye do longe in ſothe.
Yet muſte you take another poynte, conteyned in thys when:
when Rex doeth raygne and rule the roſte, and wedes oute wycked men.
You muſte not harken halfe the tale, and leaue the reſte behynde:
for than in dede you do amyſſe, and fayne woulde quareles fynde.
You Redde in faythe muche lyke the nunne, *omnia probate*:
and turned not the other ſyde *quod bonum eſt tenete.*
Redde you no more but Rex doeth raygne, and lefte the reſte vnſpyed:
is there not (too) and rule the roſte, the ſentence is ſo tyde.
And wede oute wicked worldly men, the ſpotted from the cleane:
whoſe vyce infectes the choſen lambes, lo thus did Dicar meane.

He doubted not but Rex doethe raygne, the truethe it felfe dothe fhowe:
but yet he thoughte it good to wede, oute wycked men I trowe.
And thus I fay did Dycar dreame, the fence doeth playnly tell:
yf vpryght eyes and righteous mindes, do loke and fkan him well.
If you fhulde be my iudge I fe, and deme my dremynge thus
I fhulde haue but fhort curtefy, and you my caufe difcus.
But god hath fawed your hornes fo fhort, no great hurt do you can,
he made you nether lord nor iudge, nor fkarfe an honeft man.
Whan *Rex* doth raygne and rule the roft, and out the wicked weede,
than you and many other lyke, wold fyrft of all precede.
But where you fet a fnare and net, for thefe that well intende:
to fhowe what is the very caufe, of euill and the ende.
There you your felf (and if it were, applied well in frame,
as he hath ment) fhulde certainly be catchid in the fame.
What if I fhuld caft furth the bone, you thought to choke me with:
perhappes you may repent to late, you went fo nie the pyth.
Where is your leffon now become, you lernd fo long ago,
that fpyde fuch faute in dicars dreme, and yet conceylde it fo.
Note. If it had raught to Iupiters feate, as you affirme in dede,
you ought not it haue kepte fo long, but ftraight it told with fpede.
Or if you thought you fawe the myft, that no man elles could fkrie,
there fhuld no caufe haue ftopte you fo, to tell it by and by.
If dicars when, as true it is, be clere from blame and blotte,
yet your offente is no whit leffe, by caufe you thought it not.
If ignoraunce had fayd a myffe, the fame be my defence,
yet wilfull ignoraunce in you, dothe pleade your great offence.
Behold of god the rightuoufe fcourdge, that nowe a mydde the gryn:
you layde to trappe the innocent your felfe is fallen therin.
What fay you nowe wife camelles caulfe, if rex wede wicked men,
you fhulde of right be tide to fhort, to peruerte dicars when.
But tyll fuche fpiders be wede out, and all their cobwebes to,
that fekes to trappe the fellye flies, as you begyn to do.
The barnes I fay that here do wonne, with in this bryttaine lande,
fhall byde alas thofe dredfull daies, and dicars dreme may ftande.
O Syr you toke my then in hand, wherwith my when I knit,
where I perceyue your frantike head, begins an other fyt.
Note Can you denie the plages of god, which he to vs hath fent?
and fcourgeth vs for our great finnes, from which we not repent.
Doeth not the plowe man plowe his grownde, and laborith verey fore,
the earth bringes forthe hys frute lykewyfe, encreafyng more and more
Doeth not the heauens gyue vs rayne, the watters gyues vs fyfhe?
doeth not the counfell feeke oure welth, as well as we can wifhe?
Do not they take great care and payne, all euelles to redreffe,
yes all thefe thinges doe worke as well, as mans tong can expreffe.
Yet though oure king do make good lawes, the earth bringes forth muche fede:
tyll God will take his plage awaye, oure plenty fhalbe nede.
Thus balefull barnes we be vnblyethe, and dreadfull dayes doe fee:
tyll gracious God of his goodnes, will helpe oure miferye.
Within the towne wheare you doe dwell, you know no dred nor ftryfe:
than is it fure a paradife, I laye theron my lyfe.
For I haue traueld here and theare, and fought this world full wide:
to fynde a reftyng quyet place, where I would fayn abyde.

*A bone for
Camell to
picke vpon.*

But in this wery pylgrimage, I neuer found such stay :
nor suche a vertuous towne as Lyn, yf it be as you saye.
Yf you haue done as muche in Lynne, as you in London haue :
I thinke that all your neighbours woulde, sone wyshe you in your graue.
For we were here in quyet all, vntyll you came to towne :
sence that we could not liue in rest, for suche a contrey clowne.
And Dauie Dicars dreame for soothe, was lowed of euery man :
tyll you began youre wrangling riemes, to brall vpon his whan.
Wherin you lost your honest name, you could not lose much more :
thus are you put to open shame, and haue no thanke therfore.
Go showe your councell one by one, what gayne you here haue got :
*Herman will helpe to rowe you hom, good syr nowe take your botte.
Nowe trudge a waye feare gentyll beast, and kycke no more at me :
and let them lyue in peace and rest, that thinkes no harme to the.
Thus here I take my leaue from you, wishing for grace and healthe :
to kepe my prince from all his foes, and eke the comon wealthe.

*Ad here
to wat.

Finis. (φ) Thomas Churchyard.

Imprinted in Fletstrit by Wyllyam Gryffyth, a lyttle
aboue the condit at the syne of the Gryffyn.

This ballad is probably one of the earliest examples of William Gryffyth's printing. Until 1556 his address was the sign of the Griffin in Fleet Street a little above the Conduit. In this year he transferred his press to the Falcon against St. Dunstan's Church, and for some time retained his earlier premises for the purpose of bookselling. Gryffyth was a member of the Stationers' Company at the time of its incorporation (E. Gordon Duff, *A Century of the English Book Trade*, 1905).

The ballad is printed on both sides of two sheets.

26

¶ A Farewell cauld, Churcheyeards, rounde.
From the Courte to the Cuntry grownd.

IN Courte yf Largies be
Why parte I thens fo bare
yf Lords were franke & fre
Sū dradg wold Lordings fpare
To hyme whofe tonge and penn
Myght fhowe in euery cofte
   The worthynes of men,
    And who defaruythe mofte.

Full lyttill maye be gott
Where hungry droppes do falle
Where all goes to the pott
The kitchine fefe ar fmalle
The Byrde can fpare no plumes
That fethers gaye wolde haue
   The Courttyer all confumes
    Who makes hymefelfe fo braue.

No no here lyes in dede
The padde within the ftrawe
For eche man pledithe neade
And he is held a dawe,
That gyues to fuche as wante
And thynkes hymefelfe in lacke
   This makes the world fo fkant
    And tournythe all to wracke.

For fryndfhyppe cowlde as Ife
I wayted longe and late
And gladde to playe the vice
To plefure eche eftate
And euer dyd I hope
To hitt my wyffhyd marke
   yet lo I dyd but grope
    For gnats within the darke.

Parhappes the frofte hathe nypt
Eache Noble lyberall hand
Or ellfe a waye is fkypte
Into fume other lannde
God fend a thawe a gayne
And fhyppes drawe home as faft
   That pore men for ther payne
    Maye fynde fume welthe at laft.

I faught the Prynce to farue
As all oure dutyes is
And hope I dyd defarue
A greter fute then this,
But dayes and wekes are fpente
And worne·my cotes full thyne
 And all my yearly rent
 yet founde no grace therein.

No Monftoure fure I am
Nor fowlle deformyd thynge,
No fhepe nor fuckinge lame
More lycke to farue a Kinge,
As fhall bothe hand and harte
At lengthe my wytnes be,
 When proffe in any parte
 Shall be requryde of me.

Had I but founde a wyght
In Courte when I was there,
The Lady Sydney hight
All changed had byn this gere,
What happ had I to fhue
Where no fuche helpe is founde,
 O dames yt blufhe not you
 Thought fhe in grace a bound.

Nowe from the Courte to carte
My horfe and I mufte pafe,
Who hathe the meryft harte
Who is in better cafe
My horfe or I, God knowes,
The one mufte beare his charge
 The other where he goes
 Muft pourely lyue at large.

  Finis. quod, T. Churcheyeard.

Imprinted at London in Fleteftrte | at the Faucon, ouer againfte
S. | Dunftons Churche, by | Wylliam Gryffith.

A licence for printing ' *a ffayre well called Churche-yeardes Ronde from the Couurte to the Contry grounde* ' was granted to William Gryffyth, 1565–66 (Arber's *Transcript*, i. 308).

The ballad was reprinted in J. P. Collier's ' Old Ballads ' (Percy Society, 1840), and is printed in two columns, which are separated by an ornamental border. Beneath the imprint is a woodcut of the Gemini.

27

Great thankes to the welcome,
in Churchyards behalfe:

To him that hath bleared, and cried like a Calfe.
Full well by his crying a man may now know,
Where veale may be bought of a price very low:
The head and the purtnaunce, with gather though fmall,
As cheape as a Shepes head, the hornes bought withall.

REftleffe heads, I wel perceaue,
to be acquainted fure:
Can rafhly fede on matters grofe
as meate for them vnpure.

❡ So well I doe perceaue by one,
who hath of late take payne:
By penned verce on high Churchyard
,to welcome home agayne.

❡ In tauntyng wife (alas thou foole)
what needed thus thy head
To trauaile in fuch flickeryng vearce,
fith all thy wits be fled?

Doeft thou know thou chattring Pye
on whome thou doeft thus rayle?
Or haft thou caufe by gawled backe,
to wag and wince thy tayle?

❡ As no reuenge, this men accoumpt,
to wreake thy angrie moode?
To charge him with a vowed oth,
for wearyng of a hodde.

❡ Thy nature yll, doth well declare,
thy rancour and thy fpight:
To heads that bare and naked are,
yet needs not lanthorne light.

*But canft thou fpare a hood in dede?
of hoods haft thou fuch ftore?
How can thy hornes for hoods be fene?
hufht hufht, I fay no more.

Let Churchyard liue & raigne in place
to his contented mynde,
And fo let euery horned beaft
go raunge, lyke to his kynde.

M

❡ For cloughie Clem, and William to
    neede not to take more payne,
Sith Adam Bel, for Clem of yᵉ clough
    the monſtrous Shepe hath ſlayne.

❡ And outlawes are (as I heare ſay)
    for this, ſo haynous deed :
So farewell .C. with horned cap,
    good night, and eke good ſpeed.

Thus doe I ceaſe with hoods Robin,
    now Robin Hood farewell :
And Robinſon in Churchyards ſtede
    ſhall weare the hood and bell.

❡ And yf this rude and ſimple verce
    may not a warnyng bee,
To ſtay your cockyng crackyng head
    take heed leſt that you ſee :

The cokſcōbe knockt about your pate,
    then hoods no more wyll ſeeme
Your hornes to hyde, but al men ſhall
    a monſter thee eſteeme.

And as for Churchyards cūming hom
    was not of his free wyll,
But for to pleaſe ſuch ſtats whos heſts
    may both commaund and wyll.

❡ Thus bid I thee farewell a whyle,
    as one that keepes his pen :
To aunſwer ſuch as ſhall preſume,
    to blea lyke Calues in den.

(☿) *Ra. Sm.*

❡ FINIS.

❡ Imprinted at London in little Britaine, by
Alexander Lacy, for Frauncis Coldocke, | dwellyng in Paules churchyarde, at |
the ſigne of the greene Dragon.

The Stationers' Registers for 1565–66 records that a licence was granted to Francis Coldock for this particular ballad (Arber's *Transcript*, i. 309). The full name of the author is revealed in an entry which occurs immediately afterwards, where it is mentioned that the usual sum of fourpence was 'Receuyd of Rychard Ionnes for the lycenſe for prynting of a ballet intituled *as many thankes good Maſter Smarte as late you yeelded to my ffrynde*'. Ralph Smart and his works are unknown to bibliographers. Apparently he is championing the cause of his friend Churchyard against the attack of one who, from the ballad, may have been Clement Robinſon. A ballad-writer of this name is mentioned in the 'Dictionary of National Biography', but there is nothing to lead one to suppose that he had at any time fallen foul of Churchyard.

The ballad is printed in two columns.

28

A greatter thanks, for Churchyardes
welcome home.

I Bad not Courte farewell
 for fuch hot welcome home,
But glad to leaue the coftly Courte
 and lyue lyke cuntrye mome.

¶From thence I wyllyng went:
 and thought in very deed,
To make (ere mifcheefs fel on heapes)
 a Vertue of a need.

¶But my cheeff freend came there,
 to whome for duties fake
I rode, and did (by deftinies lot)
 a further iourney make.

¶Which freend drew me by loue,
 to fee the Courte agayne:
But fens my fuddayn comming there
 doth breed in you difdayne:

I fynd more fumifh flames,
 by this fond frantike fmoke:
And fee (perhaps) a further fyer,
 then you with craft can cloke.

¶But tyll your fyngers burne,
 ye care not what ye doe:
Well, I wyll helpe to kyndle coales,
 and clap on faggots toe.

¶To bryng your handes in heat,
 becaufe the ayre is colde:
Ka. me: Knaue thee: I fay no more,
 the prouerbe is full olde.

¶Yf Crowes of Cheape cry Ka,
 the bawle doth backe rebound:
For fure I owe not all their towne,
 the halfe of twentie pound.

❡And thyrteene candels great,
   o euery pound allowe:
Then call an audite of my debt,
   and caſt my charges nowe.

❡Yet know I cut tayld Curres,
   can neuer byght in frame:
Tyll courage claps them on the backs
   and thruſts them on the game.

❡Come on you ſnarryng whelpes
   I feare your force no whit:
Though lowd ye bark ye dare not byte
   your teeth are tender yet.

❡Baight me lyke Bull at ſtake,
   I haue good fleſh and bone:
To trie it out (as hap ſhall ſerue)
   with any Dog a lone.

❡No other aunſwer ſure,
   I make: now ſkan this well:
But leaue the Lob that rayld on me,
   the bable and the bell.

*Write not to this agayne,
   in ſilence ſhall ye ſit:
As voyde of aunſwer euery way,
   as you are voyd of wyt.

(ꝙ) playne **Churchyarde.**

❡ FINIS.

❡ Imprinted at
Lonꝺon in little Britaine by Alex|ander Lacy: for Arthour Pepwel, dwel|lyng in Paules churchyard, at the | ſigne of the Kynges head.

In the Stationers' Registers for 1565–66 is an entry, 'Receuyd of Art[h]ure pepwell for his lycenſe for prynting of a ballet intituled *a greater thankes for Churchyardes Wellcome home*' (Arber's *Transcript*, i. 309).
The ballad is printed in two columns.

29

Churchyardes Lamentacion of Freyndſhyp.

IN Court ſome ſay doth freindſhyp flowe,
  And ſome to Court for freindſhyp goe:
But I that walke the worlde aboute,
  Could neuer yet fynde freyndſhyp out.
For fyneneſſe ſhewes ſo fayre a face,
  That freyndſhyp hath no dwellynge place
Yea, depe dyſſemblynge manners mylde,
  Hath fayth and freindſhyp both exylde:
The holowe harte is fowle and fell,
  Wheare freyndſhyp loketh now to dwell.
The humble ſpeche and *Syrenes* ſonge
  Hath ſhrouded freyndſhyp ouer longe,
The wylye wordes that waues wyth wynde
  Hath brought true frendſhyp out of mynde:
And to be ſhorte fayre wordes is all
  The fruite that from the tree dothe fall.
Wordes weldes the worlde, & beares the ſwaye,
  And freindſhyp daylye dothe decaye:
Yet durſte I make of it reporte,
  it is amonge the meaner ſorte,
If any faythe or freyndſhyp bee:
  But I ſo lytle freindſhyp ſee,
I feare the vertue of the ſame
  Conſyſtes but in the gentle name.
The worlde is waxen now ſo nyce
  That we haue learnd the frenche **deuyce,**
At your cōmaundement for a ſhowe,
  and meane no farther for to goe:
We are as free of promyſe ſtyll
  as though we mente a great good **wyll,**
And braue it out for gloryes ſake,
  and much adoe therof we make,
To blaſe abrode our bountye great:
  Tuſh man the fyre hath loſt his heate,
The flame yeldes furthe but ſparkles ſmal,
  theare is no fryndſhyp now at all.
Geue eare and here a pretye Ieſt:
  Theare was a man (at my requeſt)
That ſeemd an earneſt freinde in dede,
  and ſwore he wolde ſupplye my nede
Wyth all hys helpe he could deuyſe,
  and ofte to blere hys Ladyes eyes,

And make her know hys lyberall mynde :
   (for women Larges loue of kynde.)
He promyſt many a goodlye gyfte,
   but when I put hym to hys ſhyfte,
For quycke performaunce of thys geare,
   then backwarde gan he for to ſwarue
Eche worde had paſt hys mouth before.
   I pray you now if we had ſtore
Of ſuch good freinds, when nede ſhuld cum
   myght not a pore man ſtryke hys Drum
Before theyr dores wyth chereful ſprete,
   and ſounde a marche in open ſtrete
A thouſand tymes amidſte hys greefe,
   or he ſhould fynde thearby releefe?
Fyue hundred of ſuch mates as theaſe
   (whoſe freyndſhyp is not worthe a peaſe,
Whoſe brauery ſhynes beyonde the Sune,
   yet ſlypper laddes when all is done.)
My hap hath bene to mete or thys :
   beware I ſay the Iudas kyſſe,
The flyrynge face the Parate gaye,
   the bablynge tongue that hath no ſtaye,
The fawner fyne that croutcheth lowe,
   the plyant head that bendes lyke bowe,
Whoſe nature lykes not freindſhyps lawe :
   the gloryous man, the pratynge dawe.
Tut, tut, I warne thee ouerſoone,
   ful longe had nede to be the ſpoone
A man ſhould haue for euery feate
   that wyth the dyuell thynkes to eate :
For dyuels in theſe dayes are to ryfe,
   and thou muſt nedes leade out thy lyfe
Wyth depe dyſſemblers euery wayes :
   the dyuels are much more to prayſe
Then muffled men that myſcheife breedes :
   who are not knowen but by theyr deedes.
Oh frendſhyp thou art much myſuſed
   to be wyth freindes thus abuſed,
For freyndſhyp ſhould wyth open face
   be ſeene and felt in euery place.
Of playneneſſe firſt was freyndſhyp wrought,
   Iuſt as the Gods, and pure of thought :
Full free and franke as Lordes hath byn,
   full bent the peoples hartes to wynne :
Full glad to fyll the nedye hande,
   full fyrme of worde, and ſure to ſtande
As Oke that euery ſtorme wyl byde :
   not loſt with want, nor wonne wyth pryde
And welthy pompe, the pumpe of ſynne,
   that bryngeth euery myſcheife in :
But alwayes cleare from falſeheddes trayne
   Than tell me now and do not fayne :

Where do that freindſhyp buylde his bowre?
   where is ſuch freindſhyp had thys howre?
Where maketh he now hys manſyon place?
   or where (good Lord) hath men ſuch grace
To lyght vpon ſo great a blyſſe?
   mans mynde and nature altered is:
The worlde in wyckedneſſe is drounde,
   and trulye freindſhyp is vnſounde
And rotten lyke corrupted fruite,
   though gloryous men wyll beare a brute
Of freindes, theyr freyndſhyp is ſo colde
   that we therof haue lytle holde:
When it ſhould ſerue our turne (god knowes)
   we reape the weede, and plant the Roſe.
We gape for golde, and grype but glaſſe:
   now dothe ſuch wordes of offyce paſſe
Tweene all eſtates bothe farre and nere,
   that talke is nought but fayned chere
To make fayre weather for a whyle
   tyl one the other do beguyle.
I tell the man who playes the parte
   of wylye Fox, muſt lerne thys arte:
They are no ſmall byrdes (as I geſſe)
   if I in authors maye expreſſe
The ſynnes that now be kept in ſtore,
   that puts in practyſe this and more
To compaſſe cloked freindſhyp fyne
   The Fowler neuer drawes hys lyne
So ſtrayghte vpon the ſelye fowle:
   nor ſure the byas of the bowle
Goeth not ſo ſtrayghte on mayſter blocke,
   as dayly dothe thys dallyenge flocke
Vpon the polycye of the brayne
   to brynge the ſelye foole to trayne.
Men are ſo vſed theſe dayes wyth wordes,
   they take them but for ieſtes and boordes
That Chriſtmas Lordes were wonte to ſpeke.
   well, well, I ſay the worlde is weke,
And weker it is lyke to be,
   when credyte out of the worlde ſhall flye,
When truſt is gone, and trothe is dead,
   and faythfull freyndſhyp hydes hys head,
And wordes are help of none effecte,
   and promyſe faythfull is ſuſpecte.
Farewell, al earthly hope is paſt,
   I ſee our maners change ſo faſt,
And ſuche affection leades our wyll
   awrye, to fyckle freindſhyp ſtyll:
That ſure true freindſhyp ſylent ſyttes,
   and nought beares rule but wylye wyttes:
Vnſhamefaſte wayes, and meare deceyte,
   for playneneſſe ſuch a pleaſante bayte,

As choketh vp bothe hye and lowe,
  and poyſoneth all the worlde I trowe:
Wherfore ſynce freyndſhyp takes hys leaue,
  and fyneneſſe dothe vs all deceyue,
Let freyndſhyppes name be banyſhed quyte,
  for ſure it is a great dyſpyte
To ſpeke of freindſhyp any tyme,
  to make of freyndſhyp profe or ryme,
Or gyue to freyndſhyp anye prayſe,
  that is ſo fruteleſſe in our dayes.

Finis.   *qd. Churchyarde.*

¶ Imprinted at london by Thomas Col‖well for Nicolas Wyer dwelling in S. | Martyns paryſſhe nere to Charynge | Croſſe, at the ſygne of Saint | Iohn Euangeliſt.

There is an entry in the Stationers' Registers for 1565–66 'Receuyd of Nycholas Wyer for his lycenſe for prynting of a ballett intituled *the lamentation of Churchyardes fryndſhippe*' (Arber's *Transcript*, i. 310). J. P. Collier reprinted a version of this ballad, in six-line stanzas, without imprint, in his 'Roxburghe Ballads', 1847.

The ballad is printed in two columns, without border or ornament.

30

Churchyardes farewell.

AS witte is neuer good
till it bee deerely bought:
So freends vntill their truth be tride,
  may paſſe for thinges of nought.
For freendſhip all in woordes,
  a kinde of flattringe is.
And if I thinke my worthieſt freende
  may be abuſde by this,
I ought in plaine flat termes
  to ſhewe him what I thinke,
And blaze the meaninge of my minde
  by paper, pen, & Inke.
Becauſe the doores be barde,
  where my good will ſhould pas:
And buzzinge Bees do creepe in place,
  where Churcheyards credite was.
The fowlers mery pype
  betraies the careles byrde:
And fleeringe fawners lye in waite,
  to geeue their freends a gyrde.
When fortune turnes hir face,
  beware the Syrenes ſonge:
Beware the buſie Clawbackes fine
  whoſe freendſhip laſtes not longe.
Thinke you the flyes doo flocke
  aboute the fleaſhe in vaine?
Dooth not the Bee ſeeke out the flower
  ſome hony there to gayne?
Doo courtiers all for loue,
  approche the princes gates?
Dooth plainneſſe in theſe double daies,
  repaire to great eſtates?
No ſure in maſkinge robes
  goeth miſchiefe muffled nowe:
And ſubtile ſleightes with ſnakiſh ſtings,
  doo lodge in ſmilinge browe.
And your affections blinde,
  hath you bewitched ſo,
Ye haue no power to finde your freendes,
  nor to deſcerne your fo.
Ye fill the fleeſinge fiſtes,
  and let the needie lacke:
And ſharpe their teeth whoſe crafty tungs
  can byte behinde your backe.

I pray you tell me now,
  if hap woulde let you flyde,
How many would through thick & thinne
  for loue with you abide?
Perhaps a heape of fuche
  could hungry hangers on,
Whofe nature geues the courte a fygge
  when worldly hap is gon.
Can you not fee the caufe,
  that bringes them fwarminge in?
And where the wheele of Fortune fwayes
  the worlde fauour winne?
Had not your elders wife,
  good triall of fuche trafhe?
Did you not fee what woorthy wittes
  at length were lefte in lafhe:
By truftinge fome to farre,
  and heapinge hope in thofe
That feemed freends to outwarde fight,
  and yet were fecrete foes?
O let me licence haue
  to painte thefe pecocks out,
Whofe fethers wauereth with the winde
  and fo turnes taile aboute:
Yet flicker with their winges,
  to faune the face awhile,
Vntill their fodaine flight they take,
  and fo their freends beguile.
What fhould we iudge of them,
  that ftare in faces ftill:
Where lo, for all their curtfie great,
  they beare but fmall good will.
And where they feldome come,
  but when fome fute they haue:
They make a figne to fee my Lorde,
  yet feeke by fleight to craue.
What makes them watch their howres,
  and thruft in thickeft preeft.
It is for freendfhip that they beare
  vnto a certaine leafe.
My Lorde muft helpe to get,
  now crowche and kneele they all:
Now ftand they vp like fainctes in fhrine,
  or nayld againft a wall?
Now figge they here & there,
  as thornes were in their heeles
Now trudge aboute thefe whirlegigges,
  as worlde did runne on wheeles.
Now caft they freendly lookes,
  all ouer the chambers gaye.
Now geue they place as God were there,
  now turne they euery waye.

Now talke they trimme in printe,
  and prate of Robin hood :
Much like the knightes of Arthers courte,
  that knew full well their good.
Some through a finer meane,
  doo creepe in credites lappe :
And vale their bonettes by deuife,
  as fauour folowed cappe.
Suche Iuglers bleare your eies,
  and fmile within their fleeue :
When honour in his harmles moode
  Dooth beft of them beleeue.
Were you but once a daye,
  in fimple feruauntes place,
And like a looker on ye ftoode,
  to prie vpon this cafe :
Then fhould ye throughly fee,
  who plaies the wily foxe :
And how the Wolfe can frame himfelfe,
  to draw in yoke like oxe.
Then fhoulde the mufled men,
  fhew foorth their faces bare
And therby noble hartes fhoulde learne
  to knowe what flatterers are.
The glory of your ftate,
  heaues vp your hed fo hie :
That many thinges doo fcape your vewe,
  whiche we fee full with eye.
And who is now fo bolde,
  that dare flat warninge geue,
To fuche as in toppe of pompe,
  or princely plafures lyue.
I mufe what new founde chaunce,
  hath fo difguifde the ftate
That men oft times for fpeakyng plaine,
  doo purchace endleffe hate.
Whileft fraude and fained cheere
  dooth euell honour feede :
And noman dare a plaifter geue,
  to heale the wounde in deede :
Full fickle fhall you walke,
  and neuer wante difeafe.
They fhould be banifht from your courte
  that are fo glad to pleafe
With twittell twatlyng tales.
  The truth like larm bell
Should fhortly founde in tender eares
  and learne you to doo well.
But fure the fweeteft nuttes
  doo noorifhe woormes apace,
And flatterers of the fineft ftampe,
  in courte haue fineft place.

I am to plaine therefore,
  my penne hath drunke to muche?
An alie hed makes idle hande,
  the quicke to neere to touche.
Nay, nay, some one must speake,
  although the vice it bee:
Or els the play were done ye wot,
  then Lordinges pardon mee.
For free of euery Hance
  I thanke the gods I am,
And serues no turne but for a vice,
  since first to courte I came.
To make the Ladies laugh,
  that leades the retchles liues
Who late, or neuer woodcocke like
  at later Lammas thriues.
Yet if the foole had gotte,
  at his departinge thence
A night cap, or a motley coate,
  or els some spendinge pence.
It had bene well enough:
  but nothinge there I founde
For nothinge from their budgets fell
  they were so straitly bounde.
Ye lie sir Daw in deede,
  canst thou so longe be there
But needes must fall into thy handes,
  some paringe of the peare?
A hungry paringe Lorde
  he hath that there doth weight:
He watcheth like a greedy hounde
  that standeth at receight:
That oft for lacke of game,
  runnes home his panche to fill
Or sterues in forest or in parke,
  at least at kepers will.
Looke what to courte he brought
  it is consumed and gone
And there the fleash of euery iointe,
  is worne vnto the bone.
The carraine crowes of Cheape
  in fleyng bones so bare
Would clap the fell in counter too,
  to breede him further care.
Nay fie on such good hap,
  on Souldiers faith I sweare:
To sell the Courts & Cittie bothe,
  and he that takes me there.
Let him cut of mine eares,
  and slitte my nose aright
And make a curtoll of the beast,
  that hath a hed so light.

To linger out my yeeres
    for moone fhine in the well
A hood, a hood, for fuch a foole,
    a bable and a bell.
A coxcombe is to good
    for fuch a calfe I trow.
As of my Lorde my leaue I take,
    fo now againe I go.
Where fortune fhall affigne,
    my ftaffe to light or fall.
And thus I know a truer freende,
    was not amonge them all.
Then to my power I was,
    to you and all your race
Nor vnto whome I dayly wifhe,
    more bleffe happe and grace.

FINIS.   *ꝓ. Churchyarde.*

¶Printed in Fleeteftreete, for Edwarde Ruffell.

In the Registers of the Stationers' Company, 1565–66, occurs 'Receuyd of Edwarde Ruffell for his lycenfe for pryntinge of a ballett intituled Churcheyardes *ffaryre Well*' (Arber's *Transcript*, i. 308). The entry undoubtedly points to this ballad although J. P. Collier (*Extracts from the Registers of the Stationers' Company*, vol. i, p. 136) states that the original is unknown and suggests that it may refer to 'A Farewell, cauld Churchyards Rounde' printed by William Gryffyth, for which a licence was granted. The latter is one of Churchyard's ballads which are reprinted in this volume.

Edward Russell is known only by two ballads entered July 1565–July 1566: the one reprinted and another 'fhewyng how a man fhall knowe his frynde and what fryndfhippe ys &c.' (Arber, i. 305).

The ballad is printed in three columns, without border.

31

The Epitaphe of the honorable Earle

of Penbroke, Baron of Cardiffe, and Knight of the moſt Noble order of the garter.
Who dyed Lord ſtueward of the Queenes maieſties houſhold, and of her priuie counſell.

SInce playnts want power to perce the ſkyes, or rayes the dead from graue,
No teares nor ſighes may well ſuffies, to wayle the loſſe we haue.
Then lordings wype your blobbred eyen, and ſobb no more alas:
For death and deaſtnye doth aſſigne, all lyfe lyke ſhade ſhall paſſe.
No ſeat nor Scepture certayne is, the hye and lowe a lyke:
In ſpight of pompe and worldly blis, fall both amid the dyke.
But when a propp that ſtayde the ſtate, dropps downe as you do ſee:
The lokers on in muſe do ſtand, at crack of ſuch a tree.
Which leaues the world in moorning weeds, behynd to weepe the loſſe,
(Whyles frute is fled from brantch and bowe, as gold forſakes the droſſe)
O Penbroke wilt thou part ſo ſone, what haſt hath hyed thee hence:
Had I byn warnd I had perfuemd, thy Tombe with frankinſence.
But cald ſo ſwiftly to my pen, the ſweete inſence I want:
yet ſweare I by the ſacred Gods, though ſkill and ſence be ſkant.
Thou ſhalt not hyde in clotts of ciaye, thy ritch rare gyftes of kynd,
Nor ſkrawlling wormes ſhall make no praye, apon thy noble mind.
The Court that knew thy conſtant hart, bydds thee returne againe,
That art for troth and freendſhipp faſt, a parfect pattern plaine.
A father where the counſell ſate of tongue and talke deuine,
As he at byrth had ſtolne the grace, of all the Muſis nine.
His lookes dyd ſpeake when ſilent lipps, lockt vp great thinges in head,
yea eu'ry word paſt Penbrokes mouth, peyſd well a pound of lead.
No lightnes lodged in his browes, and ſure a man in deede,
That well might ryes from Troyians race, and honour Hectors ſeede.
Of nature noble voyd of blott, in Court and countrey throwe:
As curteys as the lyttell Lambe, or Faucon gentyll nowe.
In bountie dyd his harte abound, where cauſe made place before:
Not wonne by feare, but held by loue, what might be wiſhed more.
To ſuch as fau'red learnings lore, (though he no ſchole poynt knew)
His purſſe and hand as cloſly crept, as hauke weare clapt in mew.
To thoſe that ſeemd ſomwhat to be, whoſe harts he ſawe aſpier:
He gaue good hope in ſigne of happ, to further there deſier.
To Prince and countrey true as ſteell, no blaſt could beare him downe,
He kept his promiſe fayth and oth, in Court, in feeld and towne.
Deuout to God his lyfe well ſhowes, his death doth that declare,
On Chriſt alone, the corner ſtone, he onely layd his care.
O manly Penbroke yet me thinks, I ſee thee martch vpright,
Thy ieſture and thy iolly port, ſtands ſtill before my ſight.
Thy cleanly finenes trimly framd, ſprang out of noble breſt:
And all thou didſt within thy dayes, a noble mind expreſt.

But nothing here ſo cleane or gay, can kepe the lyfe alyue,
Both wealth and Lordſhipp leapes away, when death our date doth dryue.
yet death when he hath done his worſt, dare not moleſt the ſpreete:
That God doth clayme and angels thinke, for Abrams boſome meete.

FINIS.

A verſe of farwell.

I loſt a friend, you loſt no leſſe, who leaſt loſt, loſt to much,
Who lookes to light vpon the lyke, in Court ſhall find fewe ſuch.

Quoth Churchyard.

¶ Imprinted at London, in Fleteſtreat at the ſigne of the Faucon | by Wylliam Gryffith:
and are to be ſold at his ſhoppe | in S. Dunſtones Churchyard. 1570. March. 27.

The chief events in the life of William Herbert, Earl of Pembroke, are strangely similar to those which mark the careers of the Earls of Arundel and Derby, whose epitaphs also appear in this collection. Closely associated with the sovereign from their youth, all three obtained place, power, and great possessions, the latter derived principally from the suppressed monasteries. The quick changes demanded of courtiers at the succession of the children of Henry VIII found the trio equally well prepared. They openly supported Northumberland, and then at the right moment declared for Mary. By the time Elizabeth succeeded they had made their positions so strong that it was impossible for the queen to dismiss them, although, later in her reign, they fell into disgrace by reason that they had lent their support to Norfolk's proposal for marrying Mary Queen of Scots. Pembroke was a skilful military commander, and furthered his fortunes at the outset by his marriage with Anne, sister of Queen Catharine Parr. He died at Hampton Court on March 17, 1570, in his sixty-third year, and was buried in St. Paul's. His seat at Wilton, in part preserved, was erected on the site of a monastery. A licence for this ballad appears in the Registers of the Stationers' Company, 1569–70 (Arber's *Transcript*, i. 411). It is mentioned in Churchyard's 'Chance', 1580, in a list of 'Epitaphes alreadie printed, or out of my handes'.

The epitaph is printed in one column within an ornamental border.

32

Sorrowfull Verſes made on [the] death of our moſt Soueraigne Lady Queene ELIZABETH, my Gracious Miſtreſſe.

ENGLAND may mourne, as many Kingdomes may,
A loſſe of late, that Gold nor Pearle redeemes,
A gale of winde, that made Kings hoyſe vp Sayles,
When bluſtring blaſts, brought Barkes in great extreme[s,]
Her Realme ſhee rul'de, and bridled as GOD would,
With Reaſons raine, that holds backe Bayards bit,
To purchaſe peace, payd maſsie ſummes of Gold,
Did what ſhe might, to win a world with wit,
Wiſedom rules Starres, clymes vp to Heauens gate,
Makes Peace and Warres, and ſtayes a tottering State,
Her inſight ſaw, all outward flawes of winde,
Her iudgement crept, into our cunning Age,
No practize could, ſurpaſſe her Princely minde,
Her calmie wordes, could ſwelling Sea aſſwage,
Religion burnd, like Lampe in her bare breſt,
And for her faith, ſhee ſtill ſet vp her reſt,
Shee gaue great things to thouſands, world well knowes,
As at well head, and Fountaine Water flowes.
Cæſars, ſharpe Spirit, her ſpeeches vttr'ed oft,
Cyrus great power, and wealth ſhe wanted not,
Shee pluc't downe Pride, to ſet meeke hearts aloft,
Her matchles deedes, great Fame and Glorie got,
Opened her bagges, to ſuch as ſuffered wrong,
Much money lent, but felt the loſſe to long,
Eſcap't bad men, that ſought to ſhed her blood,
Forgaue great faultes, to winne worldes loue and zeale :
But when moſt ſafe, in health we thought ſhee ſtood,
Her Ghoſt paſt hence, (from Crowne and Common-weale)
To GODS high Throne, like Torch and Candle blaze,
(Loſt earthly light) and left vs in a maze.

FINIS.

T. Church-yard Eſqu[ier.]

This Phœnix *dead, from her warme Cynders ſtreight,*
In forme of Man, another Phœnix *roſe,*
Who clapt his wings, And flew vp ſuch a height,
(So neere the Sunne) that he GODS *glorie ſhowes.*

33

An admonition to Doctor Story beeing con|demned of high
Treafon, fent to him before his death, but becaufe it came to late
to his | hands: it is now put in print t[hat it may] be a warning
to all other papifts where|by they may repent and [call to God
for] mercy, cleue to his holy woord and liue ac[cording to the]
Doctrine of the fame.

BEftur your ftomp3 good Story now, ye gallous fore [by groan:]
I am fory you came fo late, that you muft hang alone.
If you had come but one yeer paft, cōpany you might [haue had]
Iohn Felton [1] & ye Nortons bothe [2], of you would haue been glad.
Alas what luck had you good man, to bide from hence fo long
And hang behinde your company, no dout you had [great   ]
But fith Dame Fortune fo dooth frown, and your [   ]
I fee that weeping wil not help, it boots not to be [   ]
Therfore I wifh you to repent, while you haue time [   ]
Lay holde on Faith in Chriftes blood, and call to God [   ]
And now prepare your felf with fpeed, to fail by Holbourn[es rill,]
And drinck you of that deadly cup, that you to vs did fil[l.]
Gods woord muft needs be prooued true, which you doo [ftoutly craue]
Such meafure as your felf did giue, fuch meafure fhall you haue.
Remember wel your crueltye, in killing of Gods Saints :
whofe blood for vēgeāuce ftil dooth cry, & god hearth their cōplaīt.
& you haue now your iuft reward, which you haue wel deferued :
Becaufe from God & princes lawes, fo tratoroufly you fwarued.
As I hear fay you doo appele, vnto your God the Pope :
But his Pardons cannot preuaile, to faue you from the rope.
Nor yet his Maffes many folde, they cannot you defend :
From Tiburn neither yet from hel, except you doo amend.
but whē thefe newes are brought to Rome, how yt you are attaīted
Of high treafon and hangd therfore, no dout you fhalbe Sainted.
Thefe names & titles fhall you haue, in Rome when you be dead :
The Pope no dout wil you inrole, vnder his bulles of lead.
A Doctor and a Confeffor, that fhall you be extolde :
A Martyr and a Saint alfo, but yet a traitor bolde.
That day that you hanged fhalbe, it fhall be holy day :
And fo ordained by the Pope, that men to you may pray.
Thus fhall you be canonized, as Saint as I haue faid :
Then to be hangd for high treafon, what need you be afraid?
For you fhall haue Trentalls great ftore, of Maffes faid & fung :
And all the belles that be in Rome, for your foule fhalbe rung.

[1] See ' The end and Confeffion of Iohn Felton'
(p. 144) and Stephen Peele's ' A letter to Rome, to
declare to ye Pope, Iohn Felton his freend is hangd in
a rope' (p. 203).

[2] See William Gibson's ' A difcription of Nortons
falcehod of Yorke fhyre, and of his fatall farewel'
(p. 149).

If some good popish catholike, of your hart could take holde:
And bring it to the Pope in Rome, it should be shrinde in golde.
Because that in the Popes defence, you dyed so bolde and stout:

The popes Heaue next house to hel.

If that your soule doo go to hel, the Pope wil Masse it out.
And place you by his owne white side, where all ye saints doo dwel
In that heauen which him self hath made, not very far from hel.

These are the Popes Saints.

Where you shall haue such plesat ioyes, Masse & mattens by note
Saint Pluto, there sings Masse him self, in a red firye cote.
Saint Dunstone is one of his clarkes, Saint Hildebrand another
There shall you see Saint Dominick, and S. Francis his brother.

Loke in Legend aurea and there shall you finde what S. Remege was.

Saint Fryer Forest is the Preest, to hear the Saints confession:
Saint Fryer Bacon beres the Crosse, before them in procession.
There shall you meete S. Thomas Becket, yt had the g[   ]eine
And S. Thomas of Harefordshere, bothe costly braue [   ]
There shall you meete S. Boniface, S. Remige and S. [   ]
Saint Brigid and S. Clare the Nun, with the holy ma[   ]

Sir Thomas More once Lord chaunceler of Englad.

There shall you meete S. Cardinall Poole, & [   ]
S. Thomas More a traitor stout, with the ho[   ]
There shall you see that blessed Saint, Pope Vr[ban   ]
Who was the first that did inuent, and make Corps Ciuile.

Loke in the Festiual for the seuen Sleepers. Boner and Gardener.

These Saints and ye[   ], with all the Sleepers seuen
Shall meete you with [   ] and welcome you to He[auen]
And there you shall [   ]ing stil, from morning v[nto euen]
And meete wt your familier freends, S. Edmond and S. [Steuen]
Saint Christopher ¹ that late was hangd, at Tiburn you [   ]
There shall you meete S. Felton to, with many [   ]

Norton.

All these Good Saints as I haue said, wil meete [   ]
And bid you welcome into Heauen, wt ioy whe you [   ]
The al these Angels & these Saints, wt great mirth [   ]
Vnto the high infernall seat, and set you next the kin [   ]
You shall be made the cheefest Saint, and sit abooue [them all]
Higher than euer Dunstone was, or any Preest of Ba[al]
You shalbe iudge of all the Saints, and highest in Commission:
Euen as you heer vpon Earth were, to maintain superstion. [sic]
But yet I dout you shall not skape, the Purgatory flame:
If Masses and Diriges doo not help, to saue you from the same.
Of whiche I knowe you shall lack none, for many wilbe fain:
To haue a thousand for your sake, to fetch you out again.
But you shall Masses great store haue, in yt heauen where you go:
That wil keep you from Purgatory, if that the Pope say no.
Thus maister Doctor haue I tolde, your ioyes after this life:
Because with Gods woord & your Prince, you dye so far at strife.
These be the ioyes yt you shall haue, in yt Popes heauen to reign:
But in Gods heauen where true ioyes be, no traitor shall remain.
No Papist nor Idolater, that doo refuse gods woord:
No worshipper of Images, shall stand before the Lord,
Nor yet Rebellious Massemonger, that dooth his Prince despise:
Against all Popish blood suckers, the Lord wil turn his eyes.
No witch nor wicked whoremoger, which your pope dooth defend
No Coniurer nor yet such like, to Gods heauen shall ascend.
No Buggerers orels yet baudes, in Gods heaue shal haue place:

¹ Christopher Norton.

No Briber nor Simoniack, nor Periurer paſt grace.
No ſuperſticious Hereticks, nor mainteners of whores :
No Sectaries nor Sodomits, ſhall come within heauen doores.
All wilful virgins with their vowes, profeſſing to liue chaſte :
That godly mariage doo contemn, from Gods heauē ſhall be caſt.
And ſuch were all your popiſh Saints, that I before haue named :
with all theſe ſinnes moſt horible, the moſte of thē were blamed
But in ſuch filthy ſtincking Saints, the Lord hath no delight :
And from the ioyes celeſtiall, he wil exclude them quite.
But theſe Saints that in Gods heauen, ſhall haue their habitatiō :
Who by true faith in Chriſtes blood, do ſeek their whole ſaluation
And ſuch as doo vnfainedly, beleeue Gods holy woord :
Whoſe life and good profeſſion, together doo accord.
And liue like ſubiects to their prince, obeying godly lawes :
Not thus to hang like traitors ſtout, as doo you popiſh dawes.
Lo maiſter Doctor theſe be they, whom we good Saints doo call :
One of theſe Saints doo pleſe God more, thē doo yᵉ popes ſaints all
And if you be vnhangd as yet, God graunt you may repent :
That you may be one of theſe Saints, of Chriſte omnipotent.
But if you be all redy hangd, I leaue you to your iudge :
And let the Papiſts by you take heed, how they doo ſpurn & grudge
Againſt God and their lawful Queene, I would not wiſh thē run
Leſt that they drink of that ſame cup, as you before haue doon.   **It is time.**
God be thanked that our Queene, begins to look about :
To draw the ſwoord out of the ſhethe, to weed ſuch trators out.
Therfore you popiſh traitors all, forſake your Romiſh ſects :
Obey your Queene like ſubiects true, or els beware your necks.
Take heed how you prouoke your Prince, at any time to wrath :   **Pro 20.**
Whoſe angre is ſaith Salomon, the meſſanger of death.
The Kings diſpleaſure is euen as, the roaring Lions voice :
Then to prouoke the Queene to wrath, papiſts doo not reioice :
Abuſe not the Queenes lenity, that ſhee to you dooth ſhowe :
What ſmall vantage is got therby, ſome papiſts late doo knowe.
Conſider what great benefits, we haue of her good grace,   **A tiborne**
Shee dooth maintain Gods holy woord, to ſhine in euery place.   **tippete.**
How godly hath ſhe ruled vs, by wiſe councels aduice :
Of ſuch a precious iewel you, papiſts knowe not the price.
Shee ſeeketh to doo harme to none, but to doo all men good :
Yea, to her foes yᵗ ſought her death, ſhe hath not ſought their **blood**
Til now of late they did rebel, high treaſon to conſpire :
Then was it time to cut them of, and hang them ſomewhat hier.
To end, God ſaue her maieſtye, from bloody papiſts vain :
And Lord ſend her olde Neſtors yeeres, wᵗ vs to liue and reigne.

FINIS.   ℈.   IOHN. CORNET. MINISTER.

❡ Imprinted at London at the long Shop adioy|ning vnto Saint Mildreds Churche in| the Pultrie, by Iohn Allde.

John Story was one of the many Roman Catholic clergy who, through unwillingness to conform, were compelled to remain abroad during the latter part of the reign of Henry VIII and throughout that of his successor. Story was appointed chancellor to Bonner, and zealously aided the bishop in the work of persecution. Toleration was shown him by Elizabeth, yet he managed to get into trouble with the authorities, and in 1563 was compelled to escape to Flanders, where he found congenial occupation. Story was appointed inquisitor by Alva, and, with other duties, undertook to search all incoming vessels for heretical books which it was known were being imported from England.

During the summer of 1570 a ship arrived at Bergen op Zoom, and while Story was making his investigations below, the hatches were suddenly clapped down, and a few days later the captive was landed at Yarmouth. The following year Story was brought to London, tried for treason, of which he was found guilty, and on June 1, 1571, was executed with the utmost barbarity.

In the Stationers' Registers, 1570–71, with other entries respecting Story, is this: 'Receuyd of Iohn alde for his lycenfe for pryntinge *an admonyffion of Doctour Storye*' (Arber's *Transcript*, i. 443). The individual referred to in ' The Troubles of Iohn Cornet ' (Foxe, *Actes and Monuments*, Book xii, A.D. 1558) may be identified with the author of this ballad. No other ballads by him are known.

It is unfortunate that the text of this ballad, which is printed in two columns, has been severely injured.

34

ஃ An Epitaph vpon the death of Richard Price.

[See facsimile.]

Sir John Price, lawyer, was a native of Brecknock-shire, and lent valuable assistance to the crown at the suppression of the monasteries and at the union of England and Wales. In addition to other grants he received the priory of Brecon, which eventually passed into the possession of the first Earl Camden through the chancellor's marriage with an heiress, Elizabeth Jeffreys, granddaughter of Sir Geoffrey Jeffreys, who had acquired it by purchase. Sir John Price published several works the most important of which are ' Hiftoriae Brytannicae defenfio' (against Polydore Vergil), 1573, and a 'Defcription of Cambria' printed with Caradoc of Llancarfan's 'Hiftorie of Cambria', 1584.

Sir John Price had several sons. Gregory, the eldest, on his marriage with a daughter of Sir Humphrey Coningsby, settled in Herefordshire; Richard, the second son, is described as a man of learning, and a frequent visitor at court in the reigns of Edward VI, Mary, and Elizabeth. He edited the 'Defensio',

and it has been suggested that he introduced Hugh Evans, a compatriot and protégé of the Prices, to Shakespeare, and furnished the poet with one of the leading characters in 'The Merry Wives of Windsor'. Richard Price lived at the priory until his death, when the property passed to John Price, a younger brother.

There are two little volumes of verse in the Britwell Library—' An Exhortation to England, to ioine for defenfe of true Religion and their natiue Countrie,' 1568, and ' A true Report of the generall Imbarre-ment of all the Englifh Shippes, vnder the dominion of the kinge of Spaine', 1585. Poth are signed R. D., and it is possible that they may have been written by the author of this epitaph. The initials also belong to Richard Davies, who wrote 'Chefters Triumph', 1610. The Britwell broadside was not in Heber's collection. It measures twelve and a half inches by eight and a half.

An Epitaph vpon the death of Richard Price Esquier (the second sonne of Sir Iohn Price Knight, deceased) which Richard left this life the fifth day of Ianuarie, 1586.

My sorrow doth suppresse my memorie,
My griefe eke grieues my hart, and all my powres,
My teares do pierce my paper thorowlie,
My Muse me failes, my woo my wit deuoures,
So as amasd I sit deuoid of might,
In verse, or prose, my meaning to indight.

Of princely iewels, precious are the price,
Of gold the gaine who wisheth not to haue,
Of house and land, and all by land that rise,
Of all for life, who seeketh not to saue:
But when I weigh the depth of mine intent,
A *Price* to prayse, I cannot but lament.

A *Price* for gentle bloud, of price he was,
A *Price* well taught in youth to liue in age,
A *Price* so fraught with vertues that surpasse,
A *Price* though yong in yeeres, in wisedom sage:
A precious *Price*, as Wales did euer yeeld,
A *Price* of peace in towne, yet fierce in field.

His vertues rare, his wisedom so profound.
His learned skill, his curtesie so seene,

His bountie great in house did so abound,
His trauell such for Countrey, and for Queene,
Made him beloued, and for his friendship fast,
So famously, as euermore shall last.

He liued no doubt with well contented mind,
He liued vpright, iust both in word and deed,
He liued a subiect true, as man may find,
He liued to God a child of *Abrahams* seed:
He liued to die, content to leaue each frend,
He died to liue in ioy, that shall not end.

His wofull wife may chiefly waile his want,
His seruants next haue greatest cause to grieue,
His country then (sith such as he be scant)
His friends each one may sorow whilest they liue:
Among the which a greater losse had none,
Then I my selfe, that causlesse do not mone.

Oh God graunt vs thy grace, and daily aide,
Oh God put feare and loue into our hart,
Oh God to sinne make vs full sore afraid,
Oh God thy loue from vs do not diuart:
Thou that from vs our peerelesse *Price* hast reft,
Be our defence, that heere behind are left.

R. D.

Imprinted at London by Iohn Charlewood.

35

¶ A new ballad Intituled, Daniels fiftyng in
thefe our dayes : aptly applyed to the true Preachers of the Gofpell.

¶ What God hath wylled vs, to that good eare geue :
For Daniels are abroad : fiftyng with their Seeue.

GOod Daniels fifting, in Gods church aboute,
The footfteps out findyng : of thofe as be ftoute.
Againft Gods word deuine, which all ought to knowe
In their owne mother toung : what duty they owe.

To God alone iuftly, to ferue hym with loue,
For all are not trufty : as his worde doth prooue.
Now yf God we obeyd, as he hath vs taught,
Then were our fayth ftayed : in him that vs bought.

¶ By Daniels, the Preachers : fo this vnderftand,
Which doo preach Chrift truly : in euery land.
Without Pope or popery, our foules for to faue,
By faith in Chrift onely, of whom we it craue.

¶ And Gods booke this Seeue is, that they in hand take,
And his word the Afhes, thereout for to fhake.
In Temples and Churches, where people refort,
To haue for their foules health : the food of comfort.

¶ The people is the ground, on whom now doth fall,
Thofe high deuine Afhes : that makes the true tryall.
Whofe footefteppes fhal apeere without frawde or guile,
Of young and olde people : now marke well this ftile.

¶ By thefe footefteppes I meane, the whole lyfe of man,
And of all women kynde : thefe things now well fcan.
Who fo in thefe Afhes, now treadeth awaye,
Their fteps fhalbe well knowne : to God & mans eye.

¶ As was in Bels Temple, a God without lyfe,
Whereas footyng was found : of Man, Chyld, & Wyfe.
Who eate vp the vittells, from that falfe God Bell,
And deceyued the Kyng : as the text doth tell.

¶ But Daniell by fiftyng, all them to lyght brought,
And alfo Bels Priftes : that wickedly wrought.
Euen fo now our Sifters, that fiftes at this day,
With Gods word fhall finde out : thofe in the brode way.

¶ When they heare the law red, vnto them full playne,
As God hath commanded : fo to be certayne.
The which law and Gofpell, receiue in good parte,
And out of the broad way : betimes looke ye ftarte.

¶ The footfteps that Adam, and Eue firft dyd trace,
To the forboden tree : brought them in woe cafe.
And all we by their fall in bondage be fet,
Day by day mafked ftyl in Sathans great net.

¶ The firfte blody footefteps, that Cayne dyd commit,
To his brother Abell : remaynes in fome yet.
As in Ruffians and Rogges, that defperate be,
Whofe footefteps from much finne cannot fcape free.

¶ The pryde of great Nemrode, that in hym dyd rayne,
Was knowne by his footefteps, and all his whole trayne,
So lykewyfe fhall theirs doe, that buyldeth exceffe,
In any kynd of trade : abufing Richeffe.

¶ Queene Iezabell that dyd, Gods true Prophets kyll,
Her footeyng was found out : agaynft her owne wyll.
The Dogs her bloud lapped in Iezraell,
This fore greuous plague : was caft on Iezabell.

¶ So lykwyfe the footfteps of Gods enemyes,
Shall well be fpyed : when as his wyll is.
And haue their reward due, for fhedyng of bloud,
Of Gods elect people : when the Lorde thinks it good.

¶ Remember how Pharao, though he was a King,
His footefteps were found out : of perfecutyng.
He with his whole army, of men drowned were,
In midft of the red fea : God dyd them not fpare.

¶ Euen fo from tyme to tyme, you may read and fee,
How God plageth Tirants : for their iniquytye.
He is the fame God ftyll, finners to correct,
Except they repent now : he wyll them reiecte.

¶ Sodome and Gomorra, their footyng was found,
What wayes they then walked : vpon the Lords ground.
They liued to them felues in the finke of finne,
Tyll fyre and brimftone : therby they dyd winne.

¶ Let this be a warnyng, fo now in lyke cafe,
To whores and whoremongers : that yet lacketh grace.
Whofe clofe trippyng footefteps, wyll fhortly appeere,
By our Daniells fiftyng : they can not fcape cleere.

¶ The coueiteous footefteps, of Ahabs great fpight,
To haue Nabaoths viniard : dyd come vnto light.
For the which the Lorde, with Ahab was wroth,
And fent to hym Elyah : who tolde hym the troth.

¶How the Lorde wold plague hym and all his houſhold,
For the death of Nabaoth: as Elyah hym tolde.
Beware now by Ahab, to get worldly muck,
For many one therby: hath had but yll lucke.

¶Syr Rapar, ſyr Capar and ſyr Tenar alſo,
And you maſter Vſerers: that now in wealth flow.
Be not imps of Ahab, common wealth to annoye,
Leaſt you with your footeſteps: the Lord doo deſtroy.

¶The Scribes, the Pharaſies, and Lawyers lykewyſe,
Their footyng was well knowne: of their enterpriſe.
How they came vnto Chriſt, to take hym in a trip,
But he ouer came them: and gaue them the ſlip.

¶So Lawyers that wreſt law, and matters prolong,
Their footeſteps wyll appeere of makyng right wrong,
Woe be to ſuch ſayeth Chriſt, whoſe ſentence is great,
Wherfore repent in tyme: and for mercy intreat.

¶Thus for to conclude now, let all men repent,
And to leade a new lyfe: by Gods Teſtament.
Ere death ſteale vpon vs, our footeſteps to finde,
Contray to Gods wyll: and to natures kinde.

¶Wherefore ſiftyng Daniells, now ply your vocations,
Declare Gods worde truely, vnto all nations.
God is your head Captayne, your ſhield and defence,
Without feare or parcialytie, now doo your dilygence.

¶By ſiftyng and ſortyng, the good from the bad,
Then God wyll be pleaſed: and his people glad.
To heare what God wylleth, to that good eare geue,
And to all ſuch Preachers, as vſe wel the Seeue.

¶ FINIS.

Imprinted at London, by Richarde | Iohnes: dwelling in the vpper end of Fleetlane, at the ſigne | of the ſpread Eagle. And are to be ſolde: at his Shop | ioynyng to the Southweſt Dore of Saint | Paules Church. The xxij day of | October. 1572.

This ballad is printed in two columns.

36

An Epitaph vpon the death of the right
honorable Edward Earle of Darby, Lorde Stanly and
Strange of Knocking, Lord and Gouernour of the Isles of Man,
Knight of the Noble order of the Garter, and one of
the Queenes Maiesties most honorable priuie
Counsell. Deceased the .xxiiij. of Nouem.
1572.

SHall shaking hande with drilling teares, deliuer rural verse:
my mourning Muse doth bid me staye, vnable to reherse.
The noble actes of Derby Earle, that late had breath and life:
   who was through Realme and forren land, beloued of man and wife.
But sure as teares doe ease the heart, that plunged is in paine:
   and Sorrow shee will belch foorth sobbes, in seeking rest againe.
Can countrie now at once refuse, with dolors thus opprest?
   To shed foorth teares, sith Darbye Earle, is thus now clapt in chest.
Who though in yeres he was, more fitter for the graue,
   then long to liue, yet may wee saye, to soone did death depraue.
This noble valiaunt Earle, of his aspiring breath:
   whose sage aduise thus lost may be, his countries seconde death.
Though hee in Ormeschurch lye, inclosed now in slime:
   yet shall his factes inforce his fame, vp to the skies to clime,
Though ougly Mors with spight, haue reft him of his life:
   yet shall his worthy deedes declare, his knowledge was full rife.
That hee in setting ioynt and bone, as stanching blooddie wounde,
   to fewe that Chirurgery doth professe, so much doth vnderstande.
Let Sicophantes that nowe doe seeke, by this his death to rayse:
   yet let them knowe his worthy factes, hath merited great prayse.
No fines no time he raysde, but Tenauntes were content:
   and yet ye shall not heare of worlde, hee greatly raysde his rent.
No toyler in the lawe, though he had profred wrong:
   nor yet would seeme to 'ppresse his foe, though he was mightie strong.
But hee by meekenesse made, his foe to be his friende:
   the wisest way, all wisemen saye, all quarrels so to ende.
You nobles doe beholde, your peere doe not forget:
   who did not long in Marchauntes booke, delight to stande in det.
Who knewe the Marchauntes trade, his money was his plow:
   and would not payment long delaye, that dishonour should not grow.
Oh noble Earle of stature meane, but yet of manly hart:
   in Scotland thou, with Northfolke Duke, at Kelzey playde thy part.
Of Darby Earle, as Lorde of man, and of the Garter Knight:
   and one that in his Princes grace, had very much delight.
Both for his fayth the which, vnto hir grace he owde:
   and also for his wisdome graue, in counsayle often showed.
A mind that did delight, in yelding Iustice dewe,
   an eare still bending downe to heare, poore Sewtors that did sewe.
A hart that rude the plight, of those that were opprest:
   a knee to bende to Princely throne, to haue their cause redrest.

A foote that readie was, to ryde, to runne, or go:
    to helpe the weake that Mydas might, was like to ouerthro.
An eye that fingle was, and not with lucre ftaind:
    a hande to helpe the hungrie poore, he in nowife refraind.
How many now fhall want, to haue wherewith to feede?
    their hungrie corpes which in his life, receyued reliefe at neede.
What mourning make his friendes, of him that are bereft?
    what mourning make his yomen all, that he behind hath left?
How doth his neyghbours all, that dwell in Lancafhire?
    with fobbes and teares they doe deplore, this death of his to heare.
With teares we all are forft, this noble Earle to wayle:
    although that death hath brought to him, a life of greater vayle.
Though Mors his corpes haue feaft, that daunger none coulde daunt:
    yet in his ende a fubiect true, as fame fhall aye auaunt.
No Traytor coulde him traine, at no time to rebell:
    nor Papift coulde him ought perfwade, he liked them not fo well.
To deale by their deuice, to holde with Scottifh dame:
    nor Duke thats dubd, nor Percies pride, that fought their countries bane.
Though Papiftes him extoll, and make the worlde beleeue:
    yet at his death he them renounft, and to his Chrift did cleaue.
Hee knewe their trafh be fuche on, Maffe he did not builde.
    but onely calde one Iefu Chrift, to helpe him win the fielde.
And thus he died in Chrift, no helpe he fought from Pope:
    but in the death and bloud of Chrift, he put his fixed hope.
Though flowe of tongue to talke, of curious queftions fine:
    yet one that read the Scriptures much, no doubt a good Diuine.
He practizd that in life, that he in Scriptures founde:
    and fo he built vpon the rocke, and not on fhiueling fonde.
No bloode he brought in Maries dayes, to burne or for to broyle:
    nor well he likt of Spanifh pride, that fought this Realme to fpoyle.
Now is this Earle from Lathum gone, tourne horfe another awaye:
    the faint is fled, though fhrine remaine, where he was woont to ftaye.
Let Lancafhyre, and Cheffhyre both, with teares bring Corpes to graue:
    For loe, his happie foule in heauen, the bleffed Aungels haue.
As hee in honour runne, a happie race to ende:
    So to his fonne now Noble Earle, God graunt him grace to bend,
To treade his Fathers trace, to ftaye in Gofpell pure:
    fo fhall he liue in fathers fame, that euer fhall endure.

Viuat poft funera Virtus.
¶ Iohn Denton Minift.

¶Imprinted at London by W. Williamfon, dwelling in Diftaffe Lane.

Edward Stanley, third Earl of Derby, began a courtier's career under the guidance of Wolsey, and though in sympathy with the Catholics he managed to retain and increase his power and possessions through the 'daungerous tymes and great rebellions' of the four Tudor sovereigns. Derby commanded the services of ten thousand men, and is said to have spent yearly four thousand pounds on his household. Holinshed contains an eulogy of the deceased nobleman, and mentions 'his cunning in fetting bones difioynted or broke, his chirurgerie and defire to helpe the poore' (*Chronicles*, 1577, vol. ii, pp. 1864–65). A full account of his funeral, which took place on December 4, 1572, at Ormskirk Church, is given in Collins's 'Peerage', 1812, vol. iii, pp. 72–78.

Of Denton, the author of the epitaph, nothing is known, nor are any other works by him extant.

The ballad is printed in two columns.

37

A lamentable Dittie compofed vpon the death of
Robert Lord Deuereux late Earle of Effex, who was beheaded in the
Tower of London, vpon *Afhwednefday* in the morning. 1601.
To the tune of Welladay.

SWeet Englands pride is gone
 welladay welladay,
Which makes her figh and grone
 euermore ftill:
He did her fame aduance,
In Ireland Spaine and France,
And now by difmall chaunce,
 is from her tane.

He was a vertuous Peere,
 welladay welladay,
And was efteemed deere
 euermore ftill:
He alwaies helpt the poore,
Which makes them figh full fore
his death they doe deplore,
 In euery place.

Braue honor grac'd him ftill
 gallantly gallantly,
He nere did deede of ill,
 well is it knowne:
But enuie that foule fiend
Whofe mallice ne're hath end,
hath brought true vertues friend
 Vnto his thrall.

At Tilt he did furpaffe
 gallantly gallantly:
all men that is and was
 euermore ftill:
One day as it was feene,
In honour of his Queene,
Such deeds hath ne're been feen,
 As he did doe.

Abroade and eke at home,
  gallantly, gallantly,
For vallour there was none,
  like him before :
In Ireland France and Spaine,
They feared great Effex name,
And England lou'd the fame,
  In euery place.

But all would not preuaile
  welladay welladay :
His deedes did nought auaile,
  more was the pittie :
He was condemn'd to die,
For treafon certainely,
But God that fits on hie
  Knoweth all things.

That Sunday in the morne,
  welladay welladay :
That he to the Cittie came,
  with all his troupe :
That firft began the ftrife,
And caufed him loofe his life,
And others did the like,
  As well as hee.

Yet her Princely Maieftie
  gratioufly, gratioufly,
Hath pardon giuen free
  to many of them :
She hath releafed them quite,
And giuen them their right,
they may pray both day & night
  God to defend her.

Shrouetewefday in the night
  welladay, welladay,
With a heauy harted fpright
  as it is fayd :
The leiftenant of the Tower
Who kept him in his power,
At ten a clocke that hour
  To him did come.

And fayd vnto him there,
  mournefully, mournfully,
My Lord you muft prepare,
  to die tomorrow :
Gods will be done quoth he,
Yet fhall you ftrangely fee,
God ftrong in me to be,
  Though I am weake.

I pray you pray for me
  welladay, welladay,
That God may ſtrengthen me,
  againſt that houre :
Then ſtraightway did he call,
The Guard vnder the wall,
And did intreate them all
  For him to pray.

For tomorrow is the day
  welladay welladay,
That I the debt muſt pay,
  which I doe owe :
It is my life I meane,
Which I muſt pay my Queene,
Euen ſoe hath iuſtice giuen,
  That I muſt doe.

In the morning was he brought,
  welladay welladay :
Where a Scaffold was ſet vp,
  within the Tower :
Many Lords were preſent then,
With other Gentlemen,
Which were appointed then
  To ſee him dye.

You noble Lords quoth he
  welladay welladay,
That muſt the witneſſe be,
  of this my death :
Know I neuer loued Papiſtrye,
  But did it ſtill defye,
And Eſſex thus did dye,
  Heere in this place.

I haue a ſinner been
  welladay welladay :
Yet neuer wrong'd my Queene
  in all my life,
My God I did offend,
Which grieues me at my end,
May all the reſt amend,
  I doe forgiue them.

To the ſtate I ne're ment ill
  welladay, welladay
Neither wiſht the commons ill
  in all my life :
But loued all with my heart,
And alwaies tooke their part,
Whereas there was deſert,
  In any place.

Then mildely did he craue
  mournefully mournefully,
He might that fauour haue
  priuate to pray:
He then prayed heartely,
And with great feruency,
To God that fits on hie,
  For to receiue him.

And then he prayed againe
  mournefully mournefully,
God to preferue his Queene
  from all her foes:
And fend her long to raigne,
True Iuftice to maintaine,
And not to let proude Spaine,
  Once to offend her.

His gowne he flipt off then
  welladay welladay,
And put off his hat and band
  and hung it by,
Praying ftill continually,
To God that fits on hie,
That he might paciently,
  There fuffer death.

My headefman that muft be,
  then faid he cheerefullie,
Let him come heere to me,
  That I may him fee:
Who kneeled to him then,
Art thou (quoth he) the man,
Which art appointed now,
  my life to free.

Yes my Lord did he fay
  welladay, welladay,
Forgiue me I you pray
  for this your death:
I heare doe thee forg[iue],
And may true iuftice liue,
No foule crime to forgiue,
  Within their [sic] place.

Then he kneeled downe againe,
  mournefully mournefully:
And was required by fome
  there ftanding by:
To forgiue his enemies,
Before death clofde his eyes,
Which he did in heartie wife,
  Thanking them for it:

That they would remember him
   welladay, welladay :
That he might forgiue all them,
   that had him wrong'd :
Now my Lords I take my leaue
Sweet Chrift my foule receiue,
Now when you wil I prepare,
   For I am readie.

He laide his head on the blocke,
   welladay welladay :
But his doublet did let the ftroke
   fome there did fay :
What muft be done (quoth he)
Shall be done prefently,
Then his doublet off put hee,
   and layde downe againe.

Then his headefman did his part
   cruelly, cruelly,
He was neuer feene to ftart,
   For all the blowes :
His foule it is at reft,
in heauen among the bleft,
Where God fend vs to reft,
   When it fhall pleafe him.

God faue the King.

FINIS.

Imprinted at London, for Margret | Allde, and are to be folde at the |
long fhop vnder Saint Mil|dreds Church in the Poul|try. 1603.

This ballad was reprinted in Ambrose Phillips's 'Collection of Old Ballads', 1723–25, vol. iii, pp. 112–17, Evans's 'Old Ballads', 1810, vol. iii, pp. 158–66, and the 'Roxburghe Ballads', vol. i, pp. 564–70. There are several editions : that at Britwell is the earliest, and a licence for it was obtained on May 18, 1603 (Arber's *Transcript*, iii. 234). Therefore it was not published until after the accession of James I and fifteen months after the earl's execution. J. P. Collier included it in 'Old Ballads' (Percy Society, 1840).

To the tune 'Well-a-day' was sung 'Essex's last good night', a ballad occasioned by the death of Walter Devereux, Earl of Essex, father of the royal favourite, and the air is also known by that name. 'Well-a-day' has an earlier origin, for it appears in ballad titles anterior to 1576, the year in which the elder Devereux died (W. Chappell, *Popular Music of the Olden Time*, vol. i, pp. 174–75).

The ballad is printed in four columns, within a border. At the head of the text is a large ornamental block rectangular in design.

38

A Prayer fayd in the kinges Chappell.

[See facsimile.]

The health of Edward the Sixth, delicate as it had been since birth, steadily grew worse through the winter of 1552–53, and by the April following, those in attendance recognized that the end could not be delayed many weeks longer. His death took place at the beginning of July, sixteen days after the publication of the Prayer.

It was general opinion at the time that Edward had been poisoned, and to this view Henry Machyn in his 'Diary' (Camden Society, 1848) clearly testifies. J. A. Froude, however, suggests (*History*, ch. 29) that the end was hastened by the attentions of a female quack, who had been admitted to the king's bedside as a last hope of saving his life, rather than that Edward had been deliberately murdered.

The Prayer was reprinted by Sir S. Egerton Brydges in the 'British Bibliographer' (vol. ii, p. 102). The broadside was not in Heber's collection; it measures twelve inches by seven and five-eighths.

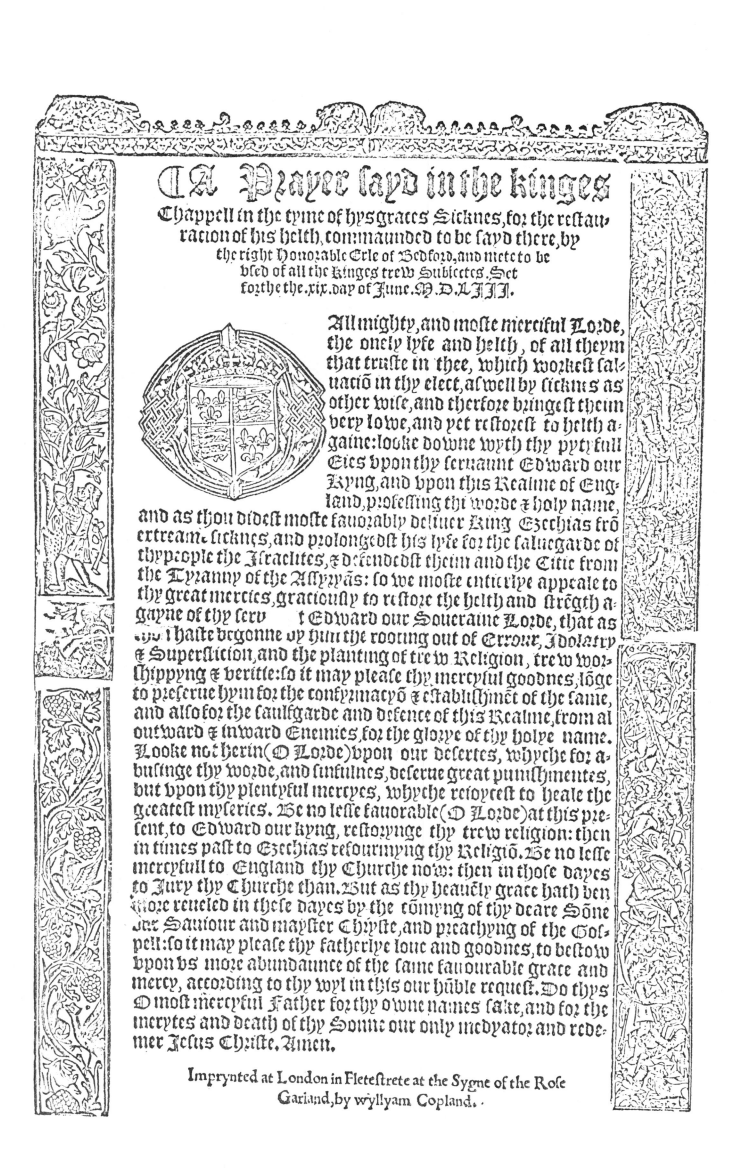

¶A Prayer ſayd in the kinges

Chappell in the tyme of hys graces Sicknes, for the reſtau-
racion of his helth, commaunded to be ſayd there, by
the right Honozable Erle of Bedford, and mete to be
vſed of all the kinges trew Subiectes. Set
forthe the .xix. day of June. M.D.LIII.

All mighty, and moſte merciful Lozde,
the onely lyfe and helth, of all theym
that truſte in thee, which workeſt ſal-
uacio in thy elect, aſwell by ſicknes as
other wiſe, and therfore bringeſt theim
very lowe, and yet reſtozeſt to helth a-
gaine: looke downe wyth thy pytyfull
Eies vpon thy ſeruaunt Edward our
Kyng, and vpon this Realme of England, pzofeſſing thi worde ₹ holy name,
and as thou dideſt moſte fauozably deliuer King Ezechias frõ
extreame ſicknes, and prolongedſt his lyfe for the ſaluegarde of
thy people the Iſraelites, ₹ defendedſt theim and the Citie from
the Tyranny of the Aſſyzyãs: ſo we moſte entierlye appeale to
thy great mercies, graciouſly to reſtoze the helth and ſtregth a-
gayne of thy ſerv   t Edward our Soueraine Lozde, that as
_ i haſte begonne vp hym the rooting out of Errour, Idolatry
₹ Superſticion, and the planting of trew Religion, trew woz-
ſhippyng ₹ veritle: ſo it may pleaſe thy mercyful goodnes, lõge
to pzeſerue hym for the confyzmacyõ ₹ eſtabliſhmet of the ſame,
and alſo for the ſaulfgarde and defence of this Realme, from al
outward ₹ inward Enemies, for the glozye of thy holye name.
Looke not herin (O Lozde) vpon our deſertes, whyche for a-
buſinge thy worde, and ſinfulnes, deſerue great puniſhmentes,
but vpon thy plentyful mercyes, whyche reioyceſt to heale the
greateſt myſeries. Be no leſſe fauozable (O Lozde) at this pze-
ſent, to Edward our kyng, reſtozynge thy trew religion: then
in times paſt to Ezechias reſourmyng thy Religiõ. Be no leſſe
mercyfull to England thy Churche now: then in thoſe dayes
to Jury thy Churche than. But as thy heauêly grace hath ben
moze reueled in theſe dayes by the cõmyng of thy deare Sõne
our Sauiour and mayſter Chzyſte, and pzeachyng of the Goſpell: ſo it may pleaſe thy fatherlye loue and goodnes, to beſtow
vpon vs moze abundaunce of the ſame fauourable grace and
mercy, according to thy wyl in this our hûble requeſt. Do thys
O moſt mercyful Father for thy owne names ſake, and for the
merytes and death of thy Sonne our only medyatoz and rede-
mer Jeſus Chziſte. Amen.

Imprynted at London in Fleteſtrete at the Sygne of the Roſe
Garland, by Wyllyam Copland.

39

ᴈ The panges of Loue and louers f[i]ttes.

WAs not good Kyng Salamon
    Rauiſhed in ſondry wyſe
with euery liuelie Paragon
That gliſtered before his eyes
If this be true as trewe it was
    Lady lady.
why ſhould not I ſerue you alas
    My deare lady.

When Paris was enamoured
With Helena dame bewties peare
Whom Venus firſt him promiſed
To venter on and not to feare
what ſturdy ſtormes endured he
    Lady lady
To winne her loue er it would be
    My deare ladye.

Knowe ye not howe Troylus
Languiſhed and loſt his ioye
with fittes and feuers meruailous
For Creſſeda that dwelt in Troye
Tyll pytie planted in her breſt
    ladie ladie.
To ſlepe with him & graunt him reſt
    My deare ladie.

I read ſomtime howe venterous
Leander was his loue to pleaſe
Who ſwomme the waters perillous
Of Abidon thoſe ſurginge ſeaſe
To come to her where as ſhe lay
    ladie ladie
Tyll he was drowned by the waye
    my deare ladie.

What ſay ye then to Priamus
That promiſed his loue to mete
And founde by fortune marueilous
A bloudie cloth before his feete
For Tyſbies ſake hymſelfe he ſlewe
    ladie ladie
To proue that he was a louer trewe
    my deare ladie.

When Hercules for Eronie
murdered a monfter fell
He put himfelfe in ieoperdie
Perillous as the ftories tell
Refkewinge her vpon the fhore
    ladie ladie.
Whiche els by lot had died therfore
    my deare ladie.

Anaxaretis bewtifull
when Iphis did beholde and fee
with fighes and fobbinges pitifull
That Paragon longe wooed he
And when he could not wynne her fo
    Ladye ladye
He went and honge him felfe for woe
    My deare ladye.

Befides thefe matters marueilous
Good Lady yet I can tell the more
The Gods haue ben full amourous
As Iupiter by learned lore
Who changed his fhape as fame hath fpred
    lady ladye.
To come to Alcumenaes bed
    My deare ladye.

And if bewtie breed fuch bliffulneffe
Euamouring [sic] both God and man
Good Lady let no wilfulneffe
Exuperate your bewtye then
To flaye the hertes that yeld & craue
    ladye ladye
The graunt of your good wil to haue
    My deare ladye.

Finis. ☞. W.E.

Imprinted at London in Smithfeld | in the parifh of Saynt Barthel|mewes Hofpitall by | Richard Lant. | An. Dñi. M.D.lix. xxij. Mar:

William Elderton, the author of five ballads in the Heber collection, is the best known and most notorious of all broadside poets. At one period Elderton led a company of comedians, and at another he is said to have filled the office of 'atturney in the Sheriffes Courtes'. His contemporaries, Gabriel Harvey and Thomas Nash, testify to his insobriety, and Elderton's 'ale-crammed nose' was proverbial, and inspired the lines quoted by Chappell in 'Popular Music of the Olden Time', vol. i, p. 107:—

'Will. Elderton's red nose is famous everywhere,
And many a ballet shows it cost him very dear;
In ale, and toast, and spice, he spent good store of coin,
Ye need not ask him twice to take a cup of wine.
But though his nose was red, his hand was very white,
In work it never sped, nor took in it delight;
No marvel therefore 'tis, that white should be his hand,
That ballets writ a score, as you well understand.'

Elderton wrote a large number of ballads. Several are in the library of the Society of Antiquaries and in the Roxburghe collection at the British Museum. Four were included by Mr. Henry Huth in 'Ancient Ballads and Broadsides' (Philobiblon Society, 1867). The Registers of the Stationers' Company mention others, but of these no copise are extant. The ballad 'The panges of Loue and louers fittes' was licensed in 1558–59 (Arber's *Transcript*, i. 96), and was reprinted in J. P. Collier's 'Old Ballads' (Percy Society, 1840), pp. 25–8. 'Lady lady' is the same tune as 'King Solomon', which took its name from the opening line of the above, and to which certain later ballads were sung.

The original is coarsely printed in two columns and without border.

40

The true fourme and ſhape of a monſterous Chyld,
Whiche was borne in Stony Stratforde, in North Hamptonſhire
The yeare of our Lord, M.CCCCC.LXV.

THis Childe was borne on Fryday, being the .xxvi. daye of Ianuary, betwyxt .vi. and vii. of the clocke in the | morninge, and lyued two howres, and was chriſtened by the Mydwyfe, and are both Women Chyldren, | hauing two bodies, ioyning togither. With .iiii. armes, and .iiii. legges perfecte, & from the Nauell vpward | one Face, two Eyes, one Noſe, and one Mouth, and three Eares, one beinge vpon the backe ſyde of the | Head, a lytle aboue the nape of the Necke, hauing heare growinge vpon the Head. Whyche Chylde was | borne out of Wedlocke. The Fathers name is Rychard Sotherne, who is now fled And the Mother is yet lyuyng | in the ſame Towne. And this Childe was brought vp to London, wheare it was ſeene of dyuers worſhipfull men | and women of the Cytie. And alſo of the Countrey. To witnes that it is a Trouth and no Fable, But a warninge of | God, to moue all people to amendment of lyfe.

YOu that ſo ſee this Childe diſfigured here,
Two Babes in one, diſguiſed to beholde,
Thinke with your ſelues, when ſuch thinges do appere
All is not well, as wiſe heades may be bolde:
But god that can in ſecretes ſhew the ſigne
Can bringe much more to pas, by poure deuine.

❡And we that lyue to ſee this wonder, howe
The gaſe is geuen, to make this meruaile great,
Let one by one that this beholdeth nowe,
Be warned as the wonder giues conceate:
To liue to mende the wonderous ſhape we ſee,
Contrarie much, in all that ought to bee.

❡For as we finde, this figure ſemeth ſtraunge,
Becauſe it ſhowes, proporſion not in vre
So bare in minde, how time can choppe and chaunce,
Diſguiſing workes, in willes that be vnſure:
From meane to more, from more to much exceſſe,
Where Nature willes, deſire ſhould be leſſe.

❡Finis.   W. Elderton.

❡Imprinted at London in Fleteſtrete beneath the Conduit: at the | ſigne of
S. Iohn Euangeliſt, by Thomas Colwell.

This ballad is entered in the Registers of the Sta-tioners' Company, 1564–65: 'Receaued of Thomas Colwell for his lycenſe for pryntinge of *a pycture of a chylde*' (Arber's *Transcript*, i. 264).

Beneath the title are two woodcuts representing the 'fore and backe' parts of the 'monſterous Chyld'.

41

¶ A ballat intituled Northomberland newes,
Wherin you maye fee what Rebelles do vfe.

¶ *Come tomblinge downe come tomblinge downe.*
That will not yet be trewe to the Crowne.

YOu Northcountrie nodies whie be ye fo bragge
To rife and raife honor to Romifh renowne
You know yᵗ at Tiborne there ftandeth a Nagge
For fuche as will neuer be trew to the crowne.
Come tomblinge. &c.

What meane ye to followe the man in the Moone,
With batt₃ bowes and arrowes and billes verye browne.
His fhyninge with fhame wilbe fhadowed fo foone,
It will greue him that euer he troubled the Crowne.
Come tomblinge. &c.

Thowghe Poperie wrought a greate while a goe,
That Percie prouoked Kinge Harry to frowne.
Yet who wolde haue thought there were any moe,
That wold not yet be trew to the Crowne.
Come tomblinge. &c.

Our Queene is the daughter of Henry theight,
Who brought euery Alter and Imagerie downe.
He lefte her and tawght her a remedie ftreight,
For anye that wold not be trew to the Crowne.
Come tombling. &c.

And though you do greete her like Traytours with treafon
To whom you owe honour with cappe and knee downe.
I am fuer that fainct Peter will faye it is reafon,
To rule ye that will not be trew to the Crowne.
Come tombling. &c.

And thoughe you do faye ther is matter amis,
Whiche you wold redreffe by noble Renowme.
What any waye wurfe then Rebellion is,
Of any that will not be true to the Crowne.
Come tomblinge. &c.

What Strangers can be, more ftraunger then ye,
That gather together bothe carter and clowne.
And ftudie to fturre to feeke and to fee,
Whiche waie to deuife to trouble the Crowne.
Come tomblinge. &c.

Syr Ihon Shorne your morowe Maſſe Prieſt,
Saythe to Lobbe looke aboute will ye knele downe?
We will haue a Maſſe before Ieſus Chriſt,
And that is the waye to trouble the Crowne.
    Come tomblinge. &c.

The Knightes to theyr knaues ſaye ſticke and be ſtowt,
Our banners and ſtaues ſhall bringe vs Renowne.
We haue Nobles and others that be as deuowt,
To helpe vs at this time to trouble the Crowne.
    Come tomblinge. &c.

The Rebelles come flinginge but what cometh after,
A ſonge worthe the ſinginge hey downe a downe downe.
A Tyborne Typpett a roope or a halter,
For anye that will not be trew to the Crowne.
    Come tomblinge. &c.

For thoughe ye ſpoile Churches and burne vp the Bible,
And worſhippe gaie Croſſes in euery towne.
Your Idolles you aſſes are neuer poſſible,
To ſaue ye that will not be trew to the Crowne.
    Come tomblinge. &c.

And thoughe ye do carie the banner of force,
And Iolie rounde Robyn vnder your gowne.
You know that ſainct George hath a praunſinge horſe,
Canne make enie Rebell to ſtoope to the Crowne.
    Come tomblinge. &c.

The Weſtmerland Bull muſt come to the ſtake,
The Lyon will rore ſtill till he be downe.
Northumberland then will tremble and quake,
For woe that he was ſo falſe to the Crowne.
    Come tomblinge. &c.

And Catholiques old that hold with the Pope,
And carie dead Images vppe and downe.
To take better holde they ſhall haue a Roope,
To teache them once to be trew to the Crowne.
    Come tomblinge. &c.

Let euery Prieſt that ſayethe anye Maſſe,
Either chuſe to take the Crucifixe downe.
Or hange as highe ac the Crucifixe was,
Except he will be trew to the Crowne.
    Come tomblinge. &c.

For God is a God of Ieloſie ſuche,
He lokes to haue his holye Renowne.
Or elles he will miſlyke verye muche,
To gyue anye one his excellente Crowne.
    Come tomblinge. &c.

God prosper the Quene as I truste that he shall,
And graunt of his mercie with blessed Renowne.
  The Northe, and West, countrie, the sowth, east, and all,
The people of Englande maye cleaue to the Crowne.
  Come tomblinge.

And I wishe that Good Preachers & other trewe teachers,
Wolde visite the vynearde whose branches be downe.
  That all the Northe Countrie yet nossled in Popeerie,
Might knowe theyr duetie to God and the Crowne.
  Come tomblinge. &c.

Finis quothe. W. E.

❧ *Imprinted at London in Paules Churcheyarde, at the signe of the*
Lucrece by Thomas Purfoote.

The above is one of the many broadsides occasioned by the series of events known as the 'Rising in the North'. During the year 1569, the Catholic nobles in England and Scotland planned to bring about a marriage between Mary Stuart and the Duke of Norfolk. It is believed that it was the intention of those concerned to acquaint Elizabeth with the proposal, but unfortunately for them the Queen received the news from a private source before this could be accomplished. Elizabeth's anger was unbounded. The Duke was sent to the Tower and the two northern lords implicated, the earls of Northumberland and Westmorland, were ordered to London to explain their share in the negotiations.

Northumberland, an amiable but weak man, panic-stricken, decided to resist violently, and persuaded Westmorland to come to his assistance. The country folk eagerly joined their standards. The rebels marched to Durham and here showed their attachment to the old religion by restoring the Mass in the cathedral. All hope of successful descent on London speedily vanished. Shortage of money and supplies, indifferent generalship, and the fact that royalists in large numbers under Sussex and Warwick were advancing from York, caused the earls to disband their followers, when many of these made their escape into Scotland. Such reprisals as were inflicted a hundred years later in the west were now carried out in the north. The marshal of Elizabeth's army boasted that he had not visited a single village in the disaffected district without holding an execution. Northumberland sought refuge across the border, and after many adventures was betrayed by a friend, taken to York, and executed. Westmorland, more fortunate, managed to reach Flanders.

In the library of the Society of Antiquaries is a ballad entitled 'Newes from Northumberland ... Qd. W. Elderton' (R. Jamieson's *Popular Ballads and Songs,* 1806, vol. ii, pp. 210–14). It was printed by Thomas Colwell, and differs entirely from the above. The licence for the Britwell ballad appears in the Stationers' Registers for 1569–70—'Receuyd of Thomas purfoote for his lycenfe for the prynting of a ballett intituled *North[um]berlandes newes by Elderton*' (Arber's *Transcript,* i. 403). Colwell's licence follows immediately afterwards.

Heber's ballad is printed in two columns within narrow ornamental borders.

42

⤷ An Epytaphe vppon the Death of the Right Reuerend and learned Father in God. I. Iuell, Doctor of Diuinitie and Bifhop of Sarifburie. Whom God called to his marcie the .22. of September. 1571.

The Iuell of our ioye is gone, the happie heauens haue wonne,
  The greateft gift that euer was, with vs beneth the fonne :
Which makes fuch weepinge eyes, in Sallefbury they faye,
  As all the ronning ftreames therof, can neuer wafhe awaye.
(Alas) is Iuell dead, the folder of the flocke,
  If Death haue caught the Diall vp, then who fhall keepe the Clocke ?
O God, what greefe is this, thye charie Churche fhould want,
  A Bifhoppe of fo good a grace, wher good men be fo fkant :
Wee feare the plague (they faye) but fuch a plague as this,
  Sithens I was borne I neuer knewe, nor neuer fhall i wis :
Yet are there fome behinde, I truft will learne to knowe,
  How Iuell to his dieng daye, his Talents did beftowe.
So bufie at his booke, to bring the truth to light,
  As they that lyke the redie way, maye looke and finde it right,
His houfe and houfholde was fo kept for his degree,
  As Paull in his Epiftles wrightes a Biffhoppes houfe fhould bee :
His Diocefe I beleeue, hee kept in fo good awe,
  As Vertue is content to fweare, they liued within her lawe.
His handes and harte were free, the needie could not lacke,
  Such peace and concorde planted hee, as nothing went to wracke :
And charie went to Churche, himfelfe by breake of daye,
  That his example might procure, the reft to go that waye :
And gaue vnto his men, their dueties when hee died,
  With large and Lordlie recompence, this can not bee denied.
(Alas) with piteous mone, all Chriftians nowe maye weepe,
  That wee haue fuch a Shepard gone : God helpe the felie fheepe :
Meethinkes I fee in heauen, triumphant truth appeare,
  And faythfulnes, which fpeake alowde, let Iuell nowe come neare.
Thappoftelles all do preafe, meethinckes to fee his face :
  And all the Angells go about to bring him to his place :
Euen Chrift him felfe mee thinkes, I fee begins to fmile,
  And faith : beholde my chofen frend, I lookte for all this while.
And Abraham rendes his clothes, and bowells out his breft,
  And fayth to Iuell iumpe in here, and take thye quiet reft.

  Finis.   Quod.   W. Elderton.

Imprynted at London, in Fleeteftreate beneath the Conduit at the | figne of
S. Iohn Euangelift by Thomas Colwell.

Befides this ballad by Elderton, there is an epitaph on Bishop Jewel, written by Nicolas Bourman, which is in this collection (p. 32). Owing to the break in the records of the Stationers' Registers it is impossible to ascertain whether one or both were licensed. Elderton's 'Epytaphe' was reprinted in 'Select Poetry, chiefly devotional, of the reign of Queen Elizabeth' (Parker Society, 1845), and again in four-line stanzas by J. P. Collier (*Book of Roxburghe Ballads*, 1847).

The ballad is printed in single column within a neat ornamental border.

43

The Lamentation of Follie:
To the tune of New Rogero.

ALas what meaneth man,
 with care and greedy paine :
To wreſt to win a worldly fame
 which is but vile and vaine.
As though he had no cauſe to doubt,
 the drift of his deſire,
Not pleaſed though he rule the route,
 but ſtill to couet higher.

And wander after will,
 farre paſſing his degree :
Not ſo contented ſtill,
 but a king himſelfe to be.
Subuerting law and right,
 detecting triall true :
Wringing euery wight,
 that all the realme dooth rue.

Whoſe deed and ill deſart,
 compact and falſe conſent :
I thinke no Chriſten heart,
 can chooſe but needs lament.
Alas it ſeemed ſtrange,
 ſuch thraldome in a realme :
Which wealthie was to waſt away,
 by will that was extreame.

Sith vertue was profeſt,
 moſt famous franke and free :
Yet men tranſpoſed cleane,
 more vile and worſe to be.
And ſuch as did pretend
 to ſhew themſelfe moſt holie :
Haue ſwarued in the end,
 and fawned after follie.

Whoſe wordes ſo diſagree,
 as waters come and go :
Their liuings to be contrary,
 that ſhould examples ſhowe.
And fawning after fame,
 purſue their owne decay :
As though there were no God,
 to call their life away.

What surety is in man,
  what truth or trust at all:
Which frameth what he can,
  to worke vnworthy thrall,
Oppreffion hath beene free,
  the poore alas be fpoyled:
Maides and wiues be rauifhed,
  the fimple are beguiled.

Lawe is made a libertie,
  and right is ouerthrowne:
Faith is but a foolifh thing,
  falfehood is alone.
Pride is counted clenlineffe,
  and theft is but a flight.
Whoredome is but wantonneffe,
  and wafte is but delight.

Spoiling is but pleafure,
  riot is but youth:
Slaunder is a laughing game,
  and lying counted trueth.
Mariage is but mockage,
  the children counted bafe:
Thus right is wronged euery way,
  in our accurfed cafe.

Flatterie is the Forte of Fame,
  and trueth is troden downe:
The innocent do beare the blame,
  the wicked winne renowne.
Thus Sathan hath preuailed long,
  and we for want of grace:
Haue troden vertue vnder foote,
  and vice hath taken place.

But God that is moft righteous,
  hath feene our fatall fall:
And fpred his mercie ouer vs,
  to fhield vs from the thrall.
Whofe mercy is fo infinite,
  to fuch as were oppreffed:
He hath reftored them to right,
  and hath their care redreffed.

And though that our vnworthineffe,
  hath not deferued fo:
Now let vs ceafe our wickedneffe,
  and graft where grace may grow.
And let vs pray for our defence,
  our worthy Queene elect:
That God may worke his will in her,
  our thraldome to correct.

That God be chiefely ſerued ſo,
　　as dooth to him belong:
That right may haue his courſe againe,
　　and vanquiſh wicked wrong.
That we may liue in feare and awe,
　　and truly to intend:
And haue the iuſtice of the lawe,
　　our cauſes to defend.

That truth may take his wonted place,
　　and faith be faſt againe:
And then repent and call for grace,
　　that wrought our care and paine.
That God ſend vs a ſhort redreſſe,
　　with wealth and great increaſe:
And to our Queene, to reigne and rule,
　　in honour, health, and peace.

FINIS.　　　　W. E.

Imprinted at London by *Edward Allde.*

Leave to print 'The Lamentation of Follie' does not appear in the Registers of the Stationers' Company. It can scarcely have been issued earlier than February 15, 1584, for on that date Edward Allde was made free of the Company and his first licence occurs on August 1, 1586 (Arber's *Transcript*, ii. 450).

This copy of the ballad is printed on the back of an imperfect copy of the first part of the ballad of 'The King and the Miller of Mansfield'. 'The Lamentation of Follie' was reprinted in J. P. Collier's 'Old Ballads' (Percy Society, 1840).

The broadside is printed in two columns.

44

The lamentable fall of Queene Elnor, who for her pride
and wickedneſſe, by Gods|Iudgment, ſunke into the ground at
Charing croſſe, and roſe vp againe at Queene hiue.

To the tune of, Gentle and Curteous.

WHen Edward was in England King
   the firſt of all that name :
Proud Elnor he made his Queene,
   a ſtately Spaniſh dame.
Whoſe wicked life and ſinfull pride,
   through England did excell :
To daintie Dames and gallant Maides
   this Queene was knowne full well.

She was the firſt that did inuent
   in Coaches braue to ride :
She was the firſt that brought this land
   the deadly ſinne of pride.
No Engliſh Taylors heere could ſerue
   to make her rich attire :
But ſent for Taylors into Spaine,
   to feede her vaine deſire.

They brought in faſhions ſtrange and new
   with golden garments bright :
The Farthingales, and mighty Ruffes,
   with Gownes of rare delight.
[The London] Dames in Spaniſh pride,
   [Did flouriſh] euerywhere,
[Our Engliſhmen, like] Women then,
   [Did wear long Lockes] of haire.

[Both Man and Child, both] maide & wife,
   [were drown'd in pride of] Spaine :
[And thought the Spaniſh] Taylors then,
   [our Engliſh men did ſtain.]
[Whereat the Queen did much] diſpite,
   [To ſee our] engliſh-men,
[In] veſtures clad, as braue to ſee
   [As] any Spaniard then.

She crau'd the King that euery man
   that wore long lockes of haire,
Might then be cut and powled all,
   or ſhauen very neare.
Whereat the King did ſeeme content,
   and ſoone thereto agreed :
And firſt commaunded that his owne,
   ſhould then be cut with ſpeed.

And after that to pleafe his Queene,
  proclaymed through the land,
That euery man that wore long haire,
  fhould powle him out of hand.
[And yet] this Spaniard not content
  [Againft] women bore a fpight:
[She then] requefted of the King
  [Againft] all law and right.

[That euery] woman-kind fhould haue,
  [Their right] breaft cut away:
[And then with] burning Irons fear'd,
  [The blood to ft]aunch and ftay.
[King Edward] then perceiuing well
  [Her fpite t]o women kind,
Deuifed foone by pollicie
  to turne her bloody minde.

He fent for burning Irons ftraight,
  all fparkling hot to fee:
And fayd, O Queene, come on thy way
  I will begin with thee.
Which wordes did much difpleafe the Queene
  that penance to begin:
But afkt him pardon on her knees,
  who gaue her grace therein.

But afterward fhe chaunft to paffe
  along braue London ftreetes:
Whereas the Maior of Londons wife,
  in ftately fort fhe meetes.
With muficke, mirth, and melodie,
  vnto the Church that went:
To giue God thanks that to L. Maior
  a noble Sonne had fent.

It grieued much this fpitefull Queene
  to fee that any one
Should fo exceede in mirth and ioy,
  except her felfe alone:
For which fhe after did deuife,
  within her bloody minde,
And practifde ftill moft fecretly
  to kill the Lady kinde.

Vnto Lord Maior of London then
  fhe fent her letters ftraight:
To fend his Lady to the Court,
  vpon her Grace to waight.
But when the London Lady came,
  before proude Elnors face:
She ftript her from her rich array,
  and kept her vile and bace.

She fent her into Wales with fpeede,
  and kept her fecret there:
And vfde her ftill more crueller
  then euer man did heare:
fhe made her wafh, fhe made her ftartch
  fhe made her drudge alway:
She made her nurfe vp children fmall,
  and labour night and day.

But this contented not the Queene,
  but fhew'd her more defpight:
She bound this Lady to a poft
  at twelue a clocke at nyght:
And as poore Lady fhe ftood bound
  the Queene in angrie mood,
Did fet two Snakes vnto her breafts,
  that fuckt away her blood.

Thus died the Maior of Londons wif
  moft greeuous for to heare:
Which made the Spaniard grow more proud
  as after fhall appeare.
The Wheate that dayly made her bred
  was boulted twentie times,
The food that fed this ftately Dame,
  was boylde in coftly wines.

The water that did fpring from ground
  fhe would not touch at all,
But wafht her handes with dew of heauen,
  that on fweete Rofes fall:
She bath'd her body many times,
  in fountaines filde with milke,
And euery day did change attire,
  in coftly median filke.

But comming then to London backe,
  within her Coach of golde:
A tempeft ftrange within the fkies,
  this Queene did there behold.
Out of which ftorme fhe could not goe
  but there remain'd a fpace,
Foure horfes could not ftirre her coach
  a foote out of that place.

A iudgement furely fent from heauen
  for fhedding guiltleffe blood,
Vpon this finfull Queene that flew
  the London Lady good:
King Edward then, as wifedome wild
  accufde her for that deede:
But fhe denied and wifht that God
  would fend his wrath with fpeede.

If that vpon ſo vile a thing,
   her hart did euer thinke,
She wiſht the ground might open wide
   and therein ſhe might ſinke :
With that at Charing croſſe ſhe ſunke
   into the ground aliue,
And after roſe with lyfe againe
   in Londan at Queene hiue.

Where after that ſhe languiſht ſore
   full twentie dayes in paine :
At laſt confeſt the Ladies blood,
   her guiltie handes did ſtaine.
And likewiſe how that by a Fryer
   ſhe had a baſe borne childe,
Whoſe ſinfull luſt and wickednes
   her mariage bed defilde.

Thus haue you heard the fall of pride
   a iuſt reward of ſinne :
For thoſe that wil forſweare theſelues
   Gods vengeance dayly winne.
Beware of Pride you London dames,
   both wiues and maydens all,
Beare this imprinted in your minde,
   that Pride will haue a fall.

FINIS.

Printed at London for William Blackwall.

It is difficult to understand why the noble and virtuous Eleanor of Castile, queen to Edward I. of England, should be presented in so unfavourable a light. Seeing that she is reported to have been the mother of a numerous progeny, her jealousy for the lady mayoress is unaccountable. Singularly enough George Peele in his play 'The Famous Chronicle of king Edward the Firſt', 1593, does the queen the same injustice. The ballad might more appropriately have been applied to Eleanor of Aquitaine. Evans in his 'Old Ballads', 1810 (vol. ii, p. 268), retails a suggestion that it was in reality aimed at Queen Mary Tudor, but Chappell is of the opinion that it was inspired by the negotiations attending the proposed marriage between Charles, Prince of Wales, with the Infanta of Spain. The earliest extant copy, now reprinted, was issued by William Blackwall, who is mentioned in the records of the Stationers' Company between the years 1586–1618, so that this surmise may be correct. A later edition, printed by the Assignes of Thomas Symcocke, without date, is in the Roxburghe collection (*Roxburghe Ballads*, vol. ii, p. 69), and another, published after the Restoration, is in the Bodleian Library. The verses appear in Ambrose Phillips's 'Collection of Old Ballads', 1723 (vol. i, p. 103). The story of Queen Eleanor, the wife of Henry II is found in 'Queen Eleanor's Confession', a ballad reprinted by F. C. Child in 'English and Scottish Popular Ballads' (No. 156), as well as by Phillips (vol. i, p. 19). The tune 'Gentle and Curteous' is not mentioned in Chappell's 'Popular Music of the Olden Time'.

The ballad is printed in three columns, the first of which has been severely mutilated. It is without border or ornament.

45

A mournefull Dittie, entituled *Elizabeths* loſſe, together
with a welcome | for King *Iames*.

To a pleaſant new tune.

FArewell, farewell, farewell,
  braue Englands ioy:
Gone is thy friend
  that kept thee from annoy.
Lament, lament, lament,
  you Engliſh Peeres,
Lament your loſſe
  poſſeſt ſo many yeeres.

Gone is thy Queene, the
  paragon of time,
On whom grim death
  hath ſpred his fatall line.
Lament, lament, &c.

Gone is that gem which
  God and man did loue,
She hath vs left
  to dwell in heauen aboue.
Lament, lament, &c.

You gallant Ladies
  of her Princely traine,
Lament your loſſe
  your loue, your hope, and gaine.
Lament, lament, &c.

Weepe wring your hands,
  all clad in mourning weeds,
Shew foorth your loue,
  in tongue in hart and deeds.
Lament, lament, &c.

Full foure and fortie yeeres
  foure moneths ſeauen dayes,
She did maintaine this realme
  in peace alwayes.
Lament, lament, &c.

In ſpite of Spaines proud Pope,
  and all the rout,
Who Lyon like ran
  ranging round about.
Lament, lament, &c.

With traiterous plots to ſlay
  her Royall grace,
Her realme, her lawes
  and Goſpell to deface,
Lament, lament, &c.

Yet time and tide God ſtill
  was her defence,
Till for himſelfe from vs
  hee tooke her hence.
Lament, lament, &c.

We neede not to rehearſe
  what care what griefe,
She ſtill endured,
  and all for our reliefe.
Lament, lament, &c.

We neede not to rehearſe
  what benefits,
You all inioyd, what pleaſures
  and what gifts.
Lament, lament, &c.

You Virgins all bewayle
  your Virgin Queene,
That Phenix rare,
  on earth but ſildome ſeene.
Lament, lament, &c.

With Angels wings ſhe pearſt
  the ſtarrie ſkie,
When death, grim death,
  hath ſhut her mortall eye.
Lament, lament, &c.

You Nimphs that ſing and bathe,
  in Fountaines cleere:
Come lend your helpe to ſing
  in mournefull cheere.
Lament, lament, &c.

All you that doe profeſſe
  ſweet muſicks Art,
Lay all aſide, your Vyoll
  Lute and Harpe.
Lament, lament, &c.

Mourne Organs, Flutes,
   mourne Sagbuts with fad foūd :
Mourne Trumpets fhrill,
   mourne Cornets mute & round.
Lament, lament, &c.

You Poets all braue Shakfpeare,
   Iohnfon, Greene,
Beftow your time to write
   for Englands Queene.
Lament, lament, &c.

Returne your fongs and Sonnets
   and your fayes :
To fet foorth fweete
   Elizabeths praife.
Lament, lament, &c.

In fine all you
   that loyall harts poffeffe,
With Rofes fweete,
   bedeck hir Princely hearfe.
Lament, lament, &c.

Bedeck that hearfe
   fprong from that famous King,
King Henrie the eight,
   whofe fame on earth doth ring.
Lament, lament, &c.

Now is the time that we
   muft all forget,
Thy facred name
   oh fweet Elizabeth.
Lament, lament, &c.

Praying for King Iames,
   as earft we prayed for thee,
In all fubmiffiue loue
   and loyaltie.
Lament, lament, &c.

Befeeching God to bleffe
   his Maieftie
With earthly peace
   and heauens felicitie.
Lament, lament, &c.

And make his raigne
   more profperous here on earth
Then was the raigne
   of late Elizabeth.
Lament, lament, &c.

Wherefore all you
    that fubiects true beare names
Still pray with me, and fay
    God faue King Iames.
Lament, lament, lament,
    you Englifh Peeres,
Lament your loffe enioyd
    fo many yeeres.

FINIS.

Imprinted at London for T. P.

The death of Queen Elizabeth in 1603, and the accession of James I occasioned the issue of a large number of ballads, many of which were licensed, although this particular one was not. Thomas Pavier published several, and there is little doubt that he was responsible for the Britwell ballad. Pavier published between the years 1600 and 1625.

The ballad is of interest from the fact that the seventeenth stanza contains a reference to Shakespeare. It is printed in three columns.

46

A new yeres Gift, intituled, a Chriſtal glas | for all Eſtates to
looke in, wherein they may plainly ſee the iuſt rewarde, for |
Vnſaciate and Abhominable Couetouſneſſe. | M.D.LXIX.

ACcordyng to my cuſtom, daily I did muſe,
Vpon Gods holy worde, which for euer ſhall endure,
I thought it the beſt exerciſe that any man could vſe,
Daily to be frequented in the Scripture,
The .xii. of Luke I beheld a place both plaine and pure,
Geuing generall warning in ſaying theſe wordes to vs,
Beware of Couetouſneſſe, ſaith Chriſt Ieſus.

It firſt confounded Adam being then in Paradice,
Coueting to be as God, and ſo began to ſlide,
He preſumed to haue knowledge, and alſo to be wiſe,
Not contented with his ſtate, nor therin did abide,
His coueting (Alas) ſet him cleane beſide,
Regarding Sathans wordes which coueted his tranſgreſſion,
Couetouſly he preſumed, to be his own confuſion.

The roote of all euill it is, as witneſſeth the Scripture,
An odious and ſecret miſcheif, as any man can ſow,
For what Bloſſom or bud, thinke ye that can proſper,
Or what Flower or Fruite, did euer man ſe grow,
But a roote it muſt haue firſt, this full wel we know,
Beware therfore of it, for this I do confeſſe,
The originall of all ſin, muſt needes be couetouſneſſe.

Of all ſin couetouſeneſſe, firſt poluted Adam,
Linked with infidelitie, Pride, and diſobedience,
Which peſtiferous ſin, dwelleth almoſt in euery man,
For lacke of grace, conſtancy, and good intelligence,
So we like Adams children, forgetting our obedience,
Seking our deſtruction, without cauſe or reward,
Like Achab, and Iezabell, coueting Nabothes vineyard.

Thus couetouſneſſe ſlew Naboth againſt all right,
The nature of it is ſuch, it neuer was founde good,
Wo be to the couetouſneſſe thou wofull wight,
That without all mercy, ſo canſt thirſt for bloud,
Thou broughteſt the generall Deluge at Noes Flud,
And Gehezie by couetouſnes, if ye herken to this ſonge,
Became a foule Lipper, euen all his life longe.

King Dauid by couetouſneſſe deceyued was,
And by concupiſcence the ſtory doth teſtify,
In coueting the onely wife of Vrias,
Greatly offended Gods deuine maieſty,
But reproued by Nathan, wept and cried bitterly,
Serche now the ſcripture, and do what you can,
For nothing is founde worſe, then a couetous man.

He that delighteth in couetoufnes, hath his foule to fell,
Thus faith Sirach, to fuch as they are,
Chrift by Iuftice muft condempne fuch to hell,
As maketh Marchandice of any fuch ware,
The couetous man doth alwaies both fcrape and fpare,
Still to fatiffie, but his greedie defire,
Which at laft fhall bring him to vnquenchable fier.

In gathering therfore of Riches, be not to bolde,
For with affurance they are but as dunge,
For when many finnes are waxen olde,
Then Couetoufneffe will feeme moft yonge,
This my Pen vttereth in fteede of my tunge,
The children of the couetous beyng ftoute and braue,
Daily wifheth in their harts, to fe there fathers graue.

Locke not in thy breaft this finfull couetoufnes,
Fofter it not vp, for any flattering fees:
Beware and be not nurce to fuch wickednes,
Leaft thou be founde as Droane amonge Bees,
Not efteemed in common wealth, but as rotten trees,
Worthy to be brent where euer thou dwell,
According to Gods prouidence, fier brandes in Hell.

Herod the kinge coueted to flea the onely Lorde,
Refifting thereby his only faluation,
As too manie there be that hateth Gods worde,
And fhall therefore receiue dampnation,
The fecond of Mathewe maketh declaracion,
How Herode coueted a kingdome not permanent,
And therfore flew many a yonge Innocent.

Some coueteth to vie both houfe and lande,
But hofpitalitee they will none keepe,
For Couetoufneffe taketh cruell thinges in hande,
Deuouring the poore as the Wolfe doth the fheepe,
In fecuritie of finne, they are rockt faft a fleape,
Night and day caringe for thinges that be vaine,
But wotteth not who fhalbe lorde of al his trauel & paine.

Sainct Barnards Chariot they will ride in,
Wherin let them continew and dwell:
Which named is Securitie of vice and fin,
Leading them poaft to the Deuill of Hell,
For fuch myzers haue their foules to fell,
Foure wheeles it hath to carie on the fame,
Of all which foure I will fhew you the name.

The firſt wheele is called Gredie deſire,
Ingratitude, and contempt of God for other twaine,
And forgetfulneſſe of Death, therto they require,
Which foure wheeles do continew and remaine,
To the Charet of Auarice which is led certaine,
By three ſtrong horſes which runneth forth the race,
Named, paſt ſhame, paſt repentaunce, and paſt grace.

To this Chariot, a careleſſe Carter they muſt haue,
Whoſe name is called Neuer contente,
His whip in his hande, like a cruell ſtaue:
With two ſtringes called wilful paine, & reſtleſſe tormēt
Theſe are ordeyned for euerlaſting puniſhment,
To belong to this Chariot, for their negligence,
To carie away couetous perſons frō good mens preſence.

This Chariot of Auarice with his horſes ſo fell,
Daily is ſet a worke toto [*sic*] in many a place:
But whether goeth this Chariot I pray you now tell,
Some thinke to Sathan to be reſident in place,
Caried away by violence from all mercy and grace,
To follow the generacion of vngodly ſtore,
Neuer to haue mercy nor ſe light any more.

Seing couetouſneſſe doth rob vs of mercie and grace,
Being the roote of all ſinne and wickedneſſe,
Let vs remember whilſt we haue ſpace,
Calling to god to be our righteouſneſſe,
To ayde and ſuccour vs, in all diſtreſſe,
And now to couet his euerlaſting preſence,
With him to raigne for euer when we depart hence.

What is the cauſe of both ſacralige and Simony,
I will now declare and manifeſtly expreſſe,
And ſhew the iniciation of deteſtable vſery,
Now being compelled the truth to confeſſe,
The origenall of both is very couetouſneſſe,
Likewiſe of Bankeroutes and Informers as I here tell,
Couetouſneſſe lately inuented by Sathans counſell.

FINIS.　　(φ) W. Fering.

❡ Imprinted at London in Fleetſtreete, | by William How, for Richarde Iohnes: | and are to be ſolde at his ſhop vnder | the Lotterie houſe.

In the Stationers' Registers for 1566–67 it is mentioned that a licence was granted to Richard Jones for printing 'a newe yeres geſte' (Arber's *Transcript*, i. 336). Again, in 1567–68, William Griffith was permitted to print 'a boke' of the same title (Arber, i. 359). There is, however, no entry of an issue in the year mentioned on the ballad.

Concerning W. Fering, the author, information is not forthcoming, nor are any other works by him known.

The ballad is printed in two columns within a line border.

47.

A Moorning Diti vpon the Deceas of the High and Mighti*| Prins Henry
Earl of Arundel, The auncient & Primer Coounte of England, and right honorabl
Baron *Mautrauers &|Clun: one of Oour moſt gracious Queen Elizabeths Maieſteez moſt honorabl
priuy Coounſel, and of the right nobl Order of*|the Garter the eldeſt Knight: that departed
in the Lord at hiz Place by Toour hil ny London, on Thurzday Saint Matthiez|day
the latter xxiiii. of February in the xxii. yeer of her highnes moſt proſperoous
Rein. 1579.

CArez & complaints that ruful moornings may purport,
 Proceding from a minde with woez oppreſt:
  A heauy hart dooun ſunk within the breſt,
A damped coountenauns deuoid of all comfort,
  May beſt beſeem the ſtate of woful wight:
And ſo may ſorroz ſmart, vs rightfully compell
  With ſighs profoound bewail in careful plight,
The late deceas of him whooz honor did excell,
Henri that nobl Prins the *Earl of Arundell.*

> Defcended
> from Caro-
> lus magnus
> who died
> at Aix. 815.

His firſt Wife Mary the Lord Marques Dorſets daughter. Lady Iane maried to Iohn Lord Lumley. Lady Mary maried to Thomas Duke of Norfolk.

Born & allyed in Line long & Heroicall,
  Coomly in foorm of featurez & perſonage,
  Matched in hy & equall mariage,
Parent to one woorthy Lord & Ladyz twoo, withall:
  For the rare bloomz of tru Nobilitee
That firſt oout budded in hiz tender ſpring,
  The Earl hiz Father yet aliue, & hee
But Lord Mautrauers: Oour late moſt famoous King
Of Callis too him gaue the truſt & goouerning.

> Henry lord
> Matrauers
>
> William
> Anno. xxx.
> Hen. viii.

The weighty charge whearof when he had vnderfong,
  He ranſakld the orderz olld & nu,
  The good he held in execution du,
The bad he brake, and ay by Iuſtis righted wrong:
  With the fine French he tempred in ſuch ſort
Az for hiz Proowes great & Pollecyz agen,
  For Fame to Prinz & ſafety to the Fort,
Both far & neer it waz pronoounced of all men,
That Callis neuer had like Capitain az then.

> **Captain of Calles v. yeeres.**

Lord Marſhall at the ſeege of Bullen. An. xxxv. Henry viii.

Oour King him made vpon this fiue yeerz nobl ſay,
  At Bullen ſeege by Marſhall of hiz hoſt:
  Wheraz hiz peinz his daungerz with the moſt,
Hiz valiauns by hart & hand waz prompt all way.
  And though a molehil to a moount be ſmall,
For certein truth yet this the writer bringz to minde,
  Whoo ſerued him thear at theez moſt actionz all:
And for the grace enteer that euer he did finde,
May moſt deplore hiz death, but honor all his kinde.

* In this copy, as well as in that belonging to the Society of Antiquaries, the words 'High and Mighti' have been erased and 'Moſt Nobl' written in their place.

xxxv. Hen.
viii.
The Prins benign anon foon az the tooun he wan,
    For feruis hy doon by this nobl Peer,
    Chaz him too be one of hiz Coounfel neer,
Lord Chamberlain allfo : which Honorz after than
    King Edward gaue him : but Queen Mary made,
Him Prezident of Coounfel and Lord Stuard too be :
Anno i.
Regine
Elizabeth.
    Of our Queen eak that dignitee he hade.
So az a thing it iz right euident to fe,
In hoow great grace With all hiz Soouerainz waz he.

The higher karged fhip, and deepar it dooth draw,
    The daunger more of ftorm of rok & fand,
    And blafts may blo that no ftate can withftand.
At anker holld of Fortitude when roze a flaw,
    He lay, with honor till he cam to port.
And az he thought none praized vertu az they ow,
    Onles their deedz tru vertu did reaport,
He furely for hiz part, commended vertu fo,
Az waz hiz Embleam, *Laus Virtutis Actio.*

For woorthy pleazurz ells : hiz Hors & Armour fitch,
    Hiz fkil profoound in both, his folem Queer
    By vois & Inftruments fo fweet to heer,
Hiz Iewelz, Antiquiteez, fo many rare & ritch,
    Hiz Tablz, Cloks, & his fymmetricall
Biildingz, fo fumptuooufly adoournd in euery part :
    For eend, his exquizit appointments all
So excellent for coft, for hy deuife & art,
Az might be fignz certain of hiz fo nobl hart.

For feruis then, for honor, or for hiz Princez pleazure,
    Hoow mooch ioyd he thear too be liberall?
    Of hart fynceer toward the Noblz all,
Too State of life he made his Birthdegree his meazure,
    Ootherz merit fmall, mooch he wolld auauns
Boounteous, benign, releeuing many greeuous gronez,
    In freendfhip firm for ony chaunge or chauns.
But ah for wo : deaf death not moouabl by monez,
All theez hiz fhining lights quite quenched hath at onez.
Twife Em-
baffadour
to King
Phillip in
Flaunderz
and cheef
Cōmifioner
in Queene
Maryes
dayes.

Obfcuring orguliooufly by dark & deadly blaft,
    The luftr of Iewell, the more ineftimabl,
    Az iz the lofs fo far irreperabl :
An Earl, a Peer, a Prins, the only & the laft
    Of that fo hy *Fitzallenz* name & blood,
But why fo fharp O Memory dooft thoou declare
    Theez groūdz of greeuez? more meet wear for thy mood
Sum *Opium* for fleep or ells white *Nenuphare,*
A fooup of *Lethes* lake for to forget thy care.

But noow, az wants a cheef one amoong the States hy,
  So Nobl youth, & all of gentl hart :
    The Herallds fage, the wize & learnd in Art,
This forlorn fkath alas bewail may rufully
  And thoou infauft day, difmoll, bifextill,
Not hallf by Charlez birth & coronation fight
  So good, az too the Earl of Flaunders ill
And too French Frauncis eak. O cruell in thy fpight
Wo woorth the tune that noow fo foon yᵗ camft too light.

Prou. 17   But fins that, heauy fprite dooth freat the minde to nought,
  Driez vp the bonez & gallz the hart fo fore,
    Healps not the cafe (God wot) a whit the more,
By wizdoom then bethink we, heerin az we ought,
  Firft yᵗ this Peer (hoow euer wear the cafe)
With looue of all Eftatz in harts finceer enrolld,
Prou.   In honor pure did run hiz nobl rafe,
Ibidem Then faw his Childerz Children (a crooun to hiz yeerz olld)
Az Graūdfire (to their glory) eak him they did behold.

Whoo wear fo vertuous all of minde & inclination
  As God took them, the fooner to be bleft :
    Yet heer left one to coounteruail the reft,
Of whooz encreafing honor fuch iz the expectation
  That in a vitall State & Dignitee
Az he fucceedz & luckily enioyz the fame,
  So hope iz that through Gods benignitee :
By him fhall glitter long in honor & in fame,
The bright fhine of yᵗ magnific *Arundelli* name.

Bethink we eak hoow well he difpozed thingz eachon,
  What tender woords our Queen vntoo him fent :
    Wherat his hart did earn, hiz eiz relent,
Reizd vp hiz febl Sprite, that then by him anon
  Intoo the Lords handz recommended is.
In Fame & in Succeffion fins heer he liueth ay,
  In Soul allfo too euerlafting blis
Let vs by folas fuppl oour forroz az we may,
And hope in Chrifte to haue a ioyful meeting day.

Deuinctiffimò (pro facultate) Arundelius. Guil. P. G.

¶ Born on Saint Georgez day 1512. Liued a Coounfeller and in great Officez 43. yeer. Buryed at Arundell in Suffex Tuifday the 22. of March An. R. R. E. 22.

¶ Imprinted at London by Iohn Allde.

(side notes:)
Borne at Gaunt 1500. Croound Emperoor at Bononi 1530.

Charlez flain by Con-fpiratoours at Burgis 1127. I. Ti. The french Kings poour flain and he takē at Paui 1525. Io.

Henry Fitz-Alan, twelfth Earl of Arundel, was a godson of King Henry VIII, and at an early age entered the royal household. He held successively the positions of deputy of Calais, 'marshal of the field' at the siege of Boulogne, and lord chamberlain. At the accession of Edward VI, he became a member of the Council where he opposed the dukes of Somerset and Northumberland. The unfounded accusations of his enemies caused him to be sent to the Tower, from whence he was eventually released.

Arundel was speedily revenged. Northumberland's attempt to place Lady Jane Grey on the throne was openly approved by Arundel, while the earl was in secret communication with Mary. When the duke left London Arundel proclaimed Mary queen, and took a prominent part in the events which terminated with the execution of his rival. Throughout Mary's reign Arundel retained influence and held many high offices, and Elizabeth, though she distrusted him and refused him in marriage, could not afford to dismiss so powerful a subject. In 1569, however, he retired from Court owing to the discovery that he was implicated in a plan for marrying Mary, Queen of Scots, to his widowed son-in-law Norfolk. Arundel was a skilful military commander, a particularly astute politician, and seems to have fairly earned Froude's verdict that 'he moved in a cloud, suspected of aims he would not avow, without a conviction, without a purpose, feared by all men and trusted by none'.

This ballad was licensed to John Allde on March 28, 1580 (Arber's *Transcript*, ii. 367). There is a second copy in the library of the Society of Antiquaries (Lemon, *Catalogue*, p. 24). J. P. Collier interpreted the signature 'Guil. P. G.' to be an abbreviation of 'Gulielmus Painter Gentleman'. It is difficult, however, to reconcile this with the statement contained in the seventh line of the fourth stanza of the ballad, for there are no grounds for supposing that the author of the 'Palace of Pleasure' was ever out of England or at any period took part in military operations.

The verses are further endowed with interest from the fact that they record an early attempt at phonetic spelling. Ten years previously John Hart published his 'Orthographie conteyning the due order and reason, howe to write or painte thimage of mannes voice, moste like to the life or nature', and in the year of Arundel's 'moorning diti' was issued 'Bullokars booke at large, for the Amendment of orthographie for Englifh fpeech'. Sir Thomas Smith and Sir John Cheke were pioneers in the same direction.

The ballad is arranged in two columns, beneath which is printed the concluding stanza.

48

≈ An Epitaph, or funerall inſcription, vpon the godlie life and death of the Right | *worſhipfull Maiſter William Lambe Eſquire, Founder of the new Conduit in Hol*|borne, &c. Deceaſed the one and twentith of April, and intumbed in S. Faiths Church | *vnder Powles, the ſixt of Maie next and immediatly following.* | Anno. 1580. Deuiſed by *Abraham Fleming.*

ALl fleſh is graſſe, the *Scripture ſaith, and vadeth like a flowre,
And nothing to be permanent, can vaunt it hath the powre.
The faireſt and the fouleſt thing, that any man can name,
Hath but a time to liue and die, in honour or in ſhame.
No artificiall workemanſhip, no notable deuiſe,
No valiant act, no noble deede, no puiſſant enterpriſe,
But as in time triumphantly, it challengeth renowne,
Euen ſo in time from honours hight, at laſt it tumbleth downe.
The doubtfull ſtate of mortall man, an argument may bee,
That nothing is perpetuall, which glanſing eie doeth ſee,
But tranſitorie, fraile, and vaine, as time demandes his fee.
The Sunne & Moone* ſhall haue their chaunge, though glorioufly they ſhine,
The gliſtering Starres in firmament, from brightnes ſhall decline,
The ſcattered cloudes, like winding worme, or ſcortched parchment ſcroll,
Shall ſhrinke together, as in ſkies they are conſtraind to roll.
Then, ſith celeſtiall creatures ſtate, ſo alterable is,
That vaine we count each earthlie thing, I iudge it not amis.
We ſee the ſeaſons of the yeare, ſucceſſiuely inſue,
Firſt nipping Winters bluſtring blaſts, with froſts as ſtiffe as glue,
Then pleaſant Spring with colours clad, of yellow, greene, and blue:
Next which comes ripening Summer in, and then doth follow faſt,
Quicke Harueſt for the huſbandman, t'acquite his charges paſt,
No time hath this prerogatiue, for euermore to laſt.
Lo thus in circle runs the yeare, with compaſſe round about,
And his appointed age the world, by portions weareth out.
Count what we can moſt excellent, needes muſt it haue an ende,
Againſt decay there is no force, nor fortreſſe to defende.
How* many Cities ſtately built, of timber, lime and ſtone,
Are come to naught, and in their place a deſert left alone?
Pompe maketh not perpetuall, although it beare a port,
A Maigame I may name it well, a paſtime and a ſport,
Whoſe glorie glides and ſlips away, whoſe pleaſure is but ſhort.
Like Plaiers in an Enterlude, vpon a common ſtage,
One repreſenting luſtie youth, another crooked age,
One royall Principalitie, another Courtlie ſtate,
One like a Iudge doth ſit on bench, another begges at gate,
Thus counterfet they all degrees, vntill the play be donne:
Euen ſo is man vpon the earth, ſince firſt his ſtocke begonne.
For Adam, though he liued long, yet dead he was at laſt,
The Patriarchs and Prophets olde, their pilgrimage haue paſt:

*Eſaie. 40. 6.
Eccl. 14. 17. 18
1 Pet. 1. 24.
Iames. 1. 10.
and in many places more, this with the like compariſons are vſuall.

* An alluſiõ to the conſummation of this world, when all things ſhal paſſe awaye & vaniſh.

* The like ſpeach is in *Tullies* Epiſtles familiar, written by *Sulpicius* to *Cicero*, touching the death of his daughter *Tullia*, wife to *Dolabella.*

(137)

Kings haue refigned vp their crownes, and titles of their thrones,
And many a politike Gouernour in graue hath laid his bones,
This proue the *fundrie writings fet, on their Sepulchre ftones.
The wifedome of the wife is vaine, the ftrong mans ftrength a toy,
If they by them as inftruments, feeke length of life t' enioy :
And as for wealth, it is but winde, for riches haue no holde,
The monied man muft thinke to die, if once he waxeth olde.
Lo, lo, a prefent patterne here, all you that lift to learne,
By viewing of this corps corrupt, what you fhall be difcearne.
Sometime he was, as others be, a quicke and liuing man,
But wounded with the dart of death, reuiue him nothing can.
His youthfull yeares, as others haue, this good Efquire hath had,
And crooked age by creeping on, with weakeneffe ficke and fad,
In winding fheete at head and foote, faft knit his corps hath clad.
Rich in his life, *poore at his death, a fteward of the Lordes,
His talent Chriftianly laide out, with Gods good will accordes.
And as in th'Actes, Cornelius deedes, beare witneffe of his faith,
(For outwarde workes before the world, beleefe within bewraith :)
So this religious Gentleman, a Patrone to the poore,
In allies and in lanes abrode, at home in th' entrie doore,
In open ftreete, in holie Church, in many a corners crooke,
(Where, for the poore and impotent, whom kith and kin forfooke,
With charitable zeale inflamde, this lowelie Lambe did looke,)
His almes he hath diftributed, and giuen as he fawe neede,
Cloth for the backe, meate for the mouth, the hungrie foule to feede.
As louing as a Lambe he liud, and verifide his name,
He was an eie vnto the blind, a legge vnto the lame,
A comfort to the comfortles, a fuccour to the ficke,
A father to the fatherles, whome nipping neede did pricke,
A hufband to the defolate, and widowe left alone,
A fauourer and a freend to all, an enimie to none,
Now *fuch as had his wooll to weare, lament of him the lacke,
His flefh did fill their bellies full, his fleefe kept warme their backe,
His pence and pounds preferued them, from many a wringing wracke.
No miffe of mercie was in him, for iointly hart and hand,
Were pliant to fupplie the wantes, of many in this land.
For this he knew, by giuing them, he lent vnto the Lord :
His humblenes no homelines, of ficklie foule abhord.
So that I may conclude of him, as needes conclude I muft,
If workes may fimply of themfelues, make righteous men and iuft,
(Which I denie, for vnto faith this office is aflinde :)
Then is he fanctifide from finne, and cleanfd in hart and minde.
The fruites of faith which flourifhed, in him whiles he did liue,
His diuerfe diftributions, and giftes which he did giue,
The monuments which he hath left, behind him being ded,
Are fignes that *Chrift our Shepherd hath, vnto his fheepfold led,
This louing Lambe, who like a Lambe dide meekely in his bed :
His bodie buried in the ground, there to confume to duft,
His foule in Abrahams bofome reftes, in quietneffe I truft :
A place allotted vnto Lambs, there to poffeffe in peace,
Such bleffings as this Lambe enioyes, whofe like the Lord increafe,
For Iefus fake the fpotleffe Lambe.   And here my penne fhall ceafe.

* Memorials of their mortalitie which fometime liued in all kind of felicitie.

* For I haue heard it credibly reported, that he left little or nothing vndiftributed.

* Poore people fhall fone feele the loffe of this Lambe by the lacke of their relief.

* For Chrift will repay ye a thoufand fold, which is giuen to ye fuccourles.

As Euening fhadowe flides,
And Seas do varie tides,
So all the pranking prides,
Of worldlie glorie glides:
Gods worde, the guide of guides,
For euermore abides.

Imprinted at London by Henrie Denham, for Thomas Turner,
and are to be folde at his fhop at Guild-hall gate.

Holinshed and Stow give full accounts of Lamb and his many benefactions: to the gift mentioned in the title of this ballad the 'Annals' (1615, p. 681) refer: 'The 26. of March, the new Conduit neare vnto Oldborne, and a ftandart with the cocke at Oldborne bridge, were begun to bee founded by William Lambe, fometime gentleman of the chappell to king Henry the eight, now citizen and clothworker of London, the water whereof is conueyed in pipes of leade from diuers fprings to one head, and from thence to the faid conduit and ftandart more then 2000. yards in length, al which of his owne cofts and charges, amounting to the fumme of 15,000. pounds, was fully finifhed the 24. of Auguft in the fame yeare.'

These conduits or leaden cisterns, castellated with stone, were fed through pipes running from springs situated in the suburbs of London. One at West Cheap is said to have been erected as early as 1285. The conduits were the city's sole source of water-supply until 1613, when Sir Hugh Middleton completed the New River canal from the Chadwell and Amwell near Ware to Islington. Lamb's name is preserved in Lamb's Conduit Street. The conduit is said to have been removed in 1746.

This Epitaph was not entered in the Registers of the Stationers' Company, although on April 28, 1580, a licence was granted for '*A memoriall of ye famous monumentes and charitable Almes deedes of ye right*

worfhipfull mafter William Lambe efquier . . . Deceafed the xxjth of Aprill 1580' (Arber's *Transcript*, ii. 369). An octavo volume by Abraham Fleming, with title answering to this description, is in the library of the British Museum.

Thomas Turner, the publisher of the 'Memoriall' and the 'Epitaph', received license to print one other book '*a pretie pallace of prudence gathered furthe of the pithie preceptes of graue* Cato' (Arber, ii. 316). He published between 1577 and 1580, and is mentioned in the Registers of the Stationers' Company as late as July 1, 1592 (Arber, ii. 710).

Abraham Fleming, the author, was born about 1552. After proceeding to Cambridge he took orders and was appointed chaplain to the Countess of Nottingham. From Archbishop Whitgift he received the rectory of St. Pancras, Soper Lane, London. Fleming died in 1607, and was buried at Bottesford in Leicestershire. He was the author of a number of historical and poetical works, a list of which is given in Cooper's 'Athenae Cantabrigienses': the more important are mentioned in the 'Dictionary of National Biography'.

The ballad is neatly printed in two columns. On the left-hand side of the six concluding lines, which are printed in the middle of the sheet, is a medallion bearing a representation of a Lamb around which are printed the words 'Sacrifizio Agnello Saluazione Mundo'; on the left hand is a shield of arms.

49

¶ A Supplication to Eldertonne, for Leaches vnlewdnes:
Defiring him to pardone, his manifeft vnrudenes.

GOod gentle maifter Eldertonne,
    may I not you intrete?
To pardō Leache yᵗ he hath dōne,
    and not with him to frete?

For I confeffe and know the fame,
    it was for lack of lewdnes:
That he fo blafde abrode your name,
    therfore forgiue his rudenes.

For you maye fee he is in deed,
    an vnrude fimple man:
Therfore of him take you no heed,
    fithe nurture none he can.

A feely fimple man hee is,
    as proof may well be made:
For no more wit he hath ywⁱˢ
    but to call a fpade, a fpade.

Therefore though that your filthy rymes,
    he filthy name to bee:
Accufe him not I fay of crimes,
    you heare his qualitie.

It was no doubt vnhomely donne,
    to chalenge in fuch cafe:
So fyne a felow as Eldertonne,
    that hath fo fayre a face.

But though your face be neuer fo riche,
    fo precious or fo gay:
Yet wil he fcratche it if it itche,
    the paines for to delay.

Wherfore you ought him thankes to geue,
    that worketh you fuche good:
And not to fhake him by the fleeue,
    to wreke your angry moode.

I may wel mufe and meruel much,
 what might be your intent:
Sith that you proue your felfe one fuch,
 as truthe cannot content.

You fhowe that Leache you doo contemne,
 euen by the felf fame reed:
Wherin you doo your felf condemne,
 I wifhe you wolde take heed.

You binde it vp with othes inow,
 in faith, in faith, faye yee:
But by fuch frutes a man may know,
 the goodnes of the tree.

A fhame it is that you fhould bring,
 thexample of Chrift I fay:
And eke forthwith the felf fame thing,
 fo fore to difobey.

For with the breache of charitie,
 you doo him fharply charge:
And by and by outragioufly,
 you raile on him at large.

Thus Sathan alfo for his turne,
 the fcriptures can out pike:
And as you wel his leffon learne,
 fo are your deedes a like.

Your harte is vaine and bent to euill,
 your toung alfo is naught:
How can it be then but the deuil,
 muft rule both toung and thought.

But hereby men may eafely fpie,
 how you doo Leache abufe:
Sith that your quarrell for to trie,
 by fcripture you refufe.

Therfore you go about I fee,
 the fcripture fet aparte:
Vnto your toies and vanitie,
 his penne for to conuart.

And if in deed you could him caufe,
 from fcripture for to flie:
No doubt forfoth but claufe by claufe,
 much brauery fhould we fee.

Then wolde you leke then wold you laffe,
  as you doo make reporte:
Then wold you anfwere euery ftaffe,
  and that in fugred forte.

In fugred forte? nay poifened then,
  I might it better call:
Although it fugred femes to men,
  which are in finfull thrall.

A worthy worke it is doubtles,
  and ful of lerned fkill:
Wherby appeareth your fhameles,
  and wilful wicked will.

And where you write that fecretly,
  your fault he fhould haue tolde;
That might not be fith openly,
  your felfe did it vpholde.

And where as he ful fkilfully,
  takes fcriptures for his ftaie:
You fay in deed that wickedly,
  he vfeth them alwaie.

It is not ftreight way proued fo,
  when that you haue it faid:
Except you bring a profe therto,
  which cannot be denaid.

As if, that I fhould fay in deed,
  you were an honeft man:
All wife men might me then deride,
  fith proue it not I can.

I wolde now wifhe you fhould forget,
  his fcience to deface:
For honeftly a man may get,
  his liuing in that race.

Muche better then the witte to fpend,
  a Parafite to play:
The bad to pleafe, the good to offend,
  and play the foole all day.

And him me thinkes you fhould not blame,
  that can wel fhape a hofe:
For he may likewife cut and frame,
  a cafe for your riche nofe.

To make a hofe is no fuche fhame,
  to Leache in his degree:
As is your nofe a glorious fame,
  vppon your face to fee.

It doth become you very ill,
  to talke fo of your taile:
But you fhal there your toung hold ftill,
  as fitte for tonges that raile.

And if you ftill thus doo deny,
  your knauerie to forbeare:
You fhal therin haue victory,
  the garland you fhall weare.

But heere I muft ful fore lament,
  the counfel you ftill geue:
To your vile Ione, not to repent,
  but beaftly ftill to liue.

O wicked man darfte thou be bolde,
  fuche finful feed to fowe?
And eke the fame for to vpholde,
  in finful hartes to growe?

Oh Lord fhal whoredom thus preuaile?
  fhal men thus finne mainteine?
Is this a chriften common weale,
  and can fuch filth fufteine?

O magiftrates play Phinehes parte?
  towardes fuche be not to milde:
Which may procure moft greuous fmart,
  to many a mothers childe.

The whoredom of one heretofore,
  Great plagues to many hath brought:
Although the lord eftfones therfore,
  in him repentance wrought.

What fhal our lot be then Oh Lord?
  which fofter fuche foule fwine:
As liue a life to bee abhorde,
  yet glory and ioye therein?

Repent (O wretche) and cal for grace,
  leaue of thefe wicked toyes:
Left Sathan reache thee fower fauce,
  to thefe thy pleafant ioyes.

Now fir, if Leache, as you doe tell,
  femes fondly thinges to knit:
It is becaufe you cannot well,
  them home with reafon hit.

A homely cloke wold ferue full wel,
  is there none to be had?
If Eldertonne of none heare tell,
  I doubt he will goe mad.

But if as you doo threaten, fo
  you fall for to bee wood:
You fhall ftreight waies to Bedlem go,
  to tame your madding mood.

Now Eldertonne I muft defire,
  you to hold Leache excufde:
For that no reafon doth appeere,
  why he fhuld fo be vfde.

And fith that I thus curteoufly,
  for Leache doo you intreat:
Your phrenfie fo to fatiffy,
  you need no more to freat.

Wherfore gentle Maifte Elderton,
  as I may doo you pleafure:
Graunt this my fupplication,
  which is not out of meafure.

    And thus fubfcribed,
    The firft day of Iune:
    At which time you faid,
    Beginneth your fume.

        φ Willyam Fulwod.

    ¶ Imprinted at London at the Long fhop
adioining vnto Saint Mildreds Church in the Pultry
          by Iohn Alde.

From this ballad it would seem that Elderton had been attacked in some insulting verses written by one Leach, a hosier, and that Fulwood, in order to keep them alive, indites others, the opening lines of which might lead one to suppose that his object was to soothe the feelings of the injured poetaster; but the later stanzas show that this was far from being his real object.

William Fulwood, merchant taylor, is known as the translator of Grataroli's 'Caftel of Memorie', 1562, and the writer of an original work entitled 'The Enímie of Idleneffe', 1568. His name appears on a curious broadside, 'A Spectacle for Pe=iu=e=s,' a copy of which is in the library of the Society of Antiquaries (R. Lemon's *Catalogue*, 1866, p. 29). From 1580 onward more than one petition was made to the Council complaining that a person named Fulwood had wrongfully withheld certain sums of money (Calendar of State Papers, *Domestic*). Two ballads reprinted by Mr. Henry Huth in 'Ancient Ballads and Broadsides'—'The Shape of ii mõfters MDLxii' and 'A new Ballad againft vnthrifts'—both published by John Allde, may be assigned to Fulwood. The 'Supplication to Eldertonne' was reprinted in J. P. Collier's 'Old Ballads' (Percy Society, 1840). It is printed in three columns.

50

The end and Confeſſion of Iohn Felton
who ſuffred in Paules Churcheyeard in London,
the .viii. of Auguſt, for high Treaſon. 1570.

EChe man deſiers to haue reporte,
  of newes both ſtrange and rare:
And couits for to know thoſe thinges,
  whereby they may be ware.
For to auoyde thoſe doynges greate,
  that might on them befall:
For by example are they taught
  to do, and what they ſhall
Receiue for their malicious mindes,
  and wicked Treaſons greate:
As now of late it hath been ſeen
  through Iuſtice iudgements ſeate.
That holdes the ſworde to do the right,
  and ſtrike where blowes ſhould fall:
And puniſh for their wicked liues,
  eche one whom ſhe doth call.
The poore, the ritche, the learnd, yᵉ wiſe
  the begger and the ſnudge:
The Kynge ſomtime too hath it felt,
  aſwell as hath the drudge.
Wherefore be lawes decreed and made
  but for to puniſh thoſe,
That will not by theyr Prince be rewld
  but ſeemes to be theyr foes.
As now is ſeene by Felton lo,
  that lately here did die,
In Paules Churchyarde he left his life,
  on Galows taule and hie.
Who from the priſon where he lay,
  was drawne on Hardell there:
For good example of all ſuch,
  that they might take the feare.
For to beware of ſuche like facte,
  as well in worde as deede:
Leaſt they for theyr like hier at laſt
  no better like to ſpeede.
Now marke his ende and what I ſhall
  reporte here of his death:
For why theſe eares of mine did here,
  and iyes while that his breath

Remained in his wicked corps,
  which ftubbornly did die:
As one me thought fomthing beftraught
  through Treafons crueltie.
His Gowne of Grograin he put of,
  which on his backe he had:
And eke his Doublet which was made
  of Sattin fomwhat fad.
Into his Shirte he then was ftript,
  and vp the Ladder he
Did mount, for to receaue that death,
  that eche man there might fe.
Thefe wordes he fpake, and faid alowde
  my Maifters all and fome:
One thinge I haue to fay to you,
  now that I here am come.
That is, I pray you all with me
  beare recorde what I fay:
I here proteft before you all,
  this prefent dieyng day,
That I was neuer Traytour fure,
  nor Treafon to my Queene
Did neuer do, nor neuer thought,
  that euer hath been feene.
And for the facte wherefore I die,
  I can it not denie:
But at the Gate where as the Bull
  was hanged, there was I,
In company, on more with me,
  did hange it vp together:
And though in place, I had not bin,
  it had not fcaped euer.
From hanging vp, for furedly,
  for that fame prefent day:
It had bin hanged, in that place,
  though I had been away.
Then fayde the Shreue, vnto him,
  Oh Felton do remember:
That thou haft bin, a Traytour great
  and to the Queene offender.
And furely thou mofte Trayteroufly,
  and ftubbornly haft thou fought,
The beft thou couldft to go aboute,
  thy Prince to bringe to nought.
And eke the Realme and all the reft,
  as mutche as in thee lay,
Thou foughft by thy Traiterous harte,
  to bringe vnto decay.
Therfore call vnto God the Lord,
  and pray him from thy hart:
That he receaue thy foule to reft,
  when thou from hence fhalt part.

Well fo I do, and here I craue,
  you all good people pray
For me, that ready is to dye,
  and then began to fay,
Into thy hands, Oh Lord my God,
  I yeeld my Soule and Breath:
For thou haft me redeemd, I fay,
  with thy moft precious death.
In manus tuas Domine,
  and fo the reft he fayde,
The Hangman then did throwe him of,
  and fo his breath was ftaide.
He hanged theare vpon the Tree,
  and in a litle fpace:
They cut him downe incontinent,
  that Iuftice might take place.
Wheras he quartred fhoulde be,
  according to the Lawe:
And to the Iudgement that he had,
  to make thofe ftande in awe.
That be of his affinitie:
  and furely there be fome,
That thinkes that he deferude not death
  in all that he hath don.
He then difmembred was ftraight way,
  when he had ended that:
His Belly ripped open wide,
  his Bowels all he gat.
And to the fire he ftraight them threwe,
  which ready there was made:
And there confumed all to duft,
  as is the fiers trade.
His Head cut of, the Hangman then,
  did take it vp in hand:
And vp alofte he did it fhowe,
  to all that there did ftand.
And then his body in Fowre partes,
  was quartred in that place:
More pitty that his Traytorous Hart,
  could take no better grace.
And thus he had his iuft defarte,
  as well he had deferued:
I would the reft that not repents,
  were likewife alfo ferued.
Beware you Papifts all beware,
  be true vnto your Queene:
Let not your Traiterous hartes be bent
  as heretofore hath been.
Stand not againft the liuing God,
  fpurne not againft his Law:
Kicke not againft the Pricke I fay,
  but haue him ftill in awe.

Be not afhamde to torne in time,
　　fet fhamefaftneffe afide:
No fhame it is to turne to God,
　　though you haue gon far wide,
The farther you haue gon aftray,
　　and wicked wayes hath led,
The ernefter you fhould returne,
　　from that moft wicked Bed,
Wherin you lay afleape long while,
　　forgetting of his grace:
Now call therefore vnto the Lord,
　　to fet you in that place,
Where you may haue eternall reft,
　　and liue in heauen hie:
And reft in Abrahams bofome too,
　　when that you needes muft dye.
And for that grace that God may geue,
　　as I haue fayde before:
I humbly pray continually,
　　both now and euermore.
Our Prince, our Queene Elizabeth,
　　a happy ftate to haue:
Let vs all pray with one accord,
　　her noble grace to faue.
And hir to keepe from all hir foes,
　　and fhield eternally:
From wicked wights that go about,
　　to feeke continually:
Hir whole decay: the Lord defend,
　　hir noble royall hart:
From yeelding to thofe Foes of hirs,
　　that daily plaies their parte.
For to bereeue her of her right,
　　and of hir ftately Crowne:
All thofe (I fay) that fo doth feke,
　　God fhortly throw them downe,
Thus here I end, and once againe,
　　the liuing God I pray:
Our noble Queene Elizabeth,
　　preferue both night and day.

FINIS.　　(ꝗ.) F. G.

❡Imprinted at London, in | Fleetftreete, by William How: | for William Pickering:
and | are to be folde at his fhop | at S. Magnus corner.

John Felton was a man of gentle birth and endowed with considerable wealth. His wife served as a maid of honour to Queen Mary and also to Queen Elizabeth. Felton, inspired by zeal for the Roman faith, in the early hours of May 15, 1570, fastened to the gates of the Bishop of London's palace a copy of the bull of excommunication issued by Pope Pius V against the English queen. The act was readily traced to Felton, who after being racked was hanged, drawn, and quartered. His behaviour at execution was dignified and clearly impressed his persecutors, a fact attested by the writer of the ballad. He is said to have sent a diamond ring to Elizabeth to show that he bore her no malice. As late as 1886 Felton was beatified by Pope Leo XIII. In 1588 a son, Thomas Felton, a Franciscan monk, shared his parent's fate for denying Elizabeth's supremacy of the Church. John Felton, who assassinated the Duke of Buckingham in 1628, may have been a connexion. Both were East Anglians.

Although Felton's acts occasioned the publication of several books and ballads, this particular ballad was not entered at Stationers' Hall. It appears, however, that permission was granted to Richard Jones 'for yᵉ pryntinge of th[e] ende and confyſſion [of] Iohn Fylton' (Arber's *Transcript*, i. 437). This licence refers to 'The ende and Confeſſion of Iohn Felton, the rank Traytour,

that ſet vp the Traiterous Bull on the Byſſhope of London his gate . . . By I. Partridge', an octavo pamphlet, consisting of eight leaves, of which a copy is in the library at St. John's College, Cambridge, reprinted in Morgan's 'Phoenix Britannicus', p. 415, and also in Howell's 'State Trials', i. 1086. Stephen Peele was the author of a ballad, 'A letter to Rome, to declare to yᵉ Pope, Iohn Felton his freend is hangd in a rope . . .', which is reprinted in this volume (p. 203). It is impossible to identify the initials at the close of the ballad. It is printed in three columns.

An exhaustive monograph on William Pickering, the publisher of the Britwell ballad, was contributed by Mr. G. J. Gray to the 'Transactions of the Bibliographical Society' (vol. iv, pp. 57–102).

𝔰𝔦

**¶A difcription of Nortons falcehod
of Yorke fhyre, and of his fatall farewel.**

The fatal fine of Traitours loe:
By Iuftice due, deferuyng foe.

OF late (alas) the great vntruth
  Of Traitours, how it fped:
Who lift to know, fhal here perceaue
  How late allegeance fled.
¶If Riuers rage againft the Sea,
  And fwell with foddeine rayne:
How glad are they to fall agayne,
  And trace their wonted traine?
If fire by force wolde forge the fall
  Of any fumptuoufe place,
If water floods byd him leaue of,
  His flames he wyll difgrace.
If God command the wyndes to ceafe,
  His blaftes are layd full low:
If God command the feas to calme,
  They wyll not rage or flow.
All thinges at Gods commandemēt be,
  If he their ftate regarde:
And no man liues whofe deftinie
  By him is vnpreparde.
But when a man forfakes the fhip,
  And rowles in wallowing waues:
And of his voluntarie wyll,
  His owne good hap depraues:
How fhal he hope to fcape the gulfe?
  How fhal he thinke to deale?
How fhal his fanfie bring him found
  To Safties fhore with fayle?
How fhall his fraight in fine fuccede?
  Alas what fhall he gayne?
What feare by ftorms do make him quake
  How ofte fubiecte to payne?
How fundrie times in Dangers den
  Is throwne the man vnwyfe?
Who climes withouten holde on hye,
  Beware, I him aduize.

All fuch as truft to falfe contracts,
   Or fecret harmes confpire?
Be fure, with Nortons they fhal tafte
   A right deferued hire.
They can not looke for better fpeede,
   No death for fuch too fell?
God grant the iuftice of the worlde
   Put by the paynes of hell.
For fuch a penfiue cafe it is,
   That Englifh harts did dare
To paffe the boundes of duties lawe,
   Or of their cuntrie care.
And mercie hath fo long releaft
   Offendours (God doth know)
And bountie of our curteous Queene
   Too long hath fpared her foe.
But God, whofe grace infpires her harte,
   Wyll not abyde the fpight
Of Rebels rage, who rampe to reach
   From her, her title quight.
Although fhee flowe in pitifull zeale,
   And loueth to fucke no blood :
Yet God a caueat wyll her lend
   T'appeafe thofe Vipers moode.
A man that fees his houfe on fire,
   Wyll feke to quench the flame :
Els from the fpoyle fome parte conuey,
   Els feke the heate to tame.
Who fees a penthoufe wether beate,
   And heares a boiftroufe wynde :
But heedefull fafetie of himfelfe,
   Wyll force him fuccour fynde?
The pitifull pacient Pellican,
   Her blood although fhee fhed :
Yet wyll fhee feme her date to end,
   Or care her young be fped.
The Eagle flynges her yong ones downe
   That fight of funne refufe :
Vnperfect fowles fhee deadly hates,
   And rightly fuch mis vfe.
The Crane wolde flye vp to the Sunne,
   I heard it once of olde :
And with the kyng of byrdes did ftriue
   By Fame, I heard it tolde.
And downe fhe wolde not fal[farre] no,
   But higher ftyll did mount :
Til paft her reach (faith olde reporte)
   Shame made a backe recou[nt.]
I touch no Armes herein at all
   But fhew a fable wyfe :
Whofe morall fence doth repro[oue]
   Of clymers hye the guyfe.

Who buyldes a houfe of many [ftore]
  and laith not ground worke [fure,]
But doth extorte the ground b[   ]g,
  His buildyng can not dure.
¶ Who fekes furmifing to dif[pofe]
  a Ruler fent by God:
Is fubiect fure, deuoide of grace
  The caufe of his owne rod.
A byrde that wyll her neft defyle
  By right fhould loofe a wyng:
And then is fhee no flying fowle,
  But flow as other thyng.
And he that lofeth all at games,
  Or fpendes in fowle exceffe:
And hopes by haps to heale his harme,
  Muft drinke of deare diftreffe.
To fpeake of brydles to reftrayne
  This wylfull wayward crewe:
They care not for the booke of God,
  To Princes, men vntrue.
To cuntrye, caufers of much woe,
  To faithfull freendes, a fall:
And to their owne eftates, a ftyng,
  To others, fharpe as gall.
O Lorde, how long thefe Lizerds lurkt,
  Good God, how great a whyle
Were they in hand with feigned harts
  Their cuntrye to defyle?
How did they frame their furniture?
  How fit they made their tooles:
How Symon fought our englyfh Troie
  To bryng to Romaine fcooles.
How Simon Magus playd his parte,
  How Babilon bawde did rage:
How Bafan bulles begon to bell,
  How Iudas fought his wage.
How Iannes and Iambres did abyde
  The brunt of braineficke acts,
How Dathan, Chore, Abiram feemd
  To dafh our Moyfes facts.
How Romaine marchant fet afrefh
  His pardons braue a fale,
How alwayes fome againft the Truth
  Wolde dreame a fenceles tale.
Gods vicar from his god receaued
  The keyes to lofe and bynd:
Baals chaplein thoght his fire wold [burne]
  Such was his pagan mynd.
Good Lorde how hits the text their acts
  That faith fuch men fhall bee
In their religion hot nor colde
  Of much varietie.

And fundry forts of fects furu[iue]
   Diuifion fhall appeare:
Againft the father, fonne fha[ll ftr]yue,
   Gainft mother, daughter [deare].
Is it not come to paffe trow you?
   Yea, baftards fure they bee,
Who our good mother Queene of [loue]
   Withftand rebelliouflie.
Can God his vengeance long retain
   Where his true feruants feele
Iniurioufe fpights of godleffe men,
   Who turne as doth a wheele?
No no, his fuffryng long (be fure)
   Wyll pay his foes at laft:
His mercye moued once away,
   He fhall them quight out caft.
With fentence iuft for their vntruth,
   And breakyng of his wyll:
The fruits of their fedicious feeds,
   The barnes of earth fhall fyll.
Their foules God wot fore clogd w^t crime
   And their pofteritie
Befpotted fore with their abufe,
   And ftand by their follie.
Their liuyngs left their name a fhame,
   Their deedes with poyfon fped:
Their deathes a wage for want of grace
   Their honours quite is dead.
Their flefh to feede the kytes and crowes
   Their armes a maze for men:
Their guerdon as examples are
   To dafh dolte Dunces den.
Throw vp your fnouts you fluggifh forte
   You mumming mafkyng route:
Extoll your exclamations vp,
   Baals chapleines, champions ftoute.
Make fute for pardons, papifts braue,
   For traitours indulgence:
Send out fome purgatorie fcraps,
   Some Bulls with Peter pence.
O fwarme of Drones, how dare ye ftyl
   With labouryng Bees contend?
You fought for honie from the hiues,
   But gall you found in end.
Thefe wafpes do waft, their ftings be out
   Their fpight wyll not auayle:
Thefe Peacocks proude are naked lefte
   Of their difplayed tayle.
Thefe Turkye cocks in cullour red,
   So long haue lurkt a loofe:
The Bear (although but flow of foote)
   Hath pluct his wynges by proofe.

The Moone her borowed light hath loft,
   Shee wayned as we fee :
Who hoped by hap of others harmes,
   A full Moone once to bee.
The Lyon fuffred long the Bull,
   His noble mynd to trye :
Vntyll the Bull was rageyng wood,
   And from his ftake did hye.
Then time it was to bid him ftay
   Perforce, his hornes to cut :
And make him leaue his rageing tunes
   In fcilence to be put.
And all the calues of Bafan kynd
   Are weaned from their wifh :
The Hircan Tigers tamed now,
   Lemathon eates no fifh.
Beholde before your balefull eyes
   The purchace of your parte,
Suruey your fodeine forrowful fight
   With fighes of dubble harte.
Lament the lacke of your alies
   Religious rebells all :
Bewepe that yll fucceffe of yours,
   Come curfe your fodeine fall.
And when ye haue your guiles out fought
   And all your craft approued,
Peccauimus fhall be your fong
   Your ground worke is remoued.
And looke how Nortons fped their wills
   Euen fo their fect fhall haue,
No better let them hope to gayne
   But gallowes without graue.

       ¶ FINIS.   q̃. William Gibfon.

¶ Imprinted at London by Alexander Lacie, for Henrie Kyrkeham, dwellyng at the figne | of the blacke Boye, at the middle North dore of Paules church.

Christopher Norton was the seventh son of Richard Norton who took part in the Pilgrimage of Grace, and is said to have had ten brothers and six sisters. The entire family was deeply attached to the Roman Catholic faith, and readily joined the rebel earls of Westmorland and Northumberland in their attempt to dethrone Elizabeth. Christopher devoted himself to the personal service of Mary, Queen of Scots, and contrived to obtain admission to Lord Scrope's guard at Bolton Castle, where Mary was in custody. Several plans were tried to effect her escape, but all failed, and Norton was removed from his post. After the collapse of the northern rebellion he and a brother, Thomas Norton, were taken prisoners, brought to London, and on May 27, 1569, executed at Tyburn with the customary barbarity of the period. Other members of the family were more fortunate, some making their escape abroad, while two received pardons. Richard Norton, the father, died at an advanced age in 1588, a pensioner of Philip the Second of Spain.

William Gibson, the author of this ballad, is unknown, and no other works by him are extant. A ballad by Leonard Gibson, entitled 'A very proper dittie : to the tune of Lightie loue', was reprinted by Mr. Henry Huth in 'Ancient Ballads and Broadsides', 1867; while Thomas and Anthony of the same name are known in literature.

In the Registers of the Stationers' Company, 1569–70, is the entry, 'Receuyd of henry kyrkam for his lycenfe for the pryntinge of a ballett intituled *a Dyfcription of Nortons in Yorke fhyre* by Gybfon' (Arber's *Transcript*, i. 414).

The ballad is printed in three columns. A part of the text has sustained some damage.

52

A Moste true and marueilous ftraunge wonder, the lyke hath | feldom ben feene, of .XVII. Monftrous fiffhes, taken in Suffolke, at Downam brydge, within a myle | of Ipfwiche. The .XI. daye of October. In the yeare of our Lorde God. M.D.LX.VIII.

FYrfte you fhall vnderftande, that the begynners firft Venterers | to take thefe fifhes, was Nycholas Gibbins, and Ihon Carnaby, | with theyr men : after came Iohn Baker, and Robert Haulley wᵗ | theyr men, being all Saylers & Shipmen dwelling in Ipfwiche, | with other, befydes manye of the countrey ther about, whyche when they | harde of it, came thyther to helpe, and fee the taking of them.

⦅ Alfo, of thefe .xvii. fyfhes, there was a male, and a female, that was | more howge and monftrous then the other .xv. For the leaft of thefe .ii. fiffhes, were .xxvii. foote longe : and as bigge in the middle eche of them, | as .iii. Buttes of Malmezie, and of a marueylous great ftrength, as it is | well known to dyuers in Ipfwich & other places, befide thofe men aboue | named. For they tyed one of thefe fyffhes to a boat, to brynge hit to Ipf|wich wharfe, and being fo tied to the boat, fwam awaye wyth the boat & | all the men that weare in it, toward the fea a maruaylous fwyft pace, for | all that they could do : this was when the tyde came in, for they had made prouifion before, whẽ the water was loo, to tie great roapes about theyr | tayles and finnes with fmall boates, and by fuch meanes as they could. | (And as I fayd before) the tyde commyng in & the fyfhe hauinge water, | fwam away with the boat fo faft toward the fea, that if ther had not byn | refcue of other boates and fuch veffels as they had thear, that boat and | all they in it, had ben loft and vtterlie caft away. But as God wold haue | it, by the helpe of thother boates or veffels, tieng the fifhe alfo. Brought | him by force to a conuenient place, and tied him faft to a tree with ftrong | Cable roapes, and fo vfyng theym one by one, founde meanes to brynge | theim to Ipfwych wharfe. Wher they were layd with great labour and | trouble, befyde breaking of theyr wyndlace & a great Cable roape, wyth | halyng them vp, they weare of fuche maruaylous greatnes, ftrength, and | wayght. Som of them laye vpon the wharfe .ii. dayes and a nyght before | they weare dead, and yet they ftrooke them wyth Axes & other weapons | to kyll them. The ryuer wherin they weare taken was coloured red, wᵗ | the blood that iffued from theyr woundes, whyle they weare a takyng, yᵉ | water beinge fo deepe that a Hoy might well ryde thearin. Thear was | alfo .iii. Butchers a hole day cutting out one of thefe fyffhes, and as ma|nye to carye it awaye with hand barous to the town warehoufe, and the | Butchers were fayne to put on bootes to ftand in to cut it out, it was fo ·| deepe & full of garbyge : this fifhe was a mans heyght in thicknes, from | the top of the backe to the bone : and his bones as harde as ftones, that the | Butchers mard al theyr Axes they occupied about them. The other .xv. | fiffhes were .xxiiii. foote longe, and fom of them, xxi. foote, and byg accor|ding to theyr length. But the .ii. biggift, male and female, was .xxvii. | foote long, and as byg in the middle as .iii. Buttes of malmfie. Hauinge | a round fnout. His mouth wyde, gapinge aboue a yeard broad. And had | xliiii. teeth, one beinge wayed & waith a pound & a halfe, viii. inches & a |

half long, and aboue .vi. inches in compas about, yet none of the biggeſt. | Alſo a great long tung, a marueylous byg head, & is a yeard betweene the | eies. Vpon theyr heds were holes, as big that a man might put in both his | fiſtes at once, out of the which they did ſpoute a great quantitie of water | whyle they were a takinge, that they had almoſte drownd .ii. boateſmen | and all, with ſpoutynge of water: for the water wold aſſende vppwarde | from the fiſſhes, as hie as any houſe, and ſo fall doun & weet all them that | were within theyr reache moſte cruellie. Alſo they were white beneath | the eyes a hand broad, theyr eies blacke, and no bigger then the eyes of a | Calfe. Theyr backes as blacke as ynke, ſo ſmoth & bryght yᵗ one myght | haue ſeene his face on it, as in a dim Glaſſe. Theyr bellies as whyte as | mylke. And vpon their backes they had eche of them one great blacke Fin | growing, and ſum of them were a yeard and a halfe long, verie thycke, & | ſtrong, and .ii. great blacke ones vnderneath the fore part of his bellye. | Alſo the male, one of the .ii. biggeſt had a yerde, that when it was out, was | more then .iii. quarters of a yearde long, and as byg toward his bodye as | a mans arme ſleeue & all, by the elboe. His tayle was .iii. yeardes long, | and .ii. yerdes broad verye thycke & blacke, & wonderfull ſtronge: for .x. | tall men ſtood vppon his tayle, & he liftng [sic] his tayle vp, ouer thrue theym | all. Alſo when he had lifted vp his tayle it was of ſuch monſtrous waight ſtrength, and bygnes, that when it fell the verye grund wold rynge, and | ſhake therwith. Thys fyſhe was cut out in peeces, and geuen away to | diuers in the towne that did eate of it, and was verye good meate, eyther roſted or bakt, (ſo much of it as was kept ſweete) and the meate of them | bakt taſted lyke red Deere. And as they cut it out it was wayed by pee|ces, ſo that the verye boddye of this one fiſhe, wayed .LII. hondred the | bare carckas, beſyde many lytle peecis that was geuen away vnwaied to | crauers that ſtood by, & beſydes a Carte loade of garbyge that came oute | of his bellye, ſo that all together was aboue threeſcore hondred and od.

If the men of Ipſwych had knowne ſo muche betyme whyle they were | ſweete, as they haue ſence, they might haue made .ii. C. marcke more of | them then is now made. But now they bee barreld vpp to make Oyle of, | and will not bee ſold for a great peece of monney.

⬛ And this you maye ſee, the perfect and true diſcripcion, of theſe ſtraunge fiſhes, wherin is to be noted, the ſtraung and marueylous handyeworkes of the Lord, bleſſed be God in all his giftes, & holye in all his workes, the Lordes name bee prayſed, in them, and for | them, for euer and euer. So be it.

Quod. Timothie Granger.

Imprynted at London in Fleeteſtreate, at the ſigne | of S. Iohn Euangeliſt by Thomas Colwell.

Stow in referring to this incident mentions 'eighteen monſtrous fiſhes' (*Annales*, 1615, p. 662), whereas Holinshed (*Chronicles*, 1577, vol. ii, p. 1839) gives the same number as the broadside.

Included in Mr. Henry Huth's 'Ancient Ballads and Broadsides' (p. 128) is a unique undated ballad entitled 'The .xxv. orders of Fooles', signed T. Gr., the original of which is now in the British Museum. This was licensed to Henry Kirkham, 1569-70 (Arber's *Transcript*, i. 414), and it is highly probable that the initials may be identified with the author of the Britwell broadside. There is also an entry in the Stationers' Registers of a licence to Peter French for printing 'a ſonge of Peters Delyueraunce out of Herodes handes, by Granger' (Arber, i. 415), but of this ballad apparently no copy survives.

The broadside reprinted above was entered in 1568-69 (Arber, i. 381). The text is printed in two parallel columns, above which is a large woodcut of a whale.

53

An excellent Ditty made vpon the great victory, which the French | king obtayned againſt the Duke de Maine, and the Romiſh Rebels in his kingdome, | vpon Aſhwedneſday being the fourth day of March laſt paſt. 1590.

To the tune of the new Tantara.

TRiumph good Chriſtians and reioyce,
 This wondrous newes to heare:
Wherein the power of mightie Ioue,
 So greatly doth appeare.
God is the ſtay and ſtrength of thoſe
 That in him puts his truſt:
And what he euer promiſte them,
 He keepeth firme and iuſt.
Let canons rore and Muſkets ſhoote,
 Let Fife and Enſignes play:
Let Trumpets ſhrill and dubbing drums,
 Sound forth this ioyfull day.

Who knows not how the Duke of Maine,
 By title from the Gwize,
Hath ſought to rule as king in Fraunce,
 And cauſed . . . .
All ioinde themſelues in battaile ray,
 Vpon firme land in Fraunce,
Entending to haue ſlaine the king,
 Yet had a worſer chaunce.
Let canons rore and Muſkets ſhoote &c.

Whereby the enemy was that time,
 Full thirtie thouſand ſtrong:
The king his power was but weake,
 To right his open wrong.
He had not paſt ten thouſand men,
 In his defence to fighte,
Which was great ods as all men knowes,
 To put all theſe to flight.
Let canons rore and Muſkets ſhoote &c.

In valiaunt ſorte he cheerd his men,
 And louingly he ſaide:
God is with vs, our quarrels good,
 Be therefore not diſmaide.
My truſt is ſtill that as the Lord,
 Hath me before defended:
So he will fighte againſt my foes,
 That haue my death pretended.
Let canons rore and Muſkets ſhoote &c.

My quarrell doth pertaine to God,
  In whom I put my truſt :
And in the promiſe he hath made,
  I know he wil be iuſt.
Be valiaunt now and fight like men,
  And God will bee your guide :
And I with you will ſpend my blood,
  And not once ſtep aſide.
Let canons rore and Muſkets ſhoote &c.

Together then the Armies went,
  Which made a wondrous ſhoe :
On either ſide they fought full fierce
  Ech fought the others woe.
The Canons roard and Muſkets ſhotte,
  And made a warlike noies :
Their Trompets ſound and dubbing drūs,
  Encreaſte the ſouldiers ioies.
Let canons rore and Muſkets ſhoote &c.

The Fife made warlike melody,
  The enſignes were diſplaied :
On either ſide they curredge cride,
  The king was not diſmaied.
But like a Souldiour and a king,
  A ſtandard he did take :
And ſlew the man that bare the ſame,
  Which made his enemies quake.
Let canons rore and Muſkets ſhoote &c.

The Duke de Maine for all his power,
  Was forſte from field to flie :
His heeles were better then his hands,
  He fought ſo valiauntly.
His power was ſtricken with ſuch feare,
  That they did flie in haſte :
Whereby the king did win the field,
  His enemies were diſgraſte,
Let canons rore and Muſkets ſhoote &c.

He and his power did follow them,
  Full fiue howres in the chaſe :
From eight at morne til toward night,
  He fought in the enemies face.
This victory he did obtaine,
  Such was his good ſucces,
And many thouſand enimies ſlaine,
  Report ſaieth ſure no les.
Let canons rore and Muſkets ſhoote &c.

What tents and furniture for warre,
    What treaſure and iewels rich :
Hereby the king and ſoldiours got,
    You may ſuppoſe was miche.
And priſoners taken of account,
    As you ſhall ſhortly heere,
Who for their treaſon to their king,
    I thinke will pay full deere.
Let canons rore and Muſkets ſhoote &c.

See here the handyworke of God,
    Who harmles ſaude the king.
And ſet him treaſure in great ſtore,
    And euery warlike thing.

[Here the verse ends]

This ballad was occasioned by the victory gained by Henry the Fourth of France at Ivry, where he defeated Charles of Lorraine, Duke of Mayenne, at the head of the army of the League. In spite of the overwhelming superiority of the latter, the royalists are said to have lost less than five hundred men. Mayenne evaded capture by flight.

The event was further celebrated by Du Bartas in a 'Canticle of the victorie obteined by the French King, Henrie the fourth at Yury . . . Tranſlated by Ioſuah Silueſter . . . London, 1590'. A copy of this book is at Britwell.

Much space of the broadside is occupied by a woodcut of two mounted knights. The imprint has been destroyed, but licences for two ballads appear in the Registers of the Stationers' Company, one granted to William Wright on March 10, 1590, and another to John Wolfe on May 19 in the same year (Arber's *Transcript*, ii. 540, 547); either may refer to the Britwell ballad, but it is more probably the later entry.

54

Luke Huttons lamentation: which he wrote the day before his death, being | condemned to be hanged at Yorke this laſt aſſiſes for his robberies and | treſpaſſes committed. To the tune of Wandering and wauering &c.

I Am a poore priſoner condemned to dye,
  ah woe is me woe is me for my great folly,
Faſt fettred in yrons in place where I lie
  Be warned yong wantons, hemp paſſeth green holly.
My parents were of good degree
  by whom I would not counſelled be,
Lord Ieſu forgiue me with mercy releeue me,
Receiue O ſweet ſauiour my ſpirit vnto thee.
❡My name is Hutton, yea Luke of bad life
  ah woe is me woe is me for my great folly :
Which on the highway robd man and wife,
  be warned yong wantons, &c.
Inticed by many a graceleſſe mate,
Whoſe counſel I repent too late.   Lord, &c.
❡Not twentie yeeres old alas was I
  ah woe is me woe is me, &c.
When I began this fellonie
  be warned yong wantons, &c.
With me went ſtil twelue yeomen, tall
Which I did my twelue Apoſtles call.   Lord, &c.
❡There was no Squire nor barron bold
  ah woe is me woe is me for my great folly :
That rode the way with ſiluer or gold,
  be warned yong wantons, &c.
But I and my twelue Apoſtles gaie,
would lighten their load ere they went away,   lord, &c.
❡This newes procured my kinſ-folkes griefe,
  ah woe is me woe is me
They hearing I was a famous theefe
  be warned yong wantons,
They wept they wailde they wrong their hands
that thus I ſhould hazard life and lands.   lord, &c.
❡They made me a Iaylor a little before,   ah woe, &c.
to keep in priſon offenders ſtore,   be warned, &c.
But ſuch a Iaylor was neuer none,
I went and let them out euerie one.   lord, &c.
❡I wiſt their ſorrow ſore grieued me
  ah woe is mee, &c.
Such proper men ſhould hanged be
  be warned yong, &c.

My office then I did defie
And ran away for company.   lord, &c.
Three yeeres I liued vpon the fpoile
  ah woe is me, &c.
Giuing many a carle the foile
  be warned yong &c.
Yet neuer did I kil man nor wife
though lewdly long I led my life.   lord, &c.
¶ But all too bad my deedes hath been,
  ah woe is me, &c.
Offending my country and my good queene,
  be warned yong, &c.
All men in Yorke-fhire talke of me,
A ftronger theefe there could not be.   lord, &c.
¶ Vpon S. Lukes day was I borne,   ah woe, &c.
whom want of grace hath made a fcorne.   bewar, &c.
  in honor of my birth day then,
I robd in a brauery nineteene men.   Lord, &c.
¶ The country weary to beare this wrong,
  ah woe is me, &c.
With hue and cries purfude me long: bewar, &c.
Though long I fcapt, yet loe at laft,
London I was in newgate caft.
There did I lye with a grieued [mi]nde,
  ah woe is me, &c.
Although the keeper was gentle and kinde,
  be warned yong, &c.
Yet was he not fo kinde as I,
to let me [out] at libertie.   lord, &c.
¶ At laft the fhiriffe of Yorke-fhire came,
  ah woe is me, &c.
And in a warrant he had my name,
  be warned yong, &c.
[Said] he at Yorke thou muft be tride,
With me therefore hence muft thou ride,   lord &c.
¶ Like the pangues of death his words did found,
  ah woe is me, &c.
My hands and armes ful faft he bound,
  be warned, &c.
Good fir quoth I, I had rather ftay,
I haue no heart to ride that way.   lord, &c.
¶ When no intreaty might preuaile,
  ah woe is me, &c.
I calde for beere, for wine and ale,
  be warned, &c.
And when my heart was in wofull cafe,
I drunke to my friends with a fmiling face.   lord, &c.
¶ With clubs and ftaues I was garded then,
  ah woe is me, &c.
I neuer before had fuch waiting men
  be warned, &c.
If they had ridden before amaine,
Befhrew me if I had cald them againe.   lord, &c.

⁋And when vnto Yorke that I was come,   ah, &c.
Each one on me did paſſe their doome.   bewar, &c.
and whilſt you liue this ſentence note,
Euill men can neuer haue good report.   lord, &c.
⁋Before the iudges when I was brought,
  ah woe is me, &c.
Be ſure I had a carefull thought,   be, &c.
Nine ſcore inditements and ſeauenteene,
againſt me there was read and ſeene.   lord, &c.
⁋And each of theſe was fellony found,
  ah woe is me, &c.
which did my heart with ſorrow wound,   be, &c.
What ſhould I heerein longer ſtay,
For this I was condemned that day.   lord, &c.
⁋My death each houre I do attend,
  ah woe is me :
In prayer and teares my time I ſpend,   be, &c.
And all my louing friends this day,
I do intreate for me to pray.   Lord &c.
⁋I haue deſerued long ſince to die,   ah woe &c.
A viler ſinner liude not then I :
On friends I hopte my life to ſaue,
But I am fitteſt for my graue :   Lord, &c.
⁋Adue my louing frends each one,
  ah woe is me woe is me for my great folly,
Thinke on my words when I am gone,
  be warned young wantons, &c.
When on the ladder you ſhal me view,
thinke I am neerer heauen then you.   Lord &c.

FINIS.   Hutton.

Printed at London for Thomas | Millington.   1598.

A brief notice of Luke Hutton is given in the 'Dictionary of National Biography', where it is mentioned on one authority that he was the son of Matthew Hutton, Archbishop of York, and on another that his father's name was Robert Hutton, a cleric of more humble position. Hutton was sent to Cambridge, but left the University to embark on the career of highwayman and housebreaker, which terminated in his execution at York in 1598. It is improbable that he had any hand in the writing of this or any other piece to which his name is attached. Copies of 'The Blacke Dogge of Newgate', without date, but printed in 1597, and of the reprint issued in 1638 under the title 'The Diſcovery of a London Monſter', of which Hutton was the reputed author, are in the Britwell Library. 'The Lamentation' was included in J. P. Collier's 'Old Ballads' (Percy Society, 1840). It is printed in two columns.

55

A Ioyful Song of the Royall receiuing of the | Queenes moſt
excellent Maieſtie into her highneſſe Campe at Tilſburie in Eſſex:
on | *Thurſday and Fryday the eight and ninth of Auguſt.* 1588.

To the Tune of Triumph and Ioy.

GOod Engliſh men whoſe valiant harts,
  With courage great and manly partes,
Doe minde to daunt the ouerthwarts,
   of any foe to England.
Attend a while and you ſhall heare,
What loue and kindneſſe doth appeare,
From the princely mind of our loue deare,
   Elizabeth Queene of England.
To cheare her ſouldiers one and all,
Of honour great or title ſmall,
Or by what name you will them call,
   [Elizabeth Queene] of England.

The time being dangerous now ye know,
That forraigne enimies to and fro,
For to inuade vs make a ſhow,
   and our good Queene of England.
Her Maieſtie by graue aduiſe,
Conſidering how the danger lyes,
By all good meanes ſhe can deuiſe,
   for the ſafetie of all England.
Hath pointed men of honour right,
With all the ſpeede they could or might,
A Campe of men there ſhould be pight,
   on Tilſburie hill in England.

Her grace being giuen to vnderſtand,
The mightie power of this her land,
And the willing harts therein ſhe fand,
   from euery ſhire in England.
The mightie troupes haue ſhewed the ſame,
That day by day to London came,
From ſhires and townes too long to name,
   to ſerue the Queene of England.
Her grace to glad their harts againe,
In princely perſon tooke the paine,
To honour the troupes and Martiall traine,
   in Tilſburie campe in England.

On Thurſday the eight of Auguſt laſt,
Her Maieſtie by water paſt,
When ſtormes of winde did blow ſo faſt
   would feare ſome folke in England.
And at her forte ſhe went on land,
That neare to Tilſburie (ſtrong) doth ſtand,
Where all things furniſht there ſhe fand,
   for the ſafe defenſe of England.
The great ſhot then, did rage and roare,
Replyed by a forte on the other ſhore,
Whoſe poudred pellets what would ye haue more,
   would feare any foe to England.

Her highneſſe then to the campe did goe,
The order there to ſee and know :
Which, her Lord generall did dutifully ſhow,
   in Tilſburie campe in England.
And euerie Captaine to her came,
And euerie Officer of fame,
To ſhow their duetie and their name,
   to their ſoueraigne Queene of England.
Of tents and cabins, thouſands three,
Some built with bowes and many a tree,
And many of canuaſſe ſhe might ſee,
   in Tilſburie campe in England.

Each Captaine had his colours braue,
Set ouer his tent in winde to waue,
With them their officers there they haue,
   to ſerue the Queene of England.
The other lodginges had their ſigne,
For ſouldiers where to ſup and dine,
And for to ſleepe: with orders fine,
   in Tilſburie Campe in England.
And vittaling boothes, there plentie were,
Where they ſold meate, bread, cheeſe and beere,
One ſhould haue been hangd for ſelling too dear
   in Tilſburie campe in England.

To tell the ioy of all and ſome,
When that her Maieſtie was come,
Such playing on phiphes and many a drum,
   to welcome the Queene of England.
Diſplaying of Enſignes verie braue,
Such throwing of hats what would ye haue,
Such cryes of ioy, God keepe and ſaue,
   our noble Queene of England.
And then to bid her grace good night,
Great Ordenance ſhot with pellets pight,
Fourteene faire peeces of great might,
   to teaze the foes of England.

Her Maieſtie went then away,
To the Court, where that her highneſſe lay,
And came againe on the next day,
   to Tilſburie campe in England.
The Captaines yerly did prepare,
To haue their battell ſet out faire,
Againſt her highneſſe comming there,
   to Tilſburie campe in England.
And long before her highneſſe came,
Each point was ordered ſo in frame,
Which ſerued to ſet forth the fame,
   of a royall campe in England.

The gallant horſemen mounted braue,
With ſtomackes ſtoute that courage haue,
Whoſe countenance ſterne might well depraue
   in fight, the foe of England.
The armde men, bowmen, and the ſhot,
Of Muſkets and Caliuers hot,
None of theſe wanted well I wot,
   in Tilſburie campe in England.
Fiftie enſignes ſpred there were,
Of ſeuerall colours fine and faire,
Of drums and phyphes, great number there,
   in Tilſburie campe in England.

The battell plac'd in order due,
   mightie hoſt I tell you true,
A famous fight it was to view,
   that royall campe in England.
The hoaſt thus ſet in battell ray,
In brauer forte then I can ſay,
For want of knowledge to diſplay,
   ſo goodly a campe in England.
How the maine battel, and the winges,
The vauntgarde, rearewarde, and ſuch things,
The horſemen whoſe ſharpe launces ſtinges,
   in fight the foe of England.

The Noble men, and men of fame,
In duetie bound did ſhow the ſame,
To waite when that her highnes came,
   our foueraigne Queene of England.
And ſhe being come into the field,
A martiall ſtaffe, my Lord did yeelde,
Vnto her highneſſe, being our ſhield,
   and marſhall chiefe of England.
Then rode ſhe along the campe to ſee,
To euerie Captaine orderly,
Amid the rankes ſo royally,
   the marſhall chiefe of England.

What princely wordes her grace declarde,
What gracious thankes in euery warde,
To euery fouldier none fhe fparde,
   that ferued anywhere for England.
With princely promiffe none fhould lacke,
Meate or drinke, or cloth for backe,
Golde and filuer fhould not flacke,
   to her marfhall men of England.
Then might fhe fee the hats to flye
And euerie fouldier fhouted hye,
For our good Queene wee'l fight or dye,
   on any foe to England.

And many a Captaine kift her hand
As fhe paft forth through euerie band,
And left her traine farre off to ftand,
   from her marfhall men of England.
Two houres fhe fpent among them there,
Her princely pleafure to declare,
Where many a one did fay and fweare,
   to liue and dye for England.
And would not afke one penny pay,
To charge her highneffe any way,
But of their owne would finde a ftay,
   to ferue her grace for England.

To my Lordes pauilion then fhe went
A fumptuous faire and famous tent,
Where dinner time her highneffe fpent,
   with martiall men of England.
In the euening when the tide was come,
Her highneffe thankt them all and fome,
With trumpets fhrile and found of drum,
   returnd the queene of England.
To the blockhoufe where fhe tooke her barge,
There diuers Captaines had their charge,
Then fhot the cannons off at large,
   to honour the queene of England.

And thus her highneffe went away,
For whofe long life all England pray,
King Henries daughter, and our ftay,
   Elizabeth queene of England.
What fubiect would not fpend his life,
And all he hath to ftay the ftrife,
Of forraigne foe that feekes fo rife,
   to inuade this realme of England.
Therefore deare countrie men I fay,
With hart to God let vs all pray,
To bleffe our Armies night and day,
   that ferue our Queene for England.

FINIS.   T. I.

LONDON.
Printed by Iohn Wolfe for Richard | Iones. 1588.

From the preceding ballad one might suppose that Elizabeth spared neither effort nor expense to render her subjects best able to resist the Armada. Such, however, was very far from being the case. Her ships, small and scanty, were inadequately provisioned, and every application for food and supplies met with the queen's resistance. But for the private liberality of the naval commanders the fleet could not have kept at sea for a week, powder and shot must have failed had the contest been ordinarily prolonged, and, when victory was won, the wounded sailors were allowed to die in the streets of the sea towns.

The land forces were in little better condition. It was only after the Armada had been sufficiently crippled to render invasion impossible that a few thousand soldiers were brought together at Tilbury under the royal favourite Leicester: here, however, Elizabeth exhibited a graciousness which aroused the highest loyalty and enthusiasm in the camp (Froude, *History*, ch. 71).

The visit to Tilbury set the ballad-writers busy. In the British Museum is a broadside entitled 'The Queenes vifiting of the Campe at Tilfburie with her entertainment there. To the Tune of Wilfons Wilde . . . T. D.' (i.e. Thomas Deloney?), and in Evans's 'Old Ballads', 1810 (vol. iii, p. 143), is re-printed a ballad, 'A Ioyful Song of the deferued praifes of good Queen Elizabeth, how princely fhe behaued herfelf at Tilbury Camp in Effex, in 1588, when the Spaniards threatened the Inuafion of this Kingdom.'

Chappell suggests that the name of the tune 'Triumph and Joy' was taken from a ballad entered in 1581, 'The Triumpe fhewed before the Queene and the French Embaffadors.' From the metre he thinks this was sung to the popular 'Green Sleeves' (*Popular Music of the Olden Time*, vol. i, p. 229), and that this air may have accompanied the Britwell ballad.

It is difficult to assign the initials of the author to any particular individual. J. P. Collier suggested Thomas Jenye, who published a translation of Pierre Ronsard's 'A difcours of the prefent troobles in Fraunce and the Miferies of this Tyme', 1568. Yet seeing that Jenye took part in the northern rebellion, and spent the rest of his life in the service of Spain, it is in the highest degree improbable that he would have sung the praises of Elizabeth. Collier reprinted this ballad in 'Old Ballads' (Percy Society, 1840).

It is printed in three columns and is decorated with a small whole length portrait of Queen Elizabeth and a broad ornamental border which has been cropped at the sides.

56

¶ An A B C to the chriſten congregacion
Or a patheway to the heauenly habitacion.

A

Act. xv. Gala. v. deu.
v. Deut. iiii. Deut.
xxvii. Act. xiiii. i. cor.
v. vi. Iames. iiii.
Apoc. xvii. Prou. xvii
Gala. v. Leuiti. xx.
Iam. ii.

ABſtayne from pryde, abſtaine from fornication
Abſtayne from couetouſnes, abſtaine frō idolatrye
Abſtayne from ſedicion, abſtayne from detraction
Abſtayne from percyalyty, abſtaine from periury.

B

1. Pet. liii. Prou. v.
Ephe. iiii. col. ii.
Gala. i. Phi. iiii.
Math. vi. Lu. xii.

¶Beware of ryot, that ſpendeth a mans thryfte
Beware of lyenge that cauſeth diſhoneſtye
Beware of vntrue making of ſhyfte
Beware of the deadly poyſon Ipocriſye

C

Eccle. vii. Proue. xiii
Deu. xxviii. i. cor. ii.
Rom. xii. Eſa. v. Le-
uit. xxvi. Prou. xxviii.
Oſee. iiii.

¶Couet for learnynge, that maketh a man wyſe
Couet the knowledge, of gods preceptes
Couet for wyſedome, cheiſe of pryce
Couet the company that honeſty gettes.

D

Math. vii. Mat. v.
Luke viii. Pet. iii.
Tob. iiii. i. Teſſa. v.

¶Do that god hathe commaunded the
Do thy duetye to euerye man
Do hurte to none, he ſayth trulye
Do good to all ſo nigh as ye can

E

1. Cor. xiii. iii
I petr. i. Phil. ii. Eph.
iiii. Iam. iii. iiii.
ii. cor. v. Math. v.
Mat. xiiii. Gal. vi.

¶Enuy not, but loue thy brother
Euery chriſtian ſainct Paule doth teache
Enuyeng is forbydde, to one another
Euery man the rewarde, of his owne burden ſhall reache

F

Gala. iii. Hebr. xiii.
Iac. ii. Act. iii. 1. Ioh.
iii. Iac. ii.

¶Fayth withoute workes auayleth not
Faythe that worketh, and is lyuelye
Faſtened on god, and loue the rote
Faſhyoneth a man to be heuenly.

G

¶ Gette the treaſure, whiche the theſe can not ſteale
Geue to the poore, geue alſo to thyne enemye
Geue god the glory, in wo and in weale
Geuyng place to thy ſuperiour declareth humilitie.

Luke. xii. Math. vi.
Luke. vi. Math xxv.
Rom. i. ii. cor. iii. act.
xiii. Luk. xiiii. 1. pet v.

H

¶ Honour thy father and mother, for ſo is it right
Helpe them in tyme of aduerſe neceſſytye
Haue gods wyl in remembraunce both day and nyghte
Heuy burdens on thy brother to put is iniquite

Math. xv. Exod. xx.
Deu. v. Ephe. v.
Marc. vii. Eccleſi. iii
Ezech. xx. Math. vii.
Ro. ii. Ia. i. Ro. xiiii.
1. cor. viii. Rom. xvi.

I

¶ Iudgement is mine, ſo ſayth the lorde
Iudge not thy brother, wherin thou haſt offended
Idell communicacion is to be abhorde
Iudge neuer any, tyl thou haſt thy ſelfe amended

Eſa. xlv. Rom. xiiii.
Iohn. v. Math. vii. a.
Luke. vi. Rom. ii.
Math. xii.

K

¶ Kepe thyne eye ſingle that thou mayſt haue lyghte
Knowledge thy faut to thy brother offended
Kepe neuer from the poore that is his righte
Kyndle charitie where hate is aſcended

Luk. xi. Math. vi. v.
Iac. v. Leui. xix. xxii.
xxiiii. Tob. iiii. Act.
xx. Math. v.

L

¶ Let hym that hath an office attende therto
Let the teachers doctryne be playne and not curious
Let loue be without dyſſymulation alſo
Let not the buſynes of Chryſt to you be tedyous

Eſa. lvi. Rom. xii.
Eze. xxxiiii. 1. cor. xiiii
1 Pet. v. 1. cor. xiii.
1 Iohn ii. Iere. xxiii.
Iohn. xii. Lu. ii.

M

¶ Mercye is a temperaunce of mynde in tyme of traunſgreſſion
Mingled with mekenes maketh great quietnes
Make no reuengyng agaynſt wrongfull oppreſſion
Make heapes of fire coles of thy enemies vnfaythfulnes

Prouer. iii. 1. pet. iiii.
Luke xiii. xv. math.
xviii. Heb. xii. Rom.
xii. Deut. xxxii. Pro.
xxv. 1. Pet. iii. Exod.
xxiii. Rom. xii. Pro-
uer. xxv.

N

¶ No man can ſerue two maſters, and at once thē pleaſe
Neuer put thy truſte in workes of mans inuenſions
Neuer ſhalte thou geue occaſion of thy brothers diſeaſe
Nether beleue the falſe prophetes, for any maner of affliccion.

Math. vi. Luke. xvi. 1
Cor. vi. math. xv. Luke.
x. Ioh. x. ii. Corin. vi.
Mar. ix. Ephe. viii. v.
col. ii. Math. xxiiii.
mar. xii. xiii. Ro. xvi.

O

¶ Open thy hande to the poore with due adminiſtracion
Obſerue chriſtes doctryne in ſcripture playnlye declared
Omytte the pope with all hys ceremonyail obſeruacion
Onles thou wylt deſerue paynes, for the deuels prepared

Rom. xii. Heb. xiii.
Baruc. vi. Eſai. xlvi.
Ecclef. xi. i. cor. iiii. col.
iii. ii. teſſa. ii. Math.
xii. Marc. vii. Apoc.
xiii. c. ii. petr. ii. Apoc.
xxii. Act. xvii. Ephe. v.

P

Colo. iii. i. cor. i. .i Cor.
vi. Exod. ii. Pe. ii. i. Cor
ii. Colo. ii.
Math. iiii. Deu. vi.
Exo. xx. i. Timo. iii. ii.
Timo. iii. Eph. iiii. ro. i.

¶ Plenteouſlye in al wiſdome let the worde of god in you dwell
Paruert not yᵉ peo[p]le wᵗ reuerent behauour idolatrye to vſe
Put no myſte before theyr eyes, peruerte neuer the goſpel
Put awaye all ignoraunce, for that ſhall neuer excuſe

Q

i. Timo. vi. i. Teſ. iiii.
Math. v. Ephe. iiii.
Colo. iiii. i. Pet. ii.
Math. v. Luke xii.
ii. Teſ. iiii. Marke. viii.
Luke. xi.

¶ Quenche the deſyre of carnall concupyſence inordinate
Quenche thy anger frō curſed ſpeaking & al maliciouſnes
Quyckly for thy offence to thy aduerſary thy ſelf proſtrate
Quit thy ſelfe from vaine ſpirites mans doctrine & Idelnes

R

Iames. iii. Gala. vi.
Prouer. xv. Mat. xviii.
Lu. xvii. Iam. iii. i. cor.
vi. Prouer. iiii.

¶ Refrayne your tongue and brydell your harte
Reporte the beſte, and iudge truelye
Raiſe no ſlaunder to your neighbours ſmert
Reape neuer to youre owne ſoule any iniquity

S

Luke. xiiii. ii. Tim. iii. i.
Pet. iiii. math. v. ii. teſ.
v. Ro. xiiii. xv. Luk. xiiii
Tob. iiii. Ia. ii. Pro. iii.

¶ Suffer Chryſtes croſſe, when it is layde on your backe
Suffer paciently, al maner trouble and aduerſyty
Suſtaine them that haue not, beare with them that lacke
Succour your poore neighbour reliefe him of hys myſery

T

i. Cor. xii. Tit. ii. i. Pe.
iiii. mat. xix. i. cor. xii. ro.
xv. i. Tim. vi. ii. Tim. ii.
Ti. iii. Act. xv. rom. xiiii.
i. Timo. i. Phil. ii. ii.
Teſſ. ii

¶ There are diuerſities of giftes, and but one ſpirit verely
The giftes of the ſpirite, are geuen to euery man
To profyte the congregacion the weke in faythe to edefye
Trouble not hys conſcyence, with queſtions of Sathan

V

Heb. iiii. Ro. iii. Rom.
iiii. Iohn. vii. ii Pet. ii.
Rom. v. Gala. iiii.

¶ Vtteraunce of wyſedome commeth of the holye ghoſte
Vpon all them that beleue, and truſt in gods promys
Vengeaunce is reſerued of god in euery coſte
Vnto the harde harted and ſuperſticious doubtles

X

i Pet. i. Phi. ii. i. cor. xv.
Heb. ix. i. Iohn. iii. xv.
Iohn. xiiii. i. Pet. ii. Eſa.
liii. Tit. iii. Act. iiii. rom
x. Rom. ix.

¶ Chriſtes bloude hathe waſhed vs from our ſynnes
Let vs folow diligently his ſteppes
Chriſt alone hathe loſed vs from payne
Let vs worſhip Chryſt and his father and his giftes

Y

ii. Cor. vi. Gal. v. i. Cor.
vi. Act. xix. ii. Pe. ii. mar.
xiii. Mat. xxiiii. Ro. iiii.

¶ Yoke neuer thy ſelfe with infidelitie
Yoke not thy ſelfe with couetous aduouterers
Yelde the to god, and thy bodye ſanctifye
Yelde thy ſpirite amonge goddes inheriters

Z

¶Zodome and gomer, plaged for theyr iniquitie
Zodometrye is a vice before god moſt deteſtable
Zeale of myſerable miſchyef ſcripture doth verefy
Zodomites a ſore warnynge, for vs moſt profitable.

Gen. xix. Rom. i. ii. pet. ii
iii. i. Cor. x. Eſa. i. mat.
xxiiii. Luke. xvii.

Finis.　　Quod　Thomas Knell.

Imprynted at London by Rycharde Kele,
dwellynge in Lombardes ſtrete nexte
vnto the ſtockes market at the
ſygne of the Egle.

This ballad is undoubtedly the most ancient in Heber's collection. Richard Kele began to print in 1542 and died in 1552. Until 1546 he printed 'at the long ſhop in the Poultry under St. Mildred's Church', and in 1547 he removed to the Eagle in Lombard Street, where he issued the 'A. B. C. to the chriſten congregacion'. The ballad is printed on the back of a portion of an impression, apparently in broadside form, of the Act of Uniformity, 2 & 3 Edw. VI, cap. 1, passed in January, 1549. It appeared, therefore, probably soon after that date. It is roughly printed in two columns without border or ornament. Thomas Knell, the author, is mentioned in connexion with the ballad following.

57

¶ An anſwer to a Papiſticall Byll, caſt in the
ſtreetes of Northampton, and brought before the Iudges
at the laſt Syſes.   1570.

The Papiſtes bill.

HOw now my maiſters maryed Prieſtes,
How like you of theſe newes?
You muſt forſake your wicked lyues,
Your wyues muſt to the ſtewes.

The Aunſwer.

How now my maſters popiſh Prieſtes,
How like you of theſe newes?
You muſt forſake your Sodomites liues,
For down is gone your ſtewes.

2. The papiſticall byll.

What neede our women now take care,
What life they now do leade?
Since euery preaching knaue muſt haue
A whoore in houſe to treade.

2. The Proteſtant.

What neede our men now to take care,
What way they go or treade,
For thoſe Prieſts which wer whormongers
Muſt now marry wife or maide.

3. The Papiſt.

There is not now a ſtrumpet whore,
In all the land to haue:
They are ſodainly ſnatched vp,
With ſome Geneua knaue.

3. The Proteſtant.

Sithe there is now no ſtrumpet whore,
In England for to haue:
Speake well then of the Goſpell good,
And do no more ſo raue.

4. The Papiſt.

Maiſter Wiborne,* alias tiborne ticke,
There dwelleth in this towne:
Which ſought by all the meanes he coulde,
The Eaſter to plucke downe.

Perceval Wiburn, puritan, took refuge abroad during the reign of Queen Mary and on the accession of Elizabeth returned to England where in 1561 he was installed a canon of Westminster.   Wiburn identified himself with nonconformity and, though he was more than once suspended from preaching, was one of the clergy chosen in 1581 to dispute with the papists.

4. The Proteſtant.

And where that godly Preacher ſought,
  That dwelling in that towne :
Your knauerie and hipocriſie,
  At Eaſter to plucke downe.

5. The papiſt.

But I of him dare well pronounce,
  And time the truth ſhall trie :
That he ſhall truſt vnto his heeles,
  Or els in Smithfield frie.

5. The proteſtant.

For this of him you dare pronounce,
  And thouſandes of his ſide :
Not like to Chriſt, but to the Pope,
  Who loues to ſee Chriſt fride.

6. The papiſt.

Not he, but thouſandes of his ſect,
  Muſt to Geneua ſeeke :
The wreſtling of the Goſpell wrong,
  Preuailes them not a leeke.

6. The Proteſtant.

If that in Rome and Geneua
  The whoores were all well ſene :
The wreſtling of the Goſpell pure,
  By that men might well deeme.

7. The Papiſt.

The Deuil when he would Chriſt attempt,
  In Scripture ſeemed wyſe :
And for him they the Scriptures take,
  To maintaine all their lyes.

7. The Proteſtant.

Chriſt, when the deuil did him tempt,
  By Scripture did confute :
But Papiſtes paſſe on that no leſſe,
  Then Fawkners on Hawkes mute.

8. The Papiſt.

Therefore be packing pratyng knaues,
  Your rayling is to playne :
Commit your Baſtards to the bag,
  And hye you hence agayne.

8. The Proteſtant.

Saint Frances preaching to the Birdes,
  All countries hath well ſpyde :
So as if Fooles ſhould be hanged vp,
  The Papiſtes ſure ſhould ryde.

9. The Papiſt.

And where I tolde you of your wyues,
    Take you for them no care:
Shift for your ſelues, and trudge with ſpede
    Leaſt halter be your ſhare.

9. The Proteſtant.

Idolatrie and adulterie,
    For them you take no care,
But euery godly common wealth,
    May wyſh ſuch tyborne fare.

10. The Papiſt.

FINIS.   ⳡ Non eſt Inuentus.

10. The proteſtant.

FINIS.   Coronat opus,
    Exitus acta probat.

❡ Three helps deⸯuiſed by the Pope for his | Mayden Prieſtes.

Firſt that Prieſtes myght | examine in con-feſſions, | wyues, & Maydes of theyr | whoredom, & by that they | knewe to make their bar|gaynes, and the people loo|king on, muſt thinke it con|feſſion, and com-mitting the | like with them, they had po|wer to geue them a knauiſh | abſolucion.

2. The ſeconde helpe ap|peareth Gloſ. in Cauſ. ii. q. 3. | cap Abſit: That if any of | hys Clergy ſhould be foūd | embraſing a woman, it muſt | be expounded and pre-ſup|poſed hee doth it to bleſſe | her.

3. The third helpe, that in | euerye Citye (lyke as it is | now in Rome) one ſtewes | at the leaſt to be permitted.

Experientia | docet.

Doctor Weſton in Eng|land, who was burnt, but | not with coales, billets, fag|gots, ſtraw, nor reedes. ‖ Alſo, the twoo Mayden | Biſhops at the laſt counſell | of Trent 1562. beyng ta|ken bleſſing mens wyues, | the one was thruſt through | wyth a Bores ſpeare, the o|ther hanged out of a wyn|dow, in the ſight of all the | people ‖ Et cetera.

Imprynted at

London by Iohn Awdely | dwellyng in litle Britain | ſtreete wythout Alderſ|gate. 1570.

In the library of St. John's College, Cambridge, is a unique tract, consisting of twelve leaves, entitled 'An anſwer at large, to a moſt hereticall, trayterous, and Papiſticall Byll in Engliſh verſe, which was caſt abroad in the ſtreetes of Northamton, and brought before the Iudges at the laſt Aſſiſes there. 1570. Imprinted at London by Iohn Awdelaye'. This is signed 'Tho Knell Iu'. The stanzas of the 'Byll' in this and the Britwell ballad are identical, but the answers in the St. John's copy are entirely different and considerably longer. The latter was included by J. Taylor in the 'Northamptonshire Reprints' (1881). The 'Dictionary of National Biography' describes the work as a reply to a Romish ballad touching the marriage of English clergy, and enumerates other works by Knell. It is, however, difficult to believe he was the author of 'An A. B. C. to the chriſten congregacion', reprinted in the present volume, and which could not have been published later than 1552, and must therefore have been issued nearly a generation earlier from the pen of Knell's father or some other writer of the same name. In the Stationers' Registers, 1570–71, is an entry 'Receuyd of Iohn awdelay for his lycenſe for pryntinge of a ballett _an anſwere to a papeſt byll in Northampton_' (Arber's _Transcript_, i. 438).

The ballad is printed in three columns contained by ornamental borders.

58

An Epitaph vpon the death of the honorable, fyr Edward Saunders | Knight, Lorde cheefe Baron of the Exchequer, who dyed the .19. of Nouember. 1576.

YOu Mufes weare your mourning weedes, ftrike on the fatal Drome,
   Sounde *Triton* out the Trumpe of Fame, in fpite of *Parcas* dome :
Diftyll *Parnaffus* pleafant droppes, poffeffe *Pierides* plafe,
   Apollo helpe with dolefull tune, to wayle this wofull cafe.
Wring hard your handes, wayle on your loffe, lament the fate that fell,
   With fobbes and fighes to *Saunders* fay, oh *Saunders* nowe farewell.
Whom *Phoebus* fed with *Pallas* pappe, as one of *Sibils* feede,
   Loe here where Death did reft his corpes, the vermines foule to feede :
Whom Impes of *Ioue* with *Nectar* fweete, long in *Libethres* nourfht,
   Behold howe dreadfull Death him brought, to that whence he came firft.
Lycurgus he for learned lawes, *Rhadamanthus* race that ranne,
   Another *Neftor* for aduife, *Zaleucus* fame that wanne.
A *Damon* deare vnto his freend, in faith like *Phocion* found,
   A *Cato* that could counfell geue, to prince a fubiect found :
Not *Athens* for their *Solon* fage, not *Rome* for *Numa* waile,
   As we for *Saunders* death haue caufe, in flooddes of teares to faile.
Not Sparta card for *Chilos* death, ne proud *Prienna* preft,
   To weepe for *Bias* as we wayle, our *Saunders* late poffeft.
His learned pathes his talentes rare, fo nowe by Death appeares,
   As he that *Salomon* fought to ferue, in prime and youthfull yeares,
His counfell fadde, his rules, his lawes, in countrey foyle fo wrought,
   As though in *Cuma* he had been, of fage Sibilla taught :
His vertuous life was fuch I fay, as Vertue did embrace,
   By Vertue taught in vertuous fchoole, to growe in vertuous race :
Might tender babes, might orphantes weake, might widowes rere the cry,
   The found thereof fhould pearce the cloudes, to fkale the empire fky :
To bidde the goddes to battel bend, and to diffend in fight,
   Though farre vnfit, and mates vnmeete, with mortall men to fight.
Too late (alas) we wyfhe his life, to foone deceiued vs Death,
   Too little witte we haue to feeke, the dead agayne to breath.
What helpleffe is, muft careleffe be, as Natures courfe dooth fhewe,
   For Death fhall reape what life hath fowen, by Nature this we knowe :
Where is that erce *Achilles* fled, where is king *Turnus* fhroude,
   What is become of *Priamus* ftate, where is *Periander* proude :
Hector, Hanno, Hanibal, dead, *Pompei, Pirrhus* fpild,
   Scipio, Cirus, Caefar flayne, and *Alexander* kild.
So long there Fortune faft dyd floe, and charged Fame to found,
   Tyll frowning Fortune foyld by fate, which fawning Fortune found :

Shun Fortunes feates, fhake Fortune of, to none is Fortune found :
    Sith none may fay of Fortune fo, I Fortune faithfull found.
Beholde where Fortune flowed fo faft, and fauoured Saunders lure,
    Tyl fickle Fortune falfe agayne, did Saunders death procure.
Lo clothed could in cloddes of clay, in droffy duft remayne,
    By fate returnd from whence he came, to his mothers wombe agayne.
Who welnigh thirtie yeeres was Iudge, before a Iudge dyd fall,
    And iudged by that mighty Iudge, which Iudge fhall iudge vs all.
The heauens may of right reioyce, and earth may it bewayle,
    Sith heauen wan, and earth hath loft, the guide and arke of vayle.
There gayne is much, our loffe is great, there myrth our mone is fuch,
    That they may laugh as caufe doo yeelde, and we may weepe as much :
O happy he, vnhappy we, his happe dooth aye encreafe,
    Happy he, and haplefle we, his hap fhall neuer ceafe.
We liue to dye, he dyed to liue, we want, and he poffeft,
    We bide in bandes, he bathes in bliffe, the gods aboue him bleft.
Being borne to liue, he liued to dye, and dyed to God fo plaine,
    That birth, that life, that death, doo fhewe, that he fhall liue agayne :
His youth to age, his age to death, his death to fame applied,
    His fame to tyme, his time to God, thus *Saunders* liued and dyed.
O happy life, O happier Death, O tenne times happy he,
    Whofe happe it was fuch happe to haue, a Iudge this age to be.
O ioyfull time, oh bleffed foyle, where *Pallas* rules with witte,
    O noble ftate, O facred feate, where *Saba* fage dooth fitte.
Like *Sufan* found, like *Sara* fadde, with *Hefters* mace in hande,
    With *Iudiths* fworde *Bellona* like, to rule this noble lande.
I had my wyll, you haue your wifhe, I laugh, reioyfe you may,
    I wan now much, you gaine no leffe, to fee this happy day.
Wherein I died, wherein you liue, Oh treble happy coft,
    Wherein I ioyed in glory greate, wherein you triumpth moft.
Kneele on your knees knocke harde your brefts, found forth yᵉ ioyful Drome,
    Clappe loude your hands, founde Eccho fay, the golden worlde is come.
Reioyce you Iudges may of right, your mirth may now be fuch,
    As neuer earft you Iudges had, in England mirth fo much.
Here *Cuma* is, here *Sibill* raignes, on *Delphos* feate to fitte,
    Here fhee like *Phoebus* rules, that can *Gordius* knotte vnknitte.
I liued to nature long yenough, I liued to honor much,
    I liued at wifh, I died at wyll, to fee my country fuch.
As neither needes it *Numas* lawes nor yet *Apollos* fweard,
    For Mauger Mars, yet Mars fhalbe of this our Queene afeard.
O peerleffe pearle, O Diamond deer, O Queene of Queenes farwell,
    Your royall Maieftie god preferue, in England long to dwell.
Farwell the *Phoenix* of the woorld, farwell my foueraigne Queene,
    Farwell moft noble vertuous prince, *Mineruas* mate I weene.
No Iuel, Gemme, no Gold to geue, no perles from *Pactolus* lo,
    No Perfian Gaze, no Indian ftones, no Tagus fandes to fhow.
But faith and will to natiue foyle a liue and dead I finde,
    My hart my mind my loue I leaue, vnto my prince behinde.
Farwell you nobles of this land, farwell you Iudges graue,
    Farwell my felowes freends and mates, your Queene I fay God faue.
What rife in time in time dooth fall, what floweth in time dooth ebbe,
    What liues in time, in time fhall die, and yeelde to *Parcas* webbe.

The funne to darkneffe fhallbe turnde, the ftarres from fkies fhall fall,
The Moone to blood, the worlde with fire fhallbe confumed all.
As fmoke or vapour vanifhe ftreight, as bubbles rife and fall,
As clowdes doo paffe, or fhadowe fhiftes we liue, we die fo all.
Our pompe our pride, our triumph moft, our glory greate herein,
Like fhattering fhadowe paffe away, as though none fuch had bin.
Earth, water, ayre, and fyre, as they were earft before,
A lumpe confufed, and *Chaos* calld, fo fhall they once be more.
And all to earth, that came from earth, and to the graue defcend,
For earth on earth, to earth fhall goe, and earth fhalbe the end :
As Chrift defcended vp in cloudes, fo Chrift in cloudes fhall come,
To iudge both good and badde on earth, at dreadfull day of dome.
From whence our flefhe fhall ryfe agayne, euen from the droffy duft,
And fo fhall paffe, I hope vnto, the manfion of the iuft.

Lodowick Lloyd.

Imprinted at London by H. S. for
Henry Difle, dwellyng at the Southweft doore | of Saint Paules Church, and are there | to be
folde. | December 3.

Sir Edward Saunders, judge, was brother to Laurence Saunders, who was burnt for heresy at Coventry in February, 1555, after trial by Bishop Gardiner. Acting in opposition to the Duke of Northumberland in his attempt to proclaim Lady Jane Grey, Saunders earned the favour of Mary Tudor and secured advancement in his profession, and received knighthood from Philip II. He appears to have made no effort to save his brother, in the year of whose death he was appointed chief justice of the Queen's Bench. He continued to hold public office under Elizabeth, but was degraded to the position of chief baron of the Exchequer in 1559. He died in 1576, and was buried in the church at Weston-under-Weatherley, Warwickshire.

Lodowick Lloyd, author of this epitaph, was an officer of Elizabeth's court, and published a number of poetical and miscellaneous works, a list of which is given in the 'Dictionary of National Biography'. 'The Pilgrimage of Princes' is perhaps the most important. The Epitaph on Saunders which was reprinted in 'The Paradyfe of daintie Deuifes', 1580, was licensed to Henry Disle, December 3, 1576 (Arber's *Transcript*, ii. 305). Henry Disle or Disley was apprenticed at Midsummer 1563 to William Jones, and published 1576–80.

The ballad is printed in two columns. Between the concluding line and the imprint appears the same cartouche which decorates the title-page of the earliest editions of the 'Paradyfe' of which Henry Disle was the publisher.

59

Remember man both night and daye,
Thou muft nedes die, there is no nay.

THy mortall body formed of clay,
  Will fone reuolue and paffe awaye:
But yet the time, houre, or day,
Vncertain is, wherfore I fay.
  Remember man.

In youth or pleafure, if thou put thy truft,
In honour, treafure, or yet in luft:
Sone all thy ioy fhall turne to duft,
For remedileffe hens thou muft.
  Remember man.

All high eftate and dignitie,
Pompe, glory, wealth and foueraintie:
It can not prolong thy life pardie,
But all fhall tourne to vanitie.
  Remember man.

The mo thy yeres, the fhorter is thy life,
Againft death there is no ftrife:
And no kin, frend, childe, nor wife,
For thy pore wil be penfife.
  Remember man.

Then helpe thy foule, while thou arte here,
For though thy frend be neuer fo nere:
When thou art dead, and laid on bere,
They all with thy goodes make good chere.
  Remember man.

Art thou fo folifh for to beleue,
That they thy foule wil releue:
Or yet thy goodes in almefe geue,
Which to forgo, did thee fore greue?
  Remember man.

Nay, nay, they wil fay openly,
It were much finne, and great folly,
On him to rue or take pity,
That kept his goodes fo nigardly.
  Remember man.

While thou haft goodes, do almes deedes,
Let vertue deftroy all vicious weedes:
And fowe in thy foule, the holfome fedes
Of forowe and repentaunce that to heauen ledes.
    Remember man.

   Send forth before to make thy way,
Charitable dedes, which fhall and may :
Conduct thee furely without delay,
Paradife to wynne, at the endleffe day.
    Remember man.

   Call alfo to thy memory,
This world fraile and tranfitory :
Ful of foule finne and mifery,
To heauenly bleffe [sic] cleane contrary.
    Remember man.

   Of Chrift Iefu the veruent loue,
Remember man all thing aboue,
Whom pity did ftire, and alfo moue :
To fuffer death for thy behoue.
    Remember man.

   This fearful day of ftrait iudgement,
Fyxe well in thy intendement:
Where man and woman fhall fore repente,
Their finfull life and time mifpent,
    Remember man.

   Forget not the infinite paines of hell,
Being fo feruent and fo fell :
That nothing can fpeake, nor yet tell,
Where dampned foules fhall euermore dwell.
    Remember man.

   Remember thy ioy ineftimable,
So pleafaunt and fo delectable,
Of paradife fo comfortable,
Prepared for perfons laudable,
    Remember man.

   Man, if thou kepe this thing in minde,
And to thy maker be not vnkinde :
Eternall ioy thou fhalt then finde,
Ordained by god for all mankinde.
    Remember man.

The ioyes of heauen, the paines of hell,
The paſſion of Chriſt, his death ſo fell :
The worlde and death, conſider thou well,
And Domes day, loue euery deale.

F I N I S.

Imprinted at London by Willyam Powell for
Willyam Pickering dwelling at Sainct
Magnus corner.   Anno. 1566. 21. Auguſt.

The Stationers' Registers, 1564–65, record that a licence was given to William Pickering for printing with others a ballad ' *Remembre man bothe nyghte and Daye thowe muſte nedes Dye thayre ys no nay &c.*' (Arber's *Transcript*, i. 262).   It appears that Heber's copy was not printed until the following year.   In the library of the Society of Antiquaries there is an earlier edition, with unimportant variants, printed by J. Tysdale for J. Charlewood, without date (Lemon's *Catalogue of Broadsides*, 1866, p. 15).

The Britwell ballad is printed in two columns within ornamental borders composed of metal cuts of French design.

60

A moſt excellent new Ballad, of an olde man and his wife, which in their olde age and miſery | ſought to their owne children for ſuccour, by whom they were diſdained & ſcornfully ſent | away ſuccourleſſe, and how the vengeance of God was iuſtly ſhewed vpon them for | the ſame.

To the tune of Priſſilla.

IT was an old man, which with his poore wife,
  in great diſtreſſe did fall:
They were ſo feeble with age God wot
  they could not worke at all
A gallant ſonne they had
  which liued wealthily
To whom they went with full intent,
  to eaſe their miſery
Alack and alas for wo,
Alack and alas for wo.

¶A hundred miles when they had gone
  with many a weary ſtep
at length they ſaw their ſonnes faire houſe
  which made their harts to leape:
They ſate them on the greene
  their ſhoes and hoſe to trim
And put cleane bands about their necke
  gainſt they ſhould enter in.   Alack &c.

¶Vnto the doore with trembling ioynts
  when this olde couple came
The woman with a ſhaking head
  the olde man blind and lame
Ful warily they did knocke
  fearing for to offend
at laſt their ſonne doth frowningly come,
  vnto them in the end.   Alack, &c.

Good folks qd he what would you haue here
  me thinkes you are too bolde
Why get you not home to your country
  now you are olde and Lame
With that they both replied
  with ſorrow care and griefe
Heere are we come to thee our ſonne
  for ſuccour and reliefe.   Alack, &c.

¶ This is thy father gentle fonne
    and I thy louing mother
That brought thee vp moft tenderly,
    and lou'd thee aboue all other
I bore thee in this wombe
    thefe breftes did nourifh thee
And as it chaunft I often daunft
    thee on my tender knee.   Alack, &c.
And humbly now we doe thee intreat,
    my deare and louing fonne
That thou wilt doe for vs in our age
    as we for thee haue done
No, no, not fo he faid
    your fute is all in vaine
Tis beft for you I tell you true
    to get you home againe.   Alacke &c.
The world is not now as when I was born
    all things are growne more deare :
My charge of Children is not fmal
    as plainely doth appeare
The beft that I can doe
    will hardly them maintaine :
Therefore I fay be packing away,
    and get you home againe.   alack, &c.
The olde man with his hat in hand
    full many a leg did make,
The woman wept and wrong her hands
    and prayd him for Chrift his fake :
Not fo to fend them back,
    diftreffed and vndone
But let vs lie in fome barne hereby
    quoth fhe my louing fonne   Alack &c.
¶ By no meenes would he thereto confent,
    but fent them foone away,
Quoth he you know the perill of Lawe
    if long time here you ftay :
The ftockes and whipping poaft
    will fall vnto your fhare
Then take you heede and with all fpeed
    to your country do repaire.   Alack &c.
¶ Away then went this woful olde man,
    full fad in heart and minde
With weeping teares his wife did lament
    their fonne was fo vnkinde.
Thou wicked child quoth they
    for this thy cruell deede :
The Lord fend thee as little pittie,
    when thou doft ftand in neede.   Alack &c.
¶ His children hearing his [sic] father fet
    his parents thus at nought
In fhort time after to haue his lands
    his death they fubtilly wrought

What caufe haue we quoth they
  more kindnes to expreffe
Then he vnto his parents did,
  in their great wretchednes   Alack, &c.
❡ They murdered him in pittifull fort
  they wayde not his intreates:
The more he prayd impaffionately
  the greater were his threates
Speake not to vs quoth they,
  for thou the death fhall die:
and with that word with Dagger & fword
  they mangled him monfteroufly   Alack &c.
When they had got his filuer and golde
  according to their minde
They buried him in a ftinking ditch
  where no man could him finde:
But now behold and fee
  Gods vengeance on them all:
To gaine that gold their couzen came,
  and flew them great and fmall.   alack, &c.
❡ He came amongft them wt a great club,
  in dead time of the night:
Yea two of the fonnes he brained therwith,
  and taking of his flight
The murderer taken was,
  and fuffered for the fame:
Deferuedly for their cruelty,
  this vengeance vpon them came.
Alack and alas therefore,
Alack and alas therefore.   Finis.

At London printed for W. B.

This ballad is extant in several editions, of which that at Britwell is probably the earliest, from the fact that the word ' new ' at the commencement of the title is wanting in all others. Copies are in the Roxburghe and Bagford collections at the British Museum, in that of Richard Rawlinson at the Bodleian, and in the Pepysian Library, Cambridge. W. Chappell, who used the earliest text for the ' Roxburghe Ballads ' (vol. ii, p. 347), is of the opinion that the story owes everything to the imagination of the poet. The tune ' Prissilla ' is not mentioned in Chappell's ' Popular Music of the Olden Time '.

The ballad may have been issued towards the close of the sixteenth or at the beginning of the seventeenth century. It is printed in two columns which are separated by a narrow typographical border.

61

The purgacion of the ryght honourable lord Wentworth, concerning the crime layde to his charge,
made the .x. of Ianuarie. Anno. M.D.L.viii.

ALas where is the man,
that liueth and doth not rue:
To fee how falfely I am charged,
with thinges that be vntrue.

My feruice true is knowen,
howe ready I haue bene:
Both with my body and my goodes,
to ferue the Kyng and Quene.

And yet fome haue deuifde,
to charge me with vntruth:
which euermore hath bene my fhielde,
euen from my very youth.

Alas to what intent,
all eyes maye eafely fee:
That theyr deuife and practife is,
to make an ende of mee.

Alas they feeke my lyfe,
and not for my defertes:
But by confent of wycked men,
which haue vngodly hartes.

Suche haue confpired my death,
as nowe euen fo beforne:
That I may fay wo woorth the tyme,
that euer they were borne.

Alas there is no man,
more innocent then I:
And yet the wicked feeke my lyfe,
and know no iuft caufe why.

For there is not a man,
that lyueth and hath breath:
Can iuftly fay for my vntrothe,
that I am worthy death.

Though they fay what they pleafe,
as they can wel deuife :
Yet all theyr trauell in this thyng,
is knowen to be but lyes.

    Alas what hartes haue they,
that cannot lyue content :
Tyll they haue fpoyled the lyfe of hym,
that is an innocent.

    As touching the fayde cryme,
or any parte therein :
I doo proteft for verye thought,
that I am voyde of fynne.

    But thys wyll not fuffife,
to mitigate theyr yre :
Nor nothing els that can be fayde,
wyll peafe theyr long defyre.

    Yet fhall my truthe appeare,
Whych they would fayne conceale :
And my obedience to the crowne,
and to the common weale.

    Though truth be now fubiect,
vnto a frowarde wyll :
Yet fhall it euermore appeare,
I neuer ment no yll.

    Eyther vnto my Prince,
to whom I am moft bounde :
Nor yet vnto the common weale,
but it muft needes be founde.

    Wherefore I faye alas,
bewaylyng my eftate :
A noble pere, a fubiect true,
rewarded thus with hate.

    And thus I make an ende,
wyth woordes that be vnfaynde :
Though I am nowe a pryfoner,
my truth cannot be ftaynde.

    God keepe our noble Queene,
God profper her intent :
God fhorten all her enmies dayes,
or graunt them to repent.

Thys is the wyſhed daye,
to ſee her in this place :
God graunt vs true obedience,
vnto her noble grace.

Finis quod Iohn Markant.

℄ Imprinted at London by Owen Ro|gers, dwellyng in Smithfield.
Anno | .M.D.L.ix. the .xxviii. of April.

Thomas, Lord Wentworth, was one of the witnesses to the settlement for placing Lady Jane Grey on the throne of England, but he speedily recognized its futility and transferred his allegiance to Queen Mary. In 1553 he was appointed deputy of Calais. How far Wentworth was responsible for its loss in 1558 is difficult to determine. He repeatedly warned the queen and government of a French attack, although he seems to have done little towards strengthening the town's defences. That he was guilty of treason, for which he was indicted and acquitted on his return to England, is highly improbable. The English possession of Calais was, and would ever have remained, a source of irritation to France. The cost of its maintenance far exceeded its intrinsic value, and the country had suffered in alien hands, yet its loss created a panic at home and set a humiliation upon Mary Tudor from which she never recovered. Wentworth held a high place in Elizabeth's court, and died early in 1584.

John Markant, or Merquaunt, was also the author of ' *a new yeres gyfte*, intituled *with ſpede Retorne to God* ', licensed in 1564–65, and ' *Verſes to diuerſe good purpoſes* ', Nov. 3, 1580 (Arber's *Transcript*, i. 267, and ii. 381). Printers of this name are mentioned in 'A Century of the English Book Trade' and 'A Dictionary of Printers and Booksellers, 1557–1640' (Bibliographical Society, 1905 and 1910).

From the Stationers' Registers, 1558–59, it appears that 'Owyn Rogers ys fyned for that he prynted a ballett of *the Lorde Wenfurthe* with out lycenſe. ijs.' (Arber, i. 101). Rogers, or Ap-Rogers, printed ' by the hoſpital in Little St. Bartholomew's Smithfield ', and afterwards moved to ' the Spread Egle near Great St. Bartholomews gate '. No reference to him is found in the Stationers' Registers after 1566.

The ballad is printed in two columns which are separated by a border consisting of a double row of typographical ornaments.

62

The true difcription of two monfterous Chyldren|Borne at Herne in Kent. The .xxvii. daie of Augufte In the yere our of [*sic*]| Lorde .M.CCCCC.LXV. They were booth women Chyldren and were|Chryftened, and lyued halfe a daye. The one departed afore | the other almofte an howre.

THe Monfterous and vnnaturall fhapes|
of thefe Chyldren & dyuers lyke
brought|foorth in our dayes (good reader)
ar not | onelye for vs to gafe and wonder
at, as | thyngs happenyng either by chaunce,
or | els by naturall reafon, as both the old,
and our Phy|lofophers alfo holde now
a dayes: and without anye | farther heede
to be had therto, or els as our common |
cuftome is, by & by to iudge god onely
offended wyth | the Parentes of the fame,
for fome notoryous vyce or | offence
reygning alone in them: But they ar
leffons | & fcholynges for vs all (as the
word monfter fhewith) | who dayly offende
as greuoufly as they do, wherby | god
almyghtye of hys greate mercy and longe
fuffe|raunce, admonyfheth vs by them to
amendmente of | our lyues, no leffe wycked,
yea many times, more then | the parentes of
fuche myfformed bee. That this is | true
they fhal wel perceyue, yᵗ ryghtly wey and
confi|der the aunfwere of oure Sauiour
Chryfte vnto hys | Dyfcyples, afkyng hym
whether we are greatter fin|ners, the blynde
hym felfe, either els hys parentes, | that he
was fo borne: To whom our fauyour Chryft|
Iohn
ix.
aunfwered, that neyther he, neyther they
were faul|tye therin, but that he was ther-
fore borne blynde, to | thend the glory of
God myghte be declared on hym, | and by
him. The fame alfo appereth in another
aun|fwere made by our fauyour Chryfte to

them, whyche | tolde hym of the Galleyans
Luke
xiii.
[*sic*], whom Pontius Pylate | put to death
for theyr rebellyon agaynfte Auguftus |
theyr Emperoure, wherein he declareth (as
alfo | by thofe .xviii. perfons on whom the
Towre by Sylo | fell) that there were as
great offenders remaynynge | alyue, as any
of them were. Wherfore he eftfones
ad|monyfhed them to amendment of lyfe
in generall: or | els by their examples
threatened them with as grea|uous dyftruc-
tyon, as fell vppon any of them. Thefe|
examples moued me (good reader) in con-
fideracyon¹ | of thefe dayes of our forget-
fulnes of duty, wherin we | fet fo lyght the
greate bounty and goodnes of God, |callyng
vs by thefe and fuch lyke examples to
repen|taunce and correction of manners, and
not ftyll to | flatter our felues whyle we
iudge others and winke | at oure owne
faultes, to caufe thefe twynnes thus to | be
portractured. And fure to hym that con-
fidereth | as he ought to do, the great decay
of harty loue and | charytie (among many
other wantes that the world | is nowe fallen
in,) and had vewed and behelde the | two
babes, the one as it were imbrafynge the
other, | and lenynge mouth to mouth,
kyffyng (as you wold | fay, one another:) it
myght feeme that God by them | eyther
dooth vpbraide vs, for our faulfe dyffem-
blynge | and Iudas condycyons & coun-
tenaunces, in freynd|ly wordes, couer-

¹ Here ends the first of the two columns of type in which this broadside is set.

ynge Caynes thoughtes and cogy|tacions, or els by theyr femblaunte and example, ex|horte vs to fincere amytie and true frendfhyp, voyde | of all counterfeytinge, or els bothe. Neyther let any | man thynke thys an obferuacyon ouer curyous, for | as much as Chrift him felfe hath by chyldren taught | vs, that vnleffe we become lyke Chyldren, wee fhall | not come in the kyngdome of heauen. God make vs | all chyldren in thys wyfe, and perfect and

Mark
x.

well lerned | men, to note and obferue to what ende he fendeth vs | fuch fightes as thefe, that hereby (put in remēbraūce | the rather of our duties both to hym and our neygh|bours) we may atteyne to lyfe euer-laftyng by Chryfte | our Lord. To whom with the holy Ghofte for thys | and all other hys workes, be all maiefty, powre glo|ry and domynyon, now and euer. Amen.

Imprinted at London
in Fletestreat by Thomas Col|well: For Owen Rogers dwelling|
at S. Sepulchers Church doore.

The following entry appears in the Stationers' Registers, 1565–66: 'Receuyd of owyn Rogers for his lycenfe for pryntinge of *a tru Dyfcription of twoo cheldren borne at Herne in Kente the xxvijth Day of augufte* anno 1565' (Arber's *Transcript*, i. 298).

Beneath the title of this broadside is a woodcut of the children exhibiting them after the manner of the Siamese twins.

63

The difcription of a rare or rather moft monftrous
fifhe taken on the Eaft coft of | Holland
the .xvii. of Nouember, Anno 1566.

The workes of God how great and ftraunge they be
A picture plaine behold heare may you fee.

HEare thou haft (gentle frend) the picture fhape and fafhion of a fifhe ftraũge and maruailous taken (as | is faide) in Holland, hauing on his finnes hard fkales in forme much like the beggers diffhes, which in | that Contrie they were wont to weare in fkoffe & derifion, his eies like an owle & mouthed as a Popin|gaye his taile reede and fower cornered like to a prieftes Cap, which fifhe hath bene feene and vewed of moft | Nobles and Peares of Flaunders, who hath plucked of his fkales lyke to diffhes and kepes them for a fhew | and for the more credit hereof, ye fhal vnderftand that the .vii of December the faid fifhe was brought to the | Citie of Antwarpt where it was openly fhewed and fene afwell of Englifhe men as other ftraungers, what | this monfter with other vncouth fights fene of late do Prognofticate and fignifye vnto vs, that I leaue to | thy coniecture (louing Reader) befeching God the Lord and gouernour of all creatures not to deale with vs | according to our defertes but for Chrift his fonnes fake to power his mercye vpon vs and graunt vs Grace | to amende and to doe thofe thinges whiche are pleafaunt and acceptable in his fight thorowe Iefus Chrifte | our Lord. Amen.

AS thou this formed fifhe doeft fee
  I Chaunged from his ftate
So many men in eche degree,
  From kynd degenerate,
To monfters men are turned now,
  Difguifed in their raye.
For in theyr fonde inuentions new
  They kepe no meane ne ftaye,
Their maners mad and monfterous,
  what fhoulde I now difcry?
Or yet their cates delitious,
  why fhoulde I them efpye?
If one that liued in thys land,
  A fortye yeares before:

Could be releafed from the band,
  To be as he was yore.
Would he not wonder wonderoufly,
  when he our monfters fpied,
In fo fmall tyme fo folyfhly
  From auntiant cuftume flyed?
Thefe monfters therfore God doth fende,
  To put vs all in minde.
Such fhaples fhapes for to amend,
  whych now are out of kynd,
Or els the God of kind and fhape
  wyll fhaples vs deteft,
And with his plage will punifhe vs.
  But more to fpeake I reft.

Imprinted at London in Pawles Churchyarde by Thomas Purfoote at the
figne of the Lucrece.

Although both Stow (*Annales*, 1615, p. 662) and Holinshed (*Chronicles*, 1577, vol. ii, p. 1839) notice the taking of certain ' monftrous fiffhes' in 1568, an event noticed by Timothy Granger, whose account is reprinted in this volume (p. 154), yet neither mention the capture of this cuttle-fish (for such it appears from a large woodcut on the broadside) in Holland during the autumn of 1566.

The author, who has not thought fit to divulge his name, clearly observed in its form much that was significant of events then in progress in the Nether-lands and elsewhere.

Thomas Purfoot obtained permission to print this ballad in 1566–67 (Arber's *Transcript*, i. 337).

64

Le vray purtraict d'un ver Monſtrueux qui a eſté
trouué dans le cœur d'un Cheual qui eſt mort
en la ville de Londres | le 17. de Mars. 1586.

VOus debues ſcauoir, Amy Lecteur, qu'au Royaume d'Angleterre il eſt advenu au temps ſuſdict,
qu'un ieune Gentilhomme nommé le Sieur Dorrington natif de la contrée appellée Spaldewick |
au Conté d'Huntington, et qui eſt de la garde du corps de ſa Maieſté, auoit entre autres vn treſbeau
& bon Cheual, lequel il tenoit fort cher, & le fayſoit curieuſement pancer, qui ſans donuer [sic] |
aucun ſigne d'eſtre malade mourut promptement, qui eſtonna tellement cedict ieune gentilhomme par
ce ſoudain euenement, que deſirant d'en ſcauoir la cauſe ſe reſolut de le faire ouurir, ce qu'ayant | eſté
faict, fut trouué au trou du cœur dudict Cheual dans lequel on apporceut vne veſſie de la groſſeur
d'un gros crapaut, dans laquelle on trouua le ver qui vous eſt icy repreſenté, qui auſſy toſt apres
l'ouuerture qui luy fut faicte ſ'eſtēdit en la forme ſemblable que le voicy, & de pareille couleur
que le poiſſon qu'on nomme Macquereau, ayant le bec, les yeux & teus ſes rameaux pareils a ce que
vous eſt | icy depainct outre il auoit en les parties de derriere quatre endpoits par leſquels il vuydoit
des gouuttes d'eau rouſſe. Sa longeur eſtoit de dixſept doigts, & ſa groſſeur de troys doigts & demy.
Et ſere|ment. De ſorte que l'on doibt eſtre eſmeu a conſyderer les ſecrets & eſmeruerillables effaits
de la puyſſance de Dieu, ſur toutes ſes createures.

Les noms de ceux qui ſe trouuerent préſens & virent le ver.

M. Dorrington & ſes gens.　　M. Pykering gentilhomme,
M. Bedels Eſquier.　　　　　　　& pluſieurs autres.
M. Worliche Eſquier.

Imprimé a Londres Chez Iean Wolfe.

Stow supplies an English version of this event in the 'Annales' (1615, p. 719): 'The 17. of March, a ſtrange thing happened, the like whereof before hath not beene heard of in our time. Maiſter Dorington of Spaldwick in the countie of Huntington eſquire, one of her Maieſties Gentlemen Penſioners, had a horſe which dyed ſuddenly, and being ripped, to ſee the cauſe of his death, there was found in the hole of the heart of the ſame horſe a ſtrange worme, which lay on a round heape in a kall or ſkinne of the likenes of a toade, which being taken out, and ſpread abroad, was in forme & faſhion not eaſie to be deſcribed, the length of which worme diuided into many greines to ye number of fiftie (ſpread from the body like the braunches of a tree) was from the ſnowte to the end of the longeſt greine 17. inches, hauing 4. iſſues in the greines, from which dropped forth a red water: the bodie in bigneſſe round about was three inches and an halfe, the colour whereof was very like a makarell. This monſtrous worme found in maner aforeſaid, crawling to haue got away, was ſtabbed in with a dagger and dyed, which after being dryed, was ſhewed to many honourable perſons of the Realme.'

On August 1, 1586, was licensed to Edward White, with thirty-five others, 'A ballad of *a worme found in ye hole of a hors hart*, etc., 1586' (Arber's *Transcript*, ii. 451). There is, however, no licence for the French version, although Wolfe published several pieces in the French language during the year 1587.

The greater part of the sheet is occupied by a woodcut of the worm. This broadside was not in Heber's collection.

65

The Map of Mortalitie.

[See facsimile.]

On May 4, 1604, the Registers of the Stationers' Company contain the following entry: 'William Lugger. Entred for his Copie vnder the handes of the wardens *The Mappe of Mortalitie*' (Arber's *Transcript*, iii. 260). The original broadside measures sixteen inches by eleven and seven-eighths.

THE MAP OF MORTALITIE.

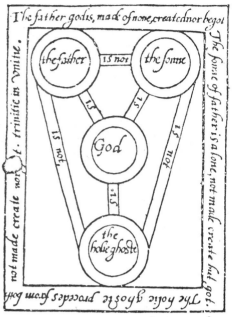

As by first Adam all doe die
So in me all are made aliue.
Death's swallowed vp in victory,
And I æternall life do giue.

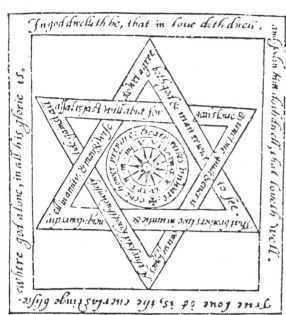

Awake from sinne,
to sleepe therin.

Earth {
goes to
treades on
as to
shall to
vpon
goes to
though on
shall from
}

EARTHE

Prepare for death but feare not

REMEMBER THINE END

{
as moulde to moulde.
glittering in goulde,
returne nere should.
goe ere he would.
Consider may,
naked away.
be stout and gay,
passe poore away.
}

A Conscience pure,
singes to last howre.

PRoude earth behould, as thou art we shall bee,
Against the graue, can no defence be made.
Dust will to dust, as thou art once were wee:
Worldes vaineglorie doth thus to nothing fade.
Man doth consume as water spilt on sande.
Like lightnings flash, his life is seene and gone:
Our part is plaide, your part is now in hand,
Death strikes vnwares, and striking spareth none.
Life is a debt to death, all men must die:
But when, where, how, the Lord alone doth knowe.
As death leaues thee, euen so vndoubtedlie
Iudgement shall find thee when last trump shall blowe.
Consider this ô man whil'st it is day,
Thine owne Christes death, for thee (if thou be his)
Vile worldes deceites, helles torments, heauens ioy.
Prouide to day: in night no comfort is,
In season calme, with Noah build an arke:
With Ioseph lay vp store in plenties tyme:
How to be sau'd, let be thy chiefest cark,
Returne to God, repent thee of thy cryme:
That come death late, earlie, or when he list,
It be birth day of thine eternitie.
Of righteous men liue thou the life in Christ.
Then sure the death of righteous shalt thou die.
Die to the world, the pompes thereof forsake,
That Christ may come and liue with thee in loue:
So in the world, when thou shalt farewell take
Thou maist goe dwell with Christ in heauen aboue.
Youth well to liue, age well to die should care:
In life, for death: in death for life prepare.

All flesh
as grasse
awaye
doth passe
and com to
nought

Gods word
most pure
aye doth
endure
not chang'd
nought

A SHROVDE TO GRAVE

MEN ONLY HAVE

Sithe Adams fall did fill the world with sinne,
Whereby mans dayes (few) dayes of sorrow bin,
His life, no life, rather calamitie,
And worldes best pleasures, but meere vanitie:
Sith beautie, strength and wit, flowers fading bee,
Man made of dust, to dust must turne againe:
Sith all must die, by gods most iust decree,
And death no torment is, but rest from paine:
Why should fraile flesh feare death, that ends all woes,
That salues all sores, and takes man from his foes?
His shape though ougly'tis, he bringeth peace,
Stints strife, ends cares, giues life, and wisht-for ease,
Men dying, sleepe: sleeping, from trauell rest,
To liue in ioy for euer with the blest.
Rather embrace, then feare so good a friend:
Yet wish not for him, that in sinne doth end:
But greater sinne, to feare him sure it is,
That troubles ends, and brings eternall blisse.
To faithfull soule, death's full of comfortes sweete,
That longeth with his Christ in Cloudes to meete.
In earth nought sweeter is to wisedomes sense,
Then to prepare for peace-full passage hence.
For, wise man all his life should meditate
On death: that come he sodaine, soone, or late,
He is prepared to entertaine him so,
As Captiues do, redeeming friends from woe.
Liue well thou maist: but canst not liue long. Euen
So liue, that death may leaue thee fit for heauen:
And feare not death; pale, ouglie though he be,
Thou art in thrall, he comes to set thee free.

Imprinted at London by R. B. for William Lugger, and are to be sould at his shop in Holborne, ouer against S. Andrewes Church.

66

◆ A memorable Epitaph, made vpon the lamentable complaint of the people of England, | for the death of the right honorable Sir Frauncis Walfingham Knight: principall Secretarie of Eftate, Chauncel|lor of her Maiefties Court for the Dutchy of Lankafter, and one of her highneffe moft honorable priuie Councell. | Who deceaffed at his houfe in London on the 7. day of Aprill laft paft. *Anno Dom.* 1590.

WHo mournes not for the prefent loffe that England dooth fuftaine?
Who hath not caufe this dolefull day, with teares for to complaine?
And waile the greeuous want of him, who was a fpeciall ftay,
And perfect piller to the ftate of England euery way.
I meane Sir Frauncis Walfingham, a Knight of great account,
Whofe wifedome in a Common wealth, moft men did fure furmount.
Of honorable place he was, beloued of Prince and Peeres,
And founde moft truftie to the ftate of England many yeeres.
His life too great a loffe, if Prince with gold might it redreffe,
His life fo deere as none but may with blubbring teares confeffe,
That England by his death hath loft a iewell of fuch ftore,
As in the feruice of his place, the like God fende vs more.
His want is great and greeuous too, this no man can denie,
When Prince and people waile his loffe with many a weeping eye.
The noble Lords of Englifh foyle: and cheefe of Englands Peeres,
Lament the death of this good Knight, and fhedde forth trickling teares.
The ftates of Scotland and of Fraunce, of Holland and the reft
Of the vnited Prouinces, with forrow haue expreft:
Gone is the cheefe of worthie Knights in whom did wifedome flowe,
Gone is Sir Frauncis Walfingham the fcourge of Englands foe.
Gone is the man that doubtleffe was a proppe to Englands ftate,
Who pittied euery ftrangers fute that came vnto his gate.
Gone is the Knight that carefull was, all futes to ende with fpeede.
As did pertaine to the releefe of thofe that ftoode in neede.
Gone is the man that watchfull was for fafetie of this lande,
To keepe the Queene and Realme in peace, and treafon to withftande,
Gone is the Knight that did rewarde all men of each degree,
That trauel'd ought for Englands good, fo good a Knight was hee.
Gone is the man that carefull was our quiet to procure,
For graue aduife and counfell good, we found him firme and fure,
The people to of Englifh foyle lament with inward greefe,
And fay he was the cheefeft ftay and ftaffe of their releefe.
They bid farewell vnto this Knight who tendred each mans cafe,
Founde free from briberie to his ende: fewe fuch will come in place.
A perfect zeale to honour good in him did alwaie reft,
And true Religion to aduaunce his loue hee ftill expreft.

He hated all Idolatours and popifh Traytors too,
He rooted out fuch wicked weedes as much as he might doo.
To fincere Preachers of Gods word, he was a fpeciall ftay,
And in his houfe he maintainde fuch, to preach Gods word each day.
Deceite he banifht from his houfe, fraude lodg'de not in his minde,
The marks of true and Chriftian life, in him each one did finde.
His iudgment floode with iuftice ftill, where as his doome was fette,
His will was ftill, each man he had, fhould pay his vtmoft debt.
To prifon he would none commit, but iuft caufe he would fee,
And what he did was alwaies doone in perfect charitie.
Which makes each man to wring his hands, & fighe with inward mone,
And faith in anguifh of theyr minde, Our cheefeft ftay is gone.
Farewell Sir Frauncis Walfingham, that vfurie fore didft hate,
That ftill didft good to rich and poore that came vnto thy gate.
Farewell the comfort of the poore, that to them almes did giue,
Farewell the ftay to Souldiers good, while he on earth did liue.
Farewell the comfort of the Court, and Londons dailie frend,
Farewell to thee that for the poore thy Letters farre would'ft fend.
Farewell the futor for the poore, that feldome let thee reft,
Farewell the freend to fatherleffe and widdowes fore oppreft.
Farewell the care for Countries good, when Corne was prifde fo hie,
Farewell the Knight that fuccourd'ft thofe that then were like to die.
Farewell and thoufand times farewell thou good and worthy Knight,
That in the caufe of poore and rich, full many a wrong didft right.
Farewell thou good and freendly Knight to Schollers poore and bare,
Of Cambridge and of Oxford to, of whom thou hadft great care,
Farewell all futors fay, he fhewed himfelfe moft kinde,
He courteoufly would take their plaints and tell them foone his mind.
His Lady wailes, his Daughter weepes, his kins-folke fighing fits,
His Seruants waile and wring their hands as folke befides their wits.
The rich doo miffe him euery day, the poore fhall want him ftill,
And many wifh him now aliue if that it were Gods will.
But teares fuffifeth not at all, let vs affured ftande,
His foule is plafte in heauen with Chrift, which fits on Gods right hand,
He liued well, and well he died, he made a godly end,
For to Almightie God his foule with zeale he did commend.
God grant her highneffe ftill may haue fuch carefull members ftore,
That fhee may liue and raigne in peace, in England euermore.
And graunt that his well gouernd life, a Loadftone ftill may be,
To fuch as fhall from time to time ferue in fuch high degree.
Graunt Lord that they may zealous be the Gofpell to defend,
And fhunne for to be couetous, euen till their liues doo end.
Then fhall her highnes liue in ioy, and England fhall be free,
From Turke, from Pope, from fword, from fire, and force of enemie.

FINIS.   Tho. Nelfon.

⸿ Printed for William Wright.

Thomas Nelson, whose name appears at the end of this ballad, was a stationer who on October 8, 1580, was admitted to the freedom of the Stationers' Company, and references to whom occur in the Registers until 1592. He was the author of 'A fhort Difcourfe: Expreffing the fubftaunce of all the late pretended Treaſons againſt the Queenes Maieſtie, and Eſtates of this Realme, by ſondry Traytors : who were executed for the ſame on the 20. and 21. daies of September laſt paſt. 1586 ... Imprinted at London by George Robinſon for Thomas Nelſon, and are to be ſolde at his Shop vpon London Bridge'. Copies of this tract are in the library of the British Museum and at Britwell, while another issue, printed by Robinson for Edward White, is mentioned in the Huth Catalogue ; the latter was formerly Corser's, and is described by him in his 'Collectanea Anglo-Poetica', vol. v, pp. 65-67. Although issued in quarto form, the poem is written in ballad style.

The British Museum possesses another of Nelson's works, 'The Deuice of the Pageant : Set forth by the Worſhipfull Companie of the Fiſhmongers, for the right honorable Iohn Allot : eſtabliſhed Lord Maior of London, and Maior of the Staple for the preſent yeere of our Lord 1590.'

The 'Dictionary of National Biography' gives a lengthy list of ballads licensed to Nelson, but whether he had any share in them beyond being their publisher it is impossible to decide.

Permission to print the Epitaph on Walsingham was given to William Wright on April 27, 1590 (Arber, ii. 545). The same event caused the appearance of Thomas Watson's 'Meliboeus', a Latin poem which its author afterwards translated into English.

The ballad is printed in two columns within a lace border.

67

¶ Of the endes and deathes of two Prifoners,
lately preffed to death in Newgate.   1569.

TRue Preachers which God liketh well,
To you I runne wyth all my hart,
Your wordes with me are like to dwell,
Vntyll thys lyfe I fhall depart.
　　As for the reft whofe tounges are tyde,
　　To them who runs, he runs far wyde.

¶ What fo doth beft commend the truth,
All falfhood lykewyfe difcommendes,
I know you Preachers tender youth,
And vifits them lyke faythfull frendes.
　　Yet if there hap a difmoll day,
　　The Wolues would teare your liues away.

¶ But they that humbly do you heare,
And eke well beare your woordes away,
Hauing their vnderftandinges cleare,
Needes neuer feare the difmoll day.
　　Nor wyll feeke peace here in this lyfe,
　　Where nought is found but war and ftrife.

¶ So they that do nor yet wyll heare,
When they be cald, and truth is told,
Ill haps to them vnwares is neare,
Yet blindnes maketh Bayardes bold.
　　But they that warned are in tyme,
　　Halfe armed are gainft daungerous crime.

¶ A tryall iuft I found of late,
Where Preachers dyd themfelues addreffe,
To fpend the day within Newgate,
To comfort two whom Law had preffe.
　　There did I fee that comfort great,
　　Whereof our Preachers oft intreat.

¶ There faw I more, do what they might,
Sharpe iudgement paft, the Preffe at hand,
The one would not remyt hys fpight
But doth the fame to vnderftand,
　　By blafphemies moft horrible,
　　And countenaunce moft terrible.

❡ Ne would beleue that he fhould dye,
Which playnly dyd to vs appeare,
By toyifh countenaunce fmylingly,
Which feemed very monftrous geare.
  And yet he was of perfect mynde,
  But thus he fhowed hys deuelifh kynde.

❡ Wyth hym perfwafions would not ferue,
In all my lyfe I faw none futch :
He fware great othes he would not fterue,
If ought there were within the hutch.
  And to it he went full egerly,
  As one that thought he fhould not dye.

❡ Anon there came a prifoner in,
That yrons had clapt on good ftore.
Gods hart quoth Wat, you wyl not lyn,
Thefe partes you playd lyke flaues before.
  And vp he fnatch coales in hand,
  To throw at one that by did ftand.

❡ This ftander by a Keeper was,
That hardly handled him alwayes :
Wherefore if he myght bring to pas,
That Keeper fhould now end hys dayes.
  Though he did burne in hell therefore.
  Sutch Keepers fhould keepe there no more.

❡ This defperate foole intreated was,
By Mafter Yong and others there,
To pray for them that dyd trefpas,
And to forgeue, fithe death is neare.
  Gods woundes quoth he, it is fhame for ye,
  That cry not agaynft this tyrannye.

❡ Why wyll not bolts or fetters ferue,
Thinke you (quoth Wat) to hold this man ?
He hath no money though he fterue,
Hys hofe and doublet muft trudge than.
  If bell there be, or plages to fall,
  Thefe Villains wyll be plaged all.

❡ For my part if I boyle in lead,
I cannot hold but brawle this out.
Would I might fight how euer I fped,
Chuld courfe that Oxe and fleering Lout.
  No more good Wat, quoth Mafter Yong,
  Thou hurtft thy felfe moft wᵗ that tong.

❡ Thus parted he and Mafter Yong,
Much greued for hys fenceles foule.
But I remayned and vfed my tong,
As God dyd force vice to controle.
  But Wat no chaungeling would not reft,
  But fell a frefh vnto a ieft.

¶As I might then I did exhort,
Them both with me to go and pray,
Where I would fpeake to their comfort,
If that the Lord dyd not fay nay.
　　The time is fhort, therefore quoth I,
　　Let vs feeke the Lord whiles he is nye.

¶I pray you be content quoth Wat,
The Lord hath mercy inough in ftore,
I may yet haue my part of that,
As he to others hath geuen before.
　　You muft repent and cal for grace,
　　(Quoth I) els neuer looke to fee Gods face.

¶Then was the tother glad of me,
And gaue to God great thankes and prayfe,
That he might haue my companye,
With hym for to remayne alwayes.
　　Wherein fuch comfort great he found,
　　That teares of ioy dropt to the ground.

¶I fee now God is good (quoth he)
And wyll not haue my foule be loft,
But hath prouided you for me,
Not fparing any payne nor coft.
　　You come from God, your words ar fwete,
　　I feele Gods grace my hart doth mete.

¶I would I had knowen you beforne,
But now it is in ryght good tyme :
For though my carcas be forlorne,
My foule to God I feele doth clyme.
　　Oh heare me (fayth he) to the reft,
　　Ill haps to me is for the beft.

¶Heare how this mifery hath wrought,
The taming of my flefh fo proud :
My foule to God that hath it bought,
I do commend with voyce fo loud.
　　Knowing that he doth heare my cry,
　　And pardons me immediately.

¶Would God the world dyd heare my voyce
And would be warned by my death,
Then would they not in euyll reioyce,
But prayfe the Lord whyles they haue breath.
　　And loue hym that hath loued them well,
　　Who hath redeemed their foules from hell.

¶O God (quoth he) is thys thy kynde,
To care for hym that knew not thee?
I neuer had thee earft in mynde,
Yet now thy grace hath healed me.
　　Due thankes to thee I cannot geue,
　　That haft now made me to beleue.

¶O tell me I pray, what is your name,
Sayth he to me vnknowen you are:
To you lykewyſe I am the ſame,
But God that knowes vs is not far.
  He wyll reward you this I truſt,
  Sith I cannot that dye needes muſt.

¶So God dealt with me yeſter day,
A frend he ſent vs in *Limbo* :
Whoſe good eſtate Gods bleſſe alway,
For that good lore that came him fro.
  Hys name was *Draper* Alderman,*
  Which was my comfort great as than.

¶He prayed wyth vs moſt earneſtly,
No ſcorne was in hys veluet cote,
Wyth teares he kyſt vs louingly,
And went with mourning chere God wote.
  So doth the power of the Lord,
  Make diuers men in truth accord.

¶Thus God hath found me out at length,
And ſtayed me of my wicked race
And me indued with perfect ſtrength
No tong can rightly prayſe ſuch grace
  I would my death were much more vile
  That others might beware therwhile.

¶So then we prayed ech one for other
Wyth trickling teares of ioye and greefe
In truth I tooke him for my brother
Though neuer ſo much he were a theefe.
  Then death to him could not come ill,
  For of Gods grace he had his fill.

¶Then foorth we went and made a fyre,
I dyned there wyth bread and cheeſe :
To ſing ſome Pſalmes was his deſyre,
So ech man ſoonge in their degrees.
  O Lord turne not away thy face,
  From hym that lyes proſtrate in place.

  But Watſon fell vnto hys foode
As one that hungry was in deede
And merely eate that he thought good,
But threw the reſt the dogs to feede.
  I ſaw no thought that he did take,
  Nor lykelyhoode from ſinne to wake.

* Sir Christopher Draper, citizen and ironmonger, was alderman of Cordwainer Ward from 1556 to 1581, in which year he died. He served the office of Sheriff in 1560–61, and of Lord Mayor in 1566–67. He was knighted Feb. 16, 1567.

❡Then vp came Maifter Yong agayne
Their deathes now being at the doore
But Watfon could not yet refrayne,
But laughes it out ftill more and more.
    Still all in vayne to hym was fayd,
    Yet all the reft downe kneeling prayde.

❡Then Skarlet tooke hym by the hande
And preached, though fmall to his regarde
Yet all the reft might vnderftande,
Hys woordes deferued to be harde.
    And yet he could not holde but fmyles,
    In deede he was begylde therwhyles.

❡A Prifoners tale that he dyd truft
Made hym that way to loofe hys lyfe
So there the matter was difcuft,
The preffe at length did end their ftryfe.
    He trufted that which was vntrue,
    Vntill it was to late to rue.

❡Lo thus much I thought good to wryte
For thofe that warned yet will be
That they in euill no more delyght,
Nor to fuch councell do agree.
    Who dyd this yll one fo peruarte,
    That heauy preffe burft Watfons harte.

❡ Imprinted at London by Iohn Awdely, dwellyng in litle Britaine
ftreete without Alderfgate.

The pressing to death mentioned in this ballad was undoubtedly the terrible *Peine forte et dure* to which were subjected all accused persons who refused to plead guilty or not guilty. Until 1772 it was within the power of a judge to order such prisoner as stood mute to be taken back to gaol and there laid on the floor with his limbs fastened towards the corners of the apartment, when increasingly heavy weights were put upon his body until he consented to plead or succumbed under the ordeal. In the event of the law failing to obtain a plead from the prisoner it was powerless to confiscate his property, and this is probably the reason why the two, who may have been ordinary malefactors, remained obdurate under the press.

In 1657 Major Strangeways, charged with the murder of his brother-in-law, died in Newgate pressed to death, and in 1721 a highwayman refused to plead until four hundredweights had been placed on his body. The Press Yard was a familiar feature of Old Newgate (Gordon, *The Old Bailey and Newgate*, 1902).

In the Registers of the Stationers' Company for 1568–69 is an entry 'Receuyd of Iohn fampfon [i. e. Awdeley] for his lycenfe for the prynting of *ye endes and Deathes of ij prifoners lately preffed to Death in Newgate*' (Arber's *Transcript*, i. 385).

The ballad is printed in three columns within a line border.

68

An Epitaphe vpon the worthy and
Honorable Lady, the Lady Knowles.

DEath with his Darte hath vs berefte,
  a Gemme of worthy fame,
A Pearle of price, an Ouche of praife,
  the Lady Knowles by name.

A Myrroure pure of womanhoode,
  a Bootreffe and a ftay,
To all that honeft were, fhe was
  I fay both locke and kaye.

Among the Troupes of Ladies all,
  and Dames of noble race,
She counted was, (and was in deede)
  in Ladie Fortunes grace.

In fauoure with our noble Queene,
  aboue the common forte,
With whom fhe was in credit greate,
  and bare a comely porte.

There feemde between our Queene & Death,
  Contencion for to be,
Which of them both more entier loue,
  to her could teftifie.

The one in ftate did her aduaunce,
  and place in dignitie,
That men thereby might knowe, to doe,
  what princes able be.

Death made her free from worldly carke,
  from ficknes, paine and ftrife,
And hath ben as a gate, to bringe
  her to eternall life.

By Death therfore fhe hath receiu'de,
  a greater boone I knowe :
For fhe hath made a chaunge, whofe bliffe,
  no mortall wight can fhowe.

She here hath lofte the companie,
  of Lords and Ladies braue,
Of hufband, Children, frendes, and kinne,
  and Courtly ftates full graue.

In Lieu wherof, fhe gained hath
  the bleffed companie
Of Sainctes, Archangels, Patriarches,
  and Angelles in degree.

With all the Troupes Seraphicall,
  which in the heauenly Bower,
Melodioufly with one accord,
  Ebuccinate Gods power.

Thus are we fure : for in this world
  fhe led a life fo right,
That ill report could not diftaine,
  nor blemifh her with fpight.

She traced had fo cunningly,
  the path of vertues lore,
Prefixing God omnipotent,
  her godly eyes before :

And all her dedes precifelie were,
  fo rulde by reafons Squire,
That all and fome might her beholde,
  from vice ftill to retire.

The vertues all, the Mufes nine,
  and Graces three agreed,
To lodge within her noble breaft,
  while fhe in Earth did feede.

A head fo ftraight and beautified,
  with wit and counfaile founde,
A minde fo cleane deuoide of guyle,
  is vneth to be founde.

But gone fhe is, and left the Stage
  of this moft wretched life,
Wherin fhe plaid a ftately part,
  till cruell Fates with knife :

Did cut the line of life in twaine,
  who fhall not after goe?
When time doth come, we muft all hence,
  Experience teacheth fo.

Examples daily manifolde,
  before our eyes we fee,
Which put vs in remembraunce,
  of our fragilitie.

And bid vs watch at euery tide,
　　for Death our lurking foe,
Sith dye we muſt, moſt certainely,
　　but when, we do not knowe.

Som which to day are luſty Brutes,
　　of age and courage ripe,
Tomorow may be layd full lowe,
　　by Death his greuous gripe.

Reſpect and parcialitie
　　of perſons is there none,
For King, or Kaiſer, rich or poore,
　　wiſe, fooliſh, all is one.

God graunt that we here left behinde,
　　this Ladies ſteppes may treade,
To liue ſo well, to die no worſe,
　　Amen, as I haue ſaide.

Then maugre Death, we ſhall be ſure,
　　when corps in earth is cloſde,
Amonge the ioyes celeſtiall,
　　our Soule ſhalbe repoſde.

FINIS.　　Tho. Newton.

Imprinted at London in
Fleetſtreete, by William How, for Ri|charde Iohnes : and are to be folde at his
Shop vnder the Lotterie houſe.

Catharine, Lady Knollys, was wife of Sir Francis Knollys, statesman and treasurer to Queen Elizabeth. She was the daughter of William Carey and Mary Boleyn, a sister of Queen Anne Boleyn. She died at Hampton Court, January 15, 1568–69, aged thirty-nine, while in attendance on Queen Elizabeth, to whom she was first cousin, and was buried in St. Edmund's Chapel, Westminster Abbey, the expenses thereof being defrayed by the Queen. Although Elizabeth showed solicitude for Lady Knollys in her last illness, and grieved at her loss, it was suggested that her decease was chiefly occasioned by the prolonged absence of her husband in the north of England, where Elizabeth had entrusted him with the custody of Mary Stuart after her flight from Scotland. (Letter from Sir N. White to Cecil. Wright's *Queen Elizabeth*, vol. i, p. 308.)

Thomas Newton, poet, physician and divine, a native of Cheshire, was born about 1542. He studied successively at Oxford and at Cambridge. The 'Dictionary of National Biography' gives a long list of his miscellaneous publications, which include translations from classical and medical writers, as well as a quantity of contributed verse. He died in 1607.

This ballad was licensed to Richard Jones in 1568–69 (Arber's *Transcript*, i. 385). It is printed in two columns, and has beneath the imprint Jones's device of the double-headed eagle.

69

A warning to London by the fall of Antwerp.

[See facsimile.]

Nowhere in the blood-stained annals of the Netherlands is there a tale equal in horror to that of the 'Spanish Fury' at Antwerp. On November 4th and 5th, 1576, six million pounds' worth of property was destroyed by fire, and a like amount secured by the Spaniards. It has been estimated that no less than eight thousand persons were slaughtered, or rather more than twice the number massacred at Paris on St. Bartholomew's Day. Every conceivable atrocity was practised on male and female. 'Of all the crimes which men can commit, whether from deliberate calculation, or in the frenzy of passion, hardly one was omitted, for riot, gaming, rape, which had been postponed to the more stringent claims of robbery and murder, were now rapidly added to the sum of atrocities. History has recorded the account indelibly on her brazen tablets; it can be adjusted only at the judgement-seat above' (J. L. Motley, *The Rise of the Dutch Republic*).

In the Stationers' Registers for 1565–66 was entered a ballad *Roowe well ye marynors*, and numerous variations of this appeared subsequently. The tune was extremely popular, as is clear from the fact that two ballads—Stephen Peele's 'A letter to Rome, to declare to ye Pope' and Thomas Preston's 'A Lamentation from Rome, how the Pope, doth bewayle'—in this collection were sung to the same air (W. Chappell, *Popular Music of the Olden Time*, vol. i, pp. 112–13).

Of Rafe Norris, the author of the ballad, nothing is known, and no other publication bearing his name is extant.

This ballad was not entered, although others referring to the same incident appear in the Stationers' Registers, including one licensed to Richard Jones and John Charlewood on Jan. 25, 1577, *A warnynge songe to Cities all to beware by Antwerps fall* (Arber's *Transcript*, ii. 308). The 'warning to London' was included in J. P. Collier's 'Old Ballads' (Percy Society, 1840). The original ballad measures twelve and three-eights inches by eight and one-eighth.

A warning to London by the fall of Antwerp

To the tune of *Rovv vvel ye Mariners.*

THe sturdy Oke at length/
When force doth fail
though nere so tall:
Resigneth vp his stregth,
By boistrous blasts vnto the fal.
The stately Stag in time dooth yeeld
Him self a pray to Dogs in feeld.
The Peccock proud, ye swelling Swan
At last dooth serue the vse of man.
Pride,pomp,plumes gay:
Must haue a fall who ere say nay,
Hye mindes,state,power:
Shall cōe to end within an houre.

¶Let *Antvverp* warning be,
thou stately *London* to beware:
Lest resting in thy glee,
thou wrapst thy self in wretched care
Be vigilant,sleepe not in sin:
Lest that thy foe doo enter in.
Keep sure thy trench,prepare thy shot:
Watch wel,so shall no foil be got.
Stand fast,play thy parte,
Quail not but shew an english hart,
Dout,dread,stil fear:
For *Antvverps* plague approcheth neer.

¶Leaue tearing of thy God,
let vain excesse be laid aside:
Els shalt thou feel the rod,
prepared for to scourge thy pride.

Forsake thy Deuilish drunken trade:
Which almoste hath the entrance made.
Erect your walles giue out your charge
Keep wel your tap,run not at large.
Faint not,fiercely fight:
Shrink not but keep your cōtries right.
Stand stout,on Iesus call:
And he no dout wil help you all.

¶Trust not a ciuil foe,
Which vnder coulour wisheth good:
For ere thy self doost knowe,
by craft he seeks to haue thy blood.
The Snake in grasse doth groueling lie:
Til for reuenge dūe time he spie.
The leering Dog doth bite more sore:
Then he that warning giues before.
Fine flattery,fair face:
Much discorde breeds in euery place.
Fire,shot,must be to hot:
For those which haue their God forgot.

¶Reioyce not if thou see,
thy neighbours house set on a flame:
For like thy luck may be,
vnlesse thou wel preuent the same.
The scourge which late on *Antvverp* fel:
Thy wrack and ruine dooth foretel.
Make not a gibing iest therat:
Lest stately *Troy* be beaten flat.
Pray God faithfully:
To saue vs from all trechery.
Dout not if we doo so:
We shall escape the forain fo.

¶Pray we with one accorde,
that God our Queene may ay defend:
From those which seek by swoord/
to bring her graces reign to end.
Cut of(O Lord)their deuilish dayes:
And graunt her life thy name to praise.
Garde her with grace her Champion be
That she may gain the victory.
Hope wel,pray stil:
God is our guide we feare none il.
Fear not,watch pray:
God sheeld this Citie from decay.

AMEN. q. *Rafe Norris.*

¶*IMPRINTED AT LONDON*
at the long Shop adioyning vnto S.
Mildreds Church in the Pultrie,
by Iohn Allde.

70

A letter to Rome, to declare to yᵉ Pope,
Iohn Felton his freend is hangd in a rope:
And farther, a right his grace to enforme,
He dyed a Papift, and feemd not to turne.

To the tune of Row well ye Mariners.

WHo keepes Saint Angell gates?
   Where lieth our holy father fay?
I muze that no man waytes,
   Nor comes to meete me on the way.
Sir Pope I fay? yf you be nere,
   Bow downe to me your liftning eare:
Come forth, befturre you then a pace,
   For I haue newes to fhow your grace.
      Stay not, come on,
That I from hence were fhortly gon:
      Harke well, heare mee,
What tidings I haue brought to thee.

❡ The Bull fo lately fent
   To England by your holy grace,
Iohn Felton may repent
   For fettyng vp the fame in place:
For. he vpon a goodly zeale
   He bare vnto your common weale
Hath ventured lyfe to pleafure you,
   And now is hangd, I tell you true.
      Wherfore, fir Pope,
In England haue you loft your hope.
      Curfe on, fpare not,
Your knights are lyke to go to pot.

❡ But further to declare,
   He dyed your obedient chylde:
And neuer feemd to fpare,
   For to exalt your doctrine wylde:
And tolde the people euery one
   He dyed your obedient fonne

And as he might, he did fet forth,
  Your dignitie thats nothyng worth.
    Your trafh, your toyes,
He toke to be his onely ioyes :
    Therfore, hath wonne,
Of you the crowne of martirdome.

¶ Let him be fhryned then
  Accordyng to his merits due,
As you haue others doen
  That proue vnto their Prince vntrue :
For thefe (fir Pope) you loue of lyfe,
  That w^t their Princes fall at ftryfe :
Defendyng of your fupreame powre,
  Yet fom haue paid ful deare therfore.
    As now, lately,
Your freend Iohn Felton feemd to try
    Therfore, I pray,
That you a maffe for him wyll fay.

¶ Ryng all the belles in Rome
  To doe his finful foule fome good,
Let that be doen right foone
  Becaufe that he hath fhed his blood,
His quarters ftand not all together
  But ye mai hap to ring them thether
In place where you wold haue them be
  Then might you doe as pleafeth ye.
    For whye ? they hang,
Vnfhryned each one vpon a ftang :
    Thus ftandes, the cafe,
On London gates they haue a place.

¶ His head vpon a pole
  Stands wauerīg in ye wherlīg wynd,
But where fhoulde be his foule
  To you belongeth for to fynd :
I wyfh you Purgatorie looke
  And fearch each corner w^t your hooke,
Left it might chance or you be ware
  The Deuyls to catce him in a fnare.
    Yf ye, him fee,
From Purgatorie fet him free :
    Let not, trudge than,
Fetch Felton out and yf ye can.

¶ I wyfh you now fir Pope
  To loke vnto your faithful freendes,
That in your Bulles haue hope
  To haue your pardon for their finnes,
For here I tell you, euery Lad
  Doth fcoff & fcorne your bulles to bad,

And thinke they fhall the better fare
For hatyng of your curfed ware.
Now doe, I end,
I came to fhow you as a frend:
whether blefſe, or curſe,
You fend to me, I am not the worſe.

℄ FINIS.　　Steuen Peele.

℄Imprinted by Alexander Lacie for | Henrie Kyrkham, dwellyng at the figne of the|
blacke Boy: at the middle North dore | of Paules church.

In Mr. Henry Huth's ' Ancient Ballads and Broad-sides', 1867, is a ballad ' The pope in his fury doth anſwer returne, To a letter yᵉ which to Rome is late come'. This is signed with the initials of Stephen Peele, and is a sequel to the Britwell broadside. Both refer to the execution of John Felton, who fastened the bull of excommunication to the gates of the Bishop of London's palace, May 15, 1570. There is also in this volume a ballad entitled ' The end and Confeſſion of Iohn Felton' (p. 144). For mention of the popular air ' Row well ye Mariners' see note to the preceding ballad.

J. P. Collier (*Extracts from the Registers of the Sta-tioners' Company*, vol. ii, p. 6) suggests that Stephen Peele was most likely father to George Peele the dramatist, but the 'Dictionary of National Biography' names that individual as James Peele, clerk of Christ's Hospital, and author of a work on bookkeeping. The fact that the son was a ' free scholar' at Christ's Hospital seems to prove that Collier was mistaken.

Stephen Peele, bookseller, is mentioned in the records of the Stationers' Company between the years 1570 and 1593. He dealt in ballads, but it is doubtful whether he can be identified with the author of the same name. J. P. Collier reprinted ' A letter to Rome' in ' Old Ballads' (Percy Society, 1840).

The ballad was licensed in 1570–71 (Arber's *Tran-script*, i. 437). It is printed in two columns, the lower portion of the ballad being decorated with three orna-mental blocks.

71

A proper new balade expreſſyng the fames,
Concerning a warning to al London dames.

To the tune of the blacke Almaine.

YOu London dames, whoſe paſſyng fames
   Through out the worlde is ſpread,
In to the ſkye, aſcendyng hye
   To euery place is fled :
For thorow each land and place,
For beauties kyndely grace :
   You are renowmed ouer all,
   You haue the prayſe and euer ſhall.
What wight on earth that can beholde
More dearer and fayrer dames then you ?
   Therfore to extoll you I may be bolde,
   Your paces and graces ſo gay to vieu.

¶ For Vertues lore, and other thinges more
   Of truth you doe excell,
I may well geſſe, for comelyneſſe
   Of all, you beare the bell :
As trim in your arraye
As be the flowres in Maye
   With roſet hew ſo brauely dight
   As twinklyng ſtarres that ſhyneth by night.
For curteſye in euery parte
Not many nor any reſemble you can,
   In lady Natures camely [*sic*] arte
   So grauely and brauely to euery man.

¶ And oft when you goe, fayre dames on a rowe
   In to the feeldes ſo greene,
You ſit and vewe the beautifull hewe
   Of flowres that there be ſeene :
Which lady Flora hath
So garnyſhed in each path
   With all the pleaſures that may be
   (Fayre dames) are there to pleaſure ye

Tyl Froſt doth come and nip the top,
And lop them and crop them, not one to be ſeene :
   So when that Death doth hap to your lot,
   Conſider and gather what beauty hath beene.

¶For as the flowre, doth change in an houre
   That was ſo fayre to ſee,
Conſyder and gather (fayre dames) the wether
   May change as well with yee :
And turne your ioyes as ſoone
As Froſt the flowres hath doone
   So ſudden Death may change as well
   Your beauties that now doth excell,
And turne your ſweetes to bitter and ſowre
When death wᵗ his breath comes ſtealing neare :
   Such haps may hap to come in an howre
   Which euer or neuer you little dyd feare.

¶Wherfore I ſay, fayre dames ſo gay
   That Death is buſyeſt now,
To catch you hence, where no defence
   May make him once to bow :
Experience well doth trye
You ſee it with your eye,
   How quickely ſome are taken hence
   Not youthfull yeares may make defence :
And ſtrange diſeaſes many are ſeene
Encreaſyng and preaſyng to vexe vs each day,
   But ſure the lyke hath euer beene
   May houe you and moue you to God to pray.

¶And learne to know, as graſſe doth grow
   And withereth in to haye,
Remember therfore, kepe vertue in ſtore
   For ſo you ſhall decaye :
And pitie on the poore
With ſome parte of your ſtore,
   Loke that your lampes may ready bee
   The dreadfull day approcheth nye :
When Chriſt ſhall come to iudge our deeds
No fairenes nor clerenes can helpe you than,
   The corne to ſeperate from the weeds
   Fayre dames, when cometh the day of dome.

¶Now that I haue ſayd, let it be wayed
   It is no ieſtyng toye,
Not all your treaſure, can you pleaſure
   It is but fadyng ioye :
Therfore remember mee
What I haue ſayd to yee,
   And thus the Lorde preſerue the Queene
   Long ſpace with vs to lyue and raigne :

As we are all bound inceſſantlie
To deſyre with prayer both night and day,
God to preſerue her maieſtie
Amen, let all her good ſubiects ſay.

⸿ FINIS.   quoth Steuen Peell.

Imprinted at S. Katherins by Alexander Lacie | for Henrie Kyrkham, dwellyng at
the middle North dore | of S. Paules church.

In the Regiſters of the Stationers' Company for 1570–71 appears the entry 'Receuyd [of] henry kyrham for his lycense for pryntinge of '*a ballett expreſ-ſynge ye fame*' (Arber's *Transcript*, i. 439). The tune is not mentioned by Chappell, nor is it known to exist. There is, however, a ballad reprinted in Mr. Henry Huth's 'Ancient Ballads and Broadsides' (Philobiblon Society, 1867) entitled ' A pleaſant poeſie, or ſweete Noſegay of fragrant ſmellyng Flowers : gathered in the garden of heauenly pleaſure, the holy and bleſſed Bible. To the Tune of the black Almayne'; and another, 'a new ballade, intituled, Agaynſt Rebellious and falſe Rumours. To the newe tune of the Blacke Almaine vpon Sciſſillia.'

J. P. Collier included this ballad in his 'Old Ballads' (Percy Society, 1840). It is printed in two columns, and within a line border.

72

A Balad intituled, A cold Pye for the Papiftes,|Wherin is
contayned: The Truft of true Subiectes for fuppreffyng of Sedicious
Papiftrie and | Rebellion: to the maintenance of the Gofpell, and the publique
Peace of Englande.

Made to be fonge to Laffiamiza Noate.

WHat Chriftian that the Lord doth feare,
Can fobs & blubbering teares forbeare,
    the time to way vprightly?
To fe how fubiects Ebbe and Flowe,
Wherby great difcord haps to growe,
    a thing God knowes vnfightly:
Wherby our Queene and Realme we fee,
By fuch (alas) difquiet be,
But God cut fhort the rage of thofe,
As feeke to be their Countreis Foes,
    Beat down their brags their boafte deface,
    Vnto our Queene Lord graunt thy grace,
    That fhe the fword from fheath may draw
    To vanquifh fuch as hate thy law,
Then fhall we be: from daunger free,
Graunt heauenly God, thus it may be.

The carelleffe Crew the fhameles Route,
Of Papifts proud whofe harts moft ftoute,
    thy Gofpell are difdaining:
Who fecretly in corners lurke,
Much mifcheife here and there to worke,
    within our land remayning:
Deface deare God for Chriftes fake,
Then fhall their Trayterous Treafon flake,
Preuent their hope wherin they ftay,
And difanull their Golden day,
    Wherof they brag: and make great boaft,
    Of Chrift and his to fcoure the Coaft,
    They truft to treade thy Gofpell downe,
    Againft our Queene they fret and frowne,
Thus thine and thee, contemned be,
From all fuch Rebels, England free.

E e

And fortefie our Queene with grace,
That fhe with fword from hence may chafe,
  all thofe that haue affented :
Againft thy word and truth to iarre,
Who feek to rayfe vp Ciuill warre,
  as people difcontented,
With thy deare gifts fo manifolde
Which they and we do well behold,
Styll giuen by thy good prouidence,
Yet fom withftand thy reuerence,
  Thy worfhip Lord they do difdaine,
  They feeke (as Truth) Lies to maintaine,
  God graunt our Queene may looke about,
  From hence to weede, fuch Papifts ftout,
Then fhall we be, from daunger free,
Graunt heauenly God fo it may be.

The difcord in the North we knowe,
Which through the Poape did fpring and grow,
  was warely preuented :
And fome that this Aduauncement fought,
A Hempen Hatchet iuftly caught,
  Becaufe they fo affented :
To take the Field agaynft all right
Againft the Trueth and Queene to fight :
But if thy worde and Gofpell deare,
Had ben fo taught and preached theare
  As it hath ben in London longe,
  They wolde haue fhund fuche Treafon ftronge,
  And duely done Obedience :
  Vnto our Queene : with reuerence :
Whofe mercye may : procure alwaye
Her Subiectes Hartes in Trueth to ftaye.

⁋ Yet many feeke for to defpyfe,
The Fowntayne, whence fuche Grace doth ryfe,
  Our Queene and Soueraygne raygnynge :
And vp and downe they vfe to goe,
Lyke Rebelles, Difcorde for to fowe
  with Lyes of their owne faynynge :
What? doth the Princeffe Curteoufie,
Of you deferue fuche Iniurie?
That fuche Rewarde ye render now,
To her, whiche fo doth tender you?
  Shall her true loue reape fuche Difdaine?
  Or thinke ye now as Lordes to raygne?
  Our Queene beares not a Sworde for nought
  Your Duties now ye wyll be taught:
I truft her Grace, within fhort fpace :
All peruers Papifts wyll hence chace.

（ 211 ）

¶ And where as mercye hath ben caufe,
That ye tranfgreffe her Highneffe Lawes:
   I truft ye fhall knowe truelye:
That Iuftice Sworde fhall cut you fhort,
Whiche to worke mifchiefe thinke it fport,
   As Rebelles moft vnrulye:
Beware therfore, ye Papifts prowde,
Whiche feeke in Dennes your felues to fhrowde,
To worke your wiles as voide of feare,
In cafting Billes now here, now there,
   Which feemes our Queene and Crowne to touch
   And ye your felues cannot aduouche,
   The hangman giue you not fuch checkes,
   That Tiburne chaunce to breake your necks,
Truft me ye may, if ye do play,
The Rebels thus, you muft that way.

¶ For when fuch Wicked plants are gone,
Englande fhall haue no caufe to mone,
   Nor future Foes be doutynge:
God graunt the Sworde may fhun the Sheathe,
And by the Rootes fuche Weedes bereaue,
   For many here are fcowtynge:
Who feeke as muche as ere they maye,
This lyttell Brittaine to betraye:
And all becaufe we Chrift profeffe,
As prefent tyme doth proue no leffe:
   But God confownde poore Englandes Foes
   And fafely keepe our Ryall Rofe:
   From fuche as woulde her highneffe harme,
   With Neftors yeares her Perfon arme:
Graunt her thy Grace, in euery place,
The Force of Rebelles to deface.

FINIS.   Iohn Phillip.

¶ Imprinted at London, by William How, for Richard Iohnes and are to be
folde, at his fhop ioyning to the Southweft doore of Paules Church.

Though J. P. Collier (*Extracts from the Registers of the Stationers' Company*, i. 128) hazards a suggestion that this ballad may be connected with 'a ballatt intituled *a monfterus pye*' for which a licence was obtained in 1565–66 (Arber's *Transcript*, i. 305), it is doubtless one of many issued at the suppression of 'the Rising in the North', yet a licence for it does not appear in the Registers for 1569–70. The tune 'Lassiamiza Noate' is not mentioned by Chappell in his 'Popular Music of the Olden Time'.

The ballad is printed in two columns, between which there is a lace border.

73

An Epytaphe, or a lamentable Difcourfe: wherein is bewayled the death of the Right worfhipfull Knight, Sir William Garrat: one of the Queens Maiefties Commiffioners, and chiefe | Alderman of the honourable Citie of London. Who deceafed. the .27. of September. 1571.

WHo can refraine from forwing plaints, and brinifh blubbring teares?
    What hart wyll now refufe to grone? and tourne from Ioy his eares.
Ne high, ne low, ne Rich, ne poore, in London that remayne,
    But haue iuft caufe for Garrats loffe, to languifh and complayne:
Helpe me therefore ye powers deuine: that in the heauens doo dwell,
    The loffe of this mofte worthy wight, in mourninge Verfe to tell.
Come now Calliope I pray, and Clio Goulden Dame:
    with Sifters thine from Helycon, aide mee frefh plaints to frame.
Stay not on Mownt Pernafo now, caft on your mournyng weede,
    conuert your Hymnes and Songs of Ioy, to wailyng woes wᵗ fpeede.
Send foorth with mee your fighing fobbes, the facred Skies to pearce:
    that vnto Goddes and mortall men, our plaints we may difpearfe.
And fayle mee not O Pallas now, amidft my griefe and woe:
    But graunt with fkyl to guide my Quil, thefe heauy Newes to fhoe.
Sith I with teares do craue your aide, let mee your fauour finde:
    The loffe of Garrat worthie Wight, help now to print in mind.
What? flie ye thus from mee? alas: why go ye backe againe?
    wyll none of you to further mee, vouchfafe to take the payne?
Alas, (vnfkilfull wretche:) Difdaine doth thee betide:
    For Meduce and Pierides, with thee in place abyde:
Thefe Dames as hard as Steele or Flint, are fixed in thy fight:
    and thou haft nought but black and white, thy meanyng to endight.
Leaue off therfore, fith Clios Spring, of Rhethorique is fled:
    thy wyll is good, but powers thyne, with Ignorance are fed.
I wept to fee my Fortune fuche, my woes did then abounde:
    But Hoape at laft to comfort mee, a prefent meane foorth fownd:
Feare not (quoth fhe) difpaire thou not, fet drowpyng dread afide,
    take Pen and write: to comfort thee, (I Hoape) a meane prouide.
Lift vp thyne eies, behold and fee, Dame Trueth is in thy fight:
    with that I rendred humble thankes, and tooke my Pen to wright.
And now, awaye ye doubtfull lettes, that clogde my hart with feares:
    By force to geue you ouerthrow, Dame Trueth in place appeares.
Should Garrats loffe vnminded bee? fuch Friend to Cōmon weale,
    Though he be gone, fhould we not way, his true and godly zeale?
Should we forget his curtefie, fo plainlie knowen and feene?
    Then moft vnkind we fhould remayne, fith he our frend hath ben.

Ye Confuls wife, ye Senatours, that Londons wealth prouide,
  Lament and wayle, for vnto you, no fmall loffe is betide.
Ye all haue loft a faithfull Frend, for Counfell fage and wife:
  In thynges of weight, ye fayled not, to folow his aduife.
But now that facred Ioue, by wifdome his [*sic*] decreed,
  That Lachefis & Clotho both, their toyle fhuld leaue in deede:
Coms Parchas fhee, with Sickle fharp, & fhreads the thred in twaine
  That three fcore yeares & vii. to weaue: they had imployd their payne.
She cutteth downe this Olyue greene, whofe Branches fayre did fhoe,
  His dayes are ron to Champian now, and Beecher he wyll goe.
Of Hayward wife, Pretorian hee, now Garrat leaue doth take
  Good Offley olde, and gentle White: by Death he muft forfake.
Eke Draper wife, and Allen hee, whofe wifdome doth excell.
  with all the Troupe of Aldermen, thus Garrat byds, Farewell.
Therfore in Senate when you fit, and want hym in your trayne:
  For wifdome his, in Memorie, let Image his remayne.
In rule, he was your equall fure: for Counfayle Solon hee,
  Then meete with teares his Abfence fhould, of you lamented bee.
No Rule, but he hath borne, that doth to London longe,
  A man vpright in Iuftice fure, that knew the right from wronge.
Moft apt was Garrat to doo good, to all and euerie wight,
  Both riche and poore, may wayle the loffe, of fuche a gentell Knight.
In Iuftice, fingle was he fure, in Iudgement alwaye fownd:
  To ceafe contendyng prone and preft, this worthie man was fownd.
To needie poore a perfite frende, to tender all their griefe,
  And fuche a one, as fpared not, to them to geue reliefe.
Vnto the Pryfoners poore, that did in captiue plight remaine:
  From bandes to free all that he could, he did imploy his payne.
But who hath loft the greateft loffe? I knowe not one, but all:
  But to his Spoufe and Ladie deare, the greateft loffe doth fall.
She wants her louyng Mate, her Friend and Turtle true:
  whofe death with fighes & forowyng fobbes, fhe ceafeth not to rew.
His Children deare their Father want, they lacke their Staffe & ftay.
  His Seruantes they, their Mafter miffe, alas and well away.
But that they loft, the Lorde hath fownd, the mightie God on hie:
  For as his lyfe was vertuous, fo godly he did die.
Amidft his bytter panges of death, that were both fharpe and ftrong:
  To fee his Chrift and heauenly Ioyes, he vehemently did longe.
And now his wifh he hath obtaind, for Death hath done his wyll:
  His Corps deuoide of breath doth reft, yet fhall his Fame lyue ftyll.
His Soule by faith the Heauens hath won, his Body fhrowdes in Clay
  This finall farewell Garrat take: I haue no more to fay.

FINIS.   I. Phillip.

⁋ Imprinted at London in the vpper end of Fleetelane: | by Richarde Iohnes, and
are to be fould at his Shop, ioynyng to the Southweft Doore of fainct|
Paules Churche. 1571.   October .4.

The 'Dictionary of National Biography' mentions
two individuals—John Phillip (fl. 1566) and John
Phillips, Philips, or Phillyps (fl. 1570–91), and from the

notices there given it appears they were both writers
of ephemeral verse.
  Mr. W. W. Greg, however, in articles published

in 'The Library' for July and October, 1910, furnishes evidence to show that Philip and Phillips may be regarded as one and the same person; and after carefully weighing the variants, and these, as may be easily understood, were numerous in the sixteenth century, he adopts as correct the spelling 'Phillip', the form accepted in the British Museum Catalogue.

Mr. Greg enumerates twenty-four articles which are associated with Phillip. Among these are the three ballads reprinted here and a poetical 'Commemoration on the life and death of . . . Sir Chriftopher Hatton', 1591, a copy of which is at Britwell, whence it came from Lamport Hall, Northamptonshire; two broadside epitaphs, one on the death of the wife of Lord Mayor Avenet (Avenon), the other on Henry, Earl of Southampton, and an octavo tract entitled 'A Frendly Larum . . . to the true harted Subiectes of England . . .' (1569–70), formerly in the Huth library; and several which are preserved in the British Museum, while others are to be found in references alone.

Nicholas Bourman was the author of another epitaph on Sir William Garrard (p. 34). Both were printed by Richard Jones and are alike in arrangement and ornament.

74

¶ An Epitaphe on the death of the right noble and moſt vertuous Lady *Margarit Duglaſis* good | grace, Countiſſe of Liuinox (& Daughter to the renowmed & moſt excellent Lady Margarit Queene, Siſter to the magnificent & moſt mighty | Prince Henry the eight of England, Fraunce and Ireland, Kinge, and by Gods permiſſion Queene of Scotland,) who diſceaſed this | life the ninth day of March. Anno. 1577. at hir mannoure in Hackny in the countye of Midelſex and lieth enterred the .3. day of April at Weſtminſter | in the Chaple of King Henry the ſeuenth, her worthie Grandfather of Englande, Fraunce and Ireland King. &c.   The yeare of our | Lorde God. 1578, and in the .20. yeare of our ſoueraigne Lady Queene Elizabeth by the grace of God of Englande, | Fraunce and Irelande, Queene, defendour of the faith. &c.

REporte run on, ringe forth thy doleful Bel,
That worldly wightes, may waile our great anoye :
In Court and Towne, our cauſe of woe do tel,
That ſtand diſtreſt bereft of al our ioye.
With care ſee that, thy ſkyl thou do imploye,
To blaſe our luckles hap throughout each land :
That mortal wightes, our grefes may vnderſtande.

Ladye Marga-
rits grace
Daugh-
ter to the
eldeſt
Daugh-
ter of
Henrye
the 7.
now diſ-
ceaſed,
borne at
Harbo-
tell three
yeares
before ill
Maye
daye.

And as we waile, ſo let conſtraint of paine,
Inforce them weepe, to thinke vpon our loſſe :
In woful wiſe, with vs, let them complaine,
That yeld of care, to beare the bitter croſſe.
Let waues of woe, their mindes in anguiſh toſſe,
Let flouds of flowing teares, each where be ſeene :
To waile this Dame, the Daughter of a Queene.

In princely place, let Prince and Peeres lament,
Let Noble Lordes, and Ladies yeld to waile :
For from the Courte a Iwel [*sic*] ritch is hent,
And ſuch a one as to her great auaile,
Deſerueth fame, though Death her life do quaile,
Wher ſhe might helpe, ſhe would no harme procure :
You all can tel, her freindſhip was moſt pure.

A foe to vice and ſuch as vitious were,
This noble dame continually did reſt :
A freendly hart ſhe did to vertue beare,
The fruites whereof did floriſh in her breſt.
To ritche and poore true frendſhip ſhe profeſt,
Her wordes with deedes confirmed were each howre :
Then nobles al lament this fragrant flowre.

Caſt of your ſilkes, your coaſtly robes forbeare,
Abandon Ioy, let myrth an exile be :
Vouchſafe a while your mourning weedes to weare,
Beweepe this dame borne of ſo hye degree.
A royal prince Henry the ſeauenth euen he,
Of England, Fraunce, and Ireland, famous kinge,
Her Gran-fyre was conſider you this thing.

Her Lady mothers grace, that Margarit hight,
Of Scotland was, whilom the crowned queene:
And fyſter to, the eight Henry by right,
Whoſe flowring fame in England ſhineth greene.
Alied by byrth this gem was to our queene,
Then noble ſtates, minde you her bloud and byrth:
And helpe with teares to bring her to the earth.

Send forth your ſobes, let floudes fal from your eyes,
This gratious gem, this pearle of prize beweepe:
And in your hartes, of Liuinox that Counteſſe wiſe,
For vertue vouch, a true recorde to keepe.
And though her corpes in earth lye cloaſed deepe,
Conſent to make memorial of her name:
That conquereth death by force of worthy fame.

Her loue to God was alwaies faithful founde,
Her lyfe ſhe led in loyalty and awe:
On trueth ſhe ſtaid, to prince her troth was founde,
And ſtoode in dread for to tranſgreſſe the lawe.
Infortune fel could not her hart with drawe,
From God nor prince, her thought could neuer chaunge,
Ne was her loue to countrey ſhowne as ſtraunge.

Then Brittaines kinde that ſytte in honors ſtal,
Forget not you, to bid this dame adew:
And you in court, that meaneſt are of al,
With teares prepare, your louing freende to rew.
Whilſt life ſhe ioyed ſhe was a freende to you,
Her hart was meeke and humble to the ende:
Iuſt cauſe you haue to weepe ſo good a freende.

You ſutors poore, haue loſt a Margarit deare,
A precious pearle, the piller of your truſt:
Who willing was, your due demaundes to heare,
And to the prince to further cauſes iuſt.
Thinke on this Phenix rare of right you muſt,
Whoſe want, with woe vouchſafe atime to waile,
Her ſhrine remaines, her preſence you do faile.

In wedlockes right, whilſt ſhe poſſeſſed life,
This pereleſſe dame moſt dutiful was founde:
Vnto her worthy ſpowſe ſhe was a conſtant wife,
Faith knit loues knot, truth was her truſtie ground
Two ſons ſhe had moſt fyt to be renownd

Henrye King of Scots. hir eldeſt ſonne.

The one of Scots the diadem did weare:
Whoſe fatal fyne is knowen to euery eare.

Whilſt he as prince did beare the royal ſway,
The commons hartes moſt curtuouſly he wonne:
But treaſon falſe in cancred hartes did ſtay,
And traitors fearce to worke his ſpoile begonne.
Yet weldeth now the ſcepter (there) his ſonne,
Whoſe death did nyp this Counteſſe to the gall:
Yet did ſhe ioy, his ſeede was ſafe from thrall.

Her other fonne Lord Charles that worthy wight,
Efpoufd fhe fee, whofe feede fhe did imbrace:
Yet death in time bereft him from her fight,
Whofe want in her a double dole did place.
Twixt thefe extremes yet did this Ladies grace,
Vfe patience fweete to falue her inward griefe:
And praifed God that was her comfort chiefe.

But as theyr race the courfe of time ware out,
And they to death conftrained were to bende:
So to her ftate (Time) his compas courft about,
And toucht her corpes with fickneffe fharp in ende.
In which by faith on Chrift fhe did depende,
Whofe onely bloud fhe did affye and truft:
By faith fhould purge, her fin and make her iuft.

**Lorde
Charles
her fon,
Earle of
Liuinox
buried at
hackney**

Her hope was heauen, this world fhe did deteft,
And when that death began to draw ful nye:
To beare his ftroke fhe patience pure poffeft,
And vnto heauen for fauegarde fweete did flye.
She vnto God with hart and minde did crye,
Preferue our queene and bleffe this little land:
Her foes confound with thy out ftretched hand.

This done fhe bids the noble Peares adew,
She takes her leaue of friends and feruants all:
My tyme is come, I take my leaue of you,
The fruite thats ripe, is foneft apt to fall.
And though to death my body now be thrall,
I dye, to liue in heauen with Chrift my loue:
And hope to refte with his elect aboue.

This faid, her breth forthwith began to fayle,
And fading life, inclines to draw to ende:
She leaues this world vnto her great auaile,
For Iefus Chrift is found her fureft frende.
From daunger great, hir foule he doth defende,
Synne is defafte by vertue of his blood:
And he alone hath done this Counteffe good.

**Wife &
Lady to
the lorde
Charles
Earle of
Liuinox**

**Charles
Kinge of
Scotlãd.**

Her Daughter deare that louinge Lady kinde,
Her Graceffe death to mourne is reddy preft:
The Lady younge that nature hath afynde,
As yet for foode to claime the Nourfes breft.
Euen as it can with forrowe is poffeft,
And Scotlands Kinge, his Gran-dames death doth mone:
In Court and Towne a caufe of care is fhowne.

Her feruants all beweepe hir noble grace,
The poore each where, her loffe with teares lament
From whom no time fhe once would turne her face
Her hart and hand they fay, each howre was bent.
Their neede to helpe, and Hackney doth affent,
with wringing hãds to waile this worthies wrack
That gaue them foode and clad the naked back.

But what can teares or pearcing plaints preuaile,
Her time was come, and death hath cut her downe:
Thre fcore, three yeres fhe liu'd til death did quaile,
The life of hir moft worthye high renowne.
And now her head of life hath got the Crowne,
Her bleffed foule before the heauenly kinge:
Doth hymes of Ioy with faints & Angels fynge.

Viuit poft funera virtus. Finis. *I. Phillips.*

Imprinted at London for Edward White and are to be folde at the little North dore
of Paules at the Signe of the Gunne.

The Countess was the only child of Archibald, nineteenth Earl of Angus by his marriage with Margaret, queen dowager of Scotland, daughter of Henry VII of England. After forming other attachments, she married in 1544 Matthew Stuart, fourth Earl of Lennox, and is best known to history as the mother of the ill-fated Lord Darnley. So long as Mary and Elizabeth Tudor were excluded by the bann of illegitimacy, Margaret was regarded as a possible successor to the throne of England, and even after her accession Mary is said to have considered the Countess's claim prior to that of her sister.

After the accession of Queen Elizabeth, Margaret retired north with other prominent Catholics, and there planned for her descendants the ultimate succession to both kingdoms. In July, 1565, Darnley and Mary of Scotland were married at Holyrood. About eighteen months later the husband was killed at Kirk o' Field. Lennox, who had been appointed Regent, was murdered in 1571. Forthwith the Countess permitted herself to become partially reconciled to Mary, actuated probably by a motive to serve her infant grandson rather than from any belief in her daughter-in-law's innocence.

Margaret's second son, Lord Charles Stuart, was created Earl of Lennox, the title having at first devolved on Darnley's infant son, James. This Earl died in 1576, leaving a daughter Arabella, who spent her last years a prisoner in the Tower.

The Countess of Lennox died at Hackney in 1578 in her sixty-third year, and was buried in Westminster Abbey. Her ambition was realized in 1603, when James VI succeeded to the throne of England.

In addition to this epitaph Phillip was the author of ' A Commemoration of the Right Noble and vertuous Ladye, Margrit Duglafis good grace, Countis of Lennox, Daughter to the . . . Princeffe Margrit, Queene of Scotland, efpowfed to King Iames the fourth . . .' (1578). Copies of this poem, printed in quarto, to which Phillip prefixed a lengthy epistle, are in the British Museum and at Britwell.

The ballad is printed in two columns on a large broadside.

75

A Lamentation from Rome, how the Pope, doth|bewayle,
That the Rebelles in England can not preuayle.

To the tune of Rowe well ye Mariners.

ALl you that newes would here,
Geue eare to me poore Fabyn Flye,
At Rome I was this yere,
And in the Pope his nofe dyd lye,
But there I could not long abide,
He blew me out of euery fide:
For furft when he had harde the newes,
That Rebelles dyd their Prince mifufe,
    Then he with ioye,
Did fporte him felfe with many a toye,
    he then fo ftout,
From that his nofe he blew me out.

¶But as he was a flepe,
Into the fame againe I goot:
I crept there in fo depe,
That I had almoft burnt my coote,
New newes to him was brought that night,
The Rebelles they weare put to flight,
But Lord how then the Pope toke one,
And called for a Mary bone,
    vp howgh make haft:
My louers all be like to wafte,
    ryfe Cardnall, vp prieft,
Saint Peter he doth what he left.

¶So then they fell to Meffe,
The Fryers one their Beades dyd praye,
The Pope began to bleffe,
At laft he weift not what to faye.
It chanced fo the next day morne,
A Poft came blowing of his Horne,
Saying Northomberland is take,
But then the Pope began to quake.
    he then rubd nofe,
With Pilgrome falue benoynt his hofe,
    runne here, runne there,
His nayles for anger gan to pare.

☞ Not Northomberland alone,
But many of his wicked ayd :
Such as thought not to grone,
They hoped well for to aplayd,
There partes to haue there hartes defire,
But now is quenched there flames of fire,
The greateft and the meane befide,
With other youths faft bound muft ride,
  Ketch faft, kepe well,
Ther youthfull bloud they long to fell,
  truft this dere Pope,
what is it than wherfore ye hope.

¶ When he perceaued well,
The newes was true to him was brought,
Vpon his knees he fell,
And then S. Peter he befought,
That he would ftand his frend in this,
To helpe to ayd thofe feruauntes his,
And he would do as much for him,
But Peter fent him to Saint Simme.
  So then he fnuft,
the Fryers all about he cuft,
  He roard he cryde,
the preifts they durft not once abide.

✠ The Cardnalles they beginnes,
To ftay and take him in there arme,
He fpurnd them on the fhinnes,
Away the trudgd for feare of harme.
So there the pope was left alone,
Good Lord how he dyd make his mone,
The Stooles againft the Walles he threwe,
And me out of his nofe he blewe.
  I hopt I fkipt,
From place to place about I whipt,
  he fwore he tare,
Till from his Crowne he pold the heare.

¶ He courft me fo about,
In the houfe I could finde no rome,
Loth I was to go out,
And fhrind my felfe vnder a Brome.
Then by and by downe he was fet,
with anger he was one a fwet,
He rubd his elbowe on the Wall
So fell a rayling on Saint Paule.
  Fye fye bloud harte,
He fcratchde him felfe till he dyd fmart,
  poll nofe rube eye,
Grafh [*sic*] the teth drawe mouth awrye.

¶ He wept and wrong his handes,
yea worſe and worſe began to fret:
Thus radging ſtill he ſtandes,
then out at doore I dyd me get,
I was not ſoner gone from thence,
But worſe and worſe was his pretence,
The poſt he plucked from the houſe,
he left no harbour for a Mouſe,
    thus now the popes mad.
Becauſe no better lucke they had,
    forlorne moleſt,
that they ſo yll their meate digeſt.

¶ When I had vewed all,
To bring this newes my winges I ſpred,
to this parplict he is fall,
I wiſh ſome would go hold his head,
For certainely he doth yll fare,
yet for the ſame I do not care,
For God his power will conuince,
And ayd with right his beloued prince,
    then Pope radge thou,
The God in heauen hath made a vowe,
    to kepe all his,
That God is iuſt our ſtay he is.

Finis. ꝓ. Thomas Preſton.

Imprinted at London, in Fleteſtrete at | the ſigne of the Faulcon by Wylliam | Gryffith, and are to be ſold at his | ſhoppe in Sainte Dunſtones Churchyard. 1570.

The rebels here mentioned are the Earls of Northumberland and Westmorland and their adherents, whose efforts to create a Catholic rising in the north of England during the autumn of 1569 had recently been suppressed.

For note of the popular tune 'Rowe well ye Mariners' see the ballad 'A warning to London by the fall of Antwerp' (p. 202).

From the 'Dictionary of National Biography' we learn that Thomas Preston was a native of Buckinghamshire and was educated at Eton. He proceeded to Cambridge, where he ultimately became vicechancellor. He was favourably noticed by Queen Elizabeth on a visit to Cambridge in 1564, when he addressed her in a Latin oration.

Preston was the author of 'a geleflower gentle or fwete mary golde Where in the frutes of terannye you may beholde', licensed to William Gryffyth in 1569-70 (Arber's *Transcript*, i. 413), but now not extant; also of 'A lamentable tragedy, mixed ful of pleaſant mirth, conteyning the life of Cambiſes King of Percia', without date, licensed to John Allde in 1569-70 (Arber, i. 400). Copies of this are in the British Museum and the Bodleian Library. A later edition, also undated, printed by Edward Allde, is at Britwell. Cambises is excessively tragic in form and language, and Falstaff refers to it when he says 'I must speak in passion and I will do it in Cambiſes way'. The 'Lamentation from Rome' was published in 1569-70 (Arber, i. 405), and was included in J. P. Collier's 'Old Ballads' (Percy Society, 1840). It was again reprinted in the 'Borderer's Table Book', vii. 154.

The ballad is printed in two columns, which are separated by a broad ornamental border in three blocks.

76

A Pſalme of thankſgiuing.

[See facsimile.]

Measurements of original, 13⅜ inches by 9¾ inches.

A Pſalme of thankſgiuing, to be ſung by

the Children of Chriſts Hoſpitall, on Munday in the Eaſter
holy dayes, at Saint Mary Spittle, for their Founders and
Benefactors. *Anno Domini.* 1610.

These two lines are to be ſung by one or two of the Children, and then repeated by the people and all the Children.

Egard O Lord from heauen aboue, accept the hartie prayſe, which

Children render for the loue, thou ſheweſt to them alwayes.

He goodnes of the Lord is ſeene, in all that he hath made, his mercy 'tis in all extreames

that ſends his creatures aide. No worme ſo ſmall, no wight ſo poore, but he preſerueth ſtill,

the ſicke he heales, the weake ſuſtaines, and hungry ſoule doth fill. Wee Orphants poore like mercy found,

when meanes and friends were ſcant, our gracious God a Prince did moue, to ſlake and eaſe our want.

Regard O Lord, &c.

(deere
The ground-worke of our good thus laid, God raiſd vs Patrons
Whoſe liberall hands did ſtil prouide, to rid our hearts from feare.
You Cittizens thoſe patrons are, by you we Orphants liue,
Foode, rayment, learning. all we want, to vs you largely giue.
Bleſſe their endeuours Lord we pray; encreaſe likewiſe their ſtore,
That thoſe in plenty may abound, which helpe to feed the poore.
Regard O Lord, &c.

(grace
O Lord vpon our Soueraigne King, powre downe thy heauenly
Preſerue his Queene, defend the Prince, bleſſe all his royall race.
Plant wiſedome in his Counſellours, graunt to his Nobles might,
Thy church maintain, thy paſtors ſaue, that they may teach aright.
On Citty, Mayor, and Aldermen, Lord let thy mercy fall,
By whome our ſtates are thus relieued, and wee releaſt from thrall.
Regard O Lord &c.

Children kept in Chriſtes Hoſpitall at this preſent   630
Children put foorth Apprentiſes, and dead this yeare out of
Chriſtes hoſpitall.   54
There hath bene cured this yeare paſt in S. Bartholmews Hoſpi-
tall of Souldiers and other diſeaſed people.   602
There is in the ſaid Hoſpitall vnder cure at this preſent.   253
There hath bene cured this yeare paſt in S. Thomas Hoſpitall of
Souldiers and other diſeaſed people.   812
There is in the ſaid Hoſpit   vnder cure at this preſent   1·6

Toward the which godly & charitable foūdation, King
Henry the eight, & King Edward the ſixt, were moſt
gratious founders and liberall benefactors.

A Report for Bridewell.

There hath bene brought to the Hoſpital of Bride-
wel within the ſpace of one yeare laſt paſt, of wā-
dring ſouldiers and other vagrant people, which haue
bene paſſed thence into their natiue countries by Paſ-
ports, according to the lawe in that caſe prouided,
to the number of 1697. of whome many haue bene
chargeable to the ſaid Hoſpitall in their dyet, for
the time of their being in the ſame: ſome more,
ſome leſſe, as they might thence be conueniently remoued, beſides other helps there miniſtred vnto many of them, as cauſe required: viz. in Hoſe, Shooes,
Shirtes, bands, money and ſuch like, which cannot
be auoyded by reaſon of their miſery, nor they thence
paſſed without charge to the ſaid Hoſpitall, in reſpect
they are to be examined, and conſidered of, to what
country to be tranſported. Alſo there is in the ſaid hoſpitall maintained and kept in Arts and occupations,
and other ſeruile workes and labours, at the charges
of the ſaid Hoſpitall, of men, women, and children. to
the number of 130. perſons, whereof 88. and vpwards
are poore boyes taken out of diuers Pariſhes and
ſtreetes of this Citty, and now bound Apprentiſes
in th ſaid   uade Freemen of this City
at the end of their ſeuerall termes.   T. S

Printed at London by *E. Alld:* for *W. Barley* dwelling in Gracious ſtreet. 1610. *Cum Priuilegio.*

77

Feare God   *And*   *Honour the King.*

A Pfalme of Prayer and praife for|the profperous and good

eftate of our Soueraigne | *Lord the King, his royall progeny, and the whole eftate* | of his Maiefties dominions and people; drawne from the *Foun|taine of Faith, for the priuate vfe of the poore Orphanes in Chrifts Hofpi|tall*; or any true Chriftian, wifhing wealth and peace to Sion.

	LOrd giue thy Iudgements to our King, therein inftruct him well
	And with his Sonne that Princely thing, Lord let thy graces dwell.
Efa. 3. 2. 1.	That they may gouerne righteoufly, and rule thy folke aright :
Pfal. 72. 1.	And fo defend with equitie, the weake, which haue no might.
Pfal. 82. 2.	The fimple heart, the Widowes poore, and Orphanes in diftreffe,
pfal. 101.	
Pfal. 12. 5.	To faue from wrong, and euill doer to punifh and repreffe.
	Direct his Nobles readily, to guide their folke in peace :
Efa. 32. 2.	And let the Magiftrates apply, in iuftice to increafe.
P[f]al. 72. 4.	That they alfo may helpe the weake, and thofe with wrong oppreft :
	From fuch as hurt and proudly fpeake, to giue them peace and reft,
Pfal. 10, 12.	
Pfal. 12. 4.	That all may know, and eke obey ; regarde and feare thy might :
Pfal. 72. 12.	So long as Sunne doeth fhine by day, or elfe the Moone by night.
Pro. 16. 15.	Lord make our king vnto the iuft, like raine on fields new mowen
Pfal. 72. 6.	And as the drops that laye the duft, and frefh the land late fowen,
Pfal. 85. 9.	That they may profper in his time, In grace, in wealth and peace :
Pfal. 10. 1.	Although the wicked doe repine, yet let them not increafe.
Pfal. 10. 15.	
Pro. 20. 26.	That thefe endes of the earth (the Weft) poffeffions of thy fonne,
Pfal. 2.	May in thy right, rule and be bleft, till date of time be done.
Pfa. 144. 15.	Plant vnitie within his Realmes, with wealth and grace deuine :
Efa. 66. 12.	Let knowledge flow like chriftall ftreames, and Babels fect decline.
Re. 18. 2.	Direct him and his royall race, thy Syon ftill to reare :
Heb. 13. 15.	In length of dayes with health and peace, in thy true faith and **feare**.
16.	
Pfal. 89. 15.	That facrifices of prayer, and prayfe, with almes may offered be :
Ieam. 1. 27.	In faith and loue, to thee alwaies, by all in each degree.

With grace & loue, with wealth and peace, this noble Citye bleffe,
And all that do our good increafe ; we pray thee Lord no leffe.
Accept our prayers, receiue our praife, which now to thee we giue,
For thefe, and all thy gifts alwaies ; and will do while wee liue.
All glorie to the Trinitie, both now and eke for aye,
To God all one, in perfons three, one effence pure we pray.

Finis.

Imprinted at London by Edward Allde.

The Easter Psalm was a feature in the early history of Christ's Hospital. The composition of these was usually the joint effort of the Song-Schoolmaster and one of the prominent scholars. Canon Pearce (*Annals of Christ's Hospital*, 1901, p. 225) names 1625 as the earliest date at which these psalms are mentioned. It was the custom to introduce extraneous matter therein, sometimes an appeal for alms on behalf of some institution, such as Bridewell, as will be seen from that of the two psalms in the Britwell collection which is facsimiled.

The opening lines of the undated psalm are accompanied by music. It is of course 'for the profperous and good eftate' of King James, although in the absence of any entry in the Stationers' Registers it is impossible to decide the precise year in which it was issued.

The broadside has a lace border.

78

¶ A short Discourse of mans fatall
end with an vnfaygned, Commendation of the worthinesse
of Syr Nicholas Bacon, Knight, Lord Keeper of the great Seale of
England : Who disceased the xx. day of February. 1578.

1. Peter. 1.   ℞ All fleshe is grasse, and all the glory of man is as the flower of
Iames. 1.   grasse, the grasse wythereth, and the flower falleth away, but the
Sira. 14.   worde of the Lorde endureth for euer.
Philip. 1.   ℞ Christ is to vs lyfe, and death to vs aduauntage.

Sira. 17.   SInce God hath fyxt our dayes and yeares, to liue and eke to dye,
Ephe. 1.   And takes his choice of vs his sheepe, what wight shal him deny?
Rom. 8.   But that he may without reiagge his creatures take and saue,
Mat. 25.   Yea heaue them vp, yea throw thē down, from life vnto the graue :
Ioh. 5.   Reioice we then among the route, which doth this thing confesse,
Rom. 8.   And pray that God may haue his will, he teacheth vs no lesse.
Sam. 12.   And thanke him to, for all his giftes, and, seeme not for to mourne,
Phil. 4.   For that which he hath in himselfe, set downe ere we were borne.
Math. 6.   All tymes with him is not one houre, to age no subiect is :
Sam. 12.   All shall decay, yea heauen and earth, such power and glory is his,
Eccle. 7.   Borne all to dye, and dye we must, all flesh shall yeeld to death,
Ephe. 1.   The promisse made welcome the tyme, with fayth let go this breath.
2. Pet. 3.   As now of late a worthy man, by God from hence is calde,
Mat. 24.   Who doth not dye, but lyue for aye, and in the heauens is stalde :
Iame. 1.   Whose lyfe on earth so well was knowne, to those of thankfull **mynde**,
Rom. 9.   That which he did that iustice had, that few lyke him I fynde.
      A subiect true, in Councell graue, in sentence briefe and sure,
Cor. 15.   A mynde bedect with equity, whose fame shall aye indure.
      To ritch and poore indifferent, respecting iustice cause,
      To mitigate extremities, he sought and had the lawes :
Pro. 1.   The patron of perswasions and enemy to all vice,
Rom. 13.   He feared God, he loud his prince, which shewde him **very wise** :
Ioh. 3.   No patch of popish mynde in him was euer found,
      But fauoured those and helpt them to, which did the **trueth expound**.
      Lo this I thinke of duty right, of him thus to reporte,
      To giue that thankes which I do owe, to all such worthy sorte :
      I not deny but greater Clarkes, may pen and paynte his prayse,
      With lofty verse heroicall, as was in Ouids dayes.
      But tell the troth, and flatter not, but speake as hart doth thinke
      A rarer man not in our dayes, nor lesse at wrong would winke :

Then would this worthy Bacon Knight, and Lord by Princes will,
Whofe bodye's dead, whofe foule doth lyue, and fame continewes ftill:

Colos. 3.
Rom. 12.
Mat. 25.
And fhall at laft ryfe vp againe, in fhape and perfect bliffe,
To take rewarde with the elect, which God doth count as his.
Rom. 13.
Deu. 28.
Vnto which hap God bring vs all, when hence that we fhall wend,
29. 30.
For Gods good feare, and honeft lyfe, doth bring a ioyfull end.

FINIS. *L. Ramfey.*

Imprinted at London for Timothy Ryder.

From a brief notice of Ramsey in the 'Dictionary of National Biography' it appears that he was prominent among the anabaptists of his time and employed his talents as a versifier in attacking the Catholics. Only one other of his productions survives, 'The Practife of the diuell,' of which there is a copy in the Bodleian Library. It is described in Sir S. Egerton Brydges's 'Restituta', vol. iii, p. 438. In the Stationers' Registers under date of August 5, 1583, there is a licence to Edward White 'vnder th[e h]ande of mafter Newbery Ramfeys *wifhinge and wouldynge*' (Arber's *Transcript*, ii. 427), and on October 7, 1588, is one to Edward Aggas 'for his Copie a ballad...entituled Ramfies *farewell to his late Lorde and mafter the erle of Leicefter whiche departed this worlde at Cornburye the iiijth of September* 1588' (Arber, ii. 502). From the latter it may be inferred that Ramsey occupied

some position in Leicester's household.

In 1563–64 Timothy Ryder, bookseller, the son of John Ryder, was apprenticed to Richard Lynnell, admitted free of the Stationers' Company in 1570–71, and filled the office of beadle from March 25, 1578. He did not obtain a licence till 1582, and his name vanishes from the Registers four years later. There is at the British. Museum, in the Huth collection, 'A merie newe Ballad intituled, the pinnyng of the Bafket: And is to bee fonge to the tune of the doune right Squire ... ℘ T. Rider', without date, which was reprinted in Mr. Henry Huth's 'Ancient Ballads and Broadsides' (Philobiblon Society, 1867).

Several ballads occasioned by Bacon's decease were licensed in 1578, but that here reprinted is not among them. It is printed in one column, within a lace border.

79

A liuing remembrance of Master Robert Rogers, Marchant
aduenturer & | Leatherfeller of London deceafed, who declared the fruites
of his faith, by his moft chriftian & charitable workes. | And left this life at his houfe in
Baffings-hall the 22. of September. And was buried in Chrift-church | on Thurfday
the 1. of October. 1601.

WHen bad men dye, the memorie remaines
Of their corruptions, and vngodly wayes,
As merit to their mifapplyed paines,
Out of ill actions, forming as ill praife.
  for vertue wounded by their deepe difgrace,
  Leaues fhame to their pofteritie and race.

When good men dye, the memorie remaines,
Of their true vertues, and moft chriftian wayes:
As a due guerdon to their godly paines,
Out of good actions, forming as good praife.
  for vertue cherifh'd by their deedes of grace,
  Leaues fame to their pofteritie and race.

Among thofe good (if goodnes may be faid,
To be among the feede of mortall men:
In vpright ballaunce of true merit wayed)
This worthy Batcheler efteeme we then.
  In whome, as in a mirrour doth appeare,
  That faith and workes did fhine in him moft cleere.

Now let vs not, as is our common vfe,
Meafure him by a many other more:
In death, to couer their lifes bad abufe,
That then flyes out fome bounty of their ftore.
  No Rogers was none fuch, as may appeare,
  By thefe true witneffes annexed heere.

Firft, as God bleft him with aboundant wealth,
Like to a carefull Steward he imployde it:
Squaring his guifts out in his beft of health,
As glad to leaue it, as when he inioyde it.
  Himfelfe prepared euery houre to die:
  And all in order pointed chriftianly.

In fundry callings and vocations,
Where he could heare of them were rightly poore:
As men decayed by their occupations,
Yet held by fhame from begging at the doore,
  Such fuccourd he, as knowing that their need,
  Stopt vp their mouthes, though made their hearts to bleede.

What fhould I fay? to what poore wanting heart,
Was he not liberall in the largeft kinde?
Such as were hopefull, and had any parte
Of chriftian zeale, felt freely his good minde.
    Preachers, poore handy-crafts, and parifhes:
    From Rogers purfe haue liberall Legacies.

In Abrahams bofome fleepes he with the bleft,
His workes do follow him, his worth furuiues:
The Angels guide him to eternall reft,
Where is no date of time, for yeares or liues.
    You that are rich, doe you as he hath done:
    and fo affure the Crowne that Chrift hath woone.

Legacies bequeathed to charitable vfes by Mafter Robert Rogers deceafed.

In primis, to the two Counters, Ludgate, Newgate, Bedlam and the Clinke.   xii. l.
Money to be prefently diftributed to the poore, in the Parifh he dwelt in.   x. l.
To prouide two dozen of bread euery Sunday for euer, to be giuen to the poore of the
    faid Parifh.   C. l.
To the Parifh of Chrift-church, to buy Coales at the beft hand for the poore yearely, to
    continue a ftocke | for euer to that vfe: x. l.
And money prefently to be diftributed to the poore in that Parifh.   v. l.
To the poor of S. George Parifh in Southwarke, the poor without Newgate, the poor
    without Cripplegate, | & the poore without Bufhops [*sic*] gate, to each Parifh xx.
    Nobles to be diftributed in money.   xxvj. l. xiij. s. iiij. d.
To the poore of two Townes in the Weft Country.   xiij. l. vj. s. viij. d.
To the poore of the towne of Poole where he was borne, to be prefently diftributed in
    money.   x. l.
More, to build almes houfes in the faid towne.   CCCxxxiij. l. vj. s. viij. d.
With exebition for twelue poore people weekely for euer.
To releeue poore Prifoners fuch as may be fet free for xx. Nobles a man, or vnder, fo
    that no Papift nor Athift | haue any benefit thereof.   CL. l.
To releeue poore Preachers of the word of God, not exceeding to any one man, aboue
    ten pound.   C. l.
To ten poore decayed Artifficers that haue charge of wife and Children ten pound a man.
    C. l.
To the company of Marchant aduenturers, for the reliefe of decayed people by him
    nominated during their | liues, and after their deceafe, to the vfe of young men free
    of the faid company.   CCCC. l.
To the Company of Leatherfellers, to giue exebition at the Vnyuerfities, to foure
    Schollers ftudents in De|uinitie for euer viz. Two in Oxford and Two in Cam-
    bridge.   CCCC. l.
To Saint George Parifh in Sowthwarke.   xxx. l.
To Saint Sepulchers Parifh.   xxx. l.
To Saint Oliffes Parifh in Sowthwarke.   xxx. l.
To Saint Gyles without Cripplegate.   xxx. l.
To Saint Leonards in Shorditch.   xxx. l.
To Saint Buttolphes without Allgate.   xx. l.
To Saint Buttolphes without Bifhopfgate.   xx. l.

Amounting to 190. l. in all, to make ftocks to buy fea-coale or other fuell in fummer at
  the beft hand, for the vfe of | the poore, and to continue for euer in that manner,
  leauing ftocks in thofe feuerall Parifhes.

To Chrifts Hofpitall (of which he was a gouernour) to purchafe land to the reliefe of that
  houfe.   CCCCC. l.

To erect Almes houfes within the Cittie of London, and for exebition weekely for xij
  poore people to be pla|ced in them.   CCCCCC. l.

The whole fumme giuen by Mafter Rogers laft Will to charitable vfes.   2960.l. 6.s. 8.d.

Imprinted at London for M. Allde, and are to be folde at her fhop vnder Saint Mildreds Church
  in the Poultry.

In 1864 Mr. Thomas Hare made a report to the
Charity Commissioners upon Rogers's Charity, and
a copy of it appears in the City of London Livery
Companies' Commission's Report, vol. v, p. 182.

From the Registers of the Stationers' Company it
would seem that a licence was not obtained for printing
this ballad. The verses are arranged in two columns,
and the sheet is decorated with an ornamental border.

80

A New Balade or Songe, of the Lambes Feaſt.

I Hearde one ſaye:
Com ᵃ now awaye,

a Math. 22. a.
Luk. 14. b.

Make no delaye:
Alack, why ſtande yee than?
All is doubtleſſe

b Eſa. 25. a.

In ᵇ redyneſſe,

c Math. 22. a.

There wantes ᶜ but Geſſe,
To the Supper of the Lamb.
For Hee is now bleſt, in verye deede,

d Apoc. 19. a.

That's found a ᵈ Geſt, in yᵉ Mariage-weede.

.2. The Scriptures all,

e Act. 3. c.

Perfourmed ᵉ ſhall
Bee, in this my Call,
Voyced-out by H. N. (than):

f i. Iohn 4. a.

I am Gods Loue ᶠ
Com from aboue,

g Math. 22. a.
Luk. 14. b.
Apoc. 19. b.

All Men to moue ᵍ
To the Supper of the Lamb.
For Hee is now bleſt. &c.

.3. Make haſte and ſpeede,
I am indeede

h Math. 22. a.

That ʰ Maryage-weede,
That Thoſe muſt putt-on, than,
Which ſhall bee fitt,
Or-els permitt

i Luk. 22. c.
Apoc. 3. c.

Downe for to ⁱ ſitt,
At the Supper of the Lamb.
For Hee is now bleſt. &c.

k Pro. i. 2.
Eccli. 6. c.

.4. Do ᵏ not diſpyſe
Thys myne Aduyſe,
Yee that bee wyſe,
And luſt for to eate than,

l Apoc. 2. a. b.

Of the¹ lyuinge Wood,
Or heauenly Food,
So pure and good,
In the Supper of the Lamb,
For Hee is now bleſt. &c.

<table>
<tr><td>m Gen. 4. d.</td><td>.5.</td><td>That Seede ^m of Seth,</td></tr>
</table>

m Gen. 4. d.
n Iohn 3. a. b.
Rom. 6.
o Gen. 15. 17. a
Rom. 4. b.
p Luk. 22 c.
Apoc. 3. c.

q 2. Tim. 4. a
1 Pet. 5. a.
Iam. i. b.

.5. That Seede *m* of Seth,
     Which paſſe thorowe *n* Death
     (In Abrahams *o* Fayth)
          To Lyfe : They onlye than,
     Shall be *p* fett-downe
     With great Renowne,
     And weare the *q* Crowne,
          In the Supper of the Lamb.
               For Hee is now bleſt. &c.

.6. All Scripture-wyfe,
     That now furmyfe,
     How to difpyfe

r 1. Cor. 1. c.   Mee, in their *r* Wyfedom, than,
     They fhall no-dout
     (Amonge all Stout)

s Math. 22. a   Bee fhutt *s* wyth-out
Luk. 14. b.   The Supper of the Lamb.
               For Hee is now bleſt. &c.

.7. For none I faye,
       Saue onlye thaye

t Mat. 22. a.   That fhall *t* obaye,
Luk. 14. b.   Myne holye Seruyce, than,
     (Which doth brynge-in

u Rom. 6.   The *u* Death of Sin.)
Col. 2. b.   Maye enter-in,
          To the Supper of the Lamb.
               For Hee is now bleſt. &c.

.8. Then all that nowe

x 2. Cor. 12. c   In *x* Stryfe do growe,
Gal. 5. c.   And wyll not *y* bowe,
y Pro. 1. c.   To My louelye Warnynges, than,
2. Teſſ. 1. a. 2 b.   Muſt now at laſt
     Cleene out bee caſt,

z Math. 22. a.   And *z* neuer taſt
Luk. 14. b.   The Supper of the Lamb.
               For Hee is now bleſt. &c.

.9. Then runne apace,
     Whylſt there is Grace,

a 2. Cor. 6. a.   Or Tyme and fpace,
Gal. 6. a.   So faſt as euer yee can,

b Eſa. 2. a. 25. b.   To Syons *b* Hyll :
     Wheare All that wyll
     May eate their fyll,
          In the Supper of the Lamb.
               For Hee is now bleſt. &c.

.10. Neglect Mee not,

c Gen. 19. b.
2. Pet. 2. a.

As they dyd ᵉ Lot
Longe paſt, yee wot,
   And perryſhed all than :
My Loue peruſe,

d Mar. 22. a.
Luk. 14. b.

Make no ᵈ excuſe,
Leſt yee refuſe
   The Supper of the Lamb.
      For Hee is now bleſt. &c.

.11. When All were ſett,
And furnyſht nett
(Both ſmall and great)
   So was it foreſeene than,
Of the Brydegroome,

e Math. 22. a.

That ther was ᵉ roome
For more to come,
   In the Supper of the Lamb.
      For Hee is now bleſt. &c.

.12. Then muſt I go

f Math. 22. a.

To the ᶠ Hye-wayes, lo,
And Hedges, tho,
   And ſeeke them-vp all than :
All Thoſe by name
That's Blynde or Lame,
And compell the ſame,
   To the Supper of the Lamb,
      For Hee is now bleſt. &c.

.13. The Lorde hath ſwore
Longe-tyme before,

g Math. 22. a.
Luk. 14. b.

That ᵍ neuermore
   Such as excuſed them than,
Shoulde taſt or eate
Of the heauenlye Meate
Or Porcion geat,
   In the Supper of the Lamb.
      For Hee is now bleſt. &c.

.14. For that all Kynges,
Vnder Loues Wynges
(Without Grudgynges)

h Sap. 6. a.

   In Peace mought ʰ gouerne, than,
Praye All : that truſt
Amonge the Iuſt,
Or haue a Luſt
   To the Supper of the Lamb.
      For Hee is now bleſt, in verye deede
      That's found a Geſt, in the Mariage-weede.

FINIS.

AN other, out of Goodwill.

a Rom. 1. a.
1. Cor. 1. a.
2. Cor. 13. c.
Ephe. 1. a.

THe Grace from God the [a] Father hye,
 Which is of Mightes moſt a,
The Mercye eake from Chriſt our Lorde,
 And Peace from the holye Goſt a,
Com to All, That now ſhall,
b Iohn. 17. c.
Rom. 12. b.
15. a.
1. Cor. 1. a.
Phil. 2. a. 3. b.
 In [b] Loue with vs agree a,
And conſent, With whole Intent,
 To the Loues Soſcietee a.

c Deu. 10. 30. b
Math. 22. c.

.2. Loue the [c] Lorde aboue al-thinge,
 Is the firſt Precept by name a :
Loue thy Neyghbour as thy-ſelfe,
 The ſecond's lyke theſame a.
Thus wee ſee, Loue to bee,
d Exo. 24. 34. c
Deut. 10. a.
e Iohn. 1. a.
f Iob. 10. c.
Eſa. 5. c. 60.
 Written with [d] Gods-his owne Hande a,
To [e] geeue vs Light, And guyde vs right,
 Eauen [f] out of that darke Lande a.

g Mat. 11. d. 18.

.3. Younge-men in your [g] Littlenes,
 Remember what is ſayde a :
Let all our Elders in the Loue,
h Heb. 12. b.
i 1. Tim. 4.
1. Ioh. 3 a. 4 b.
k Eccli. 6 d. 8. a.
9. c.
 Wyth Reuerence bee [h] obayde a.
Exercyſe, [i] Amonge the [k] Wyſe
 That holye Seruice, then a,
Which God hath wrought, And alſo tought,
 By hys Myniſter H. N. a.

l 1. Cor. 13. b.
1. Iohn. 3. 4.

.4. In Loues [l] Preceptes let vs proceede,
 And coupple arme-in-arme a,
The Serpentes Broode, that wolde deſtroye,
m Gen. 3. a.
Mark. 16. d.
 Shall ; then ; do vs [m] no harme a.
Loue ſhee ſowndes, All [n] our Woundes,
n Sap. 16. c.
 Wyth her moſt pleaſant Wine a,
o 1. Pet. 1. b.
1. Ioh. 3. 4. a b
As wee [o] obaye, And lyue alwaye,
 In her Seruice diuide a.

.5. Againſt the Sinne let vs putt-on,
p Ephe. 6. b.
 Such [p] Armour as is beſt a,
Which in the Seruice of the Loue,
 Is perfectlye expreſt a.
q Math. 6. b.
And let vs [q] praye, To God alwaye,
 Eauen-lyke as wee are taught a,
So ſhall wee fynde, Within our Mynde,
r Mich. 6. b.
 How Sinne [r] ſhall go to naught a.

s 2. Cor. 7. a.
Phil. 3. b.
t Deut. 20. a.
Efa. 41. a.
Math. 10. b.
u Pfa. 3. a. 27. a.

.6. Thus ⸱ ga-wee fourth, good willinglie,
    And haue no ᵗ doubt in mynde a,
Although fo ᵘ manye our Enemyes were,
    As Heares on Head wee fynde a :
Loue fhall make, Them all to quake,
    The Tyme is com-about a,
For with her ˣ Breath, If wee haue Faith,
    So fhall fhee caft them out a.

x Efa. 11. a. 57 b
2. Teff. 2. a

y 1. Teff. 4. a.
1. Pet. 3. 4. a.

.7. An vpright ʸ Lyfe in Lowlynes,
    Let vs expreffe alwaye a,
Amonge fuch as wee deale-with-all,
    In all Affayres I faye a :
So to ᶻ prayfe, God alwayfe,
    Eauen-as is fayde aboue a.
That's indeede, As wee reede,
    The Seruice of the Loue a.

z Pfal. 134. 136
140.
Col. 3. b.

.8. No Godferuice els do wee knowe,
    Nor none maye wee frequent a,
Without this moft holye Seruice, ᵃ
    With her godlie Intent a,
Hee is bleft, That's now preft,
    To ferue vnder Loues Bande a :
Shee fhall ᵇ byde, And neuer flyde,
    But euermore fhall ftande a.

a 1. Cor. 13.
1. Iohn. 3. 4.

b 1. Cor. 13. c.

.9. Al-though that wycked Seede of Cain,
    To ᶜ Rebellious-ftryfe aryfe a,
Yet fhall thofe feeke the ᵈ Peace and Reft,
    So manye as be wyfe a.
For all muft taft ; Now at the laft ;
    ᵉ Such Drincke as they do brue a,
And what they ᶠ feeke, That fhall them meete :
    Thys thynge is verye-true a.

c Gen. 4.
Iudæ. 1.
d Pfal. 34. c.
1. Pet. 3. b.

e Ier. 25 b. 49 b

f Mat. 10. d. 16

.10. That Wanton-luft of ᵍ Lamech Lyne,
    Expell out of your mynde a,
And ʰ vnto her Lightmyndednes,
    Bee you in no-wife kynde a :
For with all Findes, Or wycked Mindes
    (Wheare Darknes doth remayne a)
Eauen in the ⁱ Hell, Theare fhall fhee dwell,
    With all that to her pertayne a.

g Gen. 4. c.

h Ephe. 5. a.
Iudæ. 1. b.

i Math. 25.

.11. Then louinglye let vs ftande faft,
    In ᵏ brotherlye Accorde a,
Lyke-as the Seruice of the Loue,
    Requyreth in hys Worde a :
So Loue will ; Bleffe ˡ vs ftill,
    And woorke all for the beft a :
If fo bee, Wee agree ᵐ,
    And mynde the Peace and Reft a.

k Rom. 12. b
1. Teff. 3. b.
1. Pet. 2. b. 3 b.

l Rom. 8. d.

m Rom. 12. b.
Hebr. 12. b.

.12. Let vs obeye the [n] Gouernours,
    And lyue vnder their Lawes a :
And eake to them all Tribute paye,
    Eauen for the Peaces caufe a :
Yet Loue is [o] free, Though fhee agree,
    That they fhall haue fuch thynge a :
And what is right, To God alnight,
    That [p] muft wee to hym brynge a.

                                        n Rom. 13.
                                        1 Pet. 2. b.

o Math. 17. c.

p Math. 22. c.

.13. In [q] ftilnes thus let vs go-fourth,
    (With [r] Thankfulnes amonge a)
Wyth fewe Woordes, as wee are taught,
    And thus I ende my Songe a.
In Loues [s] Bande, Hande-in-hande ;
    Let vs proceede on ftill a.
O Ifraell, Take this well,
    As out of my Goodwill a.

q Pfal. 37. a.
Efa. 30. b.
r Ephe. 5. c
1. Teff. 5. b.

s Col. 3. b.

FINIS.

Per W. S. Veritatis

Amatorem.

ANNO. 1574.

Copies of ' A New Balade or Songe of the Lambes Feaft ', with that entitled ' Another, out of Goodwill ', printed on one sheet, are in the Roxburghe collection, British Museum (*Roxburghe Ballads*, vol. viii, p. 400), and in the Bodleian Library. A third copy, cut up and laid down in a quarto volume, formerly Utterson's, is described in Corser's ' Collectanea Anglo-Poetica ' (129-31), and occurs in the catalogue of his sale, 1869 (pt. ii. 797), when it was purchased by Mr. Henry Huth. A fourth copy was sold at Sotheby's in February 1896.

The ballads were probably printed at Amsterdam and are in the same type as that used for the English translations of the works of Hendrik Niclaes, the founder of the ' Family of Love ' to which they refer.

The initials W. S. may possibly be identified with William Samuel, who wrote, among other poetical pieces, ' An Abridgemēt of all the Canonical books of the olde Teftament, written in Sternholds meter . . . 1569 '.

Ebsworth, however, in his note to the Roxburghe copy, suggests William Seres the printer, who is credited by Corser (*Collectanea Anglo-Poetica*, pt. i. 73-76) with the authorship of ' An Aunfwere to the Proclamation of the Rebels in the North. 1569 '. ' A Prayer ' in verse, printed with ' A Dialogue agaynft the Tyrannye of the Papiftes. Tranflated out of Latin into Englyfhe by E. C. 1562 ', is also assigned to Seres (*Cat. Early Eng. Books*, British Museum, p. 1192).

The marginal references to the six concluding stanzas of ' AN other, out of Goodwill ' have disappeared from the right-hand side of the Britwell copy. Both ballads are printed in two columns, and are on the same sheet.

81

A Cōmendation of the aduēterus viage of
the wurthy Captain. M. Thomas Stutely Efquyer and others,
towards the Land called *Terra florida.*

IF Fortunes force procure,
The valiant noble hart:
In trauail, pain & daūgers great,
In warres to haue his part.

If loffe of goods infue,
Through valiant enterprife:
Or for flaknes, or the forefight,
Of diligent aduife.

Yet of his wurthy praife,
I can not fpeak tomiche [*sic*]:
Who ventreth bothe his goods and life,
His Contrey to enriche.

The worldly wife doo mufe,
And alfo doo inuay:
At noble harts when that their welths,
Doo fall vnto decay.

As now of late I knew,
And faw the euidence:
Of one whofe part it was to fhew,
The like experience.

A noble hart in deed,
And wurthy great renowne:
Whofe fortune was not to remain,
In Cittie nor in Towne.

A yung Eneas bolde,
With hart and courage ftout:
Whofe enterprife was only pight,
Straunge things to bring about.

And though that all men feemd,
His dooings to deride:
Yet this his fact he would not leue,
Nor throwe it fo a fide.

But ſtil he dooth procure,
  With boldned hart and minde:
That thing whiche erſt he had aſſayd,
  By trauail now to finde.

Into a land vnknowne,
  To win hym wurthy fame:
As exequies and memory,
  Of his moſte noble name.

Whiche if it fall his lot,
  With fortunes helping hand:
He may wel make a lawhing [*sic*] ſtock,
  Of them whiche him withſtand.

Sume terme it Stolida,
  And Sordida it name:
And to be plain they doo it mock,
  As at a fooliſhe game.

If reaſons fence becauſe,
  Of this foreſpoken talke:
Or fayned folly be the ground,
  Why mennes tungs thus doo walke.

Then might it ſeem to me,
  The Frenches labour loſt:
Their careful pain and trauail eke,
  That they therein haue toſt.

The cronicles alſo,
  Whiche only ſeem as trew:
And writ by them that of that place,
  Before did take the vew.

The ſpaniards eke doo ſhew,
  And verify the fame:
To be deſcribed as a thing,
  Deſeruing ſuche a name.

The Portingales doo ſay,
  The crownacles be iuſt:
And all that trauaild haue that coſte:
  The fame confes it muſt.

If that in times before,
  Through talkes men haue refraind:
Whiche for the loue of trauail ſore,
  Their harts haue long been paind.

Columbus as I reed,
  The ſpace of many yeeres:
Was counted as vnwiſe alſo,
  As in writers appeeres.

His erneſt ſute denied,
    Yet in the finall ende :
His wurds & deeds did ſeem at length,
    On reaſon to depend.

The like aſſay in hand,
    He did at laſt procure :
Whoſe life and lucky viages,
    Good fortune did aſſure.

At thend in ſauety home,
    At length he did retourn :
And quenched all their mocking harts
    Whiche erſt did ſeem to burn.

For fire of force muſt needs,
    Declare his burning heat :
Though for a time ī ſmothering ſmoke
    It ſeemes itſelf to beat.

So talk of tungs may not,
    By ſmothering through be tame :
But burſting out at length wil turn,
    Into a firye flame.

And then the mallice gon,
    The fire falleth down :
And quenched quite as by this man,
    Whiche was of great renowne.

Now Stuetley hoice thy ſail,
    Thy wiſſhed land to finde :
And neuer doo regard vain talke,
    For wurds they are but winde.

And in reproof of all,
    I wil not once refrain :
With prayer for to wiſh that thou,
    Maiſt ſafely come again.

And that ſum frute at length,
    By trauail thou maiſt finde :
With riches for to ſatiſſy,
    Thy manly modeſt minde.

      Finis.   ꝯ Robert Seall.

¶ Imprinted at Londō at the long Shop | adioyning vnto Saint Mildreds
Churche in the Pultrie, | by Iohn Alde.

Thomas Stucley was the third son of Sir Hugh Stucley, of Affeton, near Ilfracombe in the county of Devon, although it has been said that he was an illegitimate son of King Henry VIII. After serving with the army in France and Scotland, he was employed by Henry II of France as a spy to further his design on Calais, but Stucley revealed his mission to the English government, which rewarded him by transmitting his revelations to Henry with an expression of its disbelief, hoping by this means to secure the friendship of France. Stucley was detained in the Tower, but eventually obtained his release and retired to the continent to evade his creditors. Rehabilitated by a wealthy marriage, he set up as a prominent figure in London, and on June 14, 1563, he entertained Elizabeth with a sham fight on the Thames. In the same year, having spent most of his wife's money, he sought a privateering cruise under the guise of a plan for colonizing Florida. To this expedition Elizabeth subscribed one ship. For two years Stucley plundered indiscriminately, and the Queen was at length compelled to order him to be brought back to England, where he was ultimately released from custody. He transferred his services to Philip II, who listened with some attention to his proposals for an invasion of Ireland; this project, however, came to nothing.

Stucley ended a misspent life at the battle of Alcazar in 1578.

Stucley's exploits were celebrated in verse elsewhere; in 'The Famous Hiftorye of the life and death of Captaine Thomas Stukeley. . . . As it hath been Acted', 1605, a copy of which is in the British Museum, and in 'The Life and Death of the Famous Thomas Stukely, an Englifh gallant in time of Queen Elizabeth, who ended his life in a Battel of three Kings of Barbary'. The former was reprinted in Simpson's 'School of Shakespeare', 1878, while the latter was often reissued and appeared in Evans's 'Old Ballads', 1810, vol. iii, p. 148.

The 'Cōmendation' was licensed in 1562–63 (Arber's *Transcript*, i. 215), and was included in J. P. Collier's 'Old Ballads' (Percy Society, 1840). It is printed in two columns, without border or ornament.

Of the author, Robert Seall, nothing is recorded, nor is any other ballad by him known to be extant.

82

The tragical end and death of the Lord Iames | Regent of
Scotland, lately fet forth in Scottifh, and printed at Edinburgh.
1570. | And now partly turned into Englifh.

Iames Earle of Murray Regent of renowne
Now lieth dead, and wofully put downe,
  Murdred wout mercy, mourning for remaid
Who loft his life in Lythquo by a Clowne,
Giltles God wot, betrayed in to that towne.
  Was flayne by gunfhot, and fodainly put to death,
Done by the Papifts our foes, through fellonous faith.
  Hangman to Harry, now Burrio to their brother,
  Well may this murther manifeft the tother.

¶What wight a lyue would not lament his loffe?
Wo is me to want him, is the common voyce:
  For fuch a Prince fhal neuer poore man haue,
Kylled by a Traytour, ftealing vpon him clofe,
Purpofing of purpofe, life for life to lofe,
  But no comparifon twixt a Kinges fonne and a Knaue
Sith he is gone, we cannot againe him craue.
  Through al our realme I dare wel make this choife,
  Raigned not his fellow fince buried was the Bruife.

¶To keepe good rule he rode, and tooke no reft,
Both South and North, and fomtime Eaft and Weft,
  All to decore our common wealth men know:
By whom let vs fee, was Pirates fo oppreft?
Or yet the theeues fo throwne downe and dreft?
  Argyle and Huntlye hid them both for aw,
And when he might, he was tendant at Law,
  Twyfe on a day, and fleeped not in fleuth,
  To fee no fauters fhould beare them by the treuth.

¶Of this foule fact fuppofe our foes be fayne,
Yet after Moyfes, Iofua comes agayne,
  To guide the people, geue glory therfore to God.
Should they fucceede, that haue Lord Iames fo flayne?
Beware of that, leaft that ye feele the payne,
  And haue your weake ones wyrried with the Tode.
Thinke ye with reafon that fuch fhould rule the rod,
  Which with double murder haue made vs fuch ado
  And with our Kyng would play like coufonage to?

¶ Pray, if you pleafe, I warrant you ye haue neede,
To keepe our King from kankred Kedzochis feede,
  That dayly wayes inuentes to put him downe :
His Graundfire flayne at Lythquo as I it reede,
His Gudfire thrife did leaue this land in deede,
  Harry at midnight murdred in this towne,
His Coufin now laft, and yet they claime the crowne.
  Blinde locke may geffe, if thefe be godly deedes,
  Brude by that Bifhop in whō this mifchiefes breedes.

¶ Cut of that Papift Prothogal partes,
That with his leefings all the Laitie peruartes,
  Straight ioyne your forces to the fieldes without feare,
Becaufe ye take your ftoutnes al in ftartes,
To Hammilton in haft while ye haue hartes.
  Deuife fome way to pay your men of warre,
For if they once begon, ye neede not gather geare.
  Fight well, and war them, and win the riches thore,
  And if ye doe thus, in deede ye neede no more.

¶ Curft be ye both, Bifhop and Bothwell ech,
For this foule deede, your neckes the halter ftretch,
  If ye two want the withy, they do much wrong you :
Lythquo lament, your Burgefes may looke bleach,
In their fayd time your Burrow rueth the leach,
  Becaufe of this murther lately made among you,
For if I thought it helped ought to hang you,
  So fhould ye die, and fet your towne on fire,
  As fome part of punifhment to affwage Gods ire.

¶ Ouer thefe two houfes for thefe deedes inding,
The hand of God doth ouer their heades hing,
  Them to deftroy, I dout not in thefe our daies :
Hepburnis wil go to wracke, for wyrring of the King,
But Hamiltons fye, this was a fouler thing.
  Is this your firme religion, yea is, yea is ?
Such a time fhall come I trow as Thomas faies :
  Heardmen fhal hunt you vp through Garranis hill,
  Cafting their Plates and let the plough ftand ftill.

¶ Apparantly thefe plages are poured out,
To wreake this world, and wot ye where about ?
  Becaufe we want no vice vnder the heauen :
Sith double murder makers feeke to rule the rout,
With the Niniuites to our God let vs go cry and fhout,
  For to retreate the fentence iuftly geuen.
Yet thou good Lord, that iudgeth al thinges euen,
  Seing perril that ouer the people ftandes,
  Let not their blood be fought at giltles handes.

¶Now Lordes & Lordings aſſembled in this place,
Ouer long we talke of Tragedies, alas,
  Away with care, with comfort now conclude:
As good in paper, as ſpeake it to your face,
If murtherers for this geare get any grace,
  Ye ſhal be ſhent, thinke on, I ſay for good,
Sith arte and part are gilty of his blood,
    Why ſhould ye feare, or fauor them for fleiching?
    Ye herd your ſelues what Knox ſpake at the preaching.

¶Firſt on the fieldes, make ſhortly to let [lye,]
We lacke but one, and what woorſe are wee?
  Sith God was pleaſed to take him out of pine:
Al men on moold are marked for to dye,
In time and place appointed, ſo was he.
  Let not in care your couragies decline,
For want of one I would not al ſhould tine.
    Go ſeeke at Roxbrugh when the King was ſlaine
    And yet one woman wan the houſe agayne.

¶Sith then by women doughty deedes were done,
Ye Barrons be blithe, and hold your harts aboue,
  And let vs heare wherefore ye hapned hither,
They are no great partie, and ye ſpeede you ſoone,
Albeit that boyd be dayly in Denone,
  Lang or Argyle be gathered in together,
When al is done, the Counſaile may conſider,
    What is the moſt thoſe murtherers may do,
    Suppoſe that Huntly would come & help them to.

¶Had we one head would ſtoutly vndertake it,
The Barrons ſayes they ſhould be boldly backed,
  Mought they with ſpeedines trauel to theſe townes:
Why ſtand ye afeard of Traitours twiſe detracted?
Thinke ye not ſhame to heare your Lordſhips lacked?
  Some feares their fleſh, ſom gins to gather crownes
Some hides their heads, ſom girds them vp in gownes
    Looke how your enmies prides thē in their ſpurring
    Keping the fields, and frees not in their furring.

¶Wo worth the wiues that foſtred you and fed,
Ye do nothing loue but lye on ſoften bed,
  And keepe you fro cold, with cloutes in your ſhoo:
I thinke great wonder how ye can be ſo dred,
Or fray at them that laſt before you fled.
  Wanting their Quene, ſith God is gaynſt them too.
Why lye ye here, hauing here litle to do?
    The Barrons bids you ſhortly bide, or els begone,
    Courage decaies if Scotiſhmen tary long.

¶ Haue Lions lookes, and then make way forth cleare,
Be Hannibals, and hoyſe your harts with cheare.
    But be not ſtill, while thoſe Knaues do encloſe you.
He needes not worke that hath one good ouerſeer,
Nor ye neede fight, ſo that your hartes were freeer. [*sic*]
    But by my ſoule my ſelfe could neuer ruſe you:
I know wel for this crime Chriſt ſhal accuſe you.
    For ſparing Agag, Saul was puniſhed ſore,
    So ſhal he you, I dare not ſay no more.

¶ The Lord of hoſtes that heauen & earth cōmaundes,
Keepe our yong King from al vnhappy handes,
    And that good Queene of England, and her Counſel to.
Ye feare the Frenchmen ſhould ouerlay theſe landes,
But I heare ſay by ſome that vnderſtandes,
    The Doctours doubt but they haue more ado.
Our Queene is kept ſtraightly, her power is igo,
    England wil help you, and ye wil help your ſelues,
    And be the contrair, craue of them nothing els.

¶ Thus fare ye wel, I ſpare not to offend you,
In ſimple verſe this Schedul that I ſend you,
    Beſeching you to ſcanne it if ye may.
Steale ye away, the wiues wil vilypend you,
And if ye byde, the Barrons wil commend you,
    Beſt were it I thinke, we might preuent that day,
Their meeting is on Sonday I heare ſay,
    In Glaſgow towne, thinking to fight or flee,
    It lookes wel there, ye get no more of mee.

FINIS.

¶ The Tragedies | Lenuoy.

AS men recordes,
    In dede my Lordes,
        I ſhrinke not for to ſhew:
Suppoſe ye cracke,
Ye lye abacke,
    And lybelles by the Law.
Ye make not to,
As men ſhould do,
    I trow ye ſtand in ſom aw:
Suppoſe ye hight,
To ſee you fight,
    That day wil neuer daw.

Is ne remayd,
Fro [*sic*] he be dead,
   No man to feke amendes:
Or who is here,
Dare breake a fpeare,
   Vpon yone limmeris lends.
Ye dare not mum,
Tyl Sadler come,
   To fee what England fends:
Thinking to fay it,
And ay delay it,
   And fo the matter endes.

With fighes and fobs,
And belted robes,
   Ye counterfeite the dule:
What doughty deedes,
To weare fuch weedes?
   Except it were a fule.
Make to the towne,
And cow them downe,
   Now or your courage cule:
For Maddie fayes,
Bide ye few dayes,
   Ye be not ther while Zule.

Is this the thing,
Who guides the King?
   Ye cannot al agree:
Now fye for fhame,
Fetch Leuenox hame,
   Ye haue none nar nor hee.
If he want grace,
To guyde that place,
   Ther is other two or three:
Then war I fayne,
But all in vayne,
   To wyfh and wyll not bee.

And fome there bene,
Waites on the Queene,
   But gape awhil they get her:
And were fhee here,
I take no feare,
   The Fiend aby we fet her,
For we are now,
As ftark I trow,
   As farnzer whē we met her:
When all is done,
They ftart to fone,
   To boaft, & not the better.

I thinke it beſt,
Ye take no reſt,
 If ye durſt vnder take it:
And we be trew,
We are iniew,
 Ye ſhal be boldly backe it.
But ſine I ſee,
It wyll not bee,
 That metre wil not make it:
The Fiend make cair,
I ſay na mair,
 I rew that euer I ſpake it.

Finis. Rob. Sempill.

Imprinted at Lō|don
by Iohn Awdely, dwelling | in litle Britaine ſtrete, with|out Alderſgate. | 1570.

Robert Sempill, the Scottish ballad-writer, is believed to have been born about 1530. He has been connected with Robert, Lord Sempill of Beltrees, though James Paterson, in his 'Poems of the Sempills of Beltrees', 1849, denies this, and it is probable that he was illegitimate. Sempill spent a part of his earlier life in Paris, but afterwards returned to Scotland, where he secured a position at court. He was the author of a large number of ballads preserved in the Roxburghe collection, British Museum, the Public Record Office, and the library of the Society of Antiquaries. These were all issued from the press of Robert Lekpreuik and are fully described in Dickson and Edmond's 'Annals of Scottish Printing, 1890'.

'Ane new ballet ſet out be ane Fugitiue Scottiſman that fled out of Paris at this laſt Murther,' 1572, and 'Ane Complaint vpon Fortoun', without date, the originals of which are now in the British Museum, were reprinted in Mr. Henry Huth's 'Ancient Ballads and Broadsides' (Philobiblon Society, 1867). Sempill was a sturdy and indefatigable opponent of the Scottish catholics, and many of his ballads lament the loss of the Regent Moray, who was murdered on January 21, 1570, at Linlithgow, by James Hamilton of Bothwellhaugh. Sempill also wrote a short poem, 'The Sege of the caſtel of Edinburgh,' 1573, the only extant copy of which is in the British Museum. Sempill's complete works were edited by T. G. Stevenson as 'The Sempill Ballates' in 1872, and again by J. Cranstoun in 'Satirical Poems of the Time of the Reformation' for the Scottish Text Society, 1891–93.

The Britwell ballad was licensed in 1569–70 (Arber's *Transcript*, i. 411), and is an English version of 'The Regentis tragedie', a broadside issued by Lekpreuik in 1570, of which copies are to be found in the Roxburghe collection, British Museum, and in the library of the Society of Antiquaries of London. It is printed in three columns, the third containing 'The Tragedies Lenuoy'. The sheet is decorated with a narrow ornamental border.

83

¶The Confeſſion and declaration of Robert ſharpe Clerke, and other | *of that ſecte, tearmed* the Familie *of* Loue, *at Pawles|* Croſſe in London the .xij. of Iune. | An. *1575.*

WHereas I Robert Sharpe, haue hertofore vnaduiſedly, conceyued good opinion | of certayne bookes of an aucthour, otherwyſe vnknowne, ſaue onely, that hee noteth hym|ſelfe by the Letters H. N. And was induced thereunto, partly by the ſtraunge tytles that he | gyueth to himſelfe, terming hymſelfe, amongeſt other names, A Prophet rayſed vp from the | dead : Specially by God appointed, and ſtirred vppe, according to the promiſes for this tyme | which he calleth the laſt day of grace. Affirming that he hath receyued his meſſage from the | mouth of God himſelfe. And partly being alſo mooued by the noueltie of the Doctrine, and | great promiſes made, as though men might therby attayne to bee Deified, or made as God : | Now vppon conference wyth the Godly learned, (whereof ſome are in auctoritie) being admoniſhed of the ar|rogancie of the ſayde aucthour, in vſurping the ſayde tyttles, and of hys blaſphemous ſacriledge, in taking vnto | hym other greater tytles as, That he is the illuminate with the true light of the perfect being : Annointed with | goddes diuine being : One whome God hath hominified himſelf withall, and who is codeified with God himſelfe : | (For with ſuch monſtruous and vnuſed termes, he cloketh his blaſphemies, as though he were made one with | God, and God one with him) Segregating vnto himſelfe a priuate Conuenticle of ſimple deceaued men, (whom | he nameth the Familie or Comunaltie of Loue) and deteſting all wyſe and learned men, whom he tearmeth Scrip|ture learned. And alſo I being aduertiſed by the ſayde Godly learned, of a great number of deteſtable Errors | contayned in the bookes of the ſayde H. N. And ſpecially in thoſe twoo wicked Bookes. Whereof the one hee | nameth The Euangely or Goſpell of the Kingdome : As though hee had brought a newe Goſpell into the world, | (which Sainct Pawle forbiddeth, and holdeth accurſed, though it were brought by an Angell from heauen.) And | the other Booke hee calleth, The Declaration of the Maſſe. In the which twoo Bookes, and other lyke wicked | Bookes, of the ſayde aucthour, not onelye the vſurped auctoritie of the Biſhop of Rome, and his Cardinalles, | and the Sacrifice of the Maſſe, wyth manye other lyke wicked errours, but alſo diuers damned hereſies of the | Arrianes, Pelagians, and Anabaptiſtes, are maintayned : To the ouerthrow of the true doctrine of our iuſtifitacion [*sic*], and fayth in Ieſus Chriſt, and of all true Religion.||

Therefore vnderſtanding nowe my groſſe errours, I doe here before God and you vtterly deteſt, and from|my heart abhorre, as well the ſayde Aucthour, wyth all hys arrogant, and blaſphemous titles, as the inſtru|ment of Sathan, by hym ſtirred vp, to ſeduce and beguyle the ſimple people : As alſo all his Damnable errours | and Hereſies whatſoeuer. And doe confeſſe here before God and you, that I am hartily ſorye that euer I dealt | wyth any ſuch Books, or reſorted to any ſecreet Conferences, aſſemblies, or Conuenticles wyth thoſe that are | named The Familie or Comunaltie of Loue : And that thereby I haue gyuen ſo great offence vnto the Churche | of God : for the which I moſt humbly and hartily aſke forgiueneſſe both of God and you. And doe promiſe fayth|fully neuer to meddle with theſe, or any other ſuch Bookes, or with that ſecte hereafter : But vtterlye doe re|nounce and forfake the fame, and all other Errours and Herefies whatfoeuer con-trarie to the Common, Ni|cene, and Athanafius Creedes, or to the holye Scriptures con-teyned in the Bookes of the olde and newe Tefta|ment. And doe alfo forfake whatfoeuer is repugnaunt to the Doctrine nowe taught and publiquely fet foorth in | the Church of England, which Doctrine I acknowledge and confeffe, to be the true and Catholicke Doctrine, | agreeable to the Canonicall Scriptures, and that the fame of all Chriftians, ought to be profeffed, without re|fpect of any daunger to the body, whether it be by death or otherwayes. In whiche profeffion, that I maye con|ftantly remayne to my lyues ende, I doe moft hartily befeeche you, to commende me in your prayers, to the | great good-neffe and mercye of Almightye God.

Robert Sharpe.

THe fame confeffion and declaration which Robert Sharpe hath prefently made be|fore you I. A. B. Doe vnfaynedlye and willingly make I deteft all the errours and herefies be|fore by hym detefted. I do faythfully promife here before God & you whatfoeuer he hath promifed. And | wyth lyke peticion moft humbly and hartily be-feeche God and you to forgiue me. And I doe hartily de|fire you to praye vnto the Lorde for me, that he in his great mercie will pardon me, and fo guyde me | by his holy fpirite that detefting all errours, I may euer hereafter imbrace the truth of God, and con-|ftantly continue in the fame, to the ende of my lyfe. And this I craue at his mercifull handes for Iefus | Chrift his fake myne only Redeemer and Sauiour.

{ Iohn Allen. }   { Iohn Sharpe.
{ Ihon Lydye. }   { William Burwell.

❡ *Imprinted by William Seres.*

' About this Time, or somewhat before, a Sect that went by the Name of *The Family of Love*, began to be taken Notice of. It was derived from Holland; where one *H. N.* [i.e. *Henry Nicolas*] was the Founder of it. A Company of these were discovered in the Parish of *Balsham* in *Cambridgeshire*, the Bishop of Ely's Diocese. In this Society was one *Robert Sharp*, Parson of *Strethal* in *Essex*, and divers other Persons of good Reputation. These were taken up: but when they came to be examined before *Dr. Perne*, the Rector of that Parish, they were found to be none of that Sect but suspected only ... And accordingly, they made a Declaration and Confession of this, and of their sober Opinions and Doctrines; and submitted to Authority.' (Strype, *Annals of the Reformation*, 1725–31, vol. ii, p. 375.)

Hendrik Niclaes, the founder of the ' Family of Love', was born at Munster in Westphalia about the year 1502. He is described as having taught ' an anabaptist mysticism, entirely without dogma, yet of exalted ideals'. Niclaes was the author of a large number of writings, of which many were translated into English. Several of these translations are in the Britwell library. From the numerous references which appear in Holinshed the members of the Family of Love encountered severe persecution. Sir Francis Knollys, in a letter to Burghley and Leicester (Wright's *Queen Elizabeth and her Times*, 1838, vol. ii, p. 153), avows that they ' do ferue the turnes of the Papiftes, ... yet this difference is betweene the Papiftes and thofe fectaries, I do meane touching their practifes here in England; for thefe Sectaries are more hypocriticall, and woll fooner denye their doctryne and affertions to auoyde punyfhment, then the Papiftes woll'. The sect survived through persecution until the close of the seventeenth century, when the growth of religious tolerance allowed it to lapse into obscurity.

There is another copy of this broadside in the library of the Society of Antiquaries, London. It is closely printed on a small sheet, without border or ornament.

84

A moſt excellent new Dittie, wherein is ſhewed the ſage
ſayinges, and wiſe ſentences| of *Salomon*: wherein each eſtate is
taught his duetie, with ſingular counſell to his | comfort and conſolation.

To the tune of Wigmoores Galliard.

THoſe that will run a Vertuous race,
 and learne the Precepts of the ſage:
Thoſe that true wiſedome will imbrace
 and learne to liue in youth and age:
Let him approch hereto with ſpeed,
And to theſe Leſſons giue good heed:
 for bearing well theſe thinges away,
 the Lord will bleſſe them night & day.

My Sonne, ſayth Salomon the wiſe,
 if thou true Wiſedome wilt attaine:
Then feare the Lord that rules the ſkies
 for ſo the ſcripture telleth thee plaine.
Imbrace his word and him obay:
This is the chiefe and onely way:
 for they that do theſe thinges deſpiſe,
 are fooles to God, though worldly wiſe.

Vnto thy Father honour giue,
 and thou ſhalt ſurely bleſſed be:
And be obedient while you liue,
 vnto your Mother courteouſly:
Then God will ſend thee euermore
Sufficient wealth, and treaſure ſtore:
 all thinges ſhall proſper in thy hand,
 and long thou ſhalt inioy the land.

The bleſſing of thy Father deare,
 doth cauſe the childrens good ſucceſſe:
But where the Mother doth appeare,
 to curſe the childrens wickedneſſe,
Their whole foundation doth decay,
Like withered leaues they fall away:
 Then all good children learne of me,
 to loue your Parentes faythfullie.

Set not thy minde on worldly wealth,
  nor put thy confidence therein :
For Riches doth confume by ftealth,
  and Couetoufnes is counted finne :
For while thou liueft on the earth,
Thou art vncertaine of thy death :
    and when that death doth ftop thy wind
    then muft thou leaue thy goods behind.

Be friendly vnto euery man,
  but vnto few familiar be :
And try thy Friende if that thou can,
  his inward thoughts to proue and fee :
And if thou finde him iuft and true,
Change not thy old Friend for a new :
    For many promife much indeede,
    but cleane forfake thee in thy neede.

If thou haft Sonnes, inftruct them well
  but on thy Daughter neuer fmile :
Their wanton wayes do farre excell,
  let no affection thee beguile :
With due correction loue them ftill,
And giue not them their wanton will :
    for if that they do ftubborne grow,
    their duetie then they will not know.

Giue honour to the Aged fort,
  and to thy Betters alwayes bow :
So fhalt thou winne a good report,
  for God himfelfe doth him allow :
Of hatefull Pride likewife beware,
And haue an eye to after care :
    be not too rafh in anything,
    for that will foone repentance bring.

Lende not thy goodes to Mighty men,
  whofe countenance paffeth thy degree :
For it is hard to get againe,
  as we by dayly proofe may fee.
For other men giue not thy word,
No further then thou canft afford :
    leaft afterward thou chaunce to rue,
    and pay the debt when it is due.

With him that is a Maieftrate,
  in any cafe go not to law :
Leaft thou repent the fame too late,
  for he will hold thee ftill in awe :
Be alwayes wary in thy wordes,
For fpightfull tongues are euill fwords
    and looke to whom thou doft impart,
    the thoughtes and fecrets of thy hart.

Be neuer ieolous of thy Wife,
  leaſt ſhe thereby do miſchiefe learne,
For ſo thou ſhalt ſoone purchaſe ſtrife :
  then wiſely do each thing diſcerne.
And do no euill occaſion giue,
But louingly together liue :
  For where the man and wife do hate,
  the curſe of God waytes at thy gate.

On Harlots caſt not thou thy minde,
  leaſt thou thereby thy ſelfe conſume :
And waſte thy riches in the winde,
  whilſt thou in fancie fret and fume :
Their foule inticements bringeth death,
And poyſon commeth from their breath :
  their eyes are wandering too and fro,
  and euery one their faſhions know.

Prayſe no woman for her beauties ſake,
  nor diſcommende no man by light :
And with thy tongue no lying make,
  fulfill thy promiſe iuſt and right.
Be mercifull vnto the poore,
And God will thee reward therefore :
  Keepe not the Laborers wages backe
  but comfort ſuch as comfort lacke.

Grieue not the heauie harted man,
  nor ioy not at thy enemies harme :
Rebuke thy Brother friendly than,
  againſt no man vſe open charme :
Nor credite thou each tale in haſt,
Till tryall proue the matter waſt.
  Frō hateful ſlaunder keepe thy tongue
  & worke for age, whilſt thou art young.

Three things there are which God doth hate
  as holy Scripture do declare :
A man too proud in beggars ſtate,
  a Rich man for to lye and ſweare :
To ſee an Old-man giuen to luſt :
And thoſe of God are ſure acurſt.
  The lying tongue the ſoule doth quell
  but pride & luſt throwes downe to hell.

While you are liuing, call for grace,
  thy ſelfe is like the fading Flower :
Death commeth ſtealing on a pace,
  thou ſhalt not know the day nor houre.
Thy ſpeach at all times ſhall not laſt,
Vſe well the time that now thou haſt :
  and from repentance doo not ſtay,
  thou canſt no time with death delay.

If thou confider well the fame,
    and beare thefe Leffons in thy minde :
And thereunto thy felfe do frame,
    great comfort furely thou fhalt finde.
Plant well thefe fayings in thy hart,
And from thefe precepts neuer ftart :
So fhalt thou liue in perfect peace,
    and God will bleffe thee with increafe.

FINIS.

At London printed by W. W. | for T. P.

On August 1, 1586, was licensed to Edward White, with a large parcel of ballads, the ' *Sayinges and fentences of Salomon* ' (Arber's *Transcript*, ii. 451). The Britwell copy and that in the Roxburghe collection (*Roxburghe Ballads*, vol. ii, p. 539) are later editions. The earliest, printed by William White for Thomas Pavier, probably soon after 1600, is in three columns, and at the head of the text is a small biblical woodcut.

The tune ' Wigmore's Galliard ' was very popular, and there are several ballads to be sung to this tune, including Richard Harrington's ' A famous dittie of the Ioyful receauing of the Queens mofte excellent maieftie by the worthy Citizens of London, the xij. day of Nouember, 1584. at her graces comming to Saint Iames ', which was reprinted in Mr. Henry Huth's ' Ancient Ballads and Broadsides ' (Philobiblon Society, 1867), and ' A Warning for all Murderers ', without date (*Roxburghe Ballads*, vol. iii, p. 137). The name of the galliard may be connected with ' The lamentable Song of the Lord Wigmore, Gouernor of Warwick Caftle, and the Fair Maid of Dunfmore ', which was included in Evans's ' Old Ballads ', 1810 (vol. iii, p. 226). ' Wigmore's Galliard ' is given in W. Chappell's *Popular Music of the Olden Time*, vol. i, p. 242.

85

҉ The reedifying of Salomons Temple, and the Laborers therof.

WHen that the Cocke began to crow
in February laſt
It was nere dai I knewe right wel
the byrdes they ſonge ſo faſt
    For they recorded pleſauntly
when they did vnderſtande
That winters blaſtes began to ſwage
and Vere was euen at hande
    And when the Parker hard this **Cock**
eftſone he gan to ſtere
And vp he ſtart and gate him forth
to viewe and ſe the dere,
    And when he came he ſe the dere
where they were on the launde
At whome the dere were not amaſde
but ſtyll they ſtode and faunde.
    For well they wyſt this Parker came
to do his wonted feate,
And or he went from them agayne
in dede he gaue them meate.
    Which they had ſought & could not find
wherefore they loked thyn,
As though they had ben chaſt with dogs
that lately had ruſht in.
    As ſone as he was gon from them
a Scory* ſcourde the coſte,
To fray the bandogges from the Dere
for feare they ſhould be loſte.
    Whiche longe had made ſuch ſpoile of them
as like hath not ben ſene,
At euery courſe a leyſhe or two
as we full ofte haue ſene.
    This Scory ſcoured all the parke
he ſercht it rounde about.
To fortifie the walles therof
to kepe the bandogs out

*John Scory, Bishop of Rochester, 1551, Bishop of Chicester, 1552 to 1553, was deprived and recanted in the reign of Queen Mary; in 1559, however, he was elected Bishop of Hereford, and retained this see until his death in 1585.

When he had take the viewe therof,
and fawe the parke fo fcalde.
He made his fute vnto the Quene
to haue it all new palde.
    And after him there dyd fuccede
a man of auncient yeares
Which did renewe the former fute
vnto the noble Peeres.
    Whofe iudgement is profounde & depe
as all the learned fay.
And he affyrmde and proued it both
our fayth was in decaye.
Whiche is the mooft affured wall
that may or can be bylte,
Whiche wall hath ben battred at
that it was almofte fpylte,
And if this wall be not repayrde
but fall ftyll in decaye
The bandogs wyll breake in againe
and driue the deare awaye.
Thus hath this aunciēt whithed proued
with argumentes mooft ftronge,
That if this wall be not repayrde
the parke cannot ftande longe.
    Wherfore the buylders of this wall
that haue take it in hande
Haue fharpned all theyr tooles right wel
to haue this buildinge ftande.
    A Byll alfo fharped his edge
to cut the brambles downe
And to deftroy the wicked wedes
that were in hye renoume.
Thus all thefe builders work right well
for they haue begon the frame,
And all that fe theyr workmanfhip
do much commend the fame.
    They worke it artificiallye
as men experte and wyfe,
For why they builde vpon the rocke
and not vpon the yfe.
    Who hath not fene, who hath not hard
the doynges of thefe men,
What paynes they take inceffantlye
to buylde this wall agen,
    To kepe the yonge fawnes frō the fox
and from the wolues and dogges.
Lefte that the parke be foylde agayne
with fwyne and fylthy bogges.
    Marke well yᵉ grift that grind all groūd
and ye fhall vnderftande,
That he is able well to buyld
the thinge he taketh in hande.

For he hath newly bete his quernes,
wherfore it may be thought,
That he intendes to grinde the grift
that we full longe haue fought,
    But when the mighty Sampfon¹ cam
that longe had ben away.
He mufled vp the bandogges mouthes
that the had naught to faye.
    So that theyr fury is well cooled
through Sampfons force and might
For though they grin and loke awrye
they haue no power to byte,
    For nowe the dere go quietlye
within the pale and parke,
And are nothinge afrayde to here
the bandogs how they barke,
    There kepers nowe ar come agen
that longe haue ben awaye,
Wherfore the poore and fimple Dere,
are ioyfull of this daye,
    For when the Horne² was heard of thē
which founded like a bell,
The Dere that knewe the fame before
dyd like it wery [sic] well.
He blew his meafures in fuch fort
fo truly and fo trymme
That all that hard the found therof
had much delight in him,
    Befides all thefe yet are there mo,
whofe diligence and payne,
Do craue of vs etarnall prayfe
that lyue and do remayne,
Leuer³ and Sandes,⁴ for fo they hyght
whofe godly hartes and wyll
Are wholy bent vnto the truth
and to confute the yll,
    So are thefe two that yet remayne,
as it hath well bene fene,
How learnedly they fpeake their mindes
before our noble Quene.
    Pedder⁵ and Wyntrel, thefe are they
whofe memory and fame
Shalbe reuiued, when they are dead
their actes deferue the fame,
    For thefe and for the reft of them
let vs geue thankes to God,
whofe mercy towardes vs is fuche,
that he hath broke the rod,

---

¹ Thomas Sampson, Dean of Christ Church, 1561, deprived for nonconformity, 1565, and imprisoned, but released through the intercession of Archbishop Parker.
² Robert Horne, Bishop of Winchester, 1560 to 1580, who, by his obduracy towards popery and nonconformity alike, earned from his opponents the verdict that, like his name, he was 'Hard in nature and crooked in conditions'.
³ Thomas Lever, Archdeacon of Coventry, 1559 to 1577, an uncompromising puritan.
⁴ Edwin Sandys, Archbishop of York, 1576 to 1588, one of the translators of the Bishops' Bible.
⁵ John Pedder, Dean of Worcester, 1559 to 1571.

O Lorde beholde thy labourers
and now put to thy hande,
To buylde the holy Temple vp
that it may euer ſtande.

   Dryue out the ydle men thereof
ye[a] dryue them cleane awaye
Whiche long haue ſought the ſpoile of it
to bringe it to decaye.

   To whome let vs left [*sic*] vp our hartes
at morow and at euen,
That it wyll pleaſe him to preſerue
Eliſabeth our quene,

   Long to endure amongeſt vs here
and to poſſeſſe her place,
And afterwardes to Ioye with him
when ſhe hath runne her race.

Finis

God ſaue the quene.

Imprinted at London, for Wyllyam | Pickering dwellind [*sic*] at Saint | Magnus Corner.

With a number of ballads for which licences were granted to William Pickering on Sept. 4, 1564, is one 'The erydfynge of Salomans temple' (Arber's *Transcript*, i. 262). This is written much after the manner of 'The aſſault of God's Fort' (p. 5), where an allegory presents the chief partisans in the religious struggle under Mary Tudor. The ballad now reprinted indicates the difficulties which beset Parker and other leaders of the new church, ten years later, in the attempt to steer their charge betwixt Calvinism and Rome, a road shadowed by the vexed questions of ritual and vestments.

86

A moſt notable and worthy example of an vngratious Sonne,
who in the pride of his|hart denied his owne Father: and how
God for his offence turned his meate into | loathſome Toades.

To the tune of Lord Darley.

IN ſearching famous Chronicles,
  it was my chaunce to reed,
A worthy ſtorie ſtrange and true,
  whereto I tooke good heed:
Betwixt a Farmer and his Sonne,
  this rare example ſtandes:
which wel may moue the hardeſt harts
  to weepe and wring their handes.

This Farmer in the Country dwelt,
  whoſe ſubſtance did excell:
He ſent therefore his eldeſt Sonne
  In Paris for to dwell:
Where he became a Marchant man,
  and traffique great he vſd,
So that he was exceeding rich,
  till he himſelfe abuſd.

For hauing now the world at will,
  his mind was wholly bent,
To gaming, wine, and wantonneſſe,
  till all his goods were ſpent:
Yea ſuch exceſſiue riotouſneſſe,
  by him was ſhewed foorth,
That he was three times more in debt
  then all his wealth was worth.

At length his credite cleane was cract
  and he in priſon caſt:
And euery man againſt him then,
  did ſet his action faſt.
There lay he lockt in Irons ſtrong,
  for euer and for aye,
Vnable while his life did laſt,
  his greeuous debts to pay.

And lying in this carefull cafe,
   his eyes with teares befprent,
The lewdnes for [*sic*] his former life,
   too late he did repent.
And being voyde of all reliefe,
   of helpe and comfort quite,
Vnto his Father at the laft,
   he thus began to write.

Bow downe awhile your heedful eares
   my louing Father deare,
And graunt I pray in gratious fort,
   my pittious plaintes to heare.
Forgiue the foule offences all
   of thy vnthriftie Sonne :
which through the lewdnes of his life,
   hath now himfelfe vndone.

O my good Father take remorce,
   on this my extreame neede :
And fuccour his diftreffed ftate,
   whofe hart for woe doth bleed.
In dolefull dungeon heere I lie,
   my feete in fetters faft :
Whom my moft cruell creditors,
   in Prifon fo haue caft.

Let pittie therefore pearce your breft,
   and mercy moue your minde,
And to releafe my miferie,
   fome fhift fweete Father finde.
My chiefeft cheare is bread ful brown
   the boordes my fofteft bed :
And flinty ftones for pillowes ferues,
   to reft my troubled head.

My garments all are worne to rags,
   my body ftarues with cold :
And crawling vermine eates my flefh,
   moft greeuous to behold.
Deare Father come therefore with fpeed
   and rid me out of thrall,
And let me not in prifon die,
   fith for your helpe I call.

The good old man no fooner had,
   perufde this written fcrowle :
But trickling teares along his cheeks
   from watry eyes did rowle :
Alas my Sonne, my Sonne quoth he
   in whom I ioyed moft :
Thou fhalt not long in prifon be,
   what euer it doth coft.

Two hundred heads of well fed beasts
  he changed then for gold:
Foure hundred quarters eke of corne,
  for filuer there he fold.
But all the fame could not fuffize,
  that haynous debt to pay:
Till he at length conftrained was,
  to fell his land away.

Then was his Sonne releafed quite,
  his debt difcharged cleane,
And left likewife as well to liue,
  as he before had been.
Then went his louing Father home,
  who for to helpe his Sonne,
Had fold his lyuing quite away,
  and eke him felfe vndone.

So that he lyued poore and bare,
  and in fuch extreame need,
That many times he wanted food,
  his hungry corpes to feed:
His Sonne meane time in filkes did fwim,
  whofe fubftance now was fuch:
That fure within the Cittie walles,
  few men were found fo rich.

But as his goods did ftill increafe,
  and riches in did flide,
So more and more his hardned hart,
  did fwell in hatefull pride:
But it befell vpon a time,
  when ten yeeres woe was paft,
Vnto his Sonne he did repaire,
  for fome reliefe at laft.

And being come vnto his houfe,
  in very poore aray,
It chaunced fo that with his Sonne,
  great ftates fhould dine that day.
The poore old man with Hat in hand,
  did then the Porter pray,
To fhew his Sonne that at the gate,
  his Father there did ftay.

Wherat this proud difdainfull wretch
  with taunting fpeeches fayd,
That long agoe his Fathers boones,
  within the graue was layd:
What Rafcall then is that quoth he,
  that ftayneth fo my ftate?
I charge the Porter prefently
  to driue him from my gate.

Which anſwere when yᵉ old man heard
　　he was in minde diſmayde :
He wept, he waild, he wrong his hands
　　and thus at length he ſayd.
O curſed wretch, and moſt vnkind,
　　thou worker of my woe :
Thou monſter to humanitie,
　　and eke thy Fathers foe.

Haue I bin carefull of thy caſe,
　　maintayning ſtill thy ſtate ?
And doſt thou now ſo doggedly,
　　enforce me from thy gate ?
And haue I wrongd thy brethren all
　　from thrall, to ſet thee free ?
And brought my ſelfe to beggars ſtate
　　and all to ſuccour thee.

Woe worth the time when firſt of all
　　thy body I eſpide :
Which haſt in hardnes of thy hart,
　　thy Fathers face denide.
But now behold how God that time,
　　did ſhew a wonder great,
Euen when his ſon with al his friends
　　were ſetled downe to meate.

For when the faireſt Pie was cut,
　　a ſtrange and dreadfull caſe,
Moſt vglie Toads came crawling out
　　and leaped in his face.
Then did the wretch his fault confeſſe
　　and for his Father ſent
And then his great ingratitude,
　　full ſore he did repent.

All vertuous Children learne by this,
　　obedient hartes to ſhow :
And honour ſtill your Parents deare,
　　for God commaundeth ſo.
And thinke how God did turne his meate
　　to poyſond Toades indeed :
Which did his Fathers face denie,
　　becauſe he ſtood in need.

FINIS.

On August 8, 1586, the Stationers' Company granted a licence to Edward White for printing a ballad ' *A notable example of an vngratious ſonne toward his father and howe God changed his meates into* todes ' (Arber's *Transcript*, ii. 452). The entry may refer to this ballad, of which the imprint has been lost. Other and probably later editions of it are in the Roxburghe collection at the British Museum

(*Roxburghe Ballads*, vol. ii, pp. 73–79) and in the Pepysian library at Cambridge. Both these were published by Henry Gosson. Evans included it in 'Old Ballads ', 1810, vol. iii, pp. 304–11.

The tune of ' Lord Dar[n]ley ' may refer to a ballad ' A Dolefull Ditty, or forowfull Sonet of the Lord Darly, fometime King of Scots . . . and is to be fong to the tune of ' Blacke and Yellowe ' . . . Imprinted at London by Thomas Goffon ', for which a licence was granted on March 24, 1579 (Arber, ii. 349), and a copy of which is preserved in the library of the Society of Antiquaries (Lemon, *Catalogue of Broadsides*, p. 19). In the Roxburghe collection is a ballad, ' A warning to Youth . . . To the tune of the Lord Darley ' (*Ballads*, vol. iii, pp. 35–41). The tune ' I am the Duke of Norfolk ' or ' Paul's Steeple ', which William Chappell identifies with ' Blacke and Yellowe ', is given in ' Popular Music of the Olden Time ' (vol i, p. 117).

The ballad is printed in three columns on a closely cropped sheet, and is without ornament or border.

87

A briefe fonet declaring the lamentation of Beckles, a Market
Towne in | Suffolke which was in the great winde vpon S. Andrewes
eue pitifully burned with fire to the | value by eftimation of tweentie thoufande
pounds. And to the number of fourefcore dwelling houfes, | befides a great
number of other houfes. 1586. To the tune of Labandalafhotte.

MY louing good neighbours, that comes to beholde,
Me fillie poore Beckles, in cares manyfolde,
In forrow all drowned, which floated of late,
With teares all bedewed, at my wofull ftate,
With fire fo confumed, moft wofull to vewe,
Whofe fpoile thy poore people, for euer may rue,
When well you haue vewed my total decay,
And pittie haue pierced, your heartes as it may,
Say thus my good neighbours that God in his ire,
For finne hath confumed poore Beckles with Fire.

For one onely parifh, myfelfe I mought vaunt,
To match with the braueft, for who but will graunt?
The Sea and the Countrey, me fitting fo nye,
The frefh water Riuer, fo fweete running by,
My medowes and commons, fuch profpect of health,
My Fayers in fomer, fo garnifht with wealth,
My Market fo ferued, with corne, flefh, and fifh,
And all kinde of victuals, that poore men would wifh,
That who but knewe Beckles, with fighing may faye,
Would God of his mercie, had fparde my decaye.

But O my deftruction, O moft difmall day,
My temple is fpoyled, and brought in decay,
My marketfted burned, my beautie defaced,
My wealth ouerwhelmed, my people difplaced,
My muficke is wayling, my mirth it is moone,
My ioyes are departed, my comfort is gone,
My people poore creatures, are mourning in woe,
Still wandring not wotting, which waye for to goe.
Like fillie poore Troians, whom Sinon betrayde,
But God of thy mercy, releeue them with ayde.

A rude
felowe by
fiering his
chimney
procured
their ca-
lamitie.

O daye moſt vnluckie, the winde lowde in ſkie,
The water harde froſen, the houſes ſo drye,
To ſee ſuch a burning, ſuch flaming of fire,
Such wayling, ſuch crying, through ſcourge of Gods ire,
Such running, ſuch working, ſuch taking of payne,
Such whirling, ſuch haling, ſuch reauing in vaine,
Such robbing, ſuch ſtealing, from more to the leſſe,
Such diſhoneſt dealing, in time of diſtreſſe,
That who ſo hard hearted, and worne out of grace?
But pittie may pierce him to thinke of my caſe.

But O my good neighbours, that ſee mine eſtate,
Be all one as Chriſtians, not liue in debate,
With wrapping and trapping, each other in thrall,
With watching, and pryeng at each others fall,
With houing, and ſhouing, and ſtriuing in Lawe,
Of God nor his Goſpell, once ſtanding in awe,
Lyue not in heart-burning, at God neuer wreſt,
To Chriſt once be turning, not vſe him in ieſt,
Liue louely together and not in diſcorde,
Let me be your mirrour, to liue in the Lorde.

But though God haue pleaſed, for ſinne to plague me,
Let none thinke there liuing is cauſe they ſcape free,
But let them remember, how Chriſt once did tell,
Their ſinnes were not greater, on whom the wall fell,
But leaſt you repent ye, thus much he doth ſay,
Be ſure and certaine ye alſo decaye,
Let none then perſwade them, ſo free from all thrall,
But that their ill liuing, deſerueth a fall,
Thus farewell, forget not my wofull annoye,
God ſend you [good] new yeare and [bleſſe me with ioye.]

Finis ♉ D. STERRI[E].

Fœlix quem faciunt alièna pericula cautum.

Ech ſtately Towre with mightie walles vp prope
Ech loftie Roofe which golden wealth hath raiſed
All flickering wealth which flies in firmeſt hope
All glittering hew ſo haught and highly praiſde
I ſee by ſodaine ruine of Beckles towne
Is but a blaſt if mightie Ioue doe frowne.

At London,
Imprinted by Robert Robinſon for Nicholas | *Colman of Norwich, dwelling in S. Andrewes
Church yarde.*

Suckling's ' History and Antiquities of Suffolk', 1846–48 (vol. i, p. 12), describes the fire at Beccles : ' The most serious temporal calamity on record which ever visited Beccles, occurred on the 29th of November, 1586. On the eve of St. Andrew, in that year, a fire broke out in the chimney of one of the smaller houses in the town, which being fanned by a violent gale of wind blowing at that time, rapidly increased to an awful conflagration, which it was found impossible to arrest, as the river, though so early in the season, was hard frozen. It raged with greatest violence in the vicinity of the new market. The roof, seats, and wood-work of the church were consumed, though the walls and the stone-work of the windows escaped destruction. The lower part of the steeple remains blackened with smoke in a very remarkable degree to the present day. Above eighty houses fell a sacrifice to the flames; and goods and property were damaged and stolen in the confusion, to the amount of £20,000, as even then estimated.' The Huth library possessed a broadside touching the fire at Beccles entitled 'A proper newe sonet declaring the lamentation of Beckles . . . To Wilsons tune . . . T. D[eloney]', as well as a different issue of Sterrie's 'briefe sonet', which was licensed to Nicholas Colman

on Dec. 13, 1586 (Arber's *Transcript*, ii. 461). Both were reprinted in Mr. Henry Huth's 'Ancient Ballads and Broadsides' (Philobiblon Society, 1867) and are now in the library of the British Museum.

Of Sterrie, the author of this ballad, no information is forthcoming, nor are any other works by him known.

The tune of 'Labandalashotte' is not mentioned by Chappell in 'Popular Music of the Olden Time', though it is attached to 'A Song of King Edgar, shewing how he was deceived of his Loue' (Ambrose Phillips, *Collection of Old Ballads*, 1723, vol. ii, p. 25).

The ballad is printed in two columns, and at the head of the text is a woodcut of Beccles during the conflagration. The Britwell copy was not in Heber's collection.

88

[Some f]yne gloues deuifed for Newyeres gyftes to teche yonge
peo[ple to] knowe good from euyll.

[See facsimile.]

William Powell, the printer of this ballad, entered business in 1547, when he succeeded, at the sign of the George in Fleet Street, William Middleton, whose widow he had married. From 1547 to 1567 Powell is believed to have printed more than fifty books. The ballad, of which a reproduction is given, does not reveal the precise date at which it was published, nor do the Registers of the Stationers' Company throw any light thereon. It is evident that it did not appear prior to 1553, and it was possibly later than 1559, for in that year Powell printed his edition of the 'Kalendar of Shepardes', which contains from brighter impressions the blocks which decorate the text of the broadside. It is impossible to identify the author's initials with any known individual.

The original ballad measures fifteen inches by eleven inches.

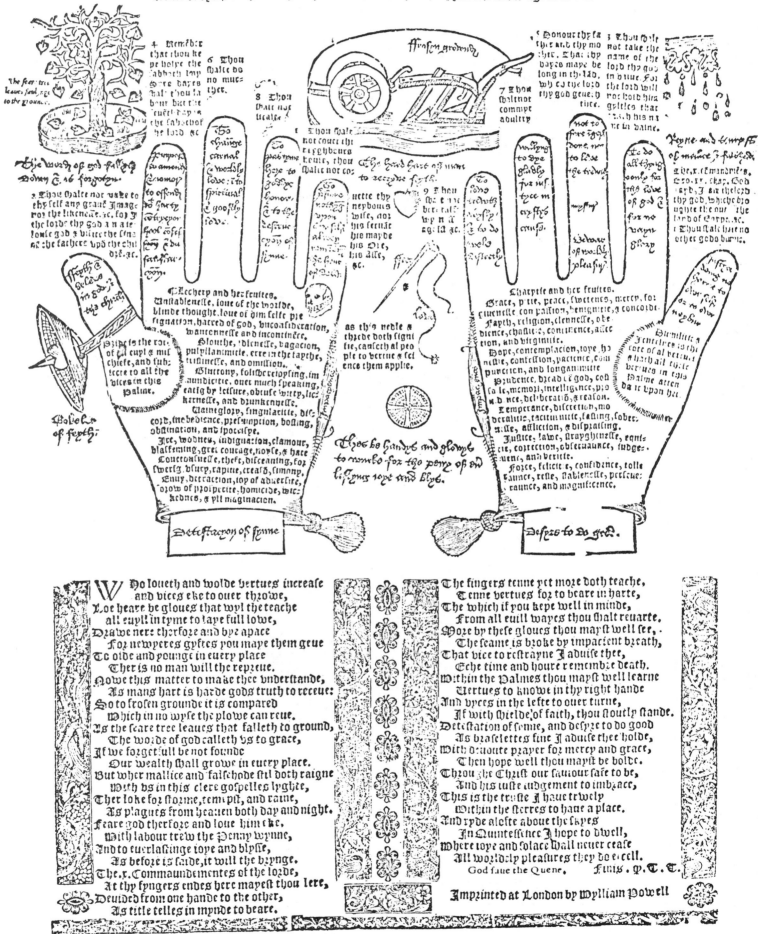

The gloues of... Newyeres gyftes to teache yonge pe[ople to]
knowe good from euyll wherby they maye learne the .x. commaundementes at theyr fyngers endes, & other
good lessons be written within the fyngers, the tree of vertues with her braunches in the right palme, and the
Roote of vyces in the lefte, with a declaration of the other pyctures folowynge in miter.

WHo loueth and wolde vertues increase
and vices eke to ouer throwe,
Loe heare be gloues that wyl the teache
all euyll in tyme to laye full lowe,
Drawe nere therfore and bye apace
For newyeres gyftes you maye them geue
To olde and younge in euery place
Ther is no man will the repreue.
Howe this matter to make thee vnderstande,
As many hart is harde gods truth to receue:
So to frosen grounde it is compared
Which in no wyse the plowe can reue.
As the seare tree leaues that falleth to ground,
The worde of god calleth vs to grace,
If we forgetfull be not founde
Our wealth shall growe in euery place.
But wher mallice and falsehode styl doth raigne
With vs in this clere gospelles lyghte,
Ther loke for storme, tempest, and raine,
As plagues from heauen both day and night.
Feare god therfore and loue him eke,
With labour trew the Peny wynne,
And to euerlastinge ioye and blysse,
As before is sayde, it will the brynge.
The .x. Commaundementes of the lorde,
At thy fyngers endes here mayest thou lere,
Deuided from one hande to the other,
As title telles in mynde to beare.

The fingers tenne yet more doth teache,
Tenne vertues for to beare in harte,
The which if you kepe well in minde,
From all euill wayes thou shalt reuarte.
More by these gloues thou mayst well see,
The seame is broke by impacient breath,
That vice to restrayne I aduise thee,
Eche time and houre remembre death.
Within the palmes thou mayst well learne
Vertues to knowe in thy right hande
And vyces in the lefte to ouer turne,
If with shielde of faith, thou stoutly stande.
Detestation of synne, and desyre to do good
As braselettes fine I aduise thee holde,
With deuoute prayer for mercy and grace,
Then hope well thou mayst be bolde.
Throu the Christ our sauiour safe to be,
And his iuste iudgement to imbrace,
This is the truste I haue truely
Within the sterres to haue a place.
And ryde aleste aboue the skyes
In Quintessence I hope to dwell,
Where ioye and solace shall neuer cease
All worldly pleasures they do excell.
God saue the Quene.   FINIS. P.T.C.

Imprinted at London by Wylliam Powell

89

¶ A very Lamentable and woful difcours of the | fierce fluds,
whiche lately flowed in Bedford fhire, in Lincoln fhire, and in many
other | places, with the great loffes of fheep and other Cattel.   The v. of October.
Anno Domini. 1570.

ALl faithful harts come waile,
    Com rent your garmēts gay :
Els nothing can preuaile,
    To turn Gods wrath away.

¶Of waters fierce and fel,
    And fluds both huge and hie :
You may report and tel ;
    Of places far and nye.

¶Of Monfters very rare,
    That are vnfeemly borne :
Whiche dooth at large declare,
    We liue as men forlorne.

¶We liue and linger ftil,
    We wander quite aftray,
We want true Chriftians fkil,
    To gide vs in the way.

¶Ful ftraunge vnfeemly fights,
    We may beholde and fee :
What mifdefourmed wights,
    Of women borne there bee.

¶Oufe bridge was lately loft,
    By force of roring ftreame :
Which many a crowne hath coft,
    In this our Englifh realme.

¶Why fhould I make delay,
    Reciting of fuch acts ?
What need I more to fay,
    Of vice and worldly facts ?

¶As erft I did pretend,
    So forward wil I glide :
To tel the totall end,
    What hapnēd at this tide.

¶By rufhing riuers late,
  In Bedford town no nay :
Ful many a woful ftate,
  May yeeld to faft and pray.

¶At twelue a clock at night,
  It flowde with fuche a hed :
Yea many a woful wight,
  Did fwim in naked bed.

¶Among the reft there was,
  A woful widow fure :
Whome God did bring to paffe,
  The death fhe did procure.

¶Widow Spencer by name,
  Afleep fhee beeing faft.
The flud fo rafhly came,
  That fhee aloft was caft.

Whiche feeing ftarted vp,
  Regarding fmall her pelf :
She lept befide her bed,
  And fo fhee drownd herfelf.

¶The houfes very ftrong,
  The cattel great and fmall :
Were quickly laid along,
  And fo they perifht all.

¶The Geldings tall and braue,
  In ftables rafhly roules,
The Churche was ouer flowed,
  In Bedford named Poules.

¶The Gardens round about,
  The fheep in marfhe or feeld,
The riuer was fo ftout,
  They knew not where to fheeld.

¶The Kine and Oxen to,
  Were all drowned by force,
They weft [*sic*] not what to doo :
  It had fo fmall remorfe.

¶O Lord this flud was ftraunge,
  And none occation why :
The wether did not chaunge,
  the winde was nothing hie.

¶There was no ſtore of raine,
 But very little ſure :
That we ſhould thus ſuſtaine,
 the loſſe we did indure.

¶The Arke of father Noy,
 was had in minde as than :
When God did clene deſtroy,
 Bothe woman childe and man.

¶But that he promis made,
 When he did heer remaine :
The world ſhould neuer vade,
 By waters force againe.

¶Els would we then haue thought,
 The dredful day of doome :
Had been bothe ſhape and wrought,
 To drown vs all and ſome.

¶Vpon the Saboth day,
 We were amaſed all :
In Church we could not pray
 But in the Iudgement hall.

¶We all aſſembled there,
 With praiers moſte deuout :
To God with many a tere,
 To tame this riuer ſtout.

¶No horſe nor man could paſſe,
 Of buſines ſmall or poſt :
For iſſue none there was,
 No way but to be loſt.

¶In Bedford town I knowe,
 This many a ſcore of yeeres :
Did neuer riuers flowe,
 To bring vs in ſuche feares.

¶By chaunce I came in place,
 This great miſchaunce to tel :
To end our crooked race,
 What fortune late befel.

¶Whiche tale no ſooner doon,
 Twoo men along did walke,
Betwixt vs wee begon,
 to raiſe ſom further talke.

¶What Cuntrey men they were,
    I did requeſt to knowe :
They ſaid of Lincoln ſhire,
    the certen trueth is ſo.

¶Quod they your loſſe is ſmall,
    But one hath loſt her life,
He aſkt what dame ſhe was,
    I ſaid one Spencers wife.

¶In Lincolnſhire (he ſaid),
    We haue ſuſtaind great loſſe,
Our ſtomacks are decaide,
    That late ſo frolick was.

¶Our Cattel in like cace,
    Are drownd and caſt away,
For oure offence in euery place,
    the dum beaſts truly pay.

¶We haue not ſcaped ſo,
    Bothe widow, man, and wife,
Since firſt this flud did flowe,
    Haue gained loſſe of life.

¶When that the water ſeaſt,
    As I and more doo knowe,
Ther did from ſkies diſcend,
    A great and greeuous ſnowe.

¶And ſo we parted then,
    Bewailing bothe togither,
Like poor and out caſt men,
    This ſudden chaunge of wether.

¶In vs therfore for ſhame,
    Let vice no more be ſeene :
and eke ourſelues ſo frame
    To ſerue aright our Queen.

Finis.   ꝓ   Richard. Tarlton.

¶ Imprinted at |
London at the long ſhop adioyning | vnto Saint Mildreds Churche | in the Pultrye, by |
Iohn Allde. 1570.

Stow (*Annales*, 1615, p. 667) refers to the great floods which rose in the low-lying counties during the autumn of 1570: 'The fift of October at night, happened a terrible tempeſt of wind and raine both on the ſea and land by meanes whereof many ſhips & other veſſels were drowned, about midnight the water ouerflowing, drowned many meddowes, paſtures, townes, villages, cattell, houſes and goods, to the vtter vndoing of a great number of fubiects of this realme: befides the loffe of many men, women, and children, fome drowned in there Beddes, and fome as they trauelled.'

Richard Tarlton, the actor, is said to have been born at Condover in Shropshire, where he minded his father's swine. Later he may have kept a tavern in Gracechurch Street, London. In 1583 he was appointed one of twelve 'queen's players', and retained the office until his death in 1588. During his lifetime Tarlton enjoyed a tremendous reputation as a comedian, and his memory lingered in ephemeral literature for more than a century afterwards. Tarlton may or may not have been responsible for the songs and ballads which are associated with his name. A list of these, some of which survive only as entries in the Registers of the Stationers' Company, is given in the 'Dictionary of National Biography'. His gift for improvisation was well known, yet the temptation to launch their own productions under the cloak of Tarlton's name may easily have proved too much for the honesty of contemporary ballad-writers.

The ballad here reprinted was licensed to John Allde in 1570–71 (Arber's *Transcript*, i. 440), and was included in J. P. Collier's 'Old Ballads' (Percy Society, 1840). It is printed in three columns within line borders.

90

A Spiritual Songe of
Thankesgiuing vnto God, for his grace and power.   Written by a
close prisonner (with a coale) for his owne | comforte

LEt others singe of this and that,
  I will singe to thy prayse,
Who doest out of aduersitie,
  Deliuer me alwayes:
And stood'st to me that Comforter,
  In all my sore temptation:
Who doeth refreshe my sinfull soule
  With spirituall consolation:
And graunt'st to me such patience,
  For all my foes despight,
As I to wayte vpon thy will,
  Doe inwardlie delight.
And when I see my nature striue
  Against thy iust correction,
Then doe I pray thy Maiestie
  To helpe myne vnsubiection,
And when my troubles most increase,
  (As who liues well and smarts not)
Then comes my Sauiour next to me,
  And stickes by me and startes not:
And when I feele my fleshe to shrinke
  Vnder thy heauie hande,
I am constrain'd my wretchednes,
  Better to vnderstande:
Calling to minde those grieuous sinns,
  I thought not on before,
Lamenting them and purposing
  To doe the like no more:
But their contrarie vertues all,
  Eftsoone to put in vre
From grace to grace, frō strength to strength,
  Whyl'st my dayes shall endure:
By thy free grace and perfect strength,
  Whereof alone I boast,
For if I should doe otherwyse,
  My labour were but loste:

Since all good giftes doe come from thee,
  And thou wilt fuffer none
To rob thee of that prayfe which doeth
  Belong to thee alone :
Yet whyl'ft by wreftling againft finne,
  Rewarde for to obtaine,
I feeke by deferte of my workes,
  Thou aunfwer'ft thus againe.

The aunfwere.

Whereas thy finnes doe farre exceede,
  My grace doeth more abounde,
And in thy weakenes moft of all,
  My power is tryed and founde :
My grace in Chrift fufficient is,
  And all my workes doeth paffe :
By it I am more glorified,
  Then ought that euer was :
And as I made all things of nought,
  And darkenes to be light,
So make I nought for to bee good,
  And feeble to bee might :
All perfons and all things on earth
  I haue fhutt vnder finne,
That by my pardon, generall,
  I might all glorie winne.
I am the firft, the middeft, and laft,
  And I am all in all,
That all at all times fhould on mee
  For helpe and mercie call.
My grace is fure full free and pure,
  Or elfe it were no grace,
It can not ftande at any hande,
  Where workes haue any place :
My power infailleable and moft incomparable
  Is of no force in deede,
When it is made of others aydes,
  To ftande in any neede :
Therefore I call the worft of all,
  And leaue the righteous ftill,
That all may fee my grace to bee
  According to my will :
Therefore I bring both Clowne and King
  To duft, to death, to nought :
That euery wight fhould knowe my might,
  All things alone hath wrought :
Wherefore bee ftill, and flee from ill,
  And doe well, but confeffe
My guiftes in thee both lent to bee,
  And marred more or leffe :

That still my grace may serue in place
  All thy defaultes to mende,
And that my power may euery hower
  Vpholde thee to the ende,
When there shalbe no sinne in thee,
  Weaknes nor wante at all,
But grace, might, wealth, peace, ioye, right,
  Health and glorie eternall.

Thus doest thou Lord direct my soule
  To quiet peace and reste,
Whereby I am assured all
  Shall fall out to the beste:
And that no shame can me defame,
  For why thou art my praise,
In life and death and all in all,
  To me at all assaies,
For thy great mercies sake in Christ,
  In whom thou art well pleafed,
The heauie harted sinners of
  Their burthens should be eafed,
And make partakers of thofe ioyes
  Vnfpeakable and rife,
Which thou doest keepe in store for them,
  After this wofull life:
And in meane while the holy ghoste
  Doeth keepe them safe and founde:
No rage nor no refistance can,
  Their happie state confounde.

Nowe whileft mine enimies seeke to driue
  Mee in defperation,
Thou forceft them againft their willes
  To further my faluation:
And thou doest turne all wiles and wrongs
  Vnto their owne difgrace:
Who feeke by all extremities,
  Thy feruauntes to deface,
And thou doest turne all other things
  To my behoofe likewife.
So that to better myne eftate,
  My harte can not deuife.
How euer wretched worldlings deeme,
  I am quite caft awaye:
And myne olde friendes a loofe from me
  Doe ftande as at a baye:
Yet thou doest ftande at my right hande,
  And compaffe me about,
And furnifhe me with diuers giftes,
  To make me ftronge and ftout:
And outwarde giftes fufficient,
  And meete for me and mine,
To ferue thy grace, and fhewe thy power
  By prouidence diuine:

Beyonde reaſon without deſert,
  Better then many moe
Of thy deare Saintes who are content,
  And ſinge for ioye alſo:

Lorde graunt wee pray that ſo we may,
  Since thou art ſtronge and kinde,
(As in our conſcience and experience
  We euerie day doe finde)
That by thinges all which doe befall,
  We may drawe neare to thee,
Till thy ſweete face in heauenly place,
  For euer wee ſhall ſee.

AMEN.

M. D. XCII.

No licence for this ballad appears in the Registers of the Stationers' Company. With the exception of the eight concluding lines it is printed in three columns, and is surrounded by a lace border.

91

❡The welſpoken Nobody.

[See facsimile.]

The character of Nobody, popular both in England and on the Continent during the sixteenth century, appears to have been the creation of a barber-poet of Strassburg, named Jörg Schan, who towards the close of the fifteenth century produced a poetical broadside which was printed at Memmingen by Albrecht Kunne, but without date, and of which the only copy extant is preserved in the Royal Library at Munich. It bears the title 'Niemants hais ich: was ieder man tut, das zücht man mich' above a large woodcut representing poor Nobody, with a padlock on his mouth, the original idea of that on the Heber broadside here given in reduced facsimile. Another reproduction, the size of the original, is to be seen in Halliwell's folio edition of Shakespeare, 1853 (i. 449). Beneath the woodcut is a metrical explanation, of which the present verses are to some extent an adaptation. The German poem has been reprinted in the 'Jahrbuch der Deutschen Shakespeare-Gesellschaft' for 1894, in an exhaustive introduction by Dr. Johannes Bolte to Ludwig Tieck's translation of the English drama 'Nobody and Somebody'.

The Stationers' Registers for 1568–69 mention that a licence was granted to Hugh Singleton 'for pryntinge of *the Retorne of olde well ſpoken No Body*' (Arber's *Transcript*, i. 387), and on August 1, 1586, Edward White received permission to print a ballad '*Nobodies Complaint*' (Arber, ii. 451).

The British Museum possesses a copy of the play 'No-body and Some-body. With the true Chronicle Hiſtorie of Elydure . . . Printed for Iohn Trundle and are to be ſold at his ſhop in Barbican, at the ſigne of No-body'. The book is without a date, but a licence was obtained for it on March 12, 1606. Other copies of it are mentioned in the Huth Catalogue and in that of the Dyce Collection.

Holbein, about 1515, painted a large panel of Nobody, which still exists in the Stadtbibliothek at Zürich, and is described in Woltmann's 'Holbein und seine Zeit', 1874.

The original ballad measures $14\frac{1}{8}$ in. by $10\frac{1}{2}$ in.

The welspoken Nobody.

God that is all good and almyghtye
Hath shewed his power vpon me Nobodye,
For whear my mouth with locke was sparred
He hath it burst and my speche restored,
Wherfor I wyll syng prayse vnto his name

Bicause I may speke withoute anye blame,
And thoughe the pope with all his trayn
Do me rebuke and against me sayen
That as tofore I shuld nowe holde my peace
Yet Gods honour to set furth I can not cease.

Many speke of Roben hoode that neuer shott in his bowe
So many haue layed faultes to me, which I did neuer knowe,
But nowe beholde here I am
Whom all the worlde doeth diffame
Long haue they also scorned me
And locked my mouthe for spekyng free
As many a Godly man they haue so serued
Which vnto them Gods truth hath shewed
Of such they haue burned and hanged some
That vnto their ydolatrye wold not come
The ladye truthe they haue locked in cage
Sayeng that of her Nobodye had knowledge
For asmuche nowe as they name Nobodye
I thinke verilye they speke of me
Wherfore to answere I nowe beginne
The locke of my mouthe is opened with ginne
Wrought by noman, but by Gods grace
Unto whom be prayse in euery place
  My Journeyes I make both far and nere
To seke whear people Gods iustice fear
In that place wolde I make my habytation
Trusting there to haue a continuall mansion
In print tofore I did neuer appere
Yet many coulde me not well bear
But no maruell for the prouerbe sayeth
All men can not abyde to here the truthe

A companyon must he be with these good fellowes,
As long as they wyll haue hym in their companyes,
But sometyme they forget hym, vntyll he be
Moulded or wormeaten, and than for here spe
They do hym burne secretely, as in the nyght
The Jewes toke Christ, so these by their myght
Followe the other, beyng sore afrayed,
Lest these their prankes shuld be bewrayed.
  In the Dedication daye, than oute of the steple
Do they hym hange to espye the people,
And with a litle bell them for to warne,
Because the prestes shuld catche no harme
In studyng Gods worde the flocke to fede,
No thys is ynough, they haue no other sede
To sowe, therfore they shall reap.
Upryde, as they sowed wynde a great heap.
Who be to me sayth Paule, yf I shuld not preache
No sayth the Pope my ceremonyes teache.
But what do they teache shew the meanynge?
Uuel, Gods worde gyueth me smellyng
That Paule and pour opinyon contrary be,
Shuld men leaue Paule, and followe the.
  On relyke Sondayes, than bryng you furth tromperp
Your relykes must be washen, that water saye yee,
Is good for synne and sicknes of beast,
Thus of Christes bloude make you a gest

So is thy soule spiritually fedde,
With Christes moost blessed bodye and bloude,
Uhich for thy synnes was offred on the rode,
Uuith whiche oblacyon Gods wrathe is satisfyed
Neuer hereafter to be offerred
For with one oblacyon by hym self made,
He hath made vs perfect, therfore be glad,
For vnto perfection nothyng can be added
Uhere be now suche, as masses haue sayed
To be propiciatory God them forgeue,
And conuert their hartes, whyles they do lyue
That they loke for none other propiciation
Than that which Christ made hym self alone,
In remembraunce, wherof to confirme our faythe
He bade vs receyue as the scripture sayeth.
Thys holpe communyon. No come and see
Stare on it (sayeth the Pope) and ones a yere take
Nay not so neyghbour take not, but gape.
Thy fynger wold rot yf thou touche but the chalyce,
O holpe Paule, thou bade men be wyse,
And ware of suche, as shuld admonyssh
From hādlyng and touchyng, which thynges dō peryssh
Euen with thabuse thou sayest. Uuell
Nowe seyng that all men begyn to smell
All you that be prestes I Nobodye praye,
To repent and be lerned, resist not I saye

92

A commendation of Muſicke,
And a confutation of them which diſprayſe it.

WHen firſt within the corps of man, dame Nature built her bower:
She ſaw that troubles eke & thral, was bent them to deuower.
To whome ſhe gaue as in reward, a pleaſaunt note or ſound:
Their carkes and cares to dryue away, wherby much eaſe was found.
Whereof in children proofe is had, whome nurſes haue in charge:
How ſoone they ſtop and ſtay their cry, when ſhe doeth ſound at large.
The Plowman eke, and Carter both, with eaſe doeth paſſe away:
In ſingyng of ſome mery note, their trauayle all the day.
Wherefore to Lady Nature I, doe render prayſe and wyll:
By whome not onely man alone, but byrdes in ſong hath ſkyll.
The Poetes fayne that _Amphion,_ who buylded Thebes towne:
Did fyrſt inuent the pleaſaunt note, whereby he got renowne.
To _Dioniſius_ ſome the name, and ſome contrary wyſe:
To _Zephus,_ who _Euſebius_ ſayth, the ſame dyd firſt deuyſe.
Solinus ſayth that men of Crete, by ryng and ſound of braſſe:
By _Thachadianes_ doeth _Polibius_ ſay, inuented firſt it was.
In deede I thinke ſoone after that, dame Nature made the ſound:
That Reaſon did the meaſure make, the concord and the ground.
And then in _Mercury_ firſt it wrought, as auctour of the ſame:
The which euen hee (as worthy prayſe) did publiſh and proclame.
Then Reaſon, as one not full ſuffyſde, did ſeeke for to deuyſe:
Some inſtrument to geue a ſound, by whome there did aryſe
A foreward wit in _Mercury,_ for to inuent the ſame:
Who made a Harpe of fyſhes bone, a _Tortes_ cald by name.
Which hee by _Nilus_ ryuer found, the fyſh was dryde away:
And nothyng but three ſinowes left, whereon he ſought to play.
But when they gaue a ſound agayne, thus doe the Poetes fayne:
He made a Harpe much lyke that bone, by thinuent of his brayne.
Three ſtrynges to it did he apply, a Treble Baſe and Meane:
The which he made for to accord, in Muſickes pleaſaunt vayne.
Then he it to _Apollo_ gaue, as gyft of wonderous weyght:
And he the ſame to _Orpheus_ handes, made redeliuery ſtreyght.
Some thinke _Amphion_ firſt it found, and ſome to that ſay no:
And ſome in _Tuball_ thinke the lyke, but that can not be ſo.
Then _Pan_ the Pype, _Apollo_ eke, the Shalme he did inuent:
Then _Dauid_ Regalles ſought to make, by Reaſones whole conſent.
And _Orphen_ firſt, with _Linus_ nexte, and _Arion_ als by name:
Timarias, and _Trezenius_ both, thereby did purchaſe fame.
Nor _Cibell_ yet, with _Piſes_ too, their labour ought did ceaſe:
But in the ſame did ſore apply, their cunnyng too encreaſe.

Thus haue we proued by Poetes lore, how auncient Muficke is :
And now I meane by Scripture playne, to proue the lyke iwis.
We read how *Dauid* daunft and foung, before the Arke of God :
And how his wyfe which flowted him, was by the Lorde forbore
For hauyng chyldren any more, but barren fhould fhe be :
Whereby I proue that God is pleafde, with fuch lyke armony.
When *Mir Iam* with the Ifraelites, the red fea deepe had paft :
And Pharaos hofte were drowned all, who did purfue them faft,
Then tooke they Timbrelles in their handes, and to yᵉ Lord fang prayfe
For that he was their ayde and fhyeld, to paffe the daungeroufe feas.
The Shepherdes eke, and Angelles both, we read how they reioyft :
When they once heard and vnderftoode, the byrth of Iefus Chrift.
We fee by this what Muficke is, we neede no better proofe :
The Scripture is a buckeler good, in Mufickes right behoofe.
In *Fucfius*, and in *Galen* both, who lyft to looke fhall fynd :
How much that Muficke doeth appeafe, the dolours of the mynd.
You know what tauntes *Themiftocles*, in banket did fuftayne :
When he good muficke did difprayfe, accoumptyng it but vayne.
They iudged his learnyng much the worfe, becaufe he did defye
That, which all men did much efteeme, regard and eke fet bye.
I pray you was not *Socrates*, whome crooked age had caught :
With Mufickes fkyll and armony, as one with Cupid fraught?
And fayd that concord was the ground, and eke the fure ftay :
Without the which nothing is good, this could that wyfe man fay.
And meafure is a mery meane, and meane who doeth embrace :
Of euery vertue hath the ground, which bryngeth man to grace.
This haue I doen in Mufickes caufe, my pen now wyll I reft :
Syth that I haue that worthy fcience, as famoufe once profeft.
And who that feekes the loffe of it, needes muft I fpeake my mynd :
A great difprayfe is to his wit, his wordes are coumpted wynd.

¶ FINIS.   (ᵠ) Nicholas Whight.

¶ Imprinted at London
in Alderfgate ftrete, by Alexander Lacy : | dwellyng befyde the Well.

The ' commendation of Muficke ' was licensed to
Lacy in 1562–63 (Arber's *Transcript*, i. 209). Although
no other work by Nicholas White survives, yet in
1565–66 Thomas Purfoote was allowed to print ' *the
ftory of Iafon, how he gotte the golden flece and how he*

Ded begyle Media, oute of laten into engleffhe by
Nycholas Whyte ' (Arber, i. 299).
The ballad is printed in single coluɯn on a narrow
slip.

93

A new yeres Gyft, intituled, A playne Pathway to perfect
reſt: Gathered out of ſundry Godly Patriarkes, and Prophets, very
comfortable | for all Chriſtians, and moſt needefull to be had in remembraunce.

To the Right honorable Lorde Rowland Hayward, Lord | Maior of the Cittie of
London, your dayly Orator | Edward Wollay, wiſheth longe life,
with in|creaſe of Fayth and Iuſtice.

I *Sraell ought to be commended by reaſon of Doctrin* | and Wiſdome, ſhewinge therfore, that
they whiche | haue it, ſhould not onely themſelues be wiſe ther|thorough, but ſhould

Eccle. ca 1.
alſo ſerue others by teaching | and preaching: that is, that Maiſters & Parentes | ſhould
inſtruct their family, and the Shepherd his ſheep, to ſaue | them from the Wolfe: what
ſtrength is the ſheepe of to eſcape | the violence or force of the Wolfe? none, ſaith
Eccleſiaſt. but euen | by his Shepherd: Euen ſo, the Miniſter & the Preacher, if they |

Iohn.
be true Preachers & true teachers, ſurelye then doth his Flocke | increaſe: & when the
Wolfe Sathan, which euer hath ben mans | Enemie ſhall come ſeekyng if he may deuoure
man, then by the | Doctrine of his Shepherde taught vnto hym, ſhall ouercome | Sathan
his Enemie. Here is the Sheep ſaued by the force | of the Shepharde: God graunt
increaſe.

Tobi. 4.
¶Let vs praiſe God for al his benefits which we haue receiued: | Conſent not vnto
ſinne. Geue Almes of thy Goods. Be mercy|ful after thy power. Be always thank-
ful vnto God for his mer|cifull benefits geuen vnto thee: vſe them well, for thou art
but a | Stewarde. God graunt yᵗ we may ſo beſtow our tyme in this | worlde, that in the
world to come we may be found good Ste|wards and haue lyfe euerlaſting. Amen.

Timo. 4.
¶O, that men were not ſo much louers of themſelues. Be not | ouercome with
Coueitouſnes: Be not Boaſters of yourſelues: | but remember who doth geue the
Acts. 26.
increaſe. Be not prowd, nor | curſed ſpeakers: Be not diſobedient to Father & mother.
Be not | vnthanckful nor vngodly. Be not vnkind, nor Truſebreakers, | Be not falſe
Accuſers, nor Riottous Perſons.

¶Be not fierce Deſpiſers of them, which are good, or do good: | but alway lay to thy
healpyng hande, incourage them to go for|wardes in their good deedes, and if thou ſe
Dauid. 9.
them ſtep backe, go | thou forwardes in their place: that is the good ſeruant, incou-|
ragyng the reſt to ſeeke their maiſters commoditie ſo muche as | in them doth lie, dealyng
truly with all men, then be you wel aſ|ſured to winne the crowne of euerlaſtyng glory,
world without | ende.

Eccle. 12.
All is but vanitie ſaith yᵉ Preacher, why be you then ſo heddy| and hie minded,
greedy vpon voluptuouſneſſe more then the lo|uers of God, hauing a ſimilitude of godli-
Peter. 12.
neſſe, but haue denied | the power therof, and ſuche you abhore. The ſeruant of the |
Lorde muſt not ſtriue, but apt to teache, be gentill vnto all men, | and one that can

ſuffer wronge with meekeneſſe : nay wee can | not do ſo, why? becauſe wee are men of corrupt mindes : but it | ſhall not longe preuayle, the euill men and deceiuers ſhall waxe | worſe and worſe : while they deceiue, they ſhal be deceiued themſelues : therfore let euery man that calleth on yᵉ name of Chriſte | flie from iniquitie.   Great are thy Iudgements (O Lorde) ther|fore men do erre that will not be reformed with thy wiſdome, God graunt wee may be reformed by him.

If thou harken vnto the voyce of the Lorde thy God : bleſſed | ſhalt thou be, but if thou knoweſt my commaundementes, ſaith | the Lorde, and keepe them not, curſed ſhalt thou be, yea curſed | ſhall be the fruite of thy ſtore :   though wee haue ſinned ſayth | Daniell yet if wee call to God in time, he will geue vs time to re|pent, to know the truth : and that wee may come to ourſelues a|gayne, to auoyde the ſnare of the Deuill, which wee are holden | captiue of him : and nothyng is able to vnlooſe vs ſaith Timothy | but a ſure faith fixed on Ieſus Chriſt, and through his precious | Bloud ſhedyng, wee are all ſaued from death, and ſhall come by | him to life euerlaſtyng.   God graunt for his ſonne Ieſus Chriſte | ſake that after this life we may com to life euerlaſting.   Amen.

TO thoſe which writers be, and perfit verſes make,
    Leaue of your triflyng toyes, and, ſuch doynges vndertake,
As ſhall both profit, and, brynge gayne to Common wealth,
Then ſhall the writers winne the prayſe and Readers ſhall gaine health,
To reade that which is good, it will their ſoules aduaunce,
And writers knowledge knit with grace, may vanquiſh ignoraunce :
    You Readers marke this well, and Printe this in your harte,
And do not as the Partridge doth, at euery thinge to ſtarte,
At euery winde that blowes, it runnes in wods to lie,
And euery Childe that throwes a ſtone, doth make the Partridge flie,
Now as I truſt you will, plante this within your breſt,
    It ſhall incourage me to write the way to perfit reſt.
¶ When I did call to minde, what cures wee haue in care,
This one chief clauſe I finde, moſt mindefull to beware,
Wee know what God hath wild to do, or to forbeare :
Yet willingly wee yeelde, from ſafetie vnto ſnare,
And therfore in this caſe, my iudgement doth aduaunce,
    That knowledge without grace, is worſe then Ignoraunce.
Wee know what thanckes wee owe, to God for all his giftes,
Yet contrary we ſhowe to him, ourſelues vnthriftes,
The good from euill we ſee, in all our daily driftes,
Yet to do good we flee, for lacke of graces giftes,
Then may we vſe this fraſe, moſt nice in remembraunce,
    That knowledge without grace, is worſe then ignoraunce.
¶ Now know wee Scripture plaine, whereas before we did not,
Yet are wee much more vaine, then when the ſame we read not,
Wee run forth hedlonge ſo, as God or man wee dreade not,
Which ſoone will plante our woe, if God the ſame forbed not,
While wee know no right race, wee runne vnder obeyſaunce,
    Our knowledge without grace, is worſe then ignoraunce.
We know wee ought to loue, although wee be not loued,
Againe no wrong to moue, though wrong to vs be moued,
Although wee be reproued, we ought not to reproue,
Theſe godly wordes approued, doth ſhow for our behoue,
Yet wanting grace, we chaſe away Gods ordinaunce,
    The knowledge without grace, is worſe then ignoraunce.
¶ Wee know wee ſhould forgeue, as wee would be forgeuen,
Yet ſtyll in yre we liue, as though our hartes were reeuen,

Reuengements we do keepe, for light occafions geuen,
Our Neighboures greefe we feeke, both euery Morne and Euen,
The more wee fpie in fpace, the leffe yet our entraunce,
    Our knowledge without grace, is worfe then ignoraunce,
All falfhood and deceite, wee fhould alfo abhorre,
Yet vfe wee more that fleight, than euer wee did before,
Lingryng ftill to view, to hurte our Neighbour fore,
So wee may them purfue, wee care not for no more
Repreffion beares the Mace, and Lucre leades the Daunce,
    Their knowledge without grace, is worfe then ignoraunce,
❡Wee know that wee fhould worke the workes of righteoufneffe,
Yet lie wee ftill and lurke in flouth and idleneffe,
Wee fhould efchew the darke, and to the light adreffe,
Yet do wee as the Turke, all godly light expreffe,
Infteede of workes wee place, our luft and daliaunce,
    Thus knowledge without grace, is worfe then ignoraunce.
Eche man accompt muft make, as he hath heare vocation,
His Talent not to flake, but turne to augmentacion,
This muft wee do I fay, in paine of our dampnacion,
Then crake no more I pray, of our iuftificacion,
Wee thinke to know the pace, difchargeth our allegiaunce.
    This knowledge without grace, is worfe then ignoraunce.
❡Better to fit euen ftill, then for to rife and fall,
So is it much leffe yll, to know nothing at all,
Then for to haue great fkyll, and then liue worft of all,
Fulfilling not Gods will, as he hath wild wee fhall,
Thus ignoraunce may face, our knowledge no entraunce,
    For knowledge without grace, is worfe then ignoraunce.
Which grace that wee now lacke, for want of calling for,
Pray wee the Lorde to graunt, to falue this forfayde fore,
That in vs he may put, repentaunce in fuch ftore,
God graunt vs out to fhut, all our wilfull errour,
All Vertue eke imbrace, and Vice away to glaunce,
    That knowledge knit with grace, may vanquifh ignoraunce.
❡Loe this much I write plaine, to fhow which way is beft,
    then folow this and do not faine, then fhall you ioy and reft,
With God which fittes aboue, with Angels round about,
    knocke and I will open, (faith he) of this haue thou no doubt,
Great compfort fure is this, then let vs cal and pray,
    for our good Queene and her Counfell, to faue them from decay.

FINIS.   (φ)   Edward Wollay.

Imprinted at London, by William How, for Richard Iohnes: and are to be folde at
his Shoppe ioyning to the Southweft doore of Paules Church. 1571.

Edward Wollay, the author of this ballad, is mentioned by Ritson (*Bibliographia Poetica*, p. 397) as having written 'An admonition to euery degree, fhewing the right way to ioy and perfite reft', and to have dedicated the same to Queen Elizabeth. It forms part of Royal MS. 17. A. xix, British Museum.

Sir Rowland Heyward, clothworker, to whom the ballad is dedicated, was elected alderman of Farringdon Without September 19, 1560; chosen Sheriff August, 1563; elected Lord Mayor September 29, 1570, and served again during a part of 1591. Heyward resided in Philip Lane, Cripplegate, and died senior alderman December 5, 1593, and was buried in St. Alphage's Church, London Wall, where a monument to his memory is preserved. His daughter Joan married Sir John Thynne, of Longleat, and was the ancestress of the Marquesses of Bath (Overall, *Remembrancia*, 1878, p. 37).

The ballad is printed in two columns upon a large sheet.

94

The maner of the world now a dayes.

SO many poynted caps
Lafed w^t double flaps
And fo gay felted hats
      Sawe I neuer.
So many good leffons
So many good fermons
And fo few deuocions
      Sawe I neuer.
So many gardes worne
Iagged and al to torne
And fo many falfly forfworne
      Sawe I neuer.
So fewe good polycies
In townes and cytyes
For kepinge of blynde hoftryes
      Sawe I neuer.
So many good warkes
So few wel lerned clarkes
And fo few that goodnes markes
      Sawe I neuer.
Suche pranked cotes & fleues
So few yonge men that preues
And fuch encreafe of theues
      Sawe I neuer.
So many garded hofe
fuch cornede fhoes
And fo many enuyous foes
      Sawe I neuer.
So many queftes fytte
With men of fmale wit
And fo many falfely quitte
      fawe I neuer.
So many gay fwordes
So many altered wordes
And fo fewe couered bordes
      Sawe I neuer.

¶So many empti purſes
ſo fewe good horſes
And ſo many curſes
      Sawe I neuer.
ſuche boſters and braggers
ſo newe faſhyoned daggers
And ſo many beggers
      Sawe I neuer.
So many proper knyues
So well apparrelled wyues
And ſo yll of theyr lyues
      Sawe I neuer.
So many cockolde makers
So many crakers
And ſo many peace breakers
      Saw I neuer.
So much vayne clothing
With cuttyng and iagging
And ſo much bragginge
      Saw I neuer.
¶So many newes and knackes
So many naughty packes
And ſo many that mony lackes
      Saw I neuer.
¶So many maidens with child
And wylfully begylde
And ſo many places vntilde
      Sawe I neuer.
ſo many women blamed
And rightuouſly defaimed
And ſo lytle aſhamed
      ſawe I neuer.
¶Widowes ſo ſone wed
After their huſbandes be deade
Hauing ſuch haſt to bed
      ſawe I neuer.
¶ſo much ſtriuinge
For goodes and for wiuinge
And ſo lytle thryuynge
      ſaw I neuer.
¶ſo many capacities
Offices and pluralites
And chaunging of dignities
      ſawe I neuer.
✠ſo many lawes to vſe
The truth to refuſe
Suche falſhead to excuſe
      ſawe I neuer.
¶Executors hauinge the ware
Taking ſo little care
Howe the ſoule doth fare
      ¶ſawe I neuer.

¶Amonge them that are riche
No frendſhyp is to kepe tuche
And ſuch fayre gloſinge ſpeche
     Saw I neuer.
 So many pore
In euery bordoure
And ſo ſmall ſoccoure
     Saw I neuer.
 So proude and ſo gaye
ſo riche in araye
And ſo ſknat [*sic*] of money
     Saw I neuer.
 So many bowyers
ſo many fletchers
And ſo few good arches [*sic*]
     ſawe I neuer.
 ſo many chepers
ſo fewe biers
And ſo many borowers
     ſawe I neuer.
 So many alle ſellers
In baudy holes and ſellers
Of yonge folkes yll counſellers
     ſawe I neuer.
 ſo many pinkers
ſo many thinkers
And ſo many good alle drinkers
     ſawe I neuer.
 ſo many wronges
ſo few mery ſonges
And ſo many yll tonges
     ſawe I neuer.
 ſo many a vacabounde
Through al this londe
And ſo many in pryſon bond
     I ſaw neuer.
¶ſo many citacions
ſo fewe oblacions
And ſo many new facions
     ſawe I neuer.
 ſo many fleyng tales
Pickers of purſes and males
And ſo many ſales
     ſaw I neuer.
 ſo much preachinge
ſpeaking fayre and teaching
And ſo ill beleuinge
     ſaw I neuer.
 ſo much wrath and enuy
Couetous and glottony
and ſo litle charitie
     ſawe I neuer.

(283)

ſo many carders
Reuelers and dicers
and ſo many yl ticers
　　　ſawe I neuer.
ſo many lollers
ſo few true tollers
ſo many baudes and pollers
　　　ſawe I neuer.
ſuch treachery
ſimony and vſury
Pouerty and lechery
　　　ſaw I neuer.
ſo many auayles
ſo many geales
And ſo many fals baylies
　　　ſawe I neuer.
By fals and ſubtyll wayes
All Englande decayes
For more enuy and lyers
　　　ſawe I neuer.
ſo new facioned iackes
With brode flappes in the neckes
And ſo gay and newe partlettes
　　　ſawe I neuer.
ſo many flutteſhe cookes
ſo few facioned tucking hookes
And ſo few biers of bookes
　　　ſaw I neuer.
ſomtime we ſong of myrth & play
But now our ioy is gone away
For ſo many fal in decay
　　　ſawe I neuer.
whither is yᵉ welth of englād gon
the ſpiritual faith they haue none
And ſo many wrongfully vndone
　　　ſaw I neuer.
It is great pitie that euery day
ſo many brybors go by the way
And ſo mani extorcioners in eche cūtrey
　　　ſaw I neuer.
To the lord I make my mone
For yᵘ maiſt healpe vs euerichone
Alas the people is ſo wo begone
　　　worſe was it neuer.

Amendment
　　Were conuenient
But it may not be
　　We haue exiled veritie
God is neither dead nor ſicke
　　He may amend al yet

And trowe ye ſo indede
  As ye beleue ye ſhal haue mede
After better I hope euer
  For worſe was it neuer.

Finis.

In the Stationers' Registers for 1561–62 (Arber's *Transcript*, i. 182), licensed to Thomas Colwell with two others, is mentioned 'a new ballett, *thus goeyth the worlde now in theſe our Dayes &c.*', which entry may possibly belong to this ballad. John Payne Collier, despite the fact that he clearly asserts his version of 'The maner of the world now a dayes', which he included in 'Old Ballads' (Percy Society, 1840), to have been taken from the Heber collection, reprints it with the addition of a colophon 'Imprinted at London in Flete Strete at the ſigne of the Roſe Garland by W. Copland'. He moreover adds the signature 'J. S.', and on the strength of this attributes the ballad to John Skelton, and he repeats the suggestion in his 'Extracts from the Registers of the Stationers' Company', 1848 (vol. i, p. 56). Alexander Dyce, in his edition of Skelton's 'Poetical Works, 1843' (vol. i, p. 48), includes the ballad with reservation, and points out that in any case it is only an adaptation of verses which are to be found in Sloane MS. 747, British Museum. It is printed in three columns, without ornament or border.

INDEX

The References are to the Numbers of the Ballads.

A

A. (I.). *See* Awdeley (John).
A B C to the christen congregacion, 56.
Against filthy writing, 13.
Answer to a Papisticall Byll, 57.
Antwerp, Fall of, 69.
Arundel, Henry Fitz-Alan, Earl of, 47.
Awdeley (John), 1, 2, 3.

B

B. (G.), 4.
Bacon (Sir Nicholas), 78.
Barker (John), 5.
Beccles, Lamentation of, 87.
Bedfordshire, Floods in, 89.
Benison (Francis), 6.
Birch (William), 7, 8, 9.
Bonner (Edmund), Bishop of London, 14.
Bourchier (Arthur), 10.
Bourman (Nicholas), 11, 12.
Breeding Larke, 10.
Brice (Thomas), 13.
Broke (Thomas), 14.
Burdet (Robert), 15.

C

Camell (Thomas), 20–25.
Children, Monstrous, 40, 62.
Christ's Hospital: Easter Psalms, 76, 77.
Christal glas for all Estates, 46.
Churchyard (Thomas), 19, 21–32.
Cold Pye for the Papistes, 72.
Complaint of a sinner, 7.
Complaynt agaynst the wicked enemies of Christ, 16.
Cornet (John), 33.
Cronycle of all the Kynges, 18.
Cruel assault of Gods Fort, 3.

D

D. (R.), 34.
Daniels siftyng in these our dayes, 35.
Dauid Dicars when, To, 20.
Dauy Dycars Dreame, 19.
Denton (John), 36.
Derby, Edward Stanley, Earl of, 36.
Downham Bridge, 52.

E

L. (W.). *See* Elderton (William).
Edward VI, King, 38.
Elderton (William), 7, 39–43, 49.
Eleanor, Queen, 44.
Elizabeth, Queen, 32, 45, 55.
England: Cronycle of all the Kynges, 18.
England, A warnyng to, 9.
Essex, Robert Devereux, Earl of, 37.

F

Familie of Loue, 80, 83.
Felton (John), 50, 70.
Fering (W.), 46.
Fishes, Monstrous, 52, 63.
Fleming (Abraham), 48.
Floods in Bedfordshire, 89.
Follie, Lamentation of, 43.
Free admonition, 4.
Fulwood (William), 49.
Fyne gloues deuised for Newyeres gyftes, 88.

G

G. (F.), 50.
G. (Guil. P.), 47.
Garrard (Sir William), 12, 73.
Gibson (William), 51.
Goodwill, An other [Balade] out of, 80.
Granger (Timothy), 52.

H

Heartie Confession of a Christian, 17.
Henry IV, King of France, 53.
Herne in Kent, 62.
Holland, East coast of, 63.
Hutton (Luke), 54.

I

I. (T.), 55.
James I, King, 45.
Jerusalem, Destruccion of, 5.
Jewel (John), Bishop of Salisbury, 11, 42.

K

Knell (Thomas), 56, 57.
Knollys (Catharine), Lady, 68.

L

Lambe (William), 48.
Lambes Feast, Songe of the, 80.
Lamentation from Rome, 75.
Lamentation of Follie, 43.
Lamentation of Freyndshyp, 29.
Larke, A breeding, 10.
Leach (—), 49.
Lennox, Margaret Douglas, Countess of, 74.
Letter to Rome, 70.
Lloyd (Lodowick), 58.
London, A warning to, 69.
London dames, A warning to al, 71.
Loue, Familie of, 80, 83.
Loue, The panges of, 39.

M

Maner of the world now a dayes, 94.
Map of Mortalitie, 65.
Markant (John), 61.
Mayenne, Charles, Duke of, 53.
Monstrous Children, 40, 62.
Monstrous Fishes, 52, 63.
Monstrous Worm, 64.
Moray, James Stewart, Earl of, 82.
Musicke, Commendation of, 92.

N

Nelson (Thomas), 66.
Newgate, Prisoners pressed to death in, 67.
Newton (Thomas), 68.
New Yeres Gift, intituled, a Christal glas for all Estates to looke in, 46.
New yeres Gyft, intituled, A playne Pathway to perfect rest, 93.
Newyeres gyftes, Fyne gloues deuised for, 88.
Nobody, The welspoken, 91.
Norris (Ralph), 69.
Northampton, 57.
Northomberland newes, 41.
Norton (Christopher), 51.

O

Olde man and his wife, 60.

P

Panges of Loue, 39.
Peele (Stephen), 70, 71.
Pembroke, William Herbert, Earl of, 31.
Phillip (John), 72, 73, 74.

Playne Pathway to perfect rest, 93.
Preston (Thomas), 75.
Price (Richard), 34.
PRINTERS AND PUBLISHERS:
  Allde (Edward), 43, 76, 77.
  Allde (John), 13, 33, 47, 49, 69, 81, 89.
  Allde (Margaret), 37, 79.
  Applay or Apple (Richard), 7.
  Awdeley (John), 1, 2, 3, 4, 6, 57, 67, 82.
  B. (R.), 65.
  B. (W.), 60.
  Barley (William), 76.
  Blackwall (William), 44.
  Charlewood (John), 34.
  Coldock (Francis), 27.
  Colman (Nicholas), 87.
  Colwell (Thomas), 5, 29, 40, 42, 52, 62.
  Copland (William), 38.
  Day (John), 14.
  Denham (Henry), 48.
  Disle (Henry), 58.
  Dyer (Nicholas), 29.
  Gryffyth (William), 25, 26, 31, 75.
  Halley (Edmund), 13.
  How (William), 46, 50, 68, 72, 93.
  Hunt (Christopher), 17.
  Jones (Richard), 10, 11, 12, 15, 35, 46, 55, 68, 72, 73, 93.
  Kele (Richard), 56.
  Kirkham (Henry), 4, 6, 51, 70, 71.
  Lacy (Alexander), 7, 8, 9, 27, 28, 51, 70, 71, 92.
  Lant (Richard), 19, 21, 23, 39.
  Lugger (William), 65.
  Millington (Thomas), 54.
  Orwin (Thomas), 17.
  Owen (William), 8, 24.
  P. (T.). See Pavier (Thomas).
  Pavier (Thomas), 45, 84.
  Pepwell (Arthur), 28.
  Pickering (William), 16, 50, 58, 85.
  Powell (William), 58, 88.
  Purfoot (Thomas), 41, 63.
  Robinson (Robert), 87.
  Rogers (Owen), 61, 62.
  Russell (Edward), 30.
  Ryder (Timothy), 78.
  S. (H.), 58.
  Seres (William), 83.
  Sutton (Henry), 20, 22, 24.
  Turner (Thomas), 48.
  W. (W.). See White (William).
  White (Edward), 74, 86.
  White (William), 84.
  Williamson (William), 36.
  Wolfe (John), 55, 64.
  Wright (William), 66.
  Wyer (Nicholas), 29.

Proper new balade expressyng the fames, 71.
Psalme of Prayer and praise, 77.
Psalme of thanksgiuing, 76.

R

Ramsey (L.), 78.
Refuge of a Sinner, 15.
Remember Death, 2.
Remember man, 59.
Rogers (Robert), 79.

S

S. (W.), 80
Samuel (William), 80.
Saunders (Sir Edward), 58.
Seall (Robert), 81.
Sempill (Robert), 82.
Sharpe (Robert), 83.
Sm. (Ra.). *See* Smart (Ralph).
Smart (Ralph), 27.
Solomon, Sage sayinges of, 84.
Solomons Temple, The re-edifying of, 85.
Songe of the Lambes Feast, 80.
Spiritual Songe of Thankesgiuing, 90.
Sterrie (D.), 87.
Stoney Stratford, 40.
Story (John), 33.
Strangways (Henry), 8.
Stucley (Thomas), 81.

T

T. (T.), 88.
Tarlton (Richard), 89.
Tilbury Camp, 55.

Tunes:
    Blacke Almaine, 71.
    Gentle and Curteous, 44.
    Labandalashotte, 87.
    Lassiamiza Noate, 72.
    Lord Darnley, 86.
    New Rogero, 43.
    New Tantara, 53.
    Pleasant new tune, 45.
    Prissilla, 60.
    Queenes Almayne, 5.
    Row well ye Mariners, 69, 70, 75.
    Triumph and Joy, 55.
    Wandering and wauering, 54.
    Welladay, 37.
    Wigmores Galliard, 84.

V

Ver monstrueux, 64.
Véron (Jean), 1.
Vngratious Sonne, 86.

W

Walsingham (Sir Francis), 66.
Warning to al London dames, 71.
Warning to London, 69.
Warnyng to England, 9.
Welspoken Nobody, 91.
Wentworth, Thomas Wentworth, Lord, 61.
Whight (Nicholas), 92.
Wollay (Edward), 93.
World, Maner of the, 94.
Worm, Monstrous, 64.
Worthy Mirrour, 10.